Understanding Global Conflict and Cooperation

Understanding Global Conflict and Cooperation

An Introduction to Theory and History

TENTH EDITION

Joseph S. Nye, Jr.
Harvard University

David A. Welch
Balsillie School of International Affairs, University of Waterloo

PEARSON

Boston Columbus Indianapolis New York San Francisco Amsterdam
Cape Town Dubai London Madrid Milan Munich Paris Montréal Toronto
Delhi Mexico City São Paulo Sydney Hong Kong Seoul Singapore Taipei Tokyo

Editorial Director: Dickson Musslewhite
Publisher: Charlyce Jones Owen
Editorial Assistant: Laura Hernandez
Program Manager: Rob DeGeorge
Project Manager: Carol O'Rourke
Field Marketing Manager: Brittany Pogue-Mohammed
Product Marketing Manager: Tricia Murphy
Product Media Editor: Tina Gagliostro
Full-Service Project Management and Composition: Cenveo® Publisher Services
Full-Service Project Manager: Cenveo® Publisher Services
Art Director: Maria Lange
Senior Operations Specialist: MaryAnn Gloriande
Cover Printer: Phoenix Color/Hagerstown
Printer/Binder: RRD-Crawfordsville

Credits and acknowledgments borrowed from other sources and reproduced, with permission, in this textbook appear on the appropriate page within text.

Library of Congress Cataloging-in-Publication Data

Names: Nye, Joseph S. | Welch, David A.
Title: Understanding global conflict and cooperation : an introduction to
    theory and history / Joseph S. Nye, Jr., Harvard University, David A.
    Welch, Balsillie School of International Affairs, University of Waterloo.
Description: Tenth edition. | Boston : Pearson, [2017] | Includes
    bibliographical references and index.
Identifiers: LCCN 2015037387 | ISBN 9780134403168
Subjects: LCSH: International relations. | War (International law) | World
    politics—20th century. | World politics—21st century.
Classification: LCC JZ1305 .N94 2016 | DDC 327.109/04--dc23
LC record available at http://lccn.loc.gov/2015037387

2   16

Student Edition:
ISBN 13: 978-0-13440316-8
ISBN 10:   0-13-440316-9
Instructor's Review Copy: Á la Carte:
ISBN 13: 978-0-13440347-2   ISBN 13: 978-0-13442225-1
ISBN 10:   0-13-440347-9   ISBN 10:   0-13-442225-2

To Stanley Hoffmann, 1928–2015
Our teacher, colleague, and friend

Brief Contents

Contents

10 What Can We Expect in the Future?   359

Preface

by Joseph S. Nye, Jr.

The fields of political science and International Relations have been criticized in recent years for a growing gap between academic theory and the real world of politics and policy. Policy makers (and students) complain about jargon-laden texts that go on and on about theory yet seem to say more and more about less and less. Do political science and International Relations have nothing to say that could help us understand whether important changes such as the recovery of Asia, Middle East turnmoil, cyberconflicts, and the growing role of nonstate actors will lead to global cooperation or conflict?

In practice, theory is unavoidable. In order to achieve your objectives, you need at least a primitive sense of cause and effect, as well as a means to simplify and interpret reality. If someone asked you to describe what happened to you in the last hour, you would have to simplify, or else you would reproduce sixty minutes of detail. If someone asked you to do something, you would need some idea of what actions would produce what results. The question is not whether theory is relevant to practice, but which theories, and in which contexts. Most people are unaware that they implicitly use theories every day. Even those who are aware often know little or nothing of the origins and limitations of the theories they inevitably use. Most practitioners seem to avoid direct contact with academic theory, and many academics disdain practice and write in a language aimed at other academics. Of the twenty-five most influential scholars recently listed by the magazine *Foreign Policy,* only four had held top-level policy positions: two in the U.S. government and two in the United Nations.

Understanding Global Conflict and Cooperation is designed to bridge that gap. It grows out of an introductory course that I taught as part of the Harvard core curriculum for more than a decade, but it is also informed by five years of experience as a policy maker at the assistant secretary level in three national security bureaucracies in Washington—the State Department, the Pentagon, and the National Intelligence Council. In that world, I discovered that theory and practice had much to contribute to each other. This book aims to introduce students to the complexities of international politics by giving them a good grounding in traditional realist theory before turning to liberal and constructivist approaches that have become more prominent after the Cold War. The aim was to present difficult concepts in clear language with historical examples so students would gain a practical understanding of the basic approaches to international politics.

Twice in the first half of the twentieth century, the great powers engaged in devastating world wars that cost nearly 50 million lives. The second half of the century was wracked by a cold war, regional wars, and the threat of nuclear weapons. Why did those conflicts happen? Could they happen again in the twenty-first century? Or will rising economic and ecological interdependence, the growth of transnational and international institutions, and the spread of democratic values bring about a new world order? How will globalization and the information revolution influence international politics in this new century? No good teacher can honestly answer such questions with certainty, but we can provide our students with conceptual tools derived from the main approaches of realism, liberalism, and constructivism that will help them shape their own answers as the future unfolds. That is the purpose of this book.

New to This Edition

This is the tenth edition of a book the first seven editions of which went by the title *Understanding International Conflicts*. For the eighth edition, I asked my friend and former student David Welch to join me as a collaborator, and we took the opportunity to change the title to *Understanding Global Conflict and Cooperation*. We did so for two reasons. First, by adding the word "cooperation," we sought to highlight more clearly the fact that conflict and cooperation are in fact two sides of the same problem: namely, resolving disputes. In world politics, disputes can be over mundane things such as technical standards or intellectual property rights, or over emotionally charged things such as territory. They can be over relatively simple problems such as protecting whales, or enormously complex problems such as balancing the interests of poor countries in economic development against the need to reduce worldwide greenhouse gas emissions. Policy makers, pundits, and professors tend to pay more attention to conflict than to cooperation, because conflict always has the potential to get out of hand. As a result, we often fail to notice that most disagreements in the world are actually handled peacefully. We also sometimes fail to notice that finding durable cooperative solutions to conflict can be just as hard as, or even harder than, avoiding wars. We added a great deal of new material designed to bring the complex relationship between conflict and cooperation into clearer view. Second, by changing "international" to "global," we wanted to highlight the fact that, in the twenty-first century, more and more problems confront the world as a whole and involve a much larger array of players than just states.

In a sense, the international is a subset of the global. While looking at the world through the former lens is still important and useful, a truly global perspective often allows us to see more. Students of world politics used to be preoccupied with conflicts between sovereign states. This made sense in the first half of the twentieth century, when sovereign states fought two devastating world wars, and it also made sense during the Cold War, when the United States and the Soviet Union had the capacity to destroy each other many times over with roughly half an hour's warning. Interstate conflict is still an important problem, of course, but the set of challenges facing humanity has both broadened and deepened. Conflict within states is now more common than between states; yet at the same time, conflict within states almost always reverberates internationally. It has the potential to affect people virtually anywhere, thanks to the speed and intensity of modern communications, the proliferation of nonstate actors, and the globalization of economic and other kinds of interests. It is getting harder to distinguish international problems from domestic ones, or local problems from regional or global ones.

Reaction to the eighth edition was strongly positive, but as with all things, improvement is always possible. This is the second revision of that book, We have gone over the text carefully, bearing in mind the very helpful feedback provided by reviewers, to update, refine, deepen, and clarify. Wherever possible we have sought to draw tighter connections between chapters and to highlight the book's main theme, which is that by reflecting jointly on history and theory it is possible to provide better explanations of events in world politics, to better understand events as they unfold, and, not least importantly, to evaluate them morally and ethically.

Highlights of the Tenth Edition

- The single most significant change to this edition is a dedicated chapter (Chapter 7) to current global flashpoints. These are the places in the world where it is easiest to imagine serious conflict between states, or conflict within states escalating to embroil whole regions. In addition to accounts of the history and dynamics of these flashpoints, we attempt to relate events in each place to the major concepts and themes animating the chapters that come before.

- We also provide new or updated chronologies to make it easier to understand how complex events have unfolded.

- Another important change is an expanded and thoroughly cross-referenced glossary. Any time you come across a word or phrase that may not be entirely clear to you, flip to the glossary, where you will find a clear and concise definition that draws your attention to important related concepts.

- New chapter learning objectives serve as a guide to the important concepts, issues, and ideas that are discussed in each major section of the text.

The interplay between theory and history as a way of seeking to explain, understand, and evaluate world events remains the pillar of this edition, as it has with the previous nine. The text itself is an example of how to think about the complex and confusing domain of international politics. It should be read not for a complete factual account, but for the way it approaches the interplay of theory and history. It is the place to start. Neither theory nor history alone is sufficient. Historians who believe that understanding comes from simply recounting the facts fail to make explicit the hidden principles by which they select some facts rather than others. Equally mistaken are political scientists who become so isolated and entangled in a maze of abstract theory that they mistake their mental constructs for reality. Only by going back and forth between history and theory can we avoid such mistakes.

This edition is designed to be able to provide the central thread for an introductory course, or for individual readers to teach themselves the equivalent of such a course; but it can also be used as a supplementary text to provide an example of one approach to the subject. Each chapter includes study questions to help guide both instructors and students, as well as suggested "follow-up" readings for students who might wish to explore certain themes in greater depth. In addition to chronologies of the historical events that we discuss in detail, it provides a selection of helpful maps, schematic figures, charts, and tables.

Our hope is that this tenth edition is the most user-friendly yet. As a work in progress of long-standing, it will, we hope, continue to evolve and improve. In fact, it will not be long before we start thinking about the eleventh edition. No doubt the headlines between now and then will give us even more grist for our particular mill—the vital interplay between theory and history.

REVEL™

Educational technology designed for the way today's students read, think, and learn

When students are engaged deeply, they learn more effectively and perform better in their courses. This simple fact inspired the creation of REVEL: an immersive learning experience designed for the way today's students read, think, and learn. Built in collaboration with educators and students nationwide, REVEL is the newest, fully digital way to deliver respected Pearson content.

REVEL enlivens course content with media interactives and assessments—integrated directly within the authors' narrative—that provide opportunities for students to read about and practice course material in tandem. This immersive educational technology boosts student engagement, which leads to better understanding of concepts and improved performance throughout the course.

Learn more about REVEL at http://www.pearsonhighered.com/revel/.

Features

As an example of a dialogue between theory and history, this book can provide the central thread for an introductory course or for individual readers to teach themselves the equivalent of such a course. It can also be used as a supplementary text in a course as an example of one approach to the subject.

Each chapter now includes specific learning objectives for each major section, as well as study questions to help guide both instructors and students. Follow-up readings strategically placed at the end of each major section are intended to steer students toward historically significant and/or cutting edge works on topics they have immediately encountered (in case they are interested in hot pursuit). You will find a variety of new maps, charts, and diagrams, many in color for the first time. You will also find updated chronologies of the historical events that the book discusses in detail. Finally, I have from time to time made use of my own reflections on my experiences in both government and the academy to illustrate the importance of taking both theory and history seriously.

Acknowledgments

This book is based on a Harvard College course titled Historical Studies A-12, *International Conflicts in the Modern World* that I sometimes co-taught with then-junior colleagues Stephan Haggard, Yuen Foong Khong, Michael Mandelbaum, and M. J. Peterson, and mounted over the years with the assistance of a number of extremely capable Head Teaching Fellows: Vin Auger, Peter Feaver, Meryl Kessler, Sean Lynn-Jones, Pam Metz, John Owen, Gideon Rose, and Gordon Silverstein. All were sources of inspiration and insight, and no doubt some of their ideas have surreptitiously crept into the text. The same can also surely be said of Stanley Hoffmann, who taught us both, and Robert Keohane—men of extraordinary intellectual creativity and generosity who have had an impact on the text more than either would imagine, even taking into account their careful reading and extensive comments.

We thank those who reviewed the manuscript in whole or in part and offered constructive feedback for this tenth edition: Holly Boux, Colorado State University; John Riley, Kutztown State University; Robert Portada, Kutztown State University; Hak-Seon Lee, James Madison University; Paul Crumby, Colorado State Univeristy; Timothy Lomperis, St. Louis University; George Guo, Guilford College; and Andrew Katz, Denison University. We remain grateful to others who have provided advice and suggestions for past editions as well: Lawrence Abraham, Emanuel Adler, Aisha Ahmad, Ihsan Alkatib, Bentley Allan, Cristina Badescu, Michael Barnett, Steven Bernstein, David Dressler, June Teufel Dreyer, Colin Dueck, Peter Feaver, Nicole Freiner, Kathie Stromile Golden, Clifford Griffin, Walter Hatch, Matthew Hoffmann, Christopher Housenick, Nathan Jensen, Kelechi Kalu, Peter Katzenstein, Elizabeth Larus, Howard Lehman, James Manicom, Charles Maier, Ernest May, Richard A. Melanson, Edward S. Mihalkanin, Kalpana Misra, Bessma Momani, Hiroshi Nakazato, J. Douglas Nelson, Carla Norrlöf, Diane Paul, Vincent Pouliot, Mark Raymond, Dan Reiter, James Ross, George Shambaugh, Aboulaye Saine, Junichiro Shiratori, Barry Stein, Janice Gross Stein, Jeffrey Togman, Theodore Vastal, Alexander Wendt, John Williams, and Melissa Williams. The book has also benefited from the expert research assistance of Chris Bordeleau, Marcel Dietsch, Zachary Karabell, Matt Kohut, Jenna Meguid, Sean Misko, Carl Nagin, Dan Philpott, Neal Rosendorf, Alex Scacco, and Richard Wood. To all, we are deeply grateful.

—*Joseph S. Nye, Jr.*

Supplements

Pearson is pleased to offer several resources to qualified adopters of *Understanding Global Conflict and Cooperation* and their students that will make teaching and learning from this book even more effective and enjoyable. Supplements for this book are available at the Instructor Resource Center (IRC), an online hub that allows instructors to quickly download book-specific supplements. Please visit the IRC welcome page at www.pearsonhighered.com/irc to register for access.

INSTRUCTORS MANUAL/TEST BANK   This resource includes learning objectives, lecture outlines, multiple-choice questions, and essay questions for each chapter. Available exclusively on the IRC.

MYTEST   This powerful assessment generation program includes all of the items in the instructor's manual/test bank. Questions and tests can be easily created, customized, saved online, and then printed, allowing flexibility to manage assessments anytime and anywhere. Available exclusively on the IRC.

LONGMAN ATLAS OF WORLD ISSUES (0-205-78020-2)   From population and political systems to energy use and women's rights, the *Longman Atlas of World Issues* features full-color thematic maps that examine the forces shaping the world. This atlas includes critical thinking exercises to promote a deeper understanding of how geography affects many global issues.

GOODE'S WORLD ATLAS (0-321-65200-2)   *Goode's World Atlas* has set the standard for college reference atlases. It features hundreds of physical, political, and thematic maps as well as graphs, tables, and a pronouncing index.

RESEARCH AND WRITING IN INTERNATIONAL RELATIONS (0-205-06065-X)   With current and detailed coverage on how to start research in the discipline's major subfields, this brief and affordable guide offers the step-by-step guidance and the essential resources needed to compose political science papers that go beyond description and into systematic and sophisticated inquiry. This text focuses on areas where students often need help—finding a topic, developing a question, reviewing the literature, designing research, and last, writing the paper.

About the Authors

Joseph S. Nye is University Distinguished Service Professor and former Dean of Harvard University's Kennedy School of Government. He also served as a Deputy to the Undersecretary of State in the Carter Administration, Assistant Secretary of Defense for International Security Affairs in the Clinton Administration, and Chair of the National Intelligence Council. His recent books include *The Power Game: A Washington Novel, The Future of Power, Presidential Leadership and the Creation of the American Era* and the latest released in 2015 *Is the American Century Over?*

David A. Welch is CIGI Chair of Global Security at the Balsillie School of International Affairs, Professor of Political Science at the University of Waterloo, and Senior Fellow at the Centre for International Governance Innovation.

Chapter 1

Are There Enduring Logics of Conflict and Cooperation in World Politics?

Photo: Alinari/Art Resource, NY.

Marble relief commemorating Athenians who died in the Peloponnesian War

Learning Objectives

1.1 Identify the distinctive features of a sovereign state system and their implications for cooperation and conflict.

1.2 Explain how history can help us understand international politics today.

1.3 Compare and contrast: (a) motives, means, and consequences; and (b) skepticism, state moralism, and cosmopolitanism.

1

The world is shrinking. The *Mayflower* took three months to cross the Atlantic. In 1924, Charles Lindbergh's flight took 33 hours. Fifty years later, the Concorde did it in three hours. Ballistic missiles can do it in 30 minutes. At the beginning of the twenty-first century, a transatlantic flight cost one-third of what it did in 1950, and a telephone call from New York to London cost only a small percentage of what it did at midcentury. Global Internet communications are nearly instantaneous, and transmission costs are negligible. An environmentalist in Asia or a human rights activist in Africa today has a power of communication once enjoyed only by large organizations such as governments or transnational corporations. On a more somber note, nuclear weapons have added a new dimension to war that one writer calls "double death," meaning that not only could individuals die, but under some circumstances the whole human species could be threatened. And as the September 11, 2001, terrorist attacks on the World Trade Center in New York and the Pentagon ("9/11") illustrated, technology is putting into the hands of nonstate actors destructive powers that once were reserved solely for governments. As the effects of distance shrink, conditions in remote, poor countries such as Afghanistan suddenly become highly relevant to people around the globe.

Yet some other things about international politics have remained the same over the ages. Thucydides' account of Sparta and Athens fighting the Peloponnesian War 2,500 years ago bears an eerie resemblance to the Arab-Israeli conflict after 1947. Pliny the Elder complained about imbalances in Rome's (mutually beneficial) trade with India nearly 2,000 years ago in almost exactly the same

Photo: David A. Welch

Marble memorial commemorating Americans who died in the Vietnam War language with which members of the U.S. Congress have complained about imbalances in the country's (mutually beneficial) trade with China. There are basic logics to conflict and cooperation that have remained surprisingly constant over the millennia, even if the forms they take and the issues that give rise to them change (the ancient world never had to worry about nuclear weapons, HIV/AIDS, or climate change). The world is a strange cocktail of continuity and change.

The task for students of world politics is to build on the past but not be trapped by it, or, in other words, to understand the continuities as well as the changes. We must learn the traditional theories and then adapt them to current circumstances. The early chapters of this book will provide you with a historical and theoretical context in which to place the phenomena of the information revolution, globalization, interdependence, and transnational actors that are discussed in the later chapters.

> *I found in my experience in government that I could ignore neither the age-old nor the brand-new dimensions of world politics.*

—JOSEPH S. NYE, JR.

World politics would be transformed if separate states were abolished, but world government is not around the corner. And although nonstate actors such as transnational corporations, nongovernmental organizations, and terrorist groups present new challenges to governments, they do not replace states. The peoples who live in the nearly 200 states on this planet want their independence, separate cultures, and different languages. In fact, rather than vanishing, nationalism and the demand for separate states have increased. Rather than fewer states, this century will probably see more. World government would not automatically solve the problem of war. Most wars today are civil or ethnic wars. Since the November 1989 fall of the Berlin Wall, 71 armed conflicts occurred in 50 different locations around the world. Eight were interstate wars, and 11 were intrastate wars with foreign intervention.[1] In fact, the bloodiest wars of the nineteenth century were not among the quarreling states of Europe; rather, they were the Taiping Rebellion in China and the American Civil War. We will continue to live in a world of rival communities and separate states for quite some time, and it is important to understand what that means for our prospects.

What Is International Politics?

1.1 **Identify the distinctive features of a sovereign state system and their implications for cooperation and conflict.**

The world has not always been divided into a system of separate states. Over the centuries, there have been three basic forms of world politics. In an *imperial system*, one government controls most of the world with which it has contact. The greatest example in the Western world was the Roman Empire, but the Sumerian,

Persian, Mongol, Chinese, Aztec, and Mayan empires fell into this category as well. None was a genuine *world* empire; each was a regional empire protected from conflict or competition for a time by lack of communication with the outside word. Their fights with barbarians on the peripheries of their empires were not the same as wars among roughly equal states.

A second basic form of international politics is a *feudal system*, in which human loyalties and political obligations are not fixed primarily by territorial boundaries. Feudalism was common in Europe after the collapse of the Roman Empire. An individual had obligations to a local lord, but might also owe other duties to some distant noble or bishop, as well as to the pope in Rome. Political obligations were determined to a large extent by what happened to one's superiors. If a ruler married, an area and its people might find their obligations rearranged as part of a wedding dowry. Townspeople born French might suddenly find themselves Flemish or even English. Cities and leagues of cities sometimes had a special semi-independent status. The crazy quilt of wars that accompanied the feudal situation did not much resemble modern territorial wars. These wars could occur within as well as across territories and were shaped by cross-cutting, nonterritorial loyalties and conflicts.

A third form of world politics is an *anarchic system of states*, composed of states that are relatively cohesive but with no higher government above them. Examples include the city-states of ancient Greece and Machiavelli's fifteenth-century Italy. Another example of an anarchic state system is the dynastic territorial state whose coherence comes from control by a ruling family. Examples can be found in India and China in the fifth century BCE. Large territorial dynasties reemerged in Europe in about 1500, and other forms of polities such as city-states and loose leagues of territories began to vanish. In 1648, the *Peace of Westphalia* ended Europe's Thirty Years' War, sometimes called the last of the great wars of religion and the first of the wars of modern states. In retrospect, we can see that the Peace of Westphalia enshrined the territorial sovereign state as the dominant political unit. What we now call the "Westphalian system" has included imperial states from time to time; the most successful by far was the nineteenth-century British empire, upon which, it was famously said, "the sun never set" (because Britain had imperial possessions in almost every time zone). Even at its peak, though, the British empire faced challenges from other strong states.

Today when we speak of the international system, we usually mean this Westphalian system of sovereign states, and we define *international politics* as politics in the absence of a common sovereign or politics among entities with no ruler above them. International politics is a self-help system. The English philosopher Thomas Hobbes (1588–1679) called such an anarchic system a "state of nature." For some, the words *state of nature* may conjure up images of a herd of cows grazing peacefully on a farm, but that is not what Hobbes meant. Think of a Texas town without a sheriff in the days of the Old West, or Lebanon after its government broke down in the 1970s, or Somalia in the 1990s. Hobbes did not think of a state of nature as benign; he saw it as a war of all against all, because there was no higher ruler to enforce order. As Hobbes famously declared, life in such a world would be nasty, brutish, and short.

Because there is no higher authority above states, there are important legal, political, and social differences between domestic and international politics. Domestic law is relatively clear and consistent. Police and courts enforce it. By contrast, international law is patchy, is incomplete, and rests on sometimes vague foundations. There is no common enforcement mechanism. The world lacks a global police force, and although there are a few international courts, they can do little when sovereign states choose to ignore them.

Force plays a different role in domestic and international politics as well. In a well-ordered domestic political system, the government has a monopoly on the legitimate use of force. In international politics, no one has such a monopoly. Because international politics is the realm of self-help and some states are stronger than others, there is always a danger that they may resort to force. When force cannot be ruled out, mistrust and suspicion are common.

Domestic and international politics also differ in their underlying sense of community. In a well-ordered domestic society, a widespread sense of community gives rise to common loyalties, standards of justice, and views of legitimate authority. On a global scale, people have competing loyalties. Any sense of global community is weak. People often disagree about what is just and legitimate. The result is a great gap between two basic political values: order and justice. In such a world, most people place national concerns before international justice. Law and ethics play roles in international politics, but in the absence of a sense of community norms, they are weaker forces than in domestic politics.

Some people speculate that of the three basic systems—world imperial, feudal, and Westphalian—the twenty-first century may see the gradual evolution of a new feudalism, or less plausibly, a new world empire. We will look at those questions in Chapter 10.

Differing Views of Anarchic Politics

International politics is anarchic in the sense that there is no government above sovereign states, but political philosophy offers different views of how harsh a state of nature need be. Hobbes, who wrote in a seventeenth-century England wracked by civil war, emphasized insecurity, force, and survival. He described humanity as being in a constant state of war. A half century later, John Locke (1632–1704), writing in a more stable England, argued that although a state of nature lacked a common sovereign, people could develop ties and make contracts; therefore, anarchy was not necessarily an obstacle to peace. Those two visions of a state of nature are the philosophical precursors of two of the most influential views of international politics, one more pessimistic and one more optimistic: *realism* and *liberalism*.

Realism has been the dominant tradition in thinking about international politics for centuries. For the realist, the central problem of international politics is war and the use of force, and the central actors are states. Among modern Americans, realism is exemplified by the writings and policies of President Richard Nixon and his secretary of state, Henry Kissinger. The realist starts from the assumption that in an anarchic system of states, the survival of the state is always at least potentially threatened by other states. Accordingly, Kissinger and Nixon sought to ensure that the United States had enough power of its own to minimize the ability of other states to jeopardize U.S. security. According to the realist, international politics is first and foremost about protecting the state from other states.

The other tradition, *liberalism*, can be traced back in Western political philosophy to Baron de Montesquieu and Immanuel Kant in eighteenth-century France and Germany, respectively, and such nineteenth-century British philosophers as Jeremy Bentham and John Stuart Mill. The best modern American examples of liberal thought can be found in the writings and policies of the political scientist and president Woodrow Wilson.

Liberals see a global society that functions alongside states and sets an important part of the context for state action. Trade crosses borders, people have contacts with one another (such as students studying in foreign countries), and international institutions such as the League of Nations and its successor the United Nations mitigate some of the harsher aspects of anarchy. Liberals complain that realists underestimate the importance of such things as people's contacts across borders and the respects in which sovereign states make up a kind of international "society." Realists, claim liberals, overstate the difference between domestic and international politics. Because the realist picture of anarchy as a Hobbesian "state of war" focuses only on extreme situations, in the liberals' view it has a hard time explaining and recognizing the importance of such things as the growth of economic interdependence and the evolution of a transnational global society, both of which can be powerful forces for peace.

Realists respond by quoting Hobbes: "Just as stormy weather does not mean perpetual rain, so a state of war does not mean constant war."[2] Just as Londoners carry umbrellas on sunny April days, the prospect of war in an anarchic system makes states keep armies even in times of peace. Realists point to

---

1910: The "Unseen Vampire" of War

If there were no other reason for making an end of war, the financial ruin it involves must sooner or later bring the civilized nations of the world to their senses. As President David Starr Jordan of Leland Stanford University said at Tufts College, "Future war is impossible because the nations cannot afford it." In Europe, he says, the war debt is $26 billion, "all owed to the unseen vampire, and which the nations will never pay and which taxes poor people $95 million a year." The burdens of militarism in time of peace are exhausting the strength of the leading nations, already overloaded with debts. The certain result of a great war would be overwhelming bankruptcy.

—*THE NEW YORK WORLD*[3]

previous liberal predictions that went awry. For example, in 1910, the president of Stanford University said that future war was no longer possible because it was too costly. Liberal writers proclaimed war obsolete; civilization had grown out of it, they argued. Economic interdependence, ties between labor unions and intellectuals, and the flow of capital all made war impossible. Of course, these predictions failed catastrophically when World War I broke out in 1914, and the realists felt vindicated.

Example

Neither history nor the argument between the realists and liberals stopped in 1914. The 1970s saw a resurgence of liberal claims that rising economic and social interdependence was changing the nature of international politics. In the 1980s, Richard Rosecrance wrote that states can increase their power in two ways: either aggressively by territorial conquest or peacefully through trade. He used the experience of Japan as an example. In the 1930s, Japan tried territorial conquest and suffered the disaster of World War II. But after the war, Japan used trade and investment to become the second largest economy in the world (measured by official exchange rates) and a significant power in East Asia. Japan succeeded while spending far less on its military, proportionately to the size of either its population or its economy, than other major powers. Thus Rosecrance and modern liberals argue that the nature of international politics is changing.

Some recent liberals look even further to the future and believe that dramatic growth in ecological interdependence will so blur the differences between domestic and international politics that humanity will evolve toward a world without borders. For example, everyone is affected by greenhouse gas emissions that warm the planet regardless of where they live. Problems such as HIV/AIDS and drugs also cross borders with such ease that we may be on our way to a different world. Professor Richard Falk of Princeton University argues that transnational problems and values will alter the state-centric orientation of the international system that has dominated for the last 400 years. Transnational forces are undoing the Peace of Westphalia, and humanity is evolving toward a new form of international politics.

In the 1980s, analysts on both sides of the realist-liberal divide attempted to emulate microeconomics by developing formal, deductive theories. *Neorealists* such as Kenneth Waltz and *neoliberals* such as Robert Keohane developed structural models of states as rational actors constrained by the international system. Neorealists and neoliberals increased the simplicity and elegance of theory, but they did so at the cost of discarding much of the rich complexity of classical realism and liberalism. As Miles Kahler put it, "By the end of the 1980s, the theoretical contest that might have been was reduced to relatively narrow disagreements within one state-centric rationalist model of international relations."[4]

These divergent views on the nature of international politics and whether (and, if so, how) it is changing will not soon be reconciled. Realists stress continuity; liberals stress change. Both claim to be more "realistic." Liberals tend to see realists as cynics whose fascination with the past blinds them to change. Realists, in turn, think liberals are utopian dreamers peddling "globaloney."

Who is right? Both are right in some respects and wrong in others. A clear-cut answer might be nice, but it would not be accurate, and it would be less interesting than a complicated one. The mix of continuity and change that characterizes today's world makes it impossible to arrive at one simple, synthetic characterization. Moreover, the world is "patchy." In some regions, such as the Middle East, international politics looks quite realist. In others, such as Western Europe, it looks more liberal.

Realism and liberalism are not the only approaches. Recently, a diverse group of theorists called *constructivists* has argued that realism and liberalism both fail to explain long-term change in world politics adequately. For example, neither realists nor liberals predicted the end of the Cold War, nor could they explain it satisfactorily after the fact. Constructivists emphasize the importance of ideas and culture in shaping both the reality and the discourse of international politics. They stress the ultimate subjectivity of interests and the ways in which interests interact with identities. A constructivist might argue, for example, that realism would do a good job of explaining international politics in a world in which states were led by people such as Richard Nixon and Henry Kissinger, while liberalism would do a good job in a world led by people such as Woodrow Wilson. Everything depends on the ideas that dominate at any given time, and ideas change.

Constructivists focus on identities, norms, culture, national interests, and international governance.[5] They believe that leaders and other people are motivated not only by material interests, but also by their sense of identity, morality, and what their society or culture considers appropriate. These norms change over time, partly through interaction with others. Constructivists agree that the international system is anarchic, but they argue that there is a spectrum of anarchies ranging from benign, peaceful, even friendly ones to bitterly hostile, competitive ones. The nature of anarchy at any given time depends on prevailing norms, perceptions, and beliefs. As the prominent constructivist scholar Alexander Wendt puts it, anarchy is what states make of it. That is why Americans worry more about one North Korean nuclear weapon than 500 British nuclear weapons and why war between France and Germany, which occurred twice in the twentieth century, seems unthinkable today.[6]

Realists and liberals take for granted that states seek to promote their "national interest," but they have little to say about how those interests are shaped or change over time. Constructivists draw on different disciplines to examine the processes by which leaders, peoples, and cultures alter their preferences, shape their identities, and learn new behaviors. For example, both slavery in the nineteenth century and racial apartheid in South Africa in the twentieth century were accepted by most states once upon a time, but both later came to be widely condemned. Constructivists ask: Why the change? What role did ideas play? Will the practice of war go the same way someday? What about the concept of the sovereign state? The world is full of political entities such as tribes, nations, and nongovernmental organizations. Only in recent centuries has the sovereign state been dominant. Constructivists suggest that concepts such as "state" and "sovereignty" that shape our understandings of world politics and that animate our theories are, in fact, socially constructed; they are not given, nor are they permanent. Even our understanding of "security" evolves. Traditional international relations theories used to understand security strictly in terms of preventing violence or war among states, but in today's world, "human security"—a relatively new concept—seems at least as problematic. Moreover, a wider range of phenomena have become "securitized," that is, treated politically as dire threats warranting extraordinary efforts to address them. Scholars and politicians worry today not only about interstate war, but also about poverty, inequality, and economic or ecological catastrophe, as we will see in Chapters 8 and 9.

Constructivism is an approach that rejects neorealism's and neoliberalism's search for scientific laws. Instead, it seeks contingent generalizations and often offers thick description as a form of explanation. Some of the most important debates in world politics today revolve around the meanings of terms such as *sovereignty*, *humanitarian intervention*, *human rights*, and *genocide*, and constructivists have much more to say about these issues than do those advocating older approaches.[7] Constructivism provides both a useful critique and an important supplement to realism and liberalism. Although sometimes loosely formulated and lacking in predictive power, constructivist approaches remind us of what realism and liberalism often miss. As we shall see in Chapter 2, it is important to look beyond the instrumental rationality of pursuing current goals and ask how changing identities and interests can sometimes lead to subtle shifts in states' policies and sometimes to profound changes in international affairs. Constructivists help us understand how preferences are formed and judgments are shaped. In that sense, constructivist thought complements rather than opposes the two main approaches. We will illustrate the questions of understanding long-term change in Chapter 2 and return to it in Chapter 10.

Realism, liberalism, and constructivism disagree on many things, but they tend to agree that the most productive way of understanding international politics is to focus on states as the main actors. Not everyone has held this view. For more than a century, *Marxism* was a popular alternative for many people. Originally developed by Karl Marx and Friedrich Engels and subsequently enhanced and adapted by other theorists, Marxism denied that states were the most important actors in international politics and insisted that economic classes—primarily capitalists and workers—were more important. Marxists were particularly interested in the domestic economic structure of capitalist states and tended to explain world politics in terms of class dynamics. Marxism's concentration on economic class, production, and property relations has sometimes been called "economic reductionism" or "historical materialism." Marxists believed that politics is a function of economics and predicted that the greed of capitalists would drive important events in international relations, ultimately proving their own undoing as socialist revolution swept the globe. But Marxists underestimated the forces of nationalism, state power, and geopolitics. Their lack of attention to the importance of diplomacy and the balance of power led to a flawed understanding of international politics and erroneous predictions. Even before the collapse of the Soviet Union in 1991, the failure of Marxist theory to account for peace among major capitalist states and warfare among various communist states undermined its explanatory value. For example, it was difficult for Marxists to explain clashes between China and the Soviet Union in 1969, the Vietnamese invasion of Cambodia in 1978, and the Sino-Vietnamese War of 1979, all of which were serious conflicts between communist states.

In the 1960s and 1970s, *dependency theory*, which builds on Marxism, was popular. It predicted that the wealthy countries in the "center" of the global marketplace would control and hold back poorer countries on the "periphery." According to dependency theorists, the global economic and political division between the First World (rich, liberal, capitalist countries) and the Third World (developing countries), also known as the North-South divide, is the result of both historical imperialism and the nature of capitalist globalization. Dependency theory enjoyed some explanatory successes, such as accounting for the failure of many poor countries to benefit from global economic liberalization to the extent that orthodox liberal economic theory predicted. It also drew attention to the curious and important phenomenon of the "dual economy" in developing countries, in which a small, wealthy, educated, urban economic elite interacted with and profited handsomely from globalization while the vast majority of impoverished, largely rural farmers, laborers, and miners did not. But although dependency theory helped illuminate some important structural causes of economic inequality, it had difficulty explaining why, in the 1980s and 1990s, "peripheral" countries in East Asia, such as South Korea, Singapore, and Malaysia, grew more rapidly than "central" countries in North America and Europe. South Korea and Singapore are now wealthy "developed" countries in their own right, and Malaysia is a rising middle-income country. These weaknesses of dependency theory were underlined when Fernando Henrique Cardoso, a leading dependency theorist in the 1970s, turned to liberal economic policies after being elected president of Brazil in the 1990s.

In contrast to Marxist scholars and dependency theorists who focus attention on economic class, *feminist* international relations scholars focus on gender. A key characteristic of virtually every society—including the anarchic society of Westphalian states—is *patriarchy*, or the systematic privileging of stereotypically "masculine" traits and virtues, such as strength, autonomy, competitiveness, and martial skill. Although everyone exhibits some mix of stereotypically "masculine" and "feminine" characteristics, patriarchy advantages men and blinds us to the rights, needs, and particular vulnerabilities of women. Feminist scholars draw our attention to systematic disparities between the sexes. In no country do women enjoy perfect equality with men. The United Nations Development Program tracks disparities by means of the "Gender Inequality Index."[8] In 2013, Slovenia came out on top, with a score of 0.021, very close to full equality; of those countries with enough reliable data to be ranked, Niger came in last with a score of 0.709. In addition to being systematically disadvantaged, women are also grossly underrepresented in positions of high political office. Out of 193 full member states of the United Nations, only 27 had female heads of state or government in 2015.[9]

Feminist critiques also illuminate problematic aspects of globalization, such as the "export" or trafficking of women and children and the use of rape as an instrument of war. Feminism gained strength as a critical approach in the early 1990s when traditional security concerns lost some of their apparent urgency in the wake of the Cold War. By focusing on social processes, nonelite issues, and transnational structures and by rejecting the established, limited focus on interstate relations, feminism aims to study world politics more inclusively and reveal "the processes through which identities and interests, not merely of states but of key social constituencies, are shaped at the global level."[10]

Theory and Practice

When I was working in Washington and helping formulate American foreign policies as an assistant secretary in the State Department and the Pentagon, I found myself borrowing elements from all three types of thinking: realism, liberalism, and constructivism. I found all of them helpful, though in different ways and in different circumstances.

—Joseph S. Nye, Jr.

> *this is so weird and narcissistic*

Sometimes practical men and women wonder why we should bother with theory at all. The answer is that theory provides a road map that allows us to make sense of unfamiliar terrain. We are lost without it. Even when we think that we are just using common sense, there is usually an implicit theory guiding our actions; we simply do not know or have forgotten what it is. If we were more conscious of the theories that guide us, we would be better able to understand their strengths and weaknesses and when best to apply them. As the British economist John Maynard Keynes once put it, practical men who consider themselves above theory are usually listening to some dead scribbler from the past whose name they have long forgotten.[11]

Building Blocks

Actors, *goals*, and *instruments* are three concepts that are basic to theorizing about international politics. As we have seen, in the traditional realist view of international politics, the only significant "actors" are the states, and only the big states really matter. This situation is changing, though. The number of states has grown enormously since World War II. In 1945, there were about 50 states in the world; today, there are almost four times that many. More important than the number of states is the rise of *nonstate actors*. Today, large multinational corporations straddle international borders and rival states in economic might (Table 1.1). Although multinational corporations lack some types of power such as military force, they are very relevant to a country's economic goals. In terms of the economy, Anheuser-Busch is more important to Belgium than is Burundi, a former Belgian colony. In fact, Anheuser-Busch's annual profit is more than five times Burundi's entire gross domestic product.[12]

Table 1.1 The World's 100 Largest Economic Units (2013)

Rank	Country or Corporation	GDP (Country) or Revenue (Corporation), US $billion
1	United States	16,768
2	China	9,240
3	Japan	4,920
4	Germany	3,730
5	France	2,806
6	United Kingdom	2,678
7	Brazil	2,246
8	Italy	2,149
9	Russia	2,097
10	India	1,877
11	Canada	1,827
12	Australia	1,560
13	Spain	1,393
14	South Korea	1,305
15	Mexico	1,261
16	Indonesia	868
17	Netherlands	854
18	Turkey	822
19	Saudi Arabia	748
20	Switzerland	685
21	Argentina	610
22	Sweden	580
23	Poland	526
24	Belgium	525
25	Nigeria	522
26	Norway	513
27	Walmart Stores	477
28	Royal Dutch Shell	451
29	Sinopec-China Petroleum	445
30	Venezuela	438
31	Austria	428
32	United Arab Emirates	402
33	Exxon Mobil Corp.	394
34	Thailand	387
35	BP	379
36	Colombia	378
37	Iran	369
38	South Africa	351

(continued)

Rank	Country or Corporation	GDP (Country) or Revenue (Corporation), US $billion
39	Denmark	336
40	PetroChina	329
41	Malaysia	313
42	Singapore	298
43	Israel	291
44	Chile	277
45	Philippines	272
46	Egypt	272
47	Finland	267
48	Volkswagen Group	262
49	Toyota Motor	256
50	Greece	242
51	Pakistan	232
52	Ireland	232
53	Kazakhstan	232
54	Iraq	229
55	Total	228
56	Portugal	227
57	Chevron	212
58	Algeria	210
59	Samsung Electronics	209
60	Czech Republic	200
61	Qatar	203
62	Peru	202
63	Romania	190
64	New Zealand	186
65	Berkshire Hathaway	179
66	Ukraine	177
67	Kuwait	176
68	Apple	174
69	Vietnam	171
70	Gazprom	165
71	E.ON	163
72	Phillips 66	158
73	Daimler	157
74	General Motors	155
75	ENI	153
76	Bangladesh	150
77	ICBC	149

(continued)

Rank	Country or Corporation	GDP (Country) or Revenue (Corporation), US $billion
78	Ford Motor	147
79	EXOR	144
80	General Electric	143
81	Rosneft	143
82	Petrobras	141
83	AXA Group	139
84	Valero Energy	138
85	Agricultural Bank of China	136
86	Hungary	133
87	Allianz	131
88	McKesson	130
89	AT&T	129
90	Hon Hai Precision	127
91	CVS Caremark	127
92	JX Holdings	125
93	Angola	124
94	BNP Paribas	123
95	Fannie Mae	123
96	UnitedHealth Group	123
97	China Construction Bank	121
98	Verizon Communications	121
99	LukOil	119
100	Honda Motor	118

Source: Forbes, World's Biggest Public Companies, http://www.forbes.com/global2000/list/ (values calculated May 2014); World Bank, GDP 2013 (current $US), http://data.worldbank.org/indicator/NY.GDP.MKTP.CD?page=5.

for reference

A picture of the Middle East without warring states and outside powers would be downright silly, but it would also be woefully inadequate if it did not include a variety of nonstate actors. Multinational oil companies such as Shell, BP, and ExxonMobil are one type of nonstate actor, but there are others. There are large intergovernmental organizations (IGOs), such as the United Nations, and smaller ones, such as the Arab League and the Organization of Petroleum Exporting Countries (OPEC). There are nongovernmental organizations (NGOs), such as the Red Cross and Amnesty International. There are also a variety of transnational ethnic groups, such as the Kurds who live in Turkey, Syria, Iran, and Iraq, and the Armenians, scattered throughout the Middle East and the Caucasus. Terrorist groups such as ISIL and al-Qaeda, drug cartels, and criminal organizations span national borders and often divide their resources among several states. International religious movements, particularly political

Islam in the Middle East and North Africa, add a further dimension to the range of nonstate actors.

The question is not whether state or nonstate groups are more important—usually the states are—but how new, complex coalitions affect the politics of a region in a way that the traditional realist views fail to disclose. States are the major actors in current international politics, but they do not have the stage to themselves.

What about goals? Traditionally, the dominant goal of states in an anarchic system has been military security. Countries today obviously care about their military security, but they often care as much or more about their economic wealth, about social issues such as stopping drug trafficking or the spread of AIDS, or about ecological changes. Moreover, as we noted above, as threats change, the definition of security changes; military security is not the only goal that states pursue. Looking at the relationship between the United States and Canada, where the prospects of war are essentially zero, a Canadian diplomat once said that his fear was not that the United States would march into Canada and sack Toronto as it did in 1813, but that Toronto would be programmed out of relevance by computers in Texas, a rather different dilemma from the traditional one of states in an anarchic system. Economic strength has not replaced military security (as Kuwait discovered when Iraq invaded it in August 1990), but the agenda of international politics has become more complex as states pursue a wider range of goals, including human security.

Along with the goals, the *instruments* of international politics are also changing. The realist view is that military force is the only instrument that really matters. Describing the world before 1914, the British historian A. J. P. Taylor defined a great power as one able to prevail in war. States obviously use military force today, but the years since World War II have seen changes in its role. Many states, particularly large ones, find it more costly to use military force to achieve their goals than was true in earlier times. As Stanley Hoffmann put it, the link between military strength and positive achievement has been loosened.

What are the reasons? One is that the ultimate means of military force, nuclear weaponry, is hopelessly muscle-bound. Although they once numbered more than 50,000, nuclear weapons have not been used in war since 1945. The disproportion between the vast devastation nuclear weapons can inflict and any reasonable political goal has made leaders understandably loath to employ them. Thus the ultimate form of military force is for all practical purposes too costly for national leaders to use in war.

Even conventional force has become more costly when used to rule nationalistic populations. In the nineteenth century, European countries conquered other parts of the globe by fielding a handful of soldiers armed with modern weapons and then administered their colonial possessions with relatively modest garrisons. But in an age of socially mobilized populations, it is difficult to rule an occupied country whose people feel strongly about their national identity. Americans

Examples found this out in Vietnam in the 1960s and 1970s; the Soviets discovered it in Afghanistan in the 1980s. Vietnam and Afghanistan had not become more powerful than the nuclear superpowers, but trying to rule these nationalistically aware populations was too expensive for either the United States or the Soviet Union. Foreign rule is very costly in an age of nationalism. In the nineteenth century, Britain was able to rule India with a handful of soldiers and civil servants, which would be impossible in today's world.

A third change in the role of force relates to internal constraints. Over time, there has been a growing ethic of antimilitarism, particularly in democracies. Such views do not prevent the use of force, but they make it a politically risky choice for leaders, particularly when it is massive or prolonged. It is sometimes said that democracies will not accept casualties, but that statement is too simple. Surveys show, for example, that the American people will accept casualties when the cause is just and military action serves a clear national interest.[13] The United States expected, and therefore was obviously prepared to accept, some 10,000 casualties when it entered the Gulf War in 1991, but it was loath to accept casualties in Somalia or Kosovo where the mission was less clear and U.S. national interests less deeply involved. Of course, in addition, if the use of force is seen as unjust or illegitimate in the eyes of other states, it can become costly for political leaders in democratic polities. Force is not obsolete, and terrorist nonstate actors are less constrained than states by such moral concerns, but force is more costly and more difficult for most states to use than in the past.

Finally, a number of issues simply do not lend themselves to forceful solutions. Take, for example, economic relations between the United States and Japan. In 1853, Commodore Matthew Perry sailed his "black ships" into the harbor at Uraga and threatened bombardment unless Japan opened its ports to trade. That would not be a very useful or politically acceptable way to solve modern-day U.S.-Japan trade disputes. Thus, although force remains a critical instrument in international politics, it is not the only instrument. The use of economic interdependence, communication, and international institutions sometimes plays a larger role than force. Military force is not obsolete as a state instrument: witness the fighting in Afghanistan, where the Taliban government had sheltered the al-Qaeda terrorist network that carried out the 9/11 attacks on the United States, or the U.S. and British use of force to overthrow Saddam Hussein in 2003. But it was easier to win the war than to win the peace in Iraq, and military force alone is not sufficient to protect against terrorism. Although military force remains the ultimate instrument in international politics, changes in its cost and effectiveness make today's international politics more complex.

The basic game of security goes on. Some political scientists argue that the balance of power is usually determined by a leading, or hegemonic, state, such as Spain in the sixteenth century, France under Louis XIV, Britain during most of the nineteenth century, and the United States in the late twentieth and early twenty-first centuries. Eventually, the top country will be challenged, and this challenge will lead to the kind of vast conflagrations that we call hegemonic, or world, wars. After world wars, a new treaty sets the new framework of order: the Treaty of Utrecht in 1713, the Congress of Vienna in 1815, the League of Nations in 1919, and the United Nations in 1945. If nothing basic has changed in international politics since the struggle for supremacy between Athens and Sparta, will a new challenge lead to another world war, or is the cycle of hegemonic war over? Will a rising China challenge the United States? Has nuclear technology made world war too devastating? Has economic interdependence made it too costly? Will nonstate actors such as terrorists force governments to cooperate? Has global society made war socially and morally unthinkable? We have to hope so, because the next hegemonic war could be the last. But first, it is important to understand the case for continuity.

Follow Up

- Kenneth Waltz, *Man, the State, and War: A Theoretical Analysis* (New York: Columbia University Press, 1959), pp. 1–15.

- Richard Ned Lebow, *A Cultural Theory of International Relations* (Cambridge: Cambridge University Press, 2008), pp. 1–28.

The Peloponnesian War

1.2 Explain how history can help us understand international politics today.

Thucydides (c. 460–400 BCE) is widely considered the inspiration for realism, the perspective most people use when thinking about international politics even when they do not know they are thinking theoretically. Theories are the indispensable tools we use to organize facts. Many of today's leaders and editorial writers use realist theories even if they have not heard of Thucydides. A member of the Athenian elite who lived during Athens' greatest age, Thucydides participated in some of the events described in his *History of the Peloponnesian War*. Robert Gilpin, a notable realist, asserted, "In honesty, one must inquire whether or not twentieth-century students of international relations know anything that Thucydides and his fifth-century [BCE] compatriots did not know about the behavior of states." He then answered his own query: "Ultimately international politics can still be characterized as it was by Thucydides."[14] Gilpin's proposition is debatable, but to debate it, we must know what Thucydides said. And what better introduction to realist theory is there than one of history's great stories? Like many great stories, it has its limits, however. One of the things we learn from the Peloponnesian War is to avoid too simplistic a reading of history.

Figure 1.1 Classical Greece

SOURCE: Brian Catchpole, *A Map History of the Modern World* (Oxford: Heinemann Publishers, 1982), reprinted with adjustments by permission.

A Short Version of a Long Story

Athens and Sparta (Figure 1.1) were allies that had cooperated to defeat the Persian Empire in 480 BCE. Sparta was a conservative, land-oriented state that turned inward after the victory over Persia; Athens was a commercial, sea-oriented state that turned outward. In the middle of the century, Athens had 50 years of growth that led to the development of an Athenian empire. Athens formed the Delian League, an alliance of states around the Aegean Sea, for mutual protection against the Persians. Sparta, in turn, organized its neighbors on the Peloponnesian Peninsula into a defensive alliance. States that had joined Athens freely for protection against the Persians soon had to pay taxes to the Athenians. Because of the growing strength of Athens and the resistance of some to its growing empire, a war broke out in 461. By 445, the first Peloponnesian War ended and was followed by a treaty that promised peace for 30 years. Thus

Greece enjoyed a period of stable peace before the second, more significant, Peloponnesian War.

In 434, a civil war broke out in the small, peripheral city-state of Epidamnus. Like a pebble that begins an avalanche, this event triggered a series of reactions that led ultimately to the second Peloponnesian War. Large conflicts are often precipitated by relatively insignificant crises in out-of-the-way places, as we shall see when we discuss World War I.

In Epidamnus, the democrats fought with oligarchs over how the country would be ruled. The democrats appealed to the city-state of Corcyra, which had helped establish Epidamnus, but were turned down. They then turned to another city-state, Corinth, and the Corinthians decided to help. This move angered the Corcyraeans, who sent a fleet to recapture Epidamnus, their former colony. In the process, the Corcyraeans defeated the Corinthian fleet. Corinth was outraged and declared war on Corcyra. Corcyra, fearing the attack from Corinth, turned to Athens for help. Both Corcyra and Corinth sent representatives to Athens.

The Athenians, after listening to both sides, were in a dilemma. They did not want to break the truce that had lasted for a decade, but if the Corinthians (who were close to the Peloponnesians) conquered Corcyra and took control of its large navy, the balance of power among the Greek states would tip against Athens. The Athenians believed that they could not risk letting the Corcyraean navy fall into the hands of the Corinthians, so they decided to become "a little bit involved." They launched a small endeavor to scare the Corinthians, sending ten ships with instructions not to fight unless attacked. But deterrence failed; Corinth attacked, and when the Corcyraeans began to lose the battle, the Athenian ships were drawn into the fray more than they had intended. The Athenian involvement infuriated Corinth, which in turn worried the Athenians. In particular, Athens worried that Corinth would stir up problems in Potidaea, which, although an Athenian ally, had historic ties to Corinth. Sparta promised to help Corinth if Athens attacked Potidaea. When a revolt did occur in Potidaea, Athens sent forces to put it down.

At that point, there was a great debate in Sparta. The Athenians appealed to the Spartans to stay neutral. The Corinthians urged the Spartans to go to war and warned them against failing to check the rising power of Athens. Megara, another important city, agreed with Corinth because contrary to the treaty, the Athenians had banned Megara's trade. Sparta was torn, but the Spartans voted in favor of war, according to Thucydides, because they were afraid that if Athenian power was not checked, Athens might control the whole of Greece. In other words, Sparta went to war to maintain the balance of power among the Greek city-states.

Bust of Thucydides

The second Peloponnesian War broke out in 431. The Athenians' mood was one of imperial greatness, with pride and patriotism about their city and their social system, and optimism that they would prevail in the war. The early phase of the war came to a stalemate. A truce was declared after ten years (421), but it was fragile, and war broke out again. In 413, Athens undertook a very risky venture. It sent two fleets and infantry to conquer Sicily, the great island off the south of Italy, which had a number of Greek colonies allied to Sparta. The result was a terrible defeat for the Athenians. At the same time, Sparta received additional money from the Persians, who were only too happy to see Athens trounced. After the defeat in Sicily, Athens was internally divided. In 411, the oligarchs overthrew the democrats, and 400 of them attempted to rule Athens. These events were not the end, but Athens never really recovered. An Athenian naval victory in 410 was followed five years later by a Spartan naval victory, and by 404, Athens was compelled to sue for peace. Sparta demanded that Athens pull down the long walls that protected it from attack by land-based powers. Athens' power was broken.

Causes and Theories

This story is dramatic and powerful. What caused the war? Thucydides is very clear. After recounting the various events in Epidamnus, Corcyra, and so forth, he said that they were not the real causes. What made the war inevitable, Thucydides insisted, was the growth of Athenian power and the fear it caused in Sparta.

Did Athens have a choice? With better foresight, could Athens have avoided this disaster? Pericles, the Athenian leader in the early days of the war, had an interesting answer for his fellow citizens. "[Y]our country has a right to your services in sustaining the glories of her position. . . . You should remember also that what you are fighting against is not merely slavery as an exchange for independence, but also loss of empire and danger from the animosities incurred in its exercise. Besides, to recede is no longer possible . . . [f]or what you hold is, to speak somewhat plainly, a tyranny; to take it was perhaps wrong, but to let it go is unsafe."[15] In other words, Pericles told his fellow Athenians that they had no choice. Perhaps they should not be where they were, but once they had an empire, there was not much they could do about it without even larger risks. Thus Pericles favored war. But there were other voices in Athens, such as those of the Athenian delegates to the debate in Sparta in 432 BCE who urged the Spartans to "consider the vast influence of accident in war, before you are engaged in it."[16] That turned out to be good advice; why didn't the Athenians heed their own counsel? Perhaps they were carried away by emotional patriotism or anger that clouded their reason. But there is a more interesting possibility. Perhaps the Athenians acted rationally but were caught in a security dilemma.

Security dilemmas are particularly acute in a Hobbesian anarchy in which there is plenty of fear but little trust. The ancient Greek city-state system was anarchical in the sense that strong city-states such as Athens and Sparta were subject to no higher authority. (The same could not be said of weaker city-states that were colonies or subjects of Athens or Sparta, of course.) Under anarchy, independent action taken by one state to increase its security may make other states less secure. If one state builds its strength to make sure that another cannot threaten it, the other, seeing the first getting stronger, may build its strength to protect itself against the first. The result is that the independent effort of each to improve its security makes both more insecure. It is an ironic result, yet neither state has acted irrationally. Neither has acted from anger or pride, but from fear caused by the threat perceived in the growth of the other. After all, building defenses is a rational response to a perceived threat. States could cooperate to avoid this security dilemma; that is, they could agree that neither should build up its defenses, and all would be better off. If it seems obvious that states should cooperate, why don't they?

An answer can be found in the game called the *Prisoner's Dilemma*. (Security dilemmas are a specific type of Prisoner's Dilemma.) The Prisoner's Dilemma scenario goes like this: Imagine that somewhere the police arrest two men who have small amounts of drugs in their possession, which would probably result in one-year jail sentences. The police have good reason to believe that these two are really drug dealers, but they do not have enough evidence for a conviction. As dealers, the two could easily get 25-year jail sentences. The police know that the testimony of one against the other would be sufficient to convict the other to a full sentence. The police offer to let each man off if he will testify that the other is a drug dealer. They tell them that if both testify, both will receive ten-year sentences. The police figure that this way these dealers will be out of commission for ten years; otherwise, they are both in jail for only one year and soon will be out selling drugs again.

The suspects are put in separate cells and are not allowed to communicate with each other. Each prisoner has the same dilemma: If the other stays silent, he can secure his own freedom by confessing, sending the other fellow to jail for 25 years; or he can stay silent and spend one year in jail. If both prisoners confess, however, they each get ten years in jail. Each prisoner thinks, "No matter what the other one does, I'm better off if I confess. If he stays quiet, I go free if I confess and spend a year in jail if I remain silent. If he confesses, I get ten years if I confess and 25 years if I don't." If both think this way, both will confess and spend ten years in jail each. If they could trust each other not to confess, however, they would both be much better off, spending only one year in jail.

That is the basic structural dilemma of independent rational action in a situation of this kind. If the two could talk to each other, they might agree to make a deal to stay silent and both spend one year in jail. But even if communication were possible, there would be another problem: trust and credibility. Continuing with the metaphor in the Prisoner's Dilemma, each suspect could say to himself, "We are both drug dealers. I have seen the way the other acts. How do I know that after we've made this deal, he won't say, 'Great! I've convinced him to stay quiet. Now I can get my best possible outcome: freedom!'?" Similarly, in an international system characterized by Hobbesian anarchy, distrust encourages states to try to provide for their own security, even though doing so may actually result in mutual insecurity. One state could say to another, "Don't build up your armaments and I will not build up my armaments, and we will both live happily ever after," but the second state may wonder whether it can afford to trust the first state.

The Athenian position in 432 looks very much like the Prisoner's Dilemma. In the middle of the century, the Athenians and Spartans agreed that they were both better off having a truce. Even after the events in Epidamnus and the dispute between Corcyra and Corinth, the Athenians were reluctant to break it. The Corcyraeans ultimately convinced the Athenians with the following argument: "[T]here are but three considerable naval powers in Hellas [Greece], Athens, Corcyra, and Corinth, and . . . if you allow two of these three to become one, and Corinth to secure us for herself, you will have to hold the sea against the united fleets of Corcyra and the Peloponnesus. But if you receive us, you will have our ships to reinforce you in the struggle."[17]

Should Athens have cooperated with the Peloponnesians by turning Corcyra down? If it had, what would have happened if the Peloponnesians had captured the Corcyraean fleet? Then the naval balance would have been two to one against Athens. Should Athens have trusted the Peloponnesians to keep their promises? The Athenians decided to ally with Corcyra, thereby risking the treaty; in our Prisoner's Dilemma scenario, it was the equivalent of squealing on the other prisoner. Thucydides explains why: "For it began now to be felt that the coming of the Peloponnesian War was only a question of time, and no one was willing to see a naval power of such magnitude as Corcyra sacrificed to Corinth."[18]

Inevitability and the Shadow of the Future

Ironically, the belief that war was inevitable, in Thucydides' view, played a major role in causing it. Athens believed that if the war was going to come, it was better to have two-to-one naval superiority rather than one-to-two naval inferiority. The belief that war was imminent and inevitable was critical to the decision. Why should that be so? Look again at the Prisoner's Dilemma. At first glance, it is best for each prisoner to cheat and let the other fellow be a sucker, but because each knows the situation, they also know that if they can trust each other, both should go for second best and cooperate by keeping silent. Cooperation is difficult to develop when playing the game only once. Playing a game time after time, people can learn to cooperate, but if it is a one-time game, whoever "defects" can get the reward and whoever trusts is a sucker. Political scientist Robert Axelrod played the Prisoner's Dilemma on a computer with different strategies. He found that after many games, on average the best results were obtained with a strategy he called *tit for tat*: "I will cooperate on my first move, and after that I will do to you what you last did to me. If on the first move you defect, I will defect. If you defect again, I will defect again. If you cooperate, I will cooperate. If you cooperate again, I cooperate again." Eventually, players find that the total benefit from the game is higher by learning to cooperate. But Axelrod warns that tit for tat is a good strategy only when you have a chance to continue the game for a long period, when there is a "long shadow of the future." On the last move, it is always rational to defect.

That is why the belief that war is inevitable is so dangerous in international politics. When you believe that war is inevitable, you believe that you are very close to the last move, and you worry about whether you can still trust your opponent. If you suspect that your opponent will defect, it is better to rely on yourself and take the risk of defecting rather than cooperating. That is what the Athenians did. Faced with the belief that war would occur, they decided that they could not afford to trust the Corinthians or the Spartans. It was better to have the Corcyraean navy on their side than against them when it looked like the last move in the game and inevitable war.

Was the Peloponnesian War really inevitable? Thucydides had a pessimistic view of human nature: "I have written my work," he wrote, "not as an essay which is to win the applause of the moment, but as a possession for all time."[19] His history shows human nature caught in the situation of the Prisoner's Dilemma then and for all time. Thucydides, like all historians, had to emphasize certain things and not others. Thucydides concluded that the cause of the war was the growth of the power of Athens and the fear it caused in Sparta. But the Yale classicist Donald Kagan argues that Athenian power was in fact *not* growing: Before the war broke out in 431 BCE, the balance of power had begun to stabilize. And although the Spartans worried about the rise of Athenian power, Kagan says, they had an even greater fear of a slave revolt. Both Athens and Sparta were slave states, and both feared that going to war might provide an opportunity for the slaves to revolt. The difference was that the slaves, or Helots, in Sparta were 90 percent of the population—far greater than Athens' slave percentage—and the Spartans had recently experienced a Helot revolt in 464 BCE.

Thus the immediate or precipitating causes of the war, according to Kagan, were more important than Thucydides' story of inevitability admits. Corinth, for example, thought that Athens would not fight; it misjudged the Athenian response, partly because it was so angry at Corcyra. Pericles overreacted; he made mistakes in giving an ultimatum to Potidaea and in punishing Megara by cutting off its trade. Those policy mistakes made the Spartans think that war might be worth the risk after all. Kagan argues that Athenian growth caused the first Peloponnesian War but that the Thirty-Year Truce doused that flame. So, to start the second Peloponnesian War, "the spark of the Epidamnian trouble needed to land on one of the rare bits of flammable stuff that had not been thoroughly drenched. Thereafter it needed to be continually and vigorously fanned by the Corinthians, soon assisted by the Megarians, Potidaeans, Aeginetans, and the Spartan War Party. Even then the spark might have been extinguished had not the Athenians provided some additional fuel at the crucial moment."[20] In other words, the war was not caused by impersonal forces but by bad decisions in difficult circumstances.

It is perhaps impudent to question Thucydides, a father figure to historians, but very little is ever truly inevitable in history. Human behavior is voluntary, although there are always external constraints. Karl Marx observed that men make history, but not in conditions of their own choosing. The ancient Greeks made flawed choices because they were caught in the situation well described by Thucydides and by the Prisoner's Dilemma. The security dilemma made war highly probable, but *highly probable* is not the same as *inevitable*. After all, the Joker in *The Dark Knight* constructed a version of the Prisoner's Dilemma for the passengers on the two Gotham City ferries wired with explosives, but (spoiler alert!) they opted to cooperate rather than defect. The 30-year unlimited war that devastated Athens was not inevitable. Human decisions mattered. Accidents and personalities make a difference even if they work within limits set by the larger structure, the situation of insecurity that resembles the Prisoner's Dilemma.

What modern lessons can we learn from this ancient history? We need to be aware of both the continuities and the changes. Some structural features of international politics predispose events in one direction rather than another. That is why it is necessary to understand security dilemmas and the Prisoner's Dilemma. On the other hand, such situations do not prove that war is inevitable. There are degrees of freedom, and human decisions can sometimes prevent the worst outcomes. Cooperation does occur in international affairs, even though the general structure of anarchy can sometimes discourage it.

It is also necessary to be wary of patently shallow historical analogies. During the Cold War, it was often popular to say that because the United States was a democracy and a sea-based power whereas the Soviet Union was a land-based power and had slave labor camps, the United States was Athens and the Soviet Union was Sparta, locked into replaying a great historical conflict. But such shallow analogies ignored that ancient Athens was a slave-holding state, wracked with internal turmoil, and that democrats were not always in control. Moreover, unlike in the Cold War, Sparta won.

Another lesson is to be aware of the selectivity of historians. No one can tell the whole story of anything. Imagine trying to tell everything that happened in the last hour, much less the entire story of your life or a whole war. Too many things happened. A second-by-second account in which everything was reported would take much longer to tell than it took for the events to happen in the first place. Thus historians always abstract. To write history, even the history of the last hour or the last day, we must simplify. We must select. What we select is obviously affected by the values, inclinations, and theories in our minds, whether explicit or inchoate.

Historians are affected by their contemporary concerns. Thucydides was concerned about how Athenians were learning the lessons of the war, blaming Pericles and the democrats for miscalculating. He therefore stressed those aspects of the situation we have described as the Prisoner's Dilemma. Although these aspects of the war were important, however, they are not the whole story. Thucydides did not write much about Athenian relations with Persia, or about the decree that cut off Megara's trade, or about Athens raising the amount of tribute that others in the Delian League had to pay. We have no reason to suspect that Thucydides' history was deliberately misleading or biased, but it is an example of how each age tends to rewrite history because the questions brought to the vast panoply of facts tend to change over time.

The need to select does not mean that everything is relative or that history is bunk. Such a conclusion is unwarranted. Good historians and social scientists do their best to ask questions honestly, objectively bringing facts to bear on their topic. But they and their students should be aware that what is selected is by necessity only part of the story. Always ask what questions the writer was asking as well as whether he or she carefully and objectively ascertained the facts. Beware of biases. Choice is a very important part of history and of writing history. The cure to misunderstanding history is to read more, not less.

Follow Up

- Robert B. Strassler, ed., *The Landmark Thucydides: A Comprehensive Guide to the Peloponnesian War*, trans. Richard Crawley (New York: Touchstone, 1996).
- Donald Kagan, *The Outbreak of the Peloponnesian War* (Ithaca, NY: Cornell University Press, 1969), pp. 31–56, 345–356.

The Rise of China

Ever since Thucydides' explanation of the Peloponnesian War, historians have known that the rise of a new power has been attended by uncertainty and anxieties. Often, though not always, violent conflict has followed. The rise in the economic and military power of China, the world's most populous country, will be a central question for Asia and for American foreign policy at the beginning of a new century. Explaining why democratic Athens decided to break a treaty that led to war, Thucydides pointed to the power of expectations of inevitable conflict. "The general belief was that whatever happened, war with the Peloponnese was bound to come," he wrote. Belief in the inevitability of conflict with China could have similar self-fulfilling effects.

—*THE ECONOMIST, JUNE 27, 1998*[21]

Ethical Questions and International Politics

1.3 Compare and contrast: (a) motives, means, and consequences; and (b) skepticism, state moralism, and cosmopolitanism.

Given the nature of the security dilemma, some realists believe that moral concerns play no role in international conflicts. However, ethics do play a role in international relations, although not quite the same role as in domestic politics.

Moral arguments have been used since the days of Thucydides. When Corcyra went to Athens to plead for help against Corinth, it used the language of ethics: "First, . . . your assistance will be rendered to a power which, herself inoffensive, is a victim to the injustice of others. Second, you will give unforgettable proof of your goodwill and create in us a lasting sense of gratitude."[22] Substitute *Ukraine* for *Corcyra* and *Russia* for *Corinth*, and those words could be uttered very recently.

Moral arguments move and constrain people. In that sense, morality is a powerful reality. However, moral arguments can also be used rhetorically as propaganda to disguise less elevated motives, and those with more power are often able to ignore moral considerations. During the Peloponnesian War, the Athenians sailed to the island of Melos to suppress a revolt. In 416 BCE, the Athenian spokesmen told the Melians that they could fight and die or they could surrender and merely be enslaved. When the Melians protested that they were fighting for their freedom, the Athenians responded that "the strong do what they can and the weak suffer what they must."[23] In essence, the Athenians stated that in a realist world, morality has little place. (People often use the phrase "might makes right" to capture this thought, although, of course, that is not quite correct. It would be more accurate to say "might ignores right.") When Iraq invaded Kuwait, or the United States invaded Grenada or Panama, or the Indonesians suppressed a revolt in East Timor, they all to some degree employed similar logic. But, in the modern world, it is increasingly less acceptable to articulate one's motives as plainly as Thucydides suggests the Athenians did in Melos. Does that mean that morality has come to occupy a more prominent place in international relations or simply that states have become more adept at propaganda? Has international politics changed dramatically, with states more attuned to ethical concerns, or is there a clear continuity between the actions of the Athenians 2,500 years ago and the actions of Iraq in 1990?

Moral arguments are not all equal. Some are more compelling than others. We ask whether they are logical and consistent. For instance, when the activist Phyllis Schlafly argued that nuclear weapons are a good thing because God gave them to the free world, we should wonder why God also gave them to Josef Stalin's Soviet Union and Mao Zedong's China.

A basic touchstone for many moral arguments is impartiality, the view that all interests are judged by the same criteria. Your interests deserve the same attention as mine. Within this framework of impartiality, however, there are two different traditions in Western political culture about how to judge moral arguments. One descends from Immanuel Kant, the eighteenth-century German philosopher, and the other from British utilitarians of the early nineteenth century such as Jeremy Bentham. As an illustration of the two approaches, imagine walking into a poor village and finding that a military officer is about to shoot three people lined up against the wall. You ask, "Why are you shooting these peasants? They look quite harmless." The officer says, "Last night somebody in this village shot one of my men. I know somebody in this village is guilty, so I am going to shoot these three to set an example." You say, "You can't do that! You're going to kill an innocent person. If only one shot was fired, then at least two of these people are innocent, perhaps all three. You just can't do that." The officer takes a rifle from one of his men and hands it to you, saying, "If you shoot one of them for me, I'll let the other two go. You can save two lives if you will shoot one of them. I'm going to teach you that in civil war you can't have these holier-than-thou attitudes."

What are you going to do? You could try to mow down all the troops in a Rambo-like move, but the officer has a soldier aiming his gun at you. So your choice is to kill one person to save two or to drop the gun and have clean hands. The Kantian tradition says that all deliberate killing is wrong, so you should refuse to perpetrate the evil deed. The utilitarian tradition suggests that if you can save two lives, you should do it.

If you sympathize with the Kantian perspective, imagine now that the numbers were increased. Suppose that there were 100 people against the wall, or imagine that you could save a city full of people from a nuclear bomb by shooting one possibly innocent person. Should you refuse to save a million people to keep your hands and conscience clean? At some point, consequences matter.

Moral arguments can be judged in three ways: by the motives or intentions involved, by the means used, and by their consequences or net effects. Although these dimensions are not always easily reconciled, good moral argument tries to take all three into account.

Limits on Ethics in International Relations

Ethics plays less of a role in international politics than in domestic politics for four reasons. One is the weak international consensus on values. There are cultural and religious differences over the justice of some acts. Second, states are not like individuals. States are abstractions, and although their leaders are individuals, statesmen are judged differently than when they act as individuals. For instance, when picking a roommate, most people want a person who believes that "thou shalt not kill." But the same people might vote against a presidential candidate who says, "Under no circumstances will I ever take an action that will lead to a death." A president is entrusted by citizens to protect their interests, and under some circumstances doing so may require the use of force. Presidents who save their own souls but fail to protect their people would not be good trustees.

In private morality, sacrifice may be the highest proof of a moral action, but should leaders sacrifice their whole people? During the Peloponnesian War, the Athenians told the leaders of the island of Melos that if they resisted, Athens would kill all the men and sell the women and children into slavery. Melos resisted and was destroyed. Should they have come to terms? In 1962, should President John Kennedy have run a risk of nuclear war to force the Soviets to remove missiles from Cuba when the United States had similar missiles in Turkey? Different people may answer these questions differently. The point is that when individuals act as leaders of states, their actions are judged somewhat differently.

A third reason ethics plays a lesser role in international politics is the complexity of causation. It is hard enough to know the consequences of actions in domestic affairs, but international relations has another layer of complexity: the interaction of states. That extra dimension makes it harder to predict consequences accurately. A famous example is the 1933 debate among students at the Oxford Union, the debating society of Oxford University. Mindful of the 20 million people killed in World War I, the majority of students voted for a resolution that they would never again fight for king and country. But someone else was listening: Adolf Hitler. He concluded that democracies were soft and that he could press them as hard as he wanted because they would not fight back. In the end, he pressed too far, and the result was World War II, a consequence not desired or expected by those students who voted never to fight for king and country. Many later did, and many died.

A more trivial example is the "hamburger argument" of the early 1970s, when people were worried about shortages of food in the world. A number of students in colleges in the United States said, "When we go to the dining hall, refuse to eat meat because a pound of beef equals eight pounds of grain, which could be used to feed poor people around the world." Many students stopped eating hamburger and felt good about themselves, but they did not help starving people in Africa or Bangladesh one bit. Why not? The grain freed up by some people not eating hamburgers in the United States did not reach the starving people in Bangladesh because those starving had no money to buy the grain. The grain was simply a surplus on the U.S. market, which meant that prices in the United States went down and farmers produced less. To help peasants in Bangladesh required getting money to them so that they could buy some of the excess grain. By launching a campaign against eating hamburger and failing to look at the complexity of the causal chain that would relate their well-intended act to its consequences, the students failed.

Finally, there is the argument that the institutions of international society are particularly weak and that the disjunction between order and justice is greater in international than in domestic politics. Order and justice are both important. In a domestic polity, we tend to take order for granted. In fact, sometimes protesters purposefully disrupt order for the sake of promoting their view of justice. But if there is total disorder, it is very hard to have any justice; witness the bombing, kidnapping, and killing by all sides in Lebanon in the 1980s, in Somalia since the end of the Cold War, and in parts of Afghanistan and Syria today. Some degree of order is a prior condition for justice. In international politics, the absence of a common legislature, central executive, or strong judiciary makes it much harder to preserve the order that precedes justice.

Three Views of the Role of Morality

At least three different views of ethics exist in international relations: those of the *skeptics*, the *state moralists*, and the *cosmopolitans*. Although there is no logical connection, people who are realists in their descriptive analysis of world politics often tend to be either skeptics or state moralists in their evaluative approach, whereas those who emphasize a liberal analysis tend toward either the state moralist or cosmopolitan moral viewpoints.

SKEPTICS   The skeptic says that moral categories have no meaning in international relations because no institutions exist to provide order. In addition, there is no sense of community, and therefore there are no moral rights and duties. For the skeptics, the classic statement about ethics in international politics was the Athenians' response to the Melians' plea for mercy: "The strong do what they can and the weak suffer what they must." That, for the skeptics, is all there is to say.

Philosophers often say that *ought* (moral obligation) implies *can* (the capacity to do something). Morality requires choice. If something is impossible, we cannot have an obligation to do it. If international relations were simply the realm of "kill or be killed," presumably there would be no real choice, and that would justify the skeptics' position. But international politics consists of more than mere survival. If choices exist in international relations, pretending that choices do not exist is merely a disguised form of choice. To think only in terms of narrow national interests is simply smuggling in values without admitting it. The French diplomat who once said, "What is moral is whatever is good for France" was ducking hard choices about why only French interests should be considered. The leader who says, "I had no choice" often did have a choice, albeit not a pleasant one. If there is some degree of order and of community in international relations—if it is not constantly "kill or be killed"—there is room for choices. Anarchy means "without government," but it does not necessarily mean chaos or total disorder. There are rudimentary practices and institutions that provide enough order to allow some important choices: balance of power, international law, and international organizations. Each is critical to understanding why the skeptical argument is not sufficient.

Thomas Hobbes argued that to escape from "the state of nature" in which anyone might kill anyone else, individuals must give up their freedom to a "leviathan," or government, for protection, because life in the state of nature is nasty, brutish, and short. Why then don't states form a superleviathan? Why isn't there a world government? The reason, Hobbes said, is that insecurity is not as great at the international level as at the individual level. Governments provide some degree of protection against the brutality of the biggest individuals taking whatever they want, and the balance of power among states provides some degree of order. Even though states are in a hostile posture of potential war, "they still uphold the daily industry of their subjects." The international state of nature does not create the day-to-day misery that would accompany a state of nature among individuals. In other words, Hobbes believed that the existence of states in a balance of power alleviates the condition of international anarchy enough to allow some degree of order.

Liberals point further to the existence of international law and customs. Even if rudimentary, such rules put a burden of proof on those who break them. Consider the Persian Gulf crisis in 1990. Saddam Hussein claimed that he annexed Kuwait to recover a province stolen from Iraq in colonial times. But because international law forbids crossing borders for such reasons, an overwhelming majority of states viewed his action as a violation of the UN charter. The 12 resolutions passed by the United Nations Security Council showed clearly that Saddam's view of the situation ran against international norms. Law and norms did not stop Saddam from invading Kuwait, but they did make it more difficult for him to recruit support, and they contributed to the creation of the coalition that expelled him from Kuwait.

International institutions, even if rudimentary, also provide a degree of order by facilitating and encouraging communication and some degree of reciprocity in bargaining. Given this situation of nearly constant communication, international politics is not always, as the skeptics claim, "kill or be killed." The energies and attention of leaders are not focused on security and survival all the time. Cooperation (as well as conflict) occurs in large areas of economic, social, and military interaction. And even though cultural differences exist about the notion of justice, moral arguments take place in international politics and principles are enshrined in international law.

Even in the extreme circumstances of war, law and morality may sometimes play a role. *Just war doctrine*, which originated in the early Christian church and became secularized after the seventeenth century, prohibits the killing of innocent civilians. The prohibition on killing innocents starts from the premise that "thou shalt not kill." But if that is a basic moral premise, how is any killing ever justified? Absolute pacifists say that no one should kill anyone else for any reason whatsoever. Usually, this view is asserted on Kantian grounds, but some pacifists add a consequentialist argument that "violence only begets more violence." Sometimes, however, the failure to respond to violence can also beget more violence. For example, it is unlikely that Osama bin Laden would have left the United States alone if President George W. Bush had turned the other cheek after 9/11. In contrast to pacifism, the just war tradition combines a concern for the intentions, means, and consequences of actions. It argues that if someone is about to kill you and you refuse to act in self-defense, the result is that evil will prevail. By refusing to defend themselves, the good die. If one is in imminent peril of being killed, it can be moral to kill in self-defense. But we must distinguish between those who can be killed and those who cannot be killed. For example, if a soldier rushes at you with a rifle, you can kill him in self-defense, but the minute the soldier drops the rifle, puts up his hands, and says, "I surrender," he is a prisoner of war and you have no right to take his life. In fact, this principle is enshrined in international law and also in the U.S. military code. A U.S. soldier who shoots an enemy soldier after he surrenders can be tried for murder in a U.S. court. Some U.S. officers in the Vietnam and Iraq wars were sent to prison for violating such laws. The prohibition against intentionally killing people who pose no harm also helps explain why terrorism is wrong. Some skeptics argue that "one man's terrorist is just another man's freedom fighter." However, under just war doctrine, you can fight for freedom, but you cannot target innocent civilians. Although they are often violated, some norms exist even under the harshest international circumstances. The rudimentary sense of justice enshrined in an imperfectly obeyed international law belies the skeptics' argument that no choices exist in a situation of war.

Just War Doctrine

Classical just war doctrine grew out of the Roman and Christian traditions. Cicero, St. Augustine, and St. Thomas Aquinas were key early thinkers. Today, just war doctrine has broad appeal. There are many possible formulations, but most have two components: principles of *jus ad bellum*, which specify the conditions under which it is morally permissible to use force, and principles of *jus in bello*, which specify how force may be used morally.

The five standard principles of *jus ad bellum* are (1) just cause, (2) right intention, (3) legitimate authority, (4) last resort, and (5) reasonable chance of success. Over the centuries, interpretations of these principles have changed. Just cause used to be restricted almost entirely to self-defense, for example, but today may include counter-intervention or preventing humanitarian catastrophe. Kings and emperors used to enjoy unquestioned legitimate authority, but increasingly world opinion requires the approval of an international body such as the United Nations Security Council.

The three standard principles of *jus in bello* are (1) observe the laws of war, (2) maintain proportionality, and (3) observe the principle of noncombatant immunity. The laws of war have also evolved over the centuries and represent a much more stringent set of constraints today than in medieval times. Modern military technology makes it more difficult in some respects to maintain proportionality and protect innocent civilians because the destructive power of modern weaponry is vastly greater than in the age of the sword and spear, but modern precision-guided munitions and advanced battlefield management systems can compensate for these issues to some extent.

We can therefore reject complete skepticism because some room exists for morality in international politics. Morality is about choice, and meaningful choice varies with the conditions of survival. The greater the threats to survival, the less room for moral choice. At the start of the Peloponnesian War, the Athenians argued, "[P]raise is due to all who, if not so superior to human nature as to refuse dominion, yet respect justice more than their position compels them to do."[24] Unfortunately, the Athenians lost sight of that wisdom later in their war, but it reminds us that situations with absolutely no choice are rare and that national security and degrees of threat are often ambiguous. Skeptics avoid hard moral choices by pretending otherwise. To sum up in an aphorism: Humans may not live wholly by the word, but neither do they live solely by the sword.

Not all realists are skeptics, but those who take morality seriously consider order at least as important. Without order, justice is difficult or impossible. Moral crusades can even cause disorder. If the United States becomes too concerned about spreading democracy or human rights throughout the world, for example, it may create disorder that will actually do more damage than good in the long run. The realist theologian and public affairs commentator Reinhold Niebuhr considered "moral and political factors" equally important. Writing in the aftermath of World War II, Niebuhr insisted that "[w]e can save mankind from another holocaust only if our nerves are steady and if our moral purpose is matched by strategic shrewdness."[25]

The realists have a valid argument, up to a point. International order is important, but it is a matter of degrees, and there are trade-offs between justice and order. How much order is necessary before we start worrying about justice? For example, after the 1990 Soviet crackdown in the Baltic republics in which a number of people were killed, some Americans urged a break in relations with the Soviet Union. In their view, Americans should express their values of democracy and human rights in foreign policy, even if that meant instability and the end of arms control talks. Others argued that although concerns for peace and for human rights were important, it was more important to control nuclear weapons and negotiate an arms reduction treaty. In the end, the U.S. government went ahead with the arms negotiations, but linked the provision of economic aid to respect for human rights. Over and over in international politics, the question is not absolute order versus justice, but how to trade off choices in particular situations. The realists have a valid point of view, but they overstate it when they argue that it has to be all order before any justice.

STATE MORALISTS *State moralists* argue that international politics rests on a society of states with certain rules, although those rules are not always perfectly obeyed. The most important rule is state sovereignty, which prohibits states from intervening across borders into others' jurisdiction. The political scientist Michael Walzer, for example, argues that national boundaries have a moral significance because states represent the pooled rights of individuals who have come together for a common life. Thus, respect for the sovereignty and territorial integrity of states is related to respect for individuals. Others argue more simply that respect for sovereignty is the best way to preserve order. "Good fences make good neighbors," in the words of the poet Robert Frost. Arguably, one reason that Eastern Europe has been able to avoid interstate war since 1945 is because of a relatively new, but very powerful norm against attempts to change borders unilaterally. The principle even held during the breakup of the Soviet Union. It is small wonder that the international community was therefore so shocked and concerned when Russia unilaterally annexed Crimea from Ukraine in 2014.

In practice, mainstream rules of state behavior are violated from time to time, sometimes on a large scale. In recent decades—to name just a few examples—Vietnam invaded Cambodia, China invaded Vietnam, Tanzania invaded Uganda, Israel invaded Lebanon, the Soviet Union invaded Afghanistan, the United States invaded Grenada and Panama, Iraq invaded Iran and Kuwait, the United States and Britain invaded Iraq, and NATO (the North Atlantic Treaty Organization) bombed Serbia because of its mistreatment of ethnic Albanians in the province of Kosovo. Determining when it is appropriate to respect another state's sovereignty is a long-standing challenge. In 1979, Americans condemned the Soviet invasion of Afghanistan in strong moral terms. The Soviets responded by pointing to the Dominican Republic, where in 1965 the United States sent 25,000 troops to prevent the formation of a communist government. The intention behind the U.S. intervention in the Dominican Republic—preventing a hostile regime from coming to power in the Caribbean—was quite similar to the intention of the Soviet Union's intervention in Afghanistan: that is, preventing the formation of a hostile government on its border.

To find differences, we have to look further than intentions. In terms of the means used, very few people were killed by the U.S. intervention in the Dominican Republic, and the U.S. forces soon withdrew. In the Afghan case, tens of thousands of people were killed, and the Soviet forces remained for nearly a decade. In the 1990s, some critics compared the Iraqi invasion of Kuwait with the U.S. invasion of Panama. In December 1989, the United States sent troops to overthrow the Panamanian dictator Manuel Noriega, and in August 1990, Iraq sent troops into Kuwait to overthrow the emir. Both the United States and Iraq violated the rule of nonintervention. But again there were differences in means and consequences. In Panama, the Americans put into office a government that had been duly elected but that Noriega had not permitted to take power. The United States did not try to annex Panama. In Kuwait, the Iraqi government tried to annex the country and caused much bloodshed in the process. Such considerations do not mean that the Panama case was all right or all wrong, but as we will see in Chapter 6, problems often arise when applying simple rules of nonintervention and sovereignty.

COSMOPOLITANS *Cosmopolitans* such as the political theorist Charles Beitz see international politics not just as a society of states, but as a society

> ## Intervention
>
> Imagine the following scene in Afghanistan in December 1979: An Afghan communist leader came to power promoting a platform of greater independence from the Soviet Union. This thought worried Soviet leaders, because an independent regime on their border might foment trouble throughout Central Asia (including Soviet Central Asia) and would create a dangerous precedent of a small communist neighbor escaping the Soviet Empire. Imagine the Russian general in charge of the Soviet invasion force confronting the renegade Afghan leader, whom he is about to kill, explaining why he is doing these things against the international rules of sovereignty and nonintervention. "As far as right goes, other countries in our sphere of influence think one has as much of it as the other, and that if any maintain their independence it is because they are strong, and that if we do not molest them it is because we are afraid; so that besides extending our empire we should gain in security by your subjection; the fact that you are a border state and weaker than others, rendering it all the more important that you should not succeed in thwarting the masters of Central Asia."
>
> Thus spoke the Athenians to the leaders of Melos (5.97), with but minor substitutions! Intervention is not a new problem.

of individuals with a set of universal human rights. When we speak about justice, say the cosmopolitans, we should speak about justice for individuals. Their main complaint against state moralism is that it makes it relatively easy for oppressive governments to hide behind the shield of state sovereignty and inflict untold horrors on their own people. They also argue that realists focus too much on issues of war and peace. Cosmopolitans contend that if realists focused on issues of distributive justice—that is, who gets what—they would pay more attention to the interdependence of the global economy. Constant economic intervention across borders can sometimes have life-or-death consequences. For example, it is a life-or-death matter if you are a peasant in the Philippines and your child dies of a curable disease because the local boy who went to medical school is now working in the United States for a much higher salary.

Cosmopolitans argue that national boundaries have no moral standing; they simply defend an inequality that should be abolished if we think in terms of distributive justice. Realists (who include both moral skeptics and some state moralists) reply that the danger in the cosmopolitans' approach is that it may lead to enormous disorder. Taken literally, efforts at radical redistribution of resources are likely to lead to violent conflict because people do not give up their wealth easily. A more limited cosmopolitan argument rests on people often having multiple loyalties: to families, friends, neighborhoods, and nations; perhaps to some transnational religious groups; and to the concept of common humanity. Most people are moved by pictures of starving Somali children or Darfur refugees, for some common community exists beyond the national level, albeit a weaker one. We are all humans.

Cosmopolitans remind us of the distributive dimensions to international relations in which morality matters as much in peace as in war. Policies can be designed to assist basic human needs and basic human rights without destroying order. And in cases of gross abuse of human rights, cosmopolitan views have been written into international laws such as the international convention against genocide. As a result, policy makers are more conscious of moral concerns. For example, Bill Clinton said that one of his worst mistakes as president was not to have done more to stop genocide in Rwanda in 1994; the United States and other countries later supported African peacekeeping troops in efforts to suppress genocidal violence in the Sudanese province of Darfur.

Of the approaches to international morality, the skeptic makes a valid point about order being necessary for justice but misses the trade-offs between order and justice. The state moralist who sees a society of states with rules against intervention illustrates an institutional approach to order but does not provide enough answers regarding when some interventions may be justified. Finally, the cosmopolitan who focuses on a society of individuals has a profound insight about common humanity but runs the risk of fomenting enormous disorder by pursuing massive redistributive policies. Most people develop a hybrid position; labels are less important than the central point that trade-offs exist among these approaches.

Because of the differences between domestic and international politics, morality is harder to apply in international politics. But just because there is a plurality of principles, it does not follow that there are no principles at all. How far should we go in applying morality to international politics? The answer is to be careful because when moral judgments determine everything, morality can lead to a sense of outrage, and outrage can lead to heightened risk. Prudence can be a virtue, particularly when the alternative is disastrous unintended consequences. After all, there are no moral questions among the dead. But we cannot honestly ignore morality in international politics. Each person must study events and make his or her own decisions about judgments and trade-offs. The enduring logic of international conflict does not remove the responsibility for moral choices, although it does require an understanding of the special setting that makes those choices difficult.

Although the specific moral and security dilemmas of the Peloponnesian War are unique, many of the issues recur over history. As we trace the evolution of international relations, we will see again and again the tension between realism and liberalism, between skeptics and cosmopolitans, between an anarchic system of states and international organizations. We will revisit the Prisoner's Dilemma and continue to grapple with the ethical conundrums of war. We will see how different actors on the world stage have approached the crises of their time and how their goals and instruments vary. As mentioned at the outset, certain variables that characterize international politics today simply did not exist in Thucydides' day: no nuclear weapons, no United Nations, no Internet, no transnational corporations, no cartels. The study of international conflict is an inexact science combining history and theory. In weaving our way through theories and examples, we try to keep in mind both what has changed and what has remained constant so that we may better understand our past and our present and better navigate the unknown shoals of the future.

Follow Up

- Joel H. Rosenthal, ed., *Ethics and International Affairs: A Reader*, 3rd ed. (Washington, DC: Georgetown University Press, 2009).
- David A. Welch, "Can We Think Systematically About Ethics and Statecraft?" *Ethics and International Affairs*, Vol. 8 (1994), pp. 23–37.

Chronology: Peloponnesian Wars

490 BCE	First Persian War
480 BCE	Second Persian War
478 BCE	Spartans abdicate leadership
476 BCE	Formation of Delian League and Athenian empire
464 BCE	Helot revolt in Sparta
461 BCE	Outbreak of first Peloponnesian War
445 BCE	Thirty-Year Truce
445–434 BCE	Ten years of peace
434 BCE	Epidamnus and Corcyra conflicts
433 BCE	Athens intervenes in Potidaea
432 BCE	Spartan Assembly debates war
431 BCE	Outbreak of second Peloponnesian War
430 BCE	Pericles' Funeral Oration
416 BCE	Melian dialogue
413 BCE	Athens' defeat in Sicily
411 BCE	Oligarchs revolt in Athens
404 BCE	Athens defeated, forced to pull down walls

Study Questions

1. What role should ethical considerations play in the conduct of international relations? What role *do* they play? Can we speak meaningfully about moral duties to other countries or their populations? What are the moral obligations of the United States in Iraq? In Afghanistan?

2. How well did the Iraq war satisfy the principles of *jus ad bellum* and *jus in bello*? What about Afghanistan?

3. Is there a difference between moral obligations in the realms of domestic politics and international politics? On the basis of the Melian dialogue, did the Athenians act ethically? Did the Melian elders?

4. What is realism? How does it differ from the liberal view of world politics? What does constructivism add to realism and liberalism?

5. What does Thucydides pinpoint as the main causes of the Peloponnesian War? Which ones were underlying causes? Which ones were triggers?

6. What sort of theory of international relations is implicit in Thucydides' account of the war?

7. Was the Peloponnesian War inevitable? If so, why and when? If not, how and when might it have been prevented?

Notes

1. Calculated from UCDP/PRIO Armed Conflict Dataset v.4-2014a, 1946–2013. See also Nils Petter Gleditsch, Peter Wallensteen, Mikael Eriksson, Margareta Sollenberg, and Håvard Strand, "Armed Conflict 1946–2001: A New Dataset," *Journal of Peace Research* 39:5 (September 2002), pp. 615–637; and Lotta Themnér and Peter Wallensteen, "Armed Conflict, 1946–2012," *Journal of Peace Research* 50:4 (July 2013), pp. 509–521.

2. Thomas Hobbes, *Leviathan*, ed. C. B. MacPherson (London: Penguin, 1981), p. 186.

3. *The New York World*, "From Our Dec. 13 Pages, 75 Years Ago," *International Herald Tribune*, December 13, 1985.

4. Miles Kahler, "Inventing International Relations: International Relations Theory after 1945," in Michael W. Doyle and G. John Ikenberry, eds., *New Thinking in International Relations Theory* (Boulder, CO: Westview, 1977), p. 38.

5. Emanuel Adler, "Constructivism in International Relations: Sources, Contributions, Debates and Future Directions," in Walter Carlsnaes, Thomas Risse, and Beth Simmons, eds., *Handbook of International Relations* (Thousand Oaks, CA: Sage, 2003).

6. Ian Hurd, quoting Alexander Wendt, "Constructivism," in Christopher Reus-Smit and Duncan Snidal, eds., *Oxford Handbook of International Relations* (Oxford: Oxford University Press, 2008).

7. Michael Barnett, "Social Constructivism," in John Baylis and Steve Smith, eds., *The Globalization of World Politics*, 3rd ed. (Oxford: Oxford University Press, 2005), p. 260.

8. See http://hdr.undp.org/en/content/table-4-gender-inequality-index.

9. See http://www.guide2womenleaders.com/Current-Women-Leaders.htm.

10. Jacqui True, "Feminism," in Scott Burchill and Andrew Linklater, eds., *Theories of International Relations*, 3rd ed. (New York: Palgrave Macmillan, 2005), p. 233.

11. John Maynard Keynes, *The General Theory of Employment, Interest and Money* (London: Macmillan, 1936), p. 383.

12. Forbes, World's Biggest Public Companies, http://www.forbes.com/global2000/list/ (values calculated May 2014); World Bank, GDP 2013 (current $US), http://data.worldbank.org/indicator/NY.GDP.MKTP.CD.

13. Peter D. Feaver and Christopher Gelpi, *Choosing Your Battles: American Civil-Military Relations and the Use of Force* (Princeton, NJ: Princeton University Press, 2004).

14. Robert Gilpin, *War and Change in World Politics* (Cambridge: Cambridge University Press, 1981), pp. 227–228.

15. Thucydides, *History of the Peloponnesian War* 2.63, trans. Richard Crawley; in Robert B. Strassler, ed., *The Landmark Thucydides: A Comprehensive Guide to the Peloponnesian War* (New York: Touchstone, 1996), pp. 125–126.

16. 1.78; ibid., p. 44.

17. 1.36; ibid., p. 24.

18. 1.44; ibid., p. 28.

19. 1.22; ibid., p. 16.

20. Donald Kagan, *The Outbreak of the Peloponnesian War* (Ithaca, NY: Cornell University Press, 1969), p. 354. For an alternative interpretation of the realities of Athenian expansion, see G. E. M. de Ste. Croix, *The Origins of the Peloponnesian War* (Ithaca, NY: Cornell University Press, 1972), pp. 60, 201–203.

21. Joseph S. Nye, Jr., "As China Rises, Must Others Bow?" *The Economist*, June 27, 1998, p. 23.

22. Thucydides, *History of the Peloponnesian War* 1.33, p. 22.

23. 5.89; ibid., p. 352.

24. 1.76; ibid., p. 43.

25. Reinhold Niebuhr, "For Peace, We Must Risk War," *Life*, September 20, 1948, p. 39.

Chapter 2

Explaining Conflict and Cooperation: Tools and Techniques of the Trade

Photo: Picture-alliance/Dpa/Newscom

German chancellor Prince Otto von Bismarck (1815–1898)

∨ Learning Objectives

2.1 Define and explain state, nation, nation-state, actor, power, authority, international system, international society, system stability, crisis stability, and "the national interest."

2.2 Distinguish the individual, state, and system levels.

2.3 Distinguish paradigms from theories and identify the key features of the realist, liberal, Marxist, and constructivist paradigms.

2.4 Explain the role of counterfactual reasoning in historical inference.

Key Concepts

2.1 Define and explain state, nation, nation-state, actor, power, authority, international system, international society, system stability, crisis stability, and "the national interest."

To make sense of something, you need an appropriate conceptual toolkit that includes a useful vocabulary, ways of drawing inferences that help you see how things work, and strategies for solving problems. Understanding global conflict and cooperation is no exception.

Unlike physicians, engineers, or natural scientists, people who study world politics have relatively little in the way of highly specialized vocabulary. We borrow words from other fields or from common usage. The upside is that the barriers to entry are low; almost anyone can have a sensible discussion about world politics. How many people can have a casual dinnertime conversation about plasmapheresis or quantum tunneling? The downside is that there is an unusually high risk of ambiguity and confusion; the same word can mean quite different things in different contexts, and many words have two or more possible meanings in the same context. Ambiguity is not something that we can purge from the English language, but we can learn to spot potentially confusing usages. Before we delve too deeply into the interplay of theory and history, it is therefore useful to spend some time exploring key concepts. We will then examine some useful tools and techniques for drawing inferences about world politics.

States, Nations, and Nation-States

Perhaps the single most important concept used in the study of world politics is the *sovereign state*. Unfortunately, it is also one of the most confusing, partly because it is two concepts bundled together: *sovereignty* and *state*. Most people would agree that the state is the most important actor in the international system (we will explore the terms *actor* and *system* more closely in a moment), although realists and liberals would disagree about the relative importance of other actors. Realists would insist that states are the only significant actors, whereas liberals would argue that states are only the most important among many. But what, exactly, *is* a "state"?

A state is a particular type of political unit that has two crucial characteristics: *territoriality* and *sovereignty*. Territoriality is straightforward: A state governs a specific, identifiable portion of Earth's surface. Sovereignty is the absolute right to govern it. In most cases, when you encounter the word *state* in a discussion of world politics, the best single synonym would be *country*. Britain, France, Argentina, and Japan are all states. Being sovereign means that they have no higher authority to which they must answer. Different countries have different political systems that locate sovereignty in different places. In traditional monarchies, kings or queens are sovereign and enjoy supreme authority over the territories they govern. In democracies, the people hold sovereignty and delegate government to their elected representatives and other state officials. But whatever the ultimate source of sovereignty, all states have governments that pass laws, enforce order, and are supposed to defend the people who live within their borders.

The United States of America is a state in this sense as well, but it is a federation of lower-level political units that rather inconveniently also happen to be called "states." The same is true for a number of other countries, such as Australia, India, and Mexico. This terminology is one obvious possible source of confusion. Michigan, New South Wales, Uttar Pradesh, and Chihuahua are all states, but they are not countries. They are territorial, but they are not sovereign. Although they have delegated areas of jurisdiction, they are answerable to their federal constitutions.

Confusing Concepts

When concepts are used in more than one way, confusion is easy. A southern colleague of mine began her university teaching career in the upper Midwest. The first course she taught was a comparative politics course titled "The State in Western Europe." In it she explored the wide variety of structures and practices of various European political systems. After a few weeks, one student timidly approached her after class with a puzzled look on his face. "Professor," he said, "I know you're from Georgia and this is Wisconsin; but when you talk about 'the state,' you do mean Wisconsin, don't you?"

—Joseph S. Nye, Jr.

A third possible source of confusion is that the word *state* is often used to refer to the *government* of a country or, more precisely, to the structure and practices of the institutions and offices that make up the government. This usage is common in the comparative politics subfield of political science, where you will often hear Singapore, for example, described as a "strong state" because its central government has a great deal of authority, whereas the United States is described as a "weak" state because of its system of checks and balances and a very generous set of constitutionally protected individual rights. Obviously, in terms of material power, the United States is much stronger than Singapore, so one must be very careful to interpret phrases such as "strong state" and "weak state" appropriately. Context is key.

Another word often used as a synonym for state is *nation*. This usage is a particularly unfortunate practice, because the word is commonly used to denote a group of people who have some combination of common language, culture, religion, history, mythology, identity, or sense of destiny. A decent but imperfect synonym for this kind of "nation" is "ethnic group."[1] Kurds, Tamils, Québécois, and Navajo are all nations in this sense, but none of them is a state. Abraham Lincoln famously said in his Gettysburg Address, "Four score and seven years ago, our forefathers brought forth upon this continent a new nation, conceived in liberty, and dedicated to the proposition that all men are created equal." It would have been much better if he had said *state* rather than *nation*, because the United States of America is a multinational state.

It was common among eighteenth- and nineteenth-century liberal political philosophers to believe that every nation should have a state of its own, and groups such as the Kurds and Tamils struggled for this goal for years. A state whose citizens are overwhelmingly members of a single nation is a *nation-state*. There are few true nation-states in the world today. Japan and the two Koreas are notable exceptions; 98.5 percent of the inhabitants of Japan are ethnic Japanese, and an even higher proportion of the inhabitants of North Korea and South Korea are ethnic Koreans. Most countries of the world today are far from being ethnically homogenous.

National groups within states often claim a right to *self-government* or *self-determination*. Self-determination is the ability to decide one's own political fate. It frequently includes a claim to a state of one's own. Québec separatists, for example, claim a right to self-determination for the purpose of carving a new country out of Canada. Sometimes groups claiming a right to self-determination seek to

Are EU Members "Sovereign States"?

The European Union (EU) is a fascinating example of supranational integration. Its 28 member states have agreed to set up supranational institutions such as the European Parliament and Council of Ministers (which are responsible for legislation), a European Commission (the EU's executive arm), and the European Court of Justice and Court of First Instance (judicial arms). The EU is a single market and customs union with free movement of goods, services, capital, and people; it attempts to harmonize policies in a wide range of issue areas; and it strives to speak with one voice on the world stage. Nineteen EU members have embraced a common currency, the euro, which is second in importance only to the U.S. dollar in the world economy. At the same time, the members only loosely coordinate their common defense and foreign policies.

Does that mean that the members are no longer sovereign states? Technically, no; every member country retains the right to withdraw from the EU at any time it chooses. Withdrawal would be very costly, however, and it is difficult to imagine anything other than very extreme circumstances prompting it. Indeed, no state is contemplating withdrawal at the moment, whereas several states, such as Turkey, are seeking entry.

The EU is the best, but not the only, example of supranational integration. Egypt and Syria formed the United Arab Republic in 1958, but it fell apart after only three years. A more interesting and somewhat more successful experiment was the East African Community (EAC) in 1967, binding Kenya, Tanzania, and Uganda. The EAC fared quite well until it was torn apart by ideological differences and personality clashes among the three countries' leaders. In 2001, the EAC was reborn, and in 2007, Burundi and Rwanda joined as well. The reincarnation of the EAC, however, still has a long way to go before it proves as effective as the EU in promoting the common and individual interests of its member states.

detach the territories in which they live from one country and join it to another, as did ethnic Germans in Austria, Czechoslovakia, and Poland between the two world wars.[2] Groups that claim a right to self-government may be happy to live within the territory of an existing multinational state, but may seek extensive rights and prerogatives to look after their own affairs. Wales, for example, is not a sovereign state—it is part of the United Kingdom—but the Welsh enjoy quite a significant degree of self-government, which is exercised by the aptly named Welsh National Assembly. Another part of the United Kingdom, Scotland, held a referendum on full independence in September 2014, which was narrowly defeated.

The difficulty with the idea of the nation-state as a philosophical ideal is that nations are often intermingled and spread out in diasporas over vast distances. It would be impossible to draw borders in such a way as to give each nation a state of its own. Even if it were possible, as we saw in Chapter 1 a powerful norm against redrawing settled borders has emerged over the last hundred years, in part in reaction to the carnage caused by the partial, inconsistent, and unsuccessful attempt to realize the nation-state ideal in Europe after World War I. In another era, Kurds and Tamils might have been in luck: Their claims to self-determination might have been greeted with sympathy from powerful countries and possibly even with active political support. Nowadays, the international community is reluctant to recognize secession in all but the most severe cases of genocide, oppression, violent state collapse, or rare mutual agreements such as the Czech and Slovak "velvet divorce" in 1993 and the division of Sudan into two countries (Sudan and South Sudan) in 2011.

For the sake of clarity, it is always important to pay careful attention to what people actually mean when they use terms such as *state*, *nation*, and *nation-state*. You will find them being used interchangeably a large proportion of the time. It does not help that the world's preeminent organization of sovereign states is called the United "Nations" (the more accurate label "United States" was already taken) or that we call what happens between states "inter*national*" politics!

How do states come to be? A group of people cannot simply mark out some turf, run up a flag, and call themselves a state (although one disgruntled Australian farmer and his family tried to do exactly that in 1970).[3] To be a state, one must be recognized *as* a state by other states. In this sense, being a state is a bit like being a member of a club: Existing members must admit you.

What do other states look at to decide whether to recognize a new sovereign state? There is no generally agreed-upon checklist, but five issues tend to dominate their deliberations: first, whether there is a government with de facto control over a certain territory; second, whether other states claim the territory, and if so, how strong their claim is; third, whether the people seeking to establish a new state are historically oppressed; fourth, whether those people consider their government legitimate; and fifth, but not least important, whether recognizing the new state as sovereign would affect their own claims and interests.

Countries such as China that face significant domestic secessionist movements are often reluctant to recognize new states out of fear of setting a precedent that could backfire, even if in other respects the case for statehood is sound. With some critical mass of recognition—being accepted as a member of the United Nations is the gold standard—a new state takes its place among the countries of the world and shoulders the rights, privileges, and obligations of statehood. Its government comes to be accepted internationally—for the most part, at any rate—as the rightful spokesperson for the inhabitants of the territory and the ultimate authority within its borders. The two newest aspirants for sovereign statehood are Kosovo, which declared unilateral independence from Serbia in 2008, and Palestine, which made a push for recognition in 2011 and was granted "non-member observer state" status by the UN General Assembly in 2012. Most observers believe that both Kosovo and Palestine will attain full UN membership eventually. Somaliland has had less luck: Despite its unilateral declaration of independence from Somalia in 1991, it remains unrecognized by any UN member state.

The club-membership dimension of statehood is functional, but not perfect; it does generate occasional anomalies. Taiwan, for example, is for all practical purposes a sovereign state, but it only has formal diplomatic relations with 21 countries and the Holy See. It does not have a seat at the UN. Because the People's Republic of China considers Taiwan a renegade province, Taiwanese officials must conduct most of their international business in a roundabout way. At the same time, there are many countries in the world—Somalia, Zimbabwe, and Afghanistan come to mind—that are recognized globally as sovereign states but that fail to satisfy the most basic condition of sovereign statehood: namely, having a legitimate government that exercises effective control within its borders.

International Actors, Power, and Authority

Earlier we saw that realists and liberals disagree on whether the state is the only significant actor in world politics. An *actor* is any person or body whose decisions and actions have repercussions for international politics. When speaking about actors in general, we don't use proper nouns; when we speak of particular actors, we do. Of course, technically only people make decisions and take actions, so when we talk of "the state" as an actor, we are abstracting for the sake of simplicity. You will commonly hear or read, for example, that Germany attacked Poland in 1939, although it would be more accurate to say that Germans attacked Poles. This kind of anthropomorphizing is very standard. It is important to be aware of it, however, because when we anthropomorphize the state—or any other collective actor, such as a multinational corporation or a nongovernmental organization (NGO)—it can incline us to assume wrongly that these players are *unitary* actors with interests, minds, and wills of their own. Very often, what happens in the world can only be understood if we pay attention to the disagreements, debates, and sometimes even struggles that take place inside states. As we shall see in Chapter 5, a major reason President John F. Kennedy and Soviet Chairman Nikita Khrushchev cut an abrupt deal to end the Cuban missile crisis in 1962 was because both had become frightened of the unanticipated, inadvertent, and sometimes insubordinate actions of their own militaries, which threatened to drag the superpowers into nuclear war. In this situation, those who should really have only been *agents* of the state (soldiers, diplomats, and bureaucrats are only ever supposed to act in accordance with superiors' instructions) were behaving inappropriately as *actors*. Of course, not all actors are anthropomorphized collectivities. Individual human beings can be international actors as well. Osama bin Laden was an international actor, as is Bono (not to put them on the same moral plane, of course!). Even movie actors can be actors.[4] Mia Farrow, for example, managed to influence China's policy on Darfur.

Although liberals are more inclined than realists to believe that multinational corporations, NGOs, churches, diasporas, transnational criminal networks, drug cartels, terrorist groups, charitable foundations, celebrities, and any number of other types of actors can do things that have real consequences in international politics, both agree that states are the most important, for four main reasons. First, all but the most "fragile" states (e.g., Somalia, Sudan, the Central African Republic))[5] have the capacity in principle to control the flow of people, goods, and money across borders. No state controls it perfectly, but most states control it fairly effectively. Second, states are usually the only actors that wield significant armies. Some other actors are capable of organized violence on a small scale, but functioning states have an unusual capacity to wield organized violence on a massive scale. (In failed states or states that are experiencing civil war, substate actors occasionally have this capacity.) Third, only states have the power to tax and spend in significant amounts. The Mafia taxes by running protection rackets, and drug cartels raise significant funds by illegal business, but on a scale dwarfed by most states and only as long as they manage to avoid or corrupt the law. Fourth, only states promulgate and enforce laws. States are answerable to no higher authority.

Systems and War

After the last war, the international system developed two rigid camps. This bipolarity led to a loss of flexibility and heightened insecurity. One of the new alliances developed around an authoritarian land-based power, the other around a democratic power with an expansive commerce and culture that held naval supremacy. Each side feared that the other would achieve a decisive advantage in the conflict that both expected. Ironically, it was civil conflict in a small, weak state threatening a marginal change in the alliances that heightened the sense of threat in both alliances and actually triggered the war.

Which war does that paragraph describe: the Peloponnesian War, World War I, or the Cold War?

These four considerations demonstrate that, compared with other actors, the state typically wields more *power*. Power is another key concept in the study of global conflict and cooperation. Like love, however, it is easier to experience than to define or measure.

Power is the ability to achieve one's purposes or goals. More specifically, it is the ability to affect others to get the outcomes one wants. Robert Dahl defined power as the ability to get others to do what they otherwise would not do. When we measure power in terms of the changed behavior of others, though, we have to know their preferences; otherwise, we may be as mistaken about our power as was the fox who thought he was hurting Br'er Rabbit when he threw him into the briar patch. Knowing in advance how other people or states would behave in the absence of our efforts is often difficult.

The behavioral definition of power can be useful to analysts and historians who devote considerable time to reconstructing the past, but to practical politicians and leaders it may seem too ephemeral. Because the ability to influence others is usually associated with the possession of certain resources, political leaders commonly define power this way. These resources include population, territory, natural resources, economic size, military forces, and political stability. This definition's virtue is that it makes power appear more concrete, measurable, and predictable than the behavioral definition. Power in this sense means holding the high cards in the international poker game. A basic rule of poker is that if your opponent is showing cards that can beat anything you hold, fold. If you know you will lose a war, don't start it.

Some wars, however, have been started by the eventual losers, which suggests that political leaders sometimes take risks or make mistakes. Japan in 1941 and Iraq in 1990 are examples. Often the opponent's cards are not all showing in the game of international politics. As in poker, bluffing and deception can make a big difference. Even without deception, mistakes can be made about which power resources are most relevant in particular situations. For example, France and Britain had more tanks than did Nazi Germany in 1940, but Adolf Hitler's tanks were better engineered, and his generals used them more effectively.

Power conversion is a problem that arises when we think of power in terms of resources. Some countries are better than others at converting their resources into effective influence over other countries' behavior, just as some skilled card players win despite being dealt weak hands. Power conversion is the capacity to convert potential power, as measured by resources, to realized power, as measured by the changed behavior of others. To predict outcomes correctly, we need to know about a country's skill at power conversion as well as its possession of power resources.

Another problem is determining which resources provide the best basis for power in any particular context. Tanks are not much good in swamps; uranium was not a power resource in the nineteenth century. In earlier periods, power resources were easier to judge. For example, in the agrarian economies of eighteenth-century Europe, population was a critical power resource because it provided a base for taxes and recruitment of infantry. In terms of population, France dominated Western Europe. Thus at the end of the Napoleonic Wars (1799–1815), Prussia presented its fellow victors at the Congress of Vienna (1815) with a precise plan for its own reconstruction to maintain the balance of power. Its plan listed the territories and populations it had lost since 1805 and the territories and populations it would need to regain equivalent numbers. In the prenationalist period, it was not significant that many of the people in those provinces did not speak German or believe themselves to be Prussian. Within half a century, however, nationalist sentiments would matter very much.

Another change of context that occurred during the nineteenth century was the growing importance of industry and rail systems that made rapid mobilization possible. In the 1860s, Chancellor Otto von Bismarck's Germany pioneered the use of railways to transport armies in Europe for quick victories. Although Russia had always had greater population resources than the rest of Europe, they were difficult to mobilize. The growth of the rail system in western Russia at the beginning of the twentieth century was one reason the Germans feared rising Russian power in 1914. Further, the spread of rail systems on the continent helped deprive Britain of the luxury of concentrating on naval power. There was no longer time, should it prove necessary, to insert an army to prevent another great power from dominating the continent.

The application of industrial technology to warfare has long had a powerful effect. Advanced science and technology have been particularly critical power resources since the beginning of the nuclear age in 1945, but the power derived from nuclear weapons has proven to be so awesome and destructive that its actual application is muscle-bound. Nuclear war is simply far too costly. Indeed, there are many situations in which any use of force may be inappropriate or too costly.

Even if the direct use of force were banned among a group of countries, military force would still play an important background role. For example, the military role of the United States in deterring threats to allies, or of assuring access to a crucial resource such as oil in the Persian Gulf, means that the provision of protective force can be used in bargaining situations. Sometimes the linkage may be direct; more often, as we will see in Chapter 8, it is a factor not mentioned openly but present in the back of leaders' minds.

Coercing other states to change is a direct or commanding method of exercising power. Such *hard power* can rest on payments ("carrots") or threats ("sticks"). But there is also a soft or indirect way to exercise power. A country may achieve its preferred outcomes in world politics because other countries want to emulate it or have agreed to a system that produces such effects. In this sense, it can be just as important to set the agenda and attract others in world politics as it is to force others to change in particular situations. This aspect of power—that is, getting others to want what you want—is called attractive or *soft power*. Soft power can rest on such resources as the appeal of one's ideas or on the ability to set the political agenda in a way that shapes the preferences that others express. Parents of teenagers know that if they have structured their children's beliefs and preferences, their power will be greater and will last longer than if they had relied only on active control. Similarly, political leaders and constructivist theorists have long understood the power that comes from setting the agenda and determining the framework of a debate. The ability to establish preferences is often associated with intangible power resources such as culture, ideology, and institutions that constructivists emphasize.

Soft power is not automatically more effective or ethical than hard power. Twisting minds is not necessarily better than twisting arms. Moral judgments depend on the purposes for which power is used. The terrorist leader bin Laden, for example, had soft power in the eyes of his followers who carried out the 9/11 attacks. Nor is soft power necessarily more closely associated with liberal than realist theory. Neorealists such as Kenneth Waltz tend to be materialists who pay little attention to the role of ideas. In their efforts to be parsimonious they impoverished realist theory. Classical realists such as Niccolò Machiavelli and Hans Morgenthau never neglected ideas as a source of power.

Power is the ability to affect others to get the outcomes you want regardless of whether its sources are tangible or not. Soft power is often more difficult for governments to wield and slower to yield results. Sometimes it is completely ineffective. But analysts ignore it at their peril. For example, in 1762, when Frederick the Great of Prussia was about to be defeated by a coalition of France, Austria, and Russia, he was saved because the new Russian tsar, Peter III (1728–1762), idolized the Prussian monarch and pulled his troops out of the anti-Prussian coalition. In 1917, Great Britain had greater soft power than Germany over American opinion, and that affected the United States' entry on Britain's side in World War I. More recently, the election of Barack Obama in 2008 gave an immediate boost to American soft power because his image and his message held great appeal even in parts of the world that had become notably hostile to U.S. policy. Translating these enhanced soft power resources into tangible outcomes has been neither linear nor easy, however.

Hard and soft power are related, but they are not the same. Material success makes a culture and ideology attractive, and decreases in economic and military success lead to self-doubt and crises of identity. But soft power does not rest solely on hard power. The soft power of the Vatican did not wane as the size of the Papal States diminished in the nineteenth century. Sweden, Norway, and the Netherlands today tend to have more influence than some other states with equivalent economic or military capability. The Soviet Union had considerable soft power in Europe after World War II but squandered it after its invasions of Hungary in 1956 and Czechoslovakia in 1968. Many would argue that the United States enjoyed enormous soft power in the immediate wake of 9/11, but squandered much of it in the aftermath through artless, muscular unilateralism.

What resources are the most important sources of power today? A look at the five centuries since the birth of the sovereign state shows that different power resources played critical roles in different periods. The sources of power are never static, and they continue to change in today's world. Moreover, they vary in different parts of the world. Soft power is becoming more important in relations among the democratic postindustrial societies in the modern information age; hard power is often more important in industrializing and preindustrial parts of the world.

In an age of information-based economies and transnational interdependence, power is becoming less transferable, less tangible, and less coercive than it ever was, as we shall see in more detail in Chapters 8 and 9. Analysts used to predict the outcome of conflict mainly on the basis of who had the bigger army or the bigger economy. Today, in conflicts such as the struggle against transnational terrorism, it is equally important whose story wins. Hard power is necessary against hardcore terrorists, but it is equally important to use soft power to win the hearts and minds of the mainstream population that might otherwise be won over by the terrorists.

> *The capacity to know when to use hard power, when to use soft power, and when to combine the two, I call smart power.*

> —JOSEPH S. NYE, JR.

The transformation of power is not the same in all parts of the world. A greater role for informational and institutional power is seen today than in previous centuries, but as events in the Middle East demonstrate, hard military power remains an important instrument. Economic scale, both in markets and in natural resources, also remains important. The service sector grows within modern economies, and the distinction between services and manufacturing continues to blur. Information will continue to become more plentiful, and the critical resource of the future will be organizational capacity for rapid and flexible response. Political cohesion will remain important, as will the nurturing of a universalistic, exportable popular culture.

Note the slightly complicated relationship between *power* and *authority*. Authority can be a power resource when others respect it, but you can have power without having authority. The United States had the power to oust the duly elected Guatemalan president, Jacobo Árbenz Guzmán, in a coup engineered by the Central Intelligence Agency in 1954, but it did not have the authority to do so. Guatemala was a sovereign state. Power is an empirical notion, whereas authority is a moral, normative, or juridical concept. Authority requires legitimacy. Although the international system of sovereign states is anarchic in the legal distribution of authority, it is never truly anarchic in the distribution of power. In *unipolar* systems, one country enjoys a preponderance of power and can effectively set the terms of international cooperation and enforce or elicit compliance. In a *bipolar* system, two countries of similar power enjoy primacy within their particular sphere or among other states aligned with them (lesser powers or client states). In a *multipolar* system, three or more countries wield an unusual degree of power. We usually call the strongest country within a unipolar system a *hegemon* (from the Greek meaning "leader"), we call the strongest countries in a modern bipolar system *superpowers*, and we call the strongest countries within multipolar systems *great powers*.

International System and International Society

We have been using the word *system* frequently to this point. What do we mean by it? According to the dictionary, a system is a set of interrelated units. The units or components of systems interact in a regular way that may be more or less complicated. We use the terms *structure* to describe the configuration of the units and *process* to capture their interactions. The distinction between structure and process at any given time can be illustrated by the metaphor of a poker game. The *structure* of a poker game is in the distribution of power, that is, how many chips the players have and how many high cards they are dealt. The *process* is how the game is played and the types of interactions among the players. (How are the rules created and understood? Are the players good bluffers? Do they obey the rules? If players cheat, are they likely to get caught?) For example, allowing the players in Prisoner's Dilemma games to communicate with each other alters the nature of the game. So, too, when states communicate with one another and reach mutually beneficial agreements or create well-understood norms and institutions, they add to the repertoire of state strategies and can thus alter political outcomes.

The international system is an example of a particular kind of system, namely, a *political* system. In contrast to many domestic political systems, which are easy to identify because of their clear institutional referents (the presidency, Congress, Parliament, etc.), the current international political system is less centralized and less tangible. Without the United Nations, an international system would still exist. Do not be misled, however, by the institutional concreteness of domestic political systems. They also include intangible aspects such as public attitudes, the role of the press, and some of the unwritten conventions of constitutions. Put another way, systems can be material, ideational, or both. Computers, human bodies, and the ecosphere are all material systems. Computers have power supplies, processors, memory chips, buses, keyboards, storage devices, and screens, all of which interact electromechanically according to the laws of physics. Languages are ideational systems; their components are words, and their processes of interaction are captured by rules of grammar and syntax. The international system is a combination of material things and ideas.

To some extent, representing something as a "system" is an exercise in mental housekeeping, because at the end of the day everything is connected to everything else. We can more easily make sense of the world, for example, by distinguishing a computer from the electrical grid required to operate it and by distinguishing the electrical grid from the hydrological processes that make it possible for dams to generate power on flowing rivers. But in fact they all interact. The international system is a mental construction as well. What happens in it is affected not only by state and nonstate actors, but also by other systems. Greenhouse gas emissions, for example, will result in climate change, altered sea levels, altered rainfall patterns, changes in vegetation, and large-scale migrations. These changes are likely to trigger intrastate conflicts, as has already happened in Darfur, and may trigger interstate conflicts as well. We might literally say that the solar system affects the international political system via the atmospheric system. But it is unwieldy and counterproductive to attempt to think of everything as part of one enormous system. Treating the international system as something discrete makes it possible to talk more sensibly of what happens in the world than would be possible otherwise, even if, in a technical sense, everything is connected to everything else.

Although the ordering principle of the international system is anarchic, the system itself is not chaotic. Most global interactions are orderly in the sense that they follow regular, largely predictable patterns. In most respects, these interactions are rule-governed. As we saw in Chapter 1, international law is a weak cousin of domestic law, but in fact rates of compliance with international law are often not that different from domestic law. If anything, egregious violations of international law are comparatively rare, whereas most countries' domestic legal systems groan under a heavy caseload of both criminal and civil violations. The marks of an orderly social system (such as the international system of sovereign states) are that institutions and practices exist for handling disputes; that most conflicts are resolved peacefully; that there exists an agreed-upon body of rules (laws, regulations, guidelines, acceptable practices, etc.); that there is a good level of compliance with the rules; and that there are methods of dealing with noncompliance. How can we explain this concept?

The answer is that relatively few parts of the world can accurately be described as being in what Thomas Hobbes called a "state of nature." The international system is not a pool table on which states-as-billiard-balls career off one another blindly in an endless series of conflicts. The international system is *social*. Just because there is no world government (i.e., the international system is anarchic in the distribution of authority) does not mean that there is no such thing as an *international society*. There are rules of conduct, an increasingly rich body of international law, well-specified rights and obligations, even rules of international etiquette—diplomatic practices, honors, and so on—in short, all the features of "polite society." Slights can trigger international conflict just as they can trigger interpersonal conflict in everyday life. Indeed, Bismarck deliberately engineered the Franco-Prussian War (1870–1871) by violating well-entrenched norms of diplomatic protocol: first by attempting to place a Prussian king on the throne of Spain without consulting France beforehand and then by leaking confidential French diplomatic communications to the international press (the famous "Ems Telegram").[6] Realists on the one hand and liberals and constructivists on the other disagree on the degree to which the international system is genuinely social. Realists think that it is social only in a thin, superficial sense, whereas liberals and constructivists think that the social constraints on action are much thicker. But virtually all agree that the social dimensions of international politics promote orderly interaction.

System Stability and Crisis Stability

International systems are stable if they are able to absorb shocks without breaking down. Systems break down when they are no longer able to serve their intended purposes. A major purpose of the international system is to safeguard the sovereignty and security of its members. Minor wars are not necessarily evidence of system breakdown, because sometimes the only way to protect the sovereignty and security of certain states is to wage war against others. For this reason, the renowned Australian scholar Hedley Bull wrote at length about war as an "institution"—in the sense of a recognized and regulated practice—for maintaining order.[7] But major wars jeopardize the sovereignty and security of most or all states and are evidence of system instability.

What makes a system stable? One important factor is the quality of the social fabric of international society. The stronger the normative and institutional threads binding states, and the denser the connections between them, the greater the stake states have in preventing system breakdown and the more avenues they have available for resolving disagreements before they can get out of hand. The weaker the social context—the more the system resembles a Hobbesian state of nature, in other words—the more states depend on self-help.

In a Hobbesian anarchy, according to systems theorists such as Waltz, distributions of power are crucial to system stability. Unipolar systems tend to erode as states try to preserve their independence by balancing against the hegemon or as a rising state eventually challenges the leader. In multipolar or dispersed-power systems, states form alliances to balance power, but alliances are flexible. Wars may occur, but they will be relatively limited in scope. In bipolar systems, alliances become more rigid, which in turn contributes to the probability of a large conflict, perhaps even a global war. Some analysts say that "bipolar systems either erode or explode." That happened in the Peloponnesian War when Athens and Sparta tightened their grips on their respective alliances. It was also true before 1914, when the multipolar European balance of power gradually consolidated into two strong alliance systems that lost their flexibility. But predictions about war based on multipolarity versus bipolarity encountered a major anomaly after 1945. During the Cold War, the world was bipolar with two big players, the United States and its allies and the Soviet Union and its allies, yet no overall central war occurred for more than four decades before the system eroded with the decline of the Soviet Union. Some people say that nuclear weapons made the prospect of global war too awful. Thus the structure of the international system offers a rough explanation for system stability, but does not explain enough all by itself.

Arguably, the Cold War system was stable because it also exhibited *crisis stability*. In a crisis-unstable situation, if two or more countries find themselves in an acute international crisis, they will feel enormous pressure to strike the first blow. To use a simple metaphor, imagine that you and an adversary are standing in the open, each armed with a gun. Neither of you is quite sure of the other's intentions. If either of you believe that there is a chance that shots might be fired, you both have a powerful incentive to shoot first. Whoever shoots first is more likely to survive. This kind of situation is very likely to escalate quickly to violence.

Now imagine that you and your adversary are locked in a room, knee-deep in gasoline, armed only with a match. In this situation, neither of you has a strong incentive to strike the first match. If you did, your adversary would surely be killed or badly injured, but so would you. You both have a powerful incentive to try to find a peaceful way out. Such a situation is highly crisis-stable.

To a very significant degree, crisis stability is a function of technology— or, perhaps more accurately, prevailing beliefs about technology—as reflected in military doctrine. When the prevailing military technology is believed to favor the offense, decision makers feel pressure to strike the first blow. When it is believed to favor the defense, they do not. As we shall see in Chapter 3, at the beginning of World War I, European leaders believed that there was a great advantage in taking the offensive, and the July crisis of 1914 escalated very quickly. (In this belief they were tragically mistaken. As the carnage of the following four years would demonstrate, well-entrenched infantry armed with machine guns and backed by mass artillery cut attacking armies to pieces.) During the Cold War, prevailing beliefs about military technology were almost certainly correct: Neither the United States nor the Soviet Union could defend against a nuclear attack, but there was little doubt that they could count on being able to launch a devastating retaliatory blow. This situation, aptly called "mutual assured destruction," or MAD, was highly crisis-stable.

The "National Interest"

The final key concept that needs clarification before we proceed further is the *national interest*. Leaders and analysts alike assert that "states act in their national interest." That statement is normally true, but it does not tell us much unless we know how states define their national interests.

Realists say that states have little choice in defining their national interest because of the international system. They must define their interest in terms of power or they will not survive, just as a company in a perfect market that wants to be altruistic rather than maximize profits will not survive. So for the realists, a state's position in the international system determines its national interests and predicts its foreign policies.

Liberals and constructivists argue that national interests are defined by much more than the state's position in the international system, and they have a richer account of how state preferences and national interests are formed. The definition of the national interest depends in large part on the type of domestic society and culture a state has. For example, a domestic society that values economic welfare and places heavy emphasis on trade, or one that views wars against other democracies as illegitimate, defines its national interests very differently from a despotic state that is similarly positioned in the international system. Liberals argue that it is particularly true if international institutions and channels of communication enable states to build trust; that helps them escape from the Prisoner's Dilemma.

Because nonpower incentives can help shape how states define their interests, it is important to know how closely a particular situation approximates a Hobbesian state of nature. In a Hobbesian system, you may be killed by your neighbor tomorrow, and limited opportunities exist for democracy or trade preferences to influence foreign policy. Survival comes first. But if institutions and stable expectations of peace moderate the Hobbesian anarchy, some of these other factors related to domestic society and culture are likely to play a larger role. Realist predictions are more likely to be accurate in the Middle East, for example, and liberal predictions in Western Europe. Knowing the context helps us gauge the likely predictive value of different theories.

It is important to bear in mind that the national interest is almost always contested. People who would agree at an abstract level that power and security are important national interests very often disagree about the concrete policies that would promote them. Sometimes policy preferences are completely opposite and incompatible. During the period between the two world wars, there was a vibrant debate in the United States between those who believed that the best way to promote American security was to avoid becoming entangled in the thorny power politics of Europe and East Asia and those who believed that American security depended on actively working with others to check the rising power and imperial ambitions of Germany and Japan. There is also a historically important debate between those who see morality and the pursuit of the national interest as separate and incompatible and those who think that a country's conception of what is right and just is a fundamental part of its national interest. What is not open for debate is that anyone seeking to promote a particular foreign policy will inevitable try to wrap it in the mantle of the national interest. The concept, in other words, is not merely a shorthand for vital state goals. It is also a playing field on which policy makers and policy entrepreneurs contend.

Follow Up

- Barry Buzan, "From International System to International Society: Structural Realism and Regime Theory Meet the English School," *International Organization*, Vol. 47, No. 3 (Summer 1993), pp. 327–352.

- Joseph S. Nye, Jr., *The Future of Power* (New York: PublicAffairs, 2011).

Levels of Analysis

2.2 Distinguish the individual, state, and system levels.

A system is greater than the sum of its parts. Systems can create consequences not intended by any of their components. Think of the market system in economics. Every firm in a perfect market tries to maximize its profits, but the market system produces competition that reduces profits to the break-even point, thereby benefiting the consumer. The businessperson does not set out to benefit the consumer, but individual firms' pattern of behavior in a perfect market leads to that effect. In other words, the system produces the consequences, which may be quite different from the intention of the actors in the system.

The international political system can similarly lead to effects the actors did not originally intend. For example, in 1917 when the Bolsheviks came to power in Russia, they regarded the whole system of interstate diplomacy that had preceded World War I as bourgeois nonsense. They intended to sweep away the interstate system and hoped that revolutions would unite all the workers of the world and abolish borders. Transnational proletarian solidarity would replace the interstate system. Indeed, when Leon Trotsky took charge of the Russian Foreign Ministry, he said that his intent was to issue some revolutionary proclamations to the peoples of the world and then "close up the joint." But the Bolsheviks found that their actions were soon affected by the nature of the interstate system. In 1922, the new communist state signed the Treaty of Rapallo with Germany. It was an alliance of the outcasts, the countries that were not accepted in the post–World War I diplomatic world. In 1939, Josef Stalin entered a pact with his ideological archenemy, Hitler, to turn Hitler westward. Soviet behavior, despite Trotsky's initial proclamations and illusions, soon became similar to that of other actors in the international system.

The distribution of power among states in an international system helps us make predictions about certain aspects of states' behavior. The tradition of *geopolitics* holds that location and proximity will tell a great deal about how states will behave. Because neighbors have more contact and points of potential friction than nonneighbors, it is not surprising that half of the military conflicts between 1816 and 1992 began between neighbors.[8] A state that feels threatened by its neighbor is likely to act in accord with the old adage that "the enemy of my enemy is my friend." This pattern has always been found in anarchic systems. For example, the Indian writer Kautilya pointed out in the third century BCE that the states of the Indian subcontinent tended to ally with distant states to protect themselves against their neighbors, thus producing a checkerboard pattern of alliances. Machiavelli noted the same behavior among the city-states in fifteenth-century Italy. In the early 1960s, as West African states emerged from colonial rule, there was a great deal of talk about African solidarity, but the new states soon began to produce a checkerboard pattern of alliances similar to what Kautilya described in ancient India. Ghana, Guinea, and Mali were ideologically radical, whereas Senegal, Ivory Coast, and Nigeria were relatively conservative, but they were also balancing against the strength of their neighbors. Another example was the pattern that developed in East Asia after the Vietnam War. If the Soviet Union were colored black, China would be red, Vietnam black, and Cambodia red. A perfect checkerboard pattern developed. Ironically, the United States entered the Vietnam War because policy makers believed in the "domino theory," according to which one state would fall to communism, leading another state to fall, and so forth. With more foresight, the United States should have realized that the game in East Asia was more like checkers than dominoes and might have stayed out. The checkerboard pattern based on "the enemy of my enemy is my friend" is an old tradition of geopolitics that helps us make useful predictions in an anarchic situation.

How can we make sense of this kind of pattern or tendency? World politics is not something one can manipulate the way a physicist or a chemist can manipulate the conditions of an experiment in the lab. What happens, happens, and we must try to make sense of it without the benefit of controlled experiments. That almost always means that we must be more guarded in our conclusions, because certain valuable strategies for identifying and ruling out spurious explanations are simply not available. We do make judgments about why things happen in world politics, however, and we never do so without reason. What tips and tricks can we use? How reliable are they?

Systems are not the only way of explaining what happens in international politics. In *Man, the State, and War*, Waltz distinguishes three levels of causation for war, which he calls "images": the *individual*, the *state*, and the *international system*. The checkerboard pattern that so frequently develops as a result of "the enemy of my enemy is my friend" could be a function of dynamics at any one (or more) of these levels of analysis. So, when attempting to determine why things happen in world politics, a good place to start is to see whether we get the most explanatory power by looking at the reasons people (such as leaders) do what they do (the individual level of analysis), by looking at what happens within individual states (the state level), or by looking at the interactions between actors (the system level).

The Individual Level

Explanations at the level of the individual are useful when it genuinely matters who is making decisions. Most analysts believe that the United States would have attacked al-Qaeda training camps in Afghanistan after 9/11 and toppled the Taliban regime if it failed to cooperate no matter who was president. If Al Gore rather than George W. Bush had won the 2000 presidential election, we probably still would have seen Operation Enduring Freedom or something very much like it. But few analysts think that a President Gore would have attacked Iraq in 2003. Neither domestic political nor systemic imperatives made that likely in the way they made Afghanistan likely. The Iraq War was very much a war of choice, and to explain it we have to look at the specific reasons why Bush and his senior advisors chose it.

There is little doubt that individuals sometimes matter. Pericles made a difference in the Peloponnesian War. In 1991, Saddam Hussein was a critical factor in the Gulf War. Sometimes individuals matter, but not in isolation from other considerations. In the 1962 Cuban missile crisis, Kennedy and Khrushchev faced the possibility of nuclear war and the ultimate decision was in their hands. But why they found themselves in that position cannot be explained at the level of individuals; something in the structure of the situation brought them to that point. Similarly, knowing something about the personality of Kaiser Wilhelm II or Hitler is necessary to an understanding of the causes of World War I and World War II, but it is not a sufficient explanation. As we see in the next chapter, it made a difference that Kaiser Wilhelm fired his chancellor, Bismarck, in 1890, but that does not mean that World War I was brought about primarily by Kaiser Wilhelm.

Although one way of using the individual level of analysis is to focus on features specific to individual people (their personalities, their life histories, etc.), another way is to look for explanations in people's common characteristics, in the "human nature" common to all individuals. For example, we could take a Calvinist view of international politics and assign the ultimate cause of war to the evil that lies within each of us. That would explain war as the result of an imperfection in human nature. But such an explanation overpredicts: It does not tell us why some evil leaders go to war and others do not or why some good leaders go to war and others do not. Sometimes generalizations about human nature lead to unfalsifiable explanations. Some realists locate the ultimate source of conflict in a relentless drive for power. The Australian historian Geoffrey Blainey, for example, argues:

> One generalization about war aims can be offered with confidence. The aims are simply varieties of power. The vanity of nationalism, the will to spread an ideology, the protection of kinsmen in an adjacent land, the desire for more territory or commerce, the avenging of a defeat or insult, the craving for greater national strength or independence, the wish to impress or cement alliances—all these represent power in different wrappings. The conflicting aims of rival nations are always conflicts of power."[9]

If every goal counts as a quest for power, the statement "the quest for power causes wars" is an unfalsifiable tautology. Something that explains everything explains nothing.

More fruitful are explanations that leverage psychological tendencies. Many students of international politics assume that psychological considerations do not matter: Leaders of states either are, or can be assumed to be, "rational" actors. If they are rational, all we need to know to understand or predict the choices they make are the costs and benefits of their options. Any rational actor facing a situation reminiscent of the Prisoner's Dilemma, according to this view, can be expected to defect rather than cooperate. But although some people do make decisions on the basis of good-quality cost-benefit analysis, there are many situations in which that is simply not possible, owing to a lack of information. In any case, we know that many people do not, or cannot, make decisions in this way even when it is possible to do so. Using psychological considerations to explain apparent deviations from "rational" actions can be very helpful.

That is precisely how the field of political psychology examines global conflict and cooperation. There are four main approaches. One is *cognitive psychology*. Cognitive psychology examines the processes by which people seek to make sense of raw information about the world. Cognitive psychologists have shown that people do so by looking for commonalities between what they are trying to make sense of and things they already know or believe: in other words, they look for connections between the unfamiliar and the familiar. Shocked by the horrors inflicted on the world by dictators such as Hitler and Benito Mussolini, for instance, Western leaders after World War II tended to think that any dictator claiming to have suffered some injustice at the hands of other countries was, in fact, an opportunistic aggressor. Sometimes they were right, but sometimes they were wrong. A case in which they were wrong was 1956, when Egyptian president Gamal Abdel Nasser asserted Egypt's right to control the Suez Canal because it cut through Egyptian territory. When Nasser nationalized the canal, French and British leaders leaped to the conclusion that Nasser was "just like Hitler" and had to be resisted. The result was an unnecessary war that greatly complicated Middle Eastern politics, divided the North Atlantic Treaty Organization, distracted the world's attention from a Soviet crackdown in Hungary, and severely damaged Britain's power and prestige.

A second approach is *motivational psychology*. Motivational psychologists explain human behavior in terms of deep-seated psychological fears, desires, and needs. These needs include self-esteem, social approval, and a sense of efficacy. Motivational psychology helps us understand, for example, why almost all German diplomats before World War I gave false or misleading reports on the likely reactions of European countries to Austrian and German military moves. The reason is that they were simply frightened of the consequences of not telling the notoriously intolerant German foreign ministry what it wanted to hear. The one German diplomat who accurately reported the likely response of Britain to a German violation of Belgian neutrality, Ambassador Prince Karl Lichnowsky in London, was dismissed in Berlin as having "gone native," a judgmental error that itself can be explained in terms of a well-documented motivational-psychological tendency: namely, the desire to avoid the psychological pain of admitting one's own error. Because Germany's entire strategy for swift victory in 1914 depended on Britain staying out of the war, Lichnowsky's accurate reports would have been extremely unsettling if they had been accepted.

A third approach, and a more recent one, is to apply insights from *behavioral economics* and particularly from *prospect theory*. Prospect theory explains deviations from rational action by noting that people make decisions very differently depending on whether they face prospects of gain or prospects of loss. Most notably, people take much greater risks to avoid losses than they would be willing to take to achieve gains. Identifying how leaders frame their choices can help us understand and even anticipate how willing they will be to take risks. Indeed, because many choice situations can be described equally well in the language of losses or gains (10 lives out of a 100 lost is the same as 90 lives saved), strategically reframing choices can induce people to make different choices. The general tendency people exhibit toward loss-aversion helps us understand, for example, why people escalate commitments to losing courses of action. The more a gambler loses at the slot machines in Las Vegas, the less willing he or she will be to stop playing, because the desire to recoup the loss gets stronger and stronger. Similarly, the more lives the United States lost in the Vietnam War, the less willing it was to throw in the towel. Unlucky gamblers and leaders who fight losing battles often quit only when they exhaust their resources.

Finally, the fourth approach, *psychobiography*, explains leaders' choices in terms of their psychodynamics. This approach locates idiosyncratic personality traits in generally recognized neuroses and psychoses. A fascinating example is Alexander and Juliette George's psychobiography of Woodrow Wilson and Colonel House, which seeks to explain the United States' heavy hand at the Paris peace talks of 1919 and its subsequent failure to join the League of Nations—the president's pet project—in terms of Wilson's need for control, his unwillingness to compromise, and his intolerance of opposition, all of which, the Georges argue, can be traced to traumatic childhood experiences at the hands of an overbearing father.[10] Equally fascinating are the many psychobiographies of Hitler, which stress the importance of his desire to compensate for self-loathing and sexual frustration.[11] It is now routine for the U.S. intelligence community to compile psychological profiles of foreign leaders with an eye toward better predicting their behavior. But even though psychobiography is always fascinating, it shares many of the weaknesses of the Freudian tradition out of which it springs, the most important of which are unfalsifiability and the difficulty of independent corroboration. When explanations for international political events rest on the subconscious fears, needs, and desires of world leaders—many of whom are dead or otherwise unavailable for close examination—it is difficult to know how to have high confidence in them.

The State Level

When we seek to explain things at the state level of analysis, we ask whether what happens in world politics is a function of domestic politics, various

Photo: Lionel Cironneau/AP Images

The Cold War ends: The Berlin wall coming down

features of domestic society, or the machinery of government. Domestic considerations clearly sometimes matter. After all, the Peloponnesian War began with a domestic conflict between the oligarchs and the democrats in Epidamnus. The domestic politics of Germany and the Austro-Hungarian Empire played significant roles in the onset of World War I. To understand the end of the Cold War, we must look inside the Soviet Union at the failure of its centrally planned economy. It is easy to find examples in which domestic considerations mattered, but can we generalize about them? After we have said that they are important, is there anything else to say?

Marxism and liberalism both put a great deal of emphasis on the state level of analysis. Both hold that states will act similarly in the international system if they are similar domestically. Marxists argue that the source of war is capitalism. In Vladimir Lenin's view, monopoly capital requires war: "Inter-imperialist alliances are inevitably nothing more than a truce in the periods between wars."[12] War can be explained by the nature of capitalist society, whose inequitable distribution of wealth leads to underconsumption, stagnation, and lack of domestic investment. As a consequence, capitalism leads to imperialist expansionism abroad, which helps sell surplus production in foreign markets, creates foreign investment opportunities, and promises access to natural resources. Such imperialism also fuels the domestic economy through higher military spending. Thus Marxism predicts arms races and conflict between capitalist states. In fact, the theory did not do a very good job of explaining the onset of World War I, which was opposed by wealthy capitalists but supported by almost everyone else. Moreover, it does not fit the experience of the second half of the twentieth century. Communist states, such as the Soviet Union, China, and Vietnam, were involved in military clashes with one another, whereas the major capitalist states in Europe, North America, and Japan maintained peaceful relations. The arguments that capitalism causes war do not stand up to historical scrutiny.

Classical liberalism, the philosophy that dominated much of British and American thought in the nineteenth century, came to the opposite conclusion: According to liberal thinkers, capitalist states tend to be peaceful because war is bad for business. One strand of classical liberalism was represented by free traders such as Richard Cobden (1804–1865), who led the successful fight to repeal England's Corn Laws, protectionist measures that had regulated Britain's international grain trade for 500 years. Like others of the Manchester School of British economists, he believed that it was better to trade and to prosper than to go to war. If we are interested in getting richer and improving the welfare of citizens, asserted Cobden, peace is best. In 1840, he expressed the classical view, saying, "We can keep the world from actual war, and I trust that the world will do that through trade."[13]

The liberal view was very powerful on the eve of World War I. A number of books, including a classic by Norman Angell, *The Great Illusion* (1910), said that war had become too expensive. To illustrate the optimism of classical liberalism on the eve of World War I, we can look at the philanthropists of that era. Andrew Carnegie, the steel magnate, established the Carnegie Endowment for International Peace in 1910. Carnegie worried about what would happen to the money he had given to this foundation after lasting peace broke out, so he put a provision in his will to cover this possibility. Edward Ginn, a Boston publisher, did not want Carnegie to get all the credit for the forthcoming permanent peace, so he set up the World Peace Foundation devoted to the same cause. Ginn also worried about what to do with the rest of the money after peace was firmly established, so he designated it for low-cost housing for young working women.

This liberal outlook was severely discredited by World War I. Even though bankers and aristocrats had frequent contact across borders and labor also had transnational contacts, none of that helped stop the European states from going to war with one another. Statistical analysis has found no strong correlation between states' involvement in war and whether they are capitalist or democratic. The classical Marxist and liberal views are opposites in their understandings of the relationship between war and capitalism, but they are similar in locating the causes of war in domestic politics and especially in the nature of the economic system.

State-level explanations of this kind suffer from some of the same difficulties as human-nature explanations. If certain types of societies cause war, why do some "bad" societies or "bad" states not go to war? And why do some "good" societies or "good" states go to war? Insert your favorite description for "good" and "bad": "democratic," "communist," "capitalist," or whatever. For example, after World War I, there was a great deal of enthusiasm for the belief that the victory of the democracies would mean less danger of war. Clearly, though, democracies can go to war and often do. After all, Athens was a democracy. Marxist theorists argued that war would be abolished when all states were communist, but obviously there have been military clashes among communist countries; witness China versus the Soviet Union or Vietnam versus Cambodia. Thus the nature of the society, democratic or capitalist or communist, is not a predictor of whether it will go to war.

One proposition (which we discuss later in this chapter) is that if *all* countries were democratic, there would be less war. In fact, cases in which liberal democracies have fought against other liberal democracies are difficult to find, although democracies have fought against authoritarian states in many situations. The reasons for this empirical finding and whether it will continue to hold in the future are not clear, but it suggests something interesting to investigate at this second level of analysis.

A relatively recent state-level line of inquiry is the *bureaucratic politics* approach. Bureaucratic politics explanations look not to the domestic political or economic arrangements of states, but to the interplay of governmental agencies and officials. One strand focuses on organizational dynamics, in particular in the routines and standard operating procedures upon which all complex organizations depend to function. Arguably, an important reason World War I broke out was because European armies in general and the German army in particular had crafted rigid military plans that limited leaders' choices in the heat of crisis. This thinking, coupled with the "cult of the offensive," which glorified the cavalry and tactics of maneuver, made the situation in July and August 1914 highly crisis-unstable. A second strand stresses the role of parochial bureaucratic interests. It is possible, for example, to explain some arms races by noting how competition for resources between branches of the military leads to escalating budgets, adversaries feeling less secure, adversaries spending more on defense, and ultimately a classic security dilemma. Perhaps the most famous insight from bureaucratic politics is captured by Miles's Law: "Where you stand depends on where you sit." If Miles's Law were correct, decision makers engaged in policy debates would seek to promote not national interests, but the interests of the departments, agencies, or branches of government that they represent. Evidence for Miles's Law is mixed. There are cases that fit the pattern. When he was the state of California's director of finance under Governor Ronald Reagan, Caspar Weinberger was known as "Cap the Knife" for the gusto with which he slashed budgets. Later, as President Reagan's secretary of defense, his enthusiastic advocacy for ever higher military spending prompted one Republican senator to call him "a draft dodger in the war on the federal deficit."[14] Yet other studies show at most a weak link between bureaucratic position and policy preferences or no link at all. In any case, although it is possible to imagine that bureaucratic considerations can help us understand specific policy choices states make, it is harder to imagine how they might be harnessed to explanations of general patterns in world politics.

The System Level

Interesting explanations often involve interplay between two or more levels of analysis. As we shall see in Chapter 3, a satisfying explanation of the outbreak of World War I might invoke a combination of three factors: rigid bipolarity (a structural feature of the international system); crisis-unstable military plans and doctrines (a result of military cultures within states, particularly Germany); and serious motivated errors of judgment by key leaders (a psychological consideration). How do we know which is most important? And where do we start when we want to explain the outbreak of war? Do we start from the outside in? That way would mean starting with system-level analysis, looking at the way the overall system constrains state action. Or do we start from the inside out? That way would mean starting with the individual or state level.

Because we often need information about more than one level of analysis, a good rule of thumb is to start with the simplest approach. If a simple explanation is adequate, it is preferable to a more complicated one. This approach is called the *rule of parsimony* or *Occam's razor*, after the philosopher William of Occam (c. 1287–1347), who argued that good explanations shave away unnecessary detail. *Parsimony*—the ability to explain a lot with a little—is only one of the criteria by which we judge the adequacy of theories. We are also interested in the *range* of a theory (how much behavior it covers) and its *explanatory fit* (how many loose ends or anomalies it accounts for). Parsimony nonetheless suggests a place to start. Because systemic explanations tend to be the simplest, they provide a good starting point. If they prove to be inadequate, we can look at the units of the system or at individual decision makers, adding complexity until a reasonable fit is obtained.

How simple or complicated should a systemic explanation be? Some neorealists, such as Waltz, argue for extreme parsimony and focus only on structure. Liberals and constructivists argue that Waltz's concept of system is so spare that it explains very little.

Economists characterize the structure of markets by the concentration of sellers' power. A monopoly has one big seller, a duopoly two big sellers, and an oligopoly several big sellers. In a perfect market, selling power is widely dispersed. Firms that maximize profits in a perfect market benefit the consumer. But the result would be different for a monopoly or oligopoly. In these systems, large firms can increase profits by restricting production to raise prices. Thus when the structure of the system is known, economists are better able to predict behavior and who will benefit. So it is that the structure of the international system can help us understand behavior within it. Note that in a perfect market, we do not need to look inside firms or at the personalities of chief executive officers to understand or predict the behavior of the market as a whole. We can assume that firms are rational, unitary actors, because over time those who do not make business decisions *as if* they were rational, unitary actors (or very close to the ideal) will fail. They will be selected out of the system, to use a Darwinian metaphor. Over the long run, only firms that respond well to the incentives of the marketplace will survive. That is not necessarily true of firms in monopolistic or oligopolistic markets. If we want to understand those markets, sometimes we must understand something about the firms and personalities that dominate them.

Does the international system resemble a perfectly competitive market? Not exactly. There are many states in the world, certainly, but they rarely get "selected out of the system," so it is more difficult to justify the assumption that they can be treated "as if" they were unitary, rational actors. Still, in a Hobbesian world, states would face powerful incentives to be on their guard, make adequate provision for their security, and take advantage of opportunities to increase their wealth and power. States that could not provide for their own security—owing, perhaps, to having much bigger and much more powerful neighbors—would face strong incentives to find allies. They might seek to balance the power of the strongest states. This logic has given rise to the most extensive body of systemic theory in the study of international politics—realist balance-of-power theory—about which we will have more to say later in this chapter and in Chapter 3.

Democracy and Peace

A coalition for democracy—it's good for America. Democracies, after all, are more likely to be stable, less likely to wage war. They strengthen civil society. They can provide people with the economic opportunities to build their own homes, not to flee their borders. Our efforts to help build democracies will make us all more secure, more prosperous, and more successful as we try to make this era of terrific change our friend and not our enemy.

—*President William J. Clinton, remarks to the 49th Session of the UN General Assembly, September 26, 1994*

The survival of liberty in our land increasingly depends on the success of liberty in other lands. The best hope for peace in our world is the expansion of freedom in all the world. America's vital interests and our deepest beliefs are now one. . . . So it is the policy of the United States to seek and support the growth of democratic movements and institutions in every nation and culture, with the ultimate goal of ending tyranny in our world.

—*President George W. Bush, second inaugural address, Washington, DC, January 20, 2005*

Non-Hobbesian systems behave very differently. The more social the system, the less the logic of self-help applies. Liberalism and constructivism are better suited to the study of highly social systems, because the interactions of the units are more reliably governed by laws, rules, norms, expectations, and taboos. Liberalism and constructivism pay a great deal of attention to the origin and evolution of these social constraints on state action. Because explaining them often requires examining the role of domestic political considerations or of individual norm entrepreneurs, liberal and constructivist theories tend to cross levels of analysis.

Follow Up

- J. David Singer, "The Levels of Analysis Problem in International Relations," in James N. Rosenau, ed., *International Politics and Foreign Policy* (New York: Free Press, 1969), pp. 20–29.

- Jack S. Levy, "Contending Theories of International Conflict: A Levels-of-Analysis Approach," in Chester A. Crocker and Fen Osler Hampson, eds., *Managing Global Chaos: Sources of and Responses to International Conflict* (Washington, DC: United States Institute of Peace, 1996), pp. 3–24.

Paradigms and Theories

2.3 Distinguish paradigms from theories and identify the key features of the realist, liberal, Marxist, and constructivist paradigms.

To study something systematically, you need a way of organizing the tools and techniques that you use. The conceptual toolkit and the "handbook" (as it were) for using the tools is called a "paradigm." As Columbia University sociologist Robert Merton put it, a paradigm is "a systematic statement of the basic assumptions, concepts, and propositions employed by a school of analysis." Paradigms, according to Merton, serve a "notational function," keeping concepts in order; they specify assumptions and the logical connections between them, they promote the cumulation of useful theories that explain things we observe in the world, they help us identify new puzzles, and they promote rigorous analysis instead of mere description.[15] Paradigms can be thought of as the foundations on which we build ever-taller (and narrower) structures of knowledge.

The structures themselves are theories. Theories are provisional statements about how the world works. We derive theories from paradigms.

We use *hypotheses* to test theories. A hypothesis is a statement about what we should expect to observe in the world if our theories were true. If our expectations are dashed, we reject the hypothesis and rework (or discard) the theory. If our expectations are met, we consider the theory confirmed and go on to expand it, refine it, or build other theories compatible with it, gradually building up a body of propositions about the world in which we can have confidence. From time to time we abandon one paradigm in favor of another if it cannot perform as well. The Newtonian paradigm dominated physics for almost 300 years, and it did an excellent job of helping us explain how the physical world worked under most conditions (indeed, it is still useful for many practical applications). But Newtonian physics could not help us explain how things behaved at extremely small time and distance scales or at speeds approaching the speed of light. A later paradigm—Einstein's relativity—performed much better.

We have already met the four dominant paradigms in the study of world politics: realism, liberalism, Marxism, and constructivism. Each begins with certain unquestioned assumptions called "axioms" (axioms are always necessary; it is impossible to question everything, because one would never actually get around to explaining anything). Each employs a particular set of concepts, although in the case of these four paradigms they often employ many of the same ones. Each generates particular bodies of theory. Table 2.1 provides a snapshot comparison.

Realism

By now the contours of realism as a paradigm should be familiar. It is worth recalling, though, that despite the apparent simplicity of realism as reflected in Table 2.1, realism is actually a fairly large tent. Realists of all stripes agree that states are the most important actors in the international system, that anarchy has a powerful effect on state behavior, and that at the end of the day all politics is power politics. But classical realism differs quite significantly from neorealism (sometimes called "structural realism"). As we noted above, classical realists such as Machiavelli and Morgenthau paid attention to ideas as well as material power. They saw foreign policy as something that could spring from domestic sources as well as from systemic pressures. They even noted the important role that considerations of ethics would play in shaping foreign policy, although they tended to bemoan that as insufficiently hard-nosed and practical. Classical realists had more of a humanistic approach to world politics than a scientific one. Many of them were prominent historians or philosophers. In contrast, neorealists seek to emulate the natural sciences and are much more concerned with generating purely systemic theories.

There are other distinctions to make within realism as well. "Defensive realists" tend to stress security as the dominant state goal, whereas "offensive" realists tended to stress power. They are both varieties of what James Mayall calls "hard realists," in contrast to "soft realists," who would include the maintenance of international order among state goals.[16] Many of the so-called English School writers on international relations, such as Bull, fall broadly within this category.

So realism is a bit like Baskin-Robbins: There may be 31 flavors, but they are all ice cream. What realists of all kinds share is a commitment to the view that there is an immutable logic to world politics that is perhaps best summed up by the aphorism inspired by an 1848 statement that Lord Palmerston made in the British House of Commons: namely, that states have no permanent friends or

Table 2.1 Key Features of Paradigms

		Realism	Liberalism	Marxism	Constructivism
Key actors		States	States, non-state actors	Economic classes	States, non-state actors
Key Axioms	Dominant human drive(s)	Fear, desire to dominate	Fear, desire to live well	Greed	Need for orderly, meaningful social life
	Actors' primary goals	Power or security	Welfare and justice in addition to security	The capital-owning class seeks to maximize profit; the working class seeks fair wages and working conditions	Actors' interests are socially constructed through interaction
	Actors' dominant instrument(s)	Military power	Military power, trade, investment, negotiation, persuasion	Wealth (capital-owning class); labor (working class)	Depends on historical period and social context
	Dominant processes of interaction	Competition	Competition and cooperation	Exploitation	Depends on historical period and social context
	Dominant structural feature of international system	Hobbesian anarchy	Non-Hobbesian anarchy	Economic inequality	Social constraints (e.g., laws, rules, norms, taboos)
Dominant bodies of theory		Balance-of-power theory; theories of hegemonic transition and hegemonic war	Neoliberal institutionalism; "Democratic Peace"	Dependency theory; theories of revolution	Structuration; theories of norm evolution

permanent enemies, merely permanent interests. But there is ample room for debate within realism and vibrant ongoing research programs that attempt to help us answer questions. For example, do states balance power, or do they balance threat? When do they balance, and when do they bandwagon? What is the fate of American leadership in the world? How will world politics change as countries such as China and India rise?

Liberalism

We have not yet had as much chance to explore liberalism as we have realism, so it would be helpful here to unpack it in somewhat more detail, particularly because it is enjoying a recent resurgence. The two world wars and the failure of collective security in the interwar period had discredited liberal theories. Most writing about international politics in the United States after World War II was strongly realist. As transnational economic interdependence increased, however, the late 1960s and 1970s saw a revival of interest in liberal theories.

There are three strands of liberal thinking: *economic*, *social*, and *political*. The political strand has two parts, one relating to institutions and the other to democracy.

The economic strand of liberalism focuses heavily on trade. Liberals argue that trade is important, not because it prevents states from going to war, but because it may lead states to define their interests in a way that makes war less important to them. Trade offers states a way to transform their position through economic growth rather than through military conquest. Richard Rosecrance points to the example of Japan.[17] In the 1930s, Japan thought that the only way to gain access to markets was to create a "Greater East Asia Co-Prosperity Sphere," which in turn required conquering its neighbors and requiring them to trade preferentially with Japan. Already in 1939, Eugene Staley, a Chicago economist, argued that part of Japan's behavior in the 1930s could be explained by economic protectionism. Staley believed that when economic walls are erected along political boundaries, possession of territory is made to coincide with economic opportunity. A better solution for avoiding war is to pursue economic growth in an open trading system without military conquest. In the postwar period, Japan successfully transformed its position in the world through trade. It is now the world's third largest national economy, measured in purchasing power parity terms, behind only the United States and China.

Realists reply that Japan was able to accomplish this amazing economic growth because somebody else was providing for its security. Specifically, Japan relied on the United States for security against its large nuclear neighbors, the Soviet Union and China. Some realists predicted that, with the Soviet Union gone, the United States would withdraw its security presence in East Asia and raise barriers against Japanese trade. Japan would remilitarize, and eventually there would be conflict between Japan and the United States. But liberals replied that modern Japan is a very different domestic society from the Japan of the 1930s. It is among the least militaristic in the world, partly because the most attractive career opportunities in Japan are in business, not in the military. Liberals argue that the realists do not pay enough attention to domestic politics and the way that Japan has changed as a result of economic opportunities. Trade may not prevent war, but it does change incentives, which in turn may lead to a social structure less inclined to war.

The second form of liberalism is social. It argues that person-to-person contacts reduce conflict by promoting understanding. Such transnational contacts occur at many levels, including through students, businesspeople, and tourists. Such contacts make others seem less foreign and less hateful than they once seemed. That, in turn, leads to a lower likelihood of conflict. The evidence for this view is mixed. After all, bankers, aristocrats, and labor union officials had broad contacts in 1914, but that did not stop them from killing one another once they put on military uniforms. Obviously, the idea that social contact breeds understanding and prevents war is far too simple, but it may nonetheless make a modest contribution to understanding. Western Europe today is very different from 1914. There are constant contacts across international borders in Europe, and textbook editors try to treat other nationalities fairly. The images of the other peoples of Europe are very different from the images of 1914. Public opinion polls show that a sense of European identity coexists with a sense of national identity. The Erasmus Program of the European Union encourages students to study in the universities of other European countries. Transnational society affects what people in a democracy want from their foreign policy. It is worth noting how France responded to the reunification of Germany in 1990. A residue of uncertainty and anxiety remained among the foreign policy experts, but public opinion polls showed that most French people welcomed German unification. Such attitudes were a sharp contrast to those when Germany first unified in 1871.

The first version of the third form of liberalism emphasizes the role of institutions; this strand is often labeled "neoliberalism." Why do international institutions matter? According to Robert Keohane, they provide information and a framework that shapes expectations.[18] They allow people to believe that there is not going to be a conflict. They lengthen the shadow of the future and reduce the acuteness of the security dilemma. Institutions mitigate the negative effects of anarchy (uncertainty and an inability to cultivate trust). Hobbes saw international politics as a state of war. He was careful to say that a state of war does not mean constant fighting, but a propensity to war, just as cloudy weather means a heightened likelihood of rain. In the same sense, a state of peace means a propensity toward peace in that people can develop peaceful expectations when anarchy is stabilized by international institutions.

Institutions stabilize expectations in four ways. First, they provide a sense of continuity; for example, most Western Europeans expect the European Union to last. It is likely to be there tomorrow. At the end of the Cold War, many Eastern European governments agreed and made plans to join the European Union. That affected their behavior even before they eventually joined in 2004. Second, institutions provide an opportunity for reciprocity. If the French get a little bit more today, the Italians might get a little more tomorrow. There is less need to worry about each transaction because over time it will likely balance out. Third, institutions provide a flow of information. Who is doing what? Are the Italians actually obeying the rules passed by the European Union? Is the flow of trade roughly equal? The institutions of the union provide information on how it is all working out. Finally, institutions provide ways to resolve conflicts. In the European Union, bargaining goes on within the Council of Ministers and in the European Commission, and there is also a European court of justice. Thus institutions create a climate in which expectations of stable peace develop.

Classical liberals also expect to see islands of peace where institutions and stable expectations have developed. The political scientist Karl Deutsch called such areas "pluralistic security communities" in which war between countries becomes so unthinkable that stable expectations of peace develop.[19] Institutions helped reinforce such expectations. The Scandinavian countries, for example, once fought one another bitterly, and the United States fought Britain and Mexico. Today such actions are unthinkable. The advanced industrial countries seem to have a propensity for peace, and institutions such as the European Union, the North American Free Trade Agreement, and the Organization of American States create a culture in which peace is expected and provide forums for negotiation. Expectations of stability can provide a way to escape the Prisoner's Dilemma.

Some realists expect the security dilemma to reemerge in Europe despite the liberal institutions of the European Union. After the high hopes that greeted European integration in 1992, some opposition arose to further unity, particularly in disputes over the single European currency, the euro, which entered circulation in 2002. Countries such as Great Britain feared that ceding further power to the European Union would jeopardize the autonomy and prosperity of the individual states. Efforts in 2003 and 2004 to develop a new European constitution proved difficult, and in 2005, voters in France and the Netherlands refused to ratify it. At the same time, Britain and others worried that if they opted out of the European Union entirely, countries such as Germany, France, and Italy that opted in would gain a competitive edge. Despite such obstacles to further integration, the former communist countries of central Europe were attracted to joining. Although the European Union is far from being a true superstate, its institutions helped transform relations between European states.

Liberals also argue that realists pay insufficient attention to democratic values. Germany today is a different country from the Germany of 1870, 1914, or 1939. It has experienced more than a half century of democracy, with parties and governments changing peacefully. Public opinion polls show that the German people do not seek an expansive international role. Thus liberals are skeptical of realist predictions that fail to account for the effects of democracy.

Is there a relationship between domestic democracy and a state's propensity to go to war? Current evidence suggests that the answer is yes, but with qualifications and for reasons that are not yet entirely clear. The Prussian philosopher Immanuel Kant (1724–1804) was among the first to suggest that democracies are less warlike than authoritarian states. Absolute rulers can easily commit their states to war, as did Frederick the Great when he wanted Silesia in 1740 or Saddam Hussein when he invaded Kuwait in 1990. But Kant and other classical liberals pointed out that in a democracy, the people can vote against war. Moreover, it is the people, rather than the rulers, who bear the heaviest costs of war. It stood to reason, Kant believed, that the people would be less inclined to war than would their leaders. But just because a country is democratic does not mean that its people will always vote against war. As we noted above, democracies are likely to be involved in wars as often as other countries, and democratic electorates often vote for war. In ancient Greece, Pericles roused the people of Athens to go to war; in 1898, the American electorate dragged a reluctant President William McKinley into the Spanish-American War. In 2003, opinion polls and a congressional vote supported Bush's calls for war against Iraq, although public opinion later soured as the conflict dragged on.

Michael Doyle offers a more limited proposition that can be derived from Kant and classical liberalism, namely, that liberal democracies do not fight *other liberal democracies*.[20] That two democratic states do not fight each other is a correlation, and some correlations are spurious. Data show that from 2000 to 2009 the divorce rate in Maine correlated almost perfectly (0.99) with the per capita consumption of margarine in the United States, but no one suspects a causal relationship between the two.[21] One possible source of spurious causation is that democratic countries tend to be rich countries, rich countries tend to be involved with trade, and according to trade liberalism, rich countries are not likely to fight one another. But that dismissal does not fit with rich countries having often fought one another; witness the two world wars. Liberals suggest that the cause behind the correlation is a question of legitimacy. Maybe people in democracies think that it is wrong to fight other democracies because there is something wrong with solving disputes through killing when the other people have the right of consent. In addition, constitutional checks and balances on making war may work better when there is widespread public debate about the legitimacy of a battle. It is harder to rouse democratic peoples when there is no authoritarian demon like Hitler or Saddam Hussein.

Although "democratic peace" theory requires further exploration and elaboration, it is striking how difficult it is to find cases of liberal democracies waging war against other liberal democracies. Whatever the reason—whether liberal democracies share and respect a common set of principles of peaceful dispute resolution, whether they identify with one another, or whether because of something else (perhaps different explanations work best in different cases)—democratic peace theory suggests that if the number of democracies in the world grows, interstate war should decline. The recent past has been somewhat encouraging. According to Freedom House, the number of "free countries"—truly liberal democracies—has risen since the end of the Cold War from 65 to 88 (i.e., from 40 percent to 45 percent).[22] But caution is in order. The democratic peace theory may be less true in the early stages of transition to democracy and may not fit states whose democratic transition is unfinished. Some of the new democracies may be plebiscitary democracies without a liberal domestic process of free press, checks on executive power, and regular elections. The warring governments of Croatia, Serbia, and Bosnia were elected, although they were far from liberal democracies. The same was true of Ecuador and Peru, which fought a border skirmish in 1995. The character of a democracy matters a great deal.

Keeping these qualifications in mind, we should be cautious about making foreign policy recommendations on the basis of the democratic peace theory alone. Elections do not guarantee peace. International democracy promotion, as advocated by presidents Clinton and Bush, may help promote peace and security in the long term, but democratic transitions may increase the proclivity for war in the early stages of transition.

Marxism

A third major paradigm of International Relations is Marxism. As we have seen, it was specific enough in its predictions about the world that we are in a fairly good position to assess it. Marxists clearly but inaccurately predicted the death of capitalism as a result of imperialism, major war, socialist revolution, and the rise of communism. Instead, we have seen changes in the nature of capitalism, an end to imperialism, the decline of major interstate war, a slowing of the rate of socialist revolution (and even the transformation of some revolutionary socialist states into liberal capitalist ones), and the collapse of communism.

Marxism appears to have suffered from three main weaknesses. First, it attempted to reduce politics to economics. People care about economics, of course, but they care about many other things as well. People's primarily loyalties rarely lie with their economic class. Second, it erred in conceiving of the state as a simple tool of a particular class. Although wealthy capitalists are often very influential in the politics of their country, their narrow, self-serving interests rarely drive foreign policy, and when they do, it is never for terribly long. (The best examples, perhaps, would be the ability of certain U.S. multinational corporations to persuade policy makers in Washington, D.C., to try to overthrow Latin American governments that had nationalized their properties, or seemed likely to do so, during the Cold War. Certainly corporate interests played a role in shaping various unsuccessful attempts to overthrow Cuban president Fidel Castro and successful attempts to overthrow socialist governments in Guatemala in 1954 and Chile in 1973.) Third, Marxism had an overly rigid understanding of the progress of history. Marx and his followers spoke at length about the inevitable collapse of capitalism and the inevitable triumph of communism, but they seem to have underestimated the role of both chance and human choice. Arguably, nothing in life is inevitable, except for death and taxes.

Still, as we saw in Chapter 1, Marxism has contributed something valuable, via dependency theory, to our understanding of patterns of development and underdevelopment and also to the problem of growing global inequality. Marx did not err when he saw the potential of capitalism to concentrate wealth, and he was certainly correct to draw our attention to the dangers of gross economic inequality, which is one of the most significant drivers of substate conflict in the world today. Smart people are rarely wrong about everything, just as no one is ever right about everything.

Constructivism

Constructivism, a relatively new paradigm for the study of world politics, draws heavily from the field of sociology. Constructivism makes use of a "thicker" understanding of "structure" than do earlier paradigms. For constructivists, structures include not just the number or configuration of units, but also the "intersubjective meanings"—the shared discourses, ideas, practices, norms, rules, and logics of appropriateness—that help make them who they are and enable them to interact in an intelligible way. Social structures thus understood shape both identities and interests. Someone who grows up in rural Afghanistan will be a dramatically different person, with rather different goals, from someone who grows up in Los Angeles.

At the same time, when people interact in a social context, they alter it, if only marginally. Accordingly, social structures change over time. The concept of agent-structure interaction is a bit like the "karma" score in the popular *Fallout* series of video games: whether your character does nice things or nasty things, thus gaining or losing karma, affects how nonplayer characters interact with you and can even affect the ending of the game.

Thus there are three crucial insights of constructivism. First, "agents" and structures interact in a cyclical and reciprocal way. Second, the identities and interests of agents are not given, but are instead the product of social interaction. Finally, over time, intersubjective meanings change as a result of social inter-action, resulting in changes in rules, norms, legitimate expectations, and even, eventually, in the very character of the international system itself.

Compared to realism, liberalism, and Marxism, constructivism is so new that there remain fundamental differences among constructivists as to its status as a paradigm. One view, championed by Alexander Wendt, is that constructivism is a purely formal approach to international politics, not a substantive one. As such, it is not directly comparable to realism, liberalism, or Marxism. Unlike these other paradigms, constructivism makes no strong assumptions about human na-ture and cannot therefore generate substantive claims or expectations about how actors behave. In this sense, it is a bit like *game theory*, which is a purely formal mathematical technique for representing interactions. Another view, however, is that constructivism merely qualifies the ways in which human nature expresses itself by noting the importance of social and cultural context. On this view, con-structivism is a bit like the "nurture" view in the nature versus nurture debate. Realism, liberalism, and Marxism all tend to cluster closer to the "nature" end of the spectrum (with neorealism arguably furthest along), but because all four per-spectives lie on a single spectrum, they are all essentially comparable.

The differences between these two views of constructivism are important to people whose primary interest is ironing out the wrinkles in International Rela-tions theory, but for someone interested primarily in explaining why things hap-pen in the world—and, if possible, anticipating how things will unfold in the future—they have a common practical implication: namely, that there is no way of avoiding hard work! We cannot simply assume that people will behave in such-and-such a way. We need to know who they are, what they want, and how they see the world to understand what they do, and to know these things, we have to understand the social and cultural contexts in which they are embedded. We have to "reconstruct" the world to explain it, and doing so requires a great deal of in-formation and a correspondingly great deal of time and energy. But constructivist scholars willing to invest the effort have succeeded in explaining things that are difficult to explain from realist, liberal, or Marxist perspectives; examples are the rise of antimilitarism in Japan; the spread of powerful international norms against slavery, territorial revision, and weapons of mass destruction; the rapid evolution of the global human rights regime; the spread of feminism and environmentalism; and the development of pluralistic security communities.[23]

Because realism packs a lot of punch into assumptions, it has a much easier time than constructivism in generating predictions. Realist predictions are not always right—the end of the Cold War did not, in fact, weaken Western solidarity, contrary to the prognostications of many prominent realists—but at least realism gives us ready tools for making predictions. One of the crucial axioms of constructivism is that international politics is "path-dependent": What will happen tomorrow is less a function of immutable mechanisms such as the balance of power than of the historical background against which leaders must choose today. Prediction, in this view, requires being able to tease out plausible future paths and identify those that are most likely. Not only is this task inherently difficult, it means that our confidence in our predictions must rapidly decline the further we project into the future.

Constructivist explanations are not always incompatible with realist, liberal, or Marxist ones. The liberal story about postwar antimilitarism in Japan, for instance—the story that appeals to economic opportunity—is fully compatible with a constructivist story that stresses the reaction of the Japanese people to the shame, betrayal, and suffering they experienced at the hands of earlier militaristic leaders. We do not have to choose between them; both stories can be true in their own way. Moreover, in some circumstances it may be possible to "nest" other paradigms' explanations within a constructivist one. There is reason to believe, for example, that realism works best when explaining periods of history in which key practitioners of diplomacy were themselves believers in realism. U.S. foreign policy was never more "realist" than when Henry Kissinger was secretary of state. Liberalism performs best when explaining periods of history in which key players were devout liberals, such as when Wilson was president. From a constructivist perspective, this strong interaction of agents and structures is hardly surprising.

Follow Up

- Annette Freyberg-Inan, Ewan Harrison, and Patrick James, eds., *Rethinking Realism in International Relations: Between Tradition and Innovation* (Baltimore, MD: Johns Hopkins University Press, 2009).

- Andrew Moravcsik, "Taking Preferences Seriously: A Liberal Theory of International Politics," *International Organization*, Vol. 51, No. 4 (Autumn 1997), pp. 513–553.

- Immanuel Wallerstein, *World-Systems Analysis: An Introduction* (Durham, NC: Duke University Press, 2004).

- Stefano Guzzini and Anna Leander, eds., *Constructivism and International Relations: Alexander Wendt and His Critics* (London: Routledge, 2006).

Counterfactuals and "Virtual History"

2.4 Explain the role of counterfactual reasoning in historical inference.

In 1990, President Václav Havel of Czechoslovakia spoke before the U.S. Congress. Six months earlier he had been a political prisoner. "As a playwright," Havel said, "I'm used to the fantastic. I dream up all sorts of implausible things and put them in my plays. So this jolting experience of going from prison to standing before you today, I can adjust to this. But pity the poor political scientists who are trying to deal with what's probable."[24] Few people, including Soviets and Eastern Europeans, predicted the collapse of the Soviet Empire in Eastern Europe in 1989. Humans sometimes make surprising choices, and human history is full of uncertainties. How can we sort out the importance of different causes at different levels of analysis?

International politics is not like a laboratory science. We cannot do controlled experiments in international politics, because it is impossible to hold other things constant while looking at one thing that changes. Aristotle said that one should be as precise in any science as the subject matter allows: Do not try to be too precise if the precision will be spurious. International politics involves so many variables, so many changes occurring at the same time, that events are often overdetermined. As analysts, though, we still want to sort out causes to get some idea of which ones are more important than others. As you will see when we look at World War I in Chapter 3, mental experiments called counterfactuals can be useful tools in helping us make those determinations.

Counterfactuals are *contrary-to-fact conditionals*, but it is simpler to think of them as thought experiments to explore causal claims. Because there is no actual, physical laboratory for international politics, we imagine situations in which one thing changes while other things are held constant, and then we construct a picture of how the world would look. In fact, we use counterfactuals every day. Many students might say, "If I had not eaten so much dinner, I could concentrate better on this reading." That is a clear counterfactual that seeks to explain inattention.

Although often without admitting it, historians use a more elaborate version of the same procedure to weigh causes. For example, imagine that Kaiser Wilhelm of Germany had not fired Bismarck as chancellor in 1890. Would that have made World War I less likely? Would Bismarck's policies have continued to lower the sense of threat that other countries felt from Germany and thus curbed the growing rigidity of the two alliance systems? In this instance, the use of a counterfactual examines how important a particular personality was in comparison to structural factors. Here is another counterfactual related to World War I: Suppose Austrian Archduke Franz Ferdinand's driver in Sarajevo on June 28, 2014, had not mistakenly turned down the wrong street, unexpectedly presenting the archduke's Serbian assassin Gavrilo Princip with a target of opportunity. Would World War I still have erupted? This counterfactual illuminates the role of the assassination (as well as the role of accident). How important was the assassination? Given the overall tensions inherent in the alliance structure, might some other spark have ignited the flame had this one not occurred? Did the assassination affect anything other than the timing of the outbreak of war?

Contrary-to-fact conditional statements provide a way to explore whether a cause is significant, but there are also pitfalls in such "iffy history." Poorly handled counterfactuals may mislead by destroying the meaning of history. In fact, once something has happened, other things are not equal, because events are path-dependent: Once something happens, the probabilities of possible futures change. Some events become more likely, others less.

Four criteria can be used to test whether our counterfactual thought experiments are good or useful. They are plausibility, proximity, theory, and facts.

Plausibility

A useful counterfactual has to be within the reasonable array of options. This criterion is sometimes called *cotenability*. It must be plausible to imagine two conditions existing at the same time. Suppose someone said that if Napoleon had had stealth bombers, he would have won the Battle of Waterloo (1815). She may say that such a counterfactual is designed to test the importance of military technology, but it makes little sense to imagine twentieth-century technology in a nineteenth-century setting. The two are not cotenable. In real life, there never was a possibility of such a conjunction.

Proximity in Time

Each major event exists in a long chain of causation, and most events have multiple causes. The further back in time we go, the more causes we must hold constant. The closer in time the questioned event is to the subject event (did A cause B?), the more likely the answer is yes. Consider Blaise Pascal's (1623–1662) famous counterfactual statement that if Cleopatra's nose had been shorter, she would have been less attractive to Marc Antony, and the history of the Roman Empire would have been different. If the history of the Roman Empire had been different, the history of Western European civilization would have been different. Thus the length of Cleopatra's nose was one of the causes of World War I. In some trivial sense, that may be true, but millions of events and causes channeled down to August 1914. The contribution of Cleopatra's nose to the outbreak of World War I is so small and so remote that the counterfactual is more amusing than interesting when we try to ascertain why the war broke out. Proximity in time means that the closeness of two events in the chain of causation allows us to better control other causes and thereby obtain a truer weighing of factors.

Relation to Theory

Good counterfactual reasoning should rely on an existing body of theory that represents a distillation of what we think we know about how things work. We should ask whether a counterfactual is plausible considering what we know about all the cases that have given rise to these theories. Theories provide coherence and organization to our thoughts about the myriad causes and help us avoid random guessing. For example, there is no theory behind the counterfactual that if Napoleon had had stealth aircraft he would have won the Battle of Waterloo. The very randomness of the example helps explain why it is amusing, but also limits what we can learn from the mental exercise.

But suppose we were considering the causes of the Cold War and asked, What if the United States had been a socialist country in 1945? Would there have been a Cold War? Or suppose the Soviet Union had come out of World War II with a capitalist government. Would there have been a Cold War? These counterfactual questions explore the theory that the Cold War was caused primarily by ideology. An alternative hypothesis is that the bipolar international structure caused the Cold War, that some sort of tension was likely even if the United States had been socialist as balance-of-power theory would predict. Counterfactual inferences can be bolstered by looking at *factual* patterns invoking factual comparisons. After the Cold War, we did not witness a wholesale reconfiguration of alliances designed to balance the now unchallenged supremacy of the United States, suggesting that ideological affinity trumps balance of power considerations at least among liberal states. But during the Cold War, at least in certain parts of the world, we did see communist states balancing against one another, and because of the Cold War both Russia and China have been wary of the United States. So we are on fairly firm ground concluding that both ideology and balance of power were relevant but that they were not equally relevant to all players. In general, counterfactuals related to theory are more interesting and more useful because the mental exercise ties into a broader body of knowledge, and by focusing our attention on theoretically informed counterfactuals, we can often come up with something new and interesting to say about the theories themselves.

Facts

It is not enough to imagine fruitful hypotheses. They must be carefully examined in relation to the known facts. Counterfactuals require accurate facts and careful history. In examining the plausibility of a mental experiment, we must ask whether what is held constant is faithful to what actually happened. We must be wary of piling one counterfactual on top of another in the same thought experiment. Such multiple counterfactuals are confusing because too many things are being changed at once, and we are unable to judge the accuracy of the exercise by a careful examination of its real historical parts.

A particularly good way of disciplining a counterfactual is *virtual history*, a term coined by historian Niall Ferguson. Done properly, it limits the dangers of implausibility and remoteness in time by answering questions about what *might* have happened strictly in terms of what *did* happen. In the 2008 film *Virtual JFK*, Koji Masutani explores the question of whether Kennedy would have committed U.S. troops heavily to the Vietnam War, as his successor did, had he lived to win reelection in 1964. He answers the question by looking carefully at what Kennedy did whenever he faced a decision about committing U.S. troops to battle overseas. Six times in his presidency, Kennedy confronted just such a decision; all six times he avoided it. Not only did Kennedy demonstrate a powerful aversion to militarizing disputes, he also displayed deep skepticism about the advice he was receiving from his military and intelligence officials who were urging him to do so. By extrapolating from Kennedy's actual behavior and known disposition, it is possible to discipline the counterfactual in a way that increases our confidence in the judgment that Kennedy would not have committed large numbers of U.S. troops to Vietnam.[25]

Some historians claim to dismiss counterfactuals. They insist that history is about what actually happened, not what might have happened. This objection, however, misses the point that we should try to understand not just *what* happened, but *why* it happened. Any time you say "A caused B," you are logically implying that "if there had not been A, there would not have been B." By exploring that counterfactual, you can often gauge the plausibility of the causal claim. In fact, we know of no historian who shies away from making causal claims, and even those who voice skepticism of counterfactuals routinely use them. The skeptics do us a service when they warn us against what Richard Ned Lebow calls "magical" counterfactuals such as Napoleon's stealth bombers. But, as we see in Chapter 3, there is a distinction between saying that some counterfactual analysis is trivial and saying that you can make causal inferences against the background of a fixed historical record without disciplined counterfactual analysis.

Follow Up

- Philip E. Tetlock and Aaron Belkin, eds., *Counterfactual Thought Experiments in World Politics: Logical, Methodological, and Psychological Perspectives* (Princeton, NJ: Princeton University Press, 1996).

- Niall Ferguson, *Virtual History: Alternatives and Counterfactuals* (New York: Basic Books, 1999).

Study Questions

1. What are the relationships among the concepts "state," "nation," and "nation-state"?

2. How might authority be a source of power? Would it be a source of hard power or soft power?

3. What is the relationship between system stability and crisis stability?

4. What are Waltz's three images? Can they be combined? If so, how?

5. Why do liberals think democracy can prevent war? What are the limits to their view?

6. What is the difference between the structure and process of an international system? Is constructivism useful for understanding how processes change?

7. What is counterfactual history? Can you use it to explain the causes of the Peloponnesian War or the Iraq War?

Notes

1. A nation is an "imagined community," in the words of Benedict Anderson, so it is often difficult to define objectively; to some extent, a nation is a self-defined entity. Benedict Anderson, *Imagined Communities: Reflections on the Origin and Spread of Nationalism* (London: Verso, 1991).

2. A claim by one state to the territory of another state on grounds of self-determination of the inhabitants is called *irredentism*, from the Italian *irredenta*, meaning "unredeemed."

3. See http://www.hutt-river-province.com/.

4. Andrew F. Cooper, *Celebrity Diplomacy* (Boulder, CO: Paradigm Publishers, 2008).

5. We used to use the term "failed" state to refer to what we now call the most "fragile." See http://fsi.fundforpeace.org/rankings-2015.

6. David A. Welch, *Justice and the Genesis of War* (Cambridge: Cambridge University Press, 1993), pp. 76–94.

7. Hedley Bull, *The Anarchical Society: A Study of Order in World Politics* (London: Macmillan, 1977).

8. Paul R. Hensel, "Territory: Theory and Evidence on Geography and Conflict," in John A. Vazquez, ed., *What Do We Know About War?* (New York: Rowman & Littlefield, 2000), p. 62.

9. Geoffrey Blainey, *The Causes of War* (New York: Free Press, 1973), p. 150.

10. Alexander L. George and Juliette L. George, *Woodrow Wilson and Colonel House* (New York: John Day Co., 1956).

11. Perhaps the best is Fritz Redlick, *Hitler: Diagnosis of a Destructive Prophet* (New York: Oxford University Press, 1999).

12. V. I. Lenin, *Imperialism: The Highest Stage of Capitalism* (New York: International Publishers, 1977), p. 119.

13. Richard Cobden, quoted in Kenneth N. Waltz, *Man, the State, and War: A Theoretical Analysis* (New York: Columbia University Press, 1959), p. 104.

14. Barry M. Blechman, *The Politics of National Security: Congress and U.S. Defense Policy* (New York: Oxford University Press, 1990), pp. 36–37.

15. Robert K. Merton, *Social Theory and Social Structure*, rev. and enl. ed. (New York: Free Press, 1965), pp. 12–16.

16. James Mayall, *Nationalism and International Society* (Cambridge: Cambridge University Press, 1990), p. 15.

17. Richard Rosecrance, *The Rise of the Trading State: Commerce and Conquest in the Modern World* (New York: Basic, 1986), p. ix.

18. Robert O. Keohane, *After Hegemony: Cooperation and Discord in the World Political Economy* (Princeton, NJ: Princeton University Press, 1984).

19. Karl W. Deutsch, *Political Community and the North Atlantic Area: International*

Organization in the Light of Historical Experience (Princeton, NJ: Princeton University Press, 1957).

20. Michael Doyle, "Liberalism and World Politics," *American Political Science Review*, Vol. 80, No. 4 (December 1986), pp. 1151–1169.

21. See http://www.tylervigen.com/view_correlation?id=1703.

22. Freedom House, *Freedom in the World 2014*, https://freedomhouse.org/report/freedom-world/freedom-world-2014.

23. Peter J. Katzenstein, *Rethinking Japanese Security: Internal and External Dimensions* (New York: Routledge, 2008); Margaret E. Keck and Kathryn Sikkink, *Activists Beyond Borders: Advocacy Networks in International Politics* (Ithaca, NY: Cornell University Press, 1998); Martha Finnemore, *The Purpose of Intervention: Changing Beliefs About the Use of Force* (Ithaca, NY: Cornell University Press, 2003); Matthew J. Hoffmann, *Ozone Depletion and Climate Change: Constructing a Global Response* (Albany: State University of New York Press, 2005); Emanuel Adler and Michael Barnett, *Security Communities* (Cambridge: Cambridge University Press, 1998).

24. Václav Havel, "Address to U.S. Congress," *Congressional Record*, February 21, 1990, pp. S1313–1315.

25. See also James G. Blight, janet M. Lang, and David A. Welch, *Virtual JFK: Vietnam If Kennedy Had Lived* (Lanham, MD: Rowman & Littlefield, 2010).

Chapter 3

From Westphalia to World War I

World War I: The aftermath of battle

Learning Objectives

3.1 Distinguish four different senses of "balance of power": (1) as a description, (2) as a policy, (3) as a theory, and (4) as a particular geopolitical period.

3.2 Understand the structures and processes of different phases of the nineteenth-century balance of power.

3.3 Identify deep, intermediate, and proximate causes of World War I at various levels of analysis and assess whether the war was inevitable.

The primary political unit has varied in human history from time to time and from place to place. In isolated, rural, hunter-gatherer societies, small-scale groups such as tribes or even extended family units tended to dominate. With urbanization and the development of more specialized social and economic roles, larger-scale units such as city-states and small kingdoms came to the fore. As societies advanced technologically, organizationally, and militarily, they sometimes exercised dominion over vast areas. The largest contiguous political unit of all time was the Mongol Empire, which at its height in 1279 stretched from the Sea of Japan to the Baltic and from the South China Sea to the Persian Gulf. The British Empire in 1922 covered nearly one-fourth of Earth's surface and ruled over nearly a fourth of the human population. Typically, different political units would dominate in different places at the same time. Although Kublai Khan ruled the territorially well-defined Mongol Empire, Europe was a patchwork of feudal kingdoms, bishoprics, principalities, and lesser fiefdoms, and North America was home to mostly nomadic or seminomadic tribes. Only in the twentieth century did a single form of political organization come to dominate the entire globe: namely, the sovereign state. Today, the entire land mass of the planet—with the exception of Antarctica, which by treaty has been off-limits to territorial claims since 1961—is under the jurisdiction of a sovereign state or (as in the case of Taiwan) its functional equivalent. How did that come to be?

Although many political units all over the globe throughout history have been well defined territorially, ruled internally, and subservient to no outside authority, the modern sovereign state as we know it, with its specified rights, privileges, and obligations to international society, is a European creation. In fact, one might go so far as to say that it is Europe's most successful export. For hundreds of years after Europe had abandoned feudalism for the Westphalian system, powerful European countries ventured abroad and directly or indirectly ruled virtually the entire world. Countries committed to respecting the autonomy of other polities in their home neighborhood, in other words, very much ignored it elsewhere. In the wake of World War II, European empires gradually collapsed. Nationalist groups worldwide fought for or negotiated formal independence. Although eager to throw off colonial yokes, independence movements were just as eager to adopt the Westphalian model.

The Peace of Westphalia was actually a set of treaties, of which the two most important, the treaties of Osnabrück and Münster (1648), ended the *Thirty Years' War*.[1] Although there are no precise figures for casualties, the Thirty Years' War was certainly one of the deadliest in European history. Most of the destruction occurred in the territory of modern Germany, or what was then called the Holy Roman Empire (about which Voltaire once quipped that it was "neither holy, nor Roman, nor an empire"). There were as many issues and stakes as participants, but one important underlying conflict was religious. The Peace of Westphalia effectively entrenched the principle of *cuius regio, eius religio*, whereby each ruler would have the right to determine the religion of his or her own state. The treaties did not quite amount to a full endorsement of the principle of state sovereignty as we know it today, as they contained rights of intervention to enforce their terms, but, as Kalevi J. Holsti puts it, "By providing a legal basis for the developing territorial particularisms of Europe, and by terminating the vestiges of relations between superiors and inferiors, with authority emanating downward from the Emperor and the Pope, the documents licensed an anarchical dynastic states system and the internal consolidation of its members."[2]

Although political philosophers would later justify the principle of state sovereignty with reference to the rights of political communities to regulate their own affairs according to their own visions of the good life, there is a good case to be made that it was, in fact, appealing primarily because it would empower and enrich rulers. Charles Tilly compares the state with a protection racket in which rulers justify extracting "rents" (i.e., surplus funds) from hapless citizens by pleading the necessities of state security.[3] It was also part of the attraction of sovereign statehood for some rapacious Third World leaders during the period after decolonization, several of whom managed to enrich themselves considerably.

The Peace of Westphalia did not eliminate war from Europe, but it did moderate its severity and intensity. The European great powers continued to vie for primacy. The Netherlands enjoyed a brief period of commercial hegemony in the seventeenth century, thanks largely to the efforts of the Dutch East India Company. The Dutch were among the first Europeans (along with the Portuguese) to establish a long-lasting imperial presence overseas. France under Louis XIV (1638–1715) attained a degree of preeminence in Europe; succeeded in engineering a centralized, modern bureaucratic state; and colonized much of North America. Britain, which contended with both the Netherlands and France for maritime supremacy (despite its formidable economic and naval power and its astonishing success in acquiring overseas colonial territory, it never became a major land power in Europe), gradually established its claim for preeminence in the eighteenth and nineteenth centuries by defeating French forces on the Plains of Abraham in Québec (1759), by defeating the combined French and Spanish fleets in the Battle of Trafalgar (1805), and by helping defeat Napoleon at the Battle of Waterloo (1815). Despite its embarrassing and costly loss of colonies in the American Revolutionary War, Britain became the world's most powerful country in the nineteenth century because of its early industrialization, its control of the seas, its dominance of capital markets, and the embrace of the pound as the world's reserve currency.

Most of the wars fought in Europe between the Thirty Years' War and the Napoleonic Wars (1799–1815) were short, sharp, and geographically limited. They were fought over dynastic issues, territorial disputes, and sometimes merely to prevent certain states from becoming too powerful. In this period, European states did not have wars whose purpose was to rewrite the fundamental rules of the game. Put another way, it was a very stable international system. European leaders did not have revolutionary goals. In the eighteenth century, for example, the basic rules of the game were to protect the legitimacy of monarchical states—the divine right of rulers—and maintain a balance of power among them (the 1713 *Treaty of Utrecht* referred explicitly to the importance of the balance of power). Consider Frederick the Great of Prussia (1740–1786) and the way he treated his neighbor Maria Theresa (1717–1780) of Austria. In 1740, Frederick decided that he wanted Silesia, a province belonging to Maria Theresa. Frederick had no great revolutionary cause, only a simple goal of aggrandizement. He did not try to incite a popular revolution against Maria Theresa by appealing to the people in Silesia to overthrow the German-speaking autocrats of Vienna. After all, Frederick was a German-speaking autocrat in Berlin. He took Silesia because he wanted it and was careful not to do anything else that would damage Austria or the basic principle of monarchical legitimacy.

Compare that to the French Revolution (1789–1799) half a century later, when the prevailing view in France was that all monarchs should be sent to the gallows or the guillotine and that power should instead emanate from the people. Napoleon spread this revolutionary idea of popular sovereignty throughout Europe, and the Napoleonic Wars posed an enormous challenge to both the rules of the game and the balance of power. The moderate process and stable balance of the system in the middle of the century changed to a revolutionary process and unstable balance at the end of the century. We refer to changes like the French Revolution as *exogenous* to a structural theory because they cannot be explained inside the theory. This example illustrates how a realist structural theory can be supplemented by constructivist work. Constructivism is well suited to explaining phenomena such as the rise of a norm of popular (as opposed to monarchical) sovereignty.

In addition to changing their goals, states can also change their means. The process of a system is also affected by the nature of the instruments actors use. As we saw in Chapter 2, different means can have stabilizing or destabilizing effects. Some instruments change because of technology. For example, the development of new weapons such as the machine gun made World War I a particularly bloody encounter. Means can also change because of new social organization. In the eighteenth century, Frederick the Great not only had limited goals, he was also limited by his means. He had a mercenary army with limited loyalties and poor logistics. Eighteenth-century armies generally campaigned in the summer, when food was readily available or when the treasury had accumulated enough gold to pay soldiers, many of whom were often from the fringes of society. When the food or the gold ran out, the soldiers deserted. The French Revolution changed the social organization of war to what the French called the *levée en masse*, or what we call "conscription" or "the draft." As constructivists point out, soldiers' sense of identity changed. People came to understand themselves as citizens, rallied to the concept of a national homeland, and believed that all should participate. War was no longer a matter among a few thousand mercenaries who campaigned far away; war now involved nearly everyone. This large-scale involvement and mass support overwhelmed the old mercenary infantries. The change in the means available to states also helped change certain processes of the eighteenth-century international system.

Managing Great Power Conflict: The Balance of Power

3.1   Distinguish four different senses of "balance of power": (1) as a description, (2) as a policy, (3) as a theory, and (4) as a particular geopolitical period.

The European system of sovereign states was stable from Westphalia to the Napoleonic Wars in large part because of the fairly effective operation of the *balance of power*.

What exactly is the balance of power? It is one of the most frequently used concepts in international politics, but it is also one of the most confusing. The term is loosely used to describe and justify all sorts of things. The eighteenth-century British philosopher David Hume characterized the balance of power as a constant rule of prudent politics, but the nineteenth-century British liberal Richard Cobden called it "a chimera—an undescribed, indescribable, incomprehensible nothing."[4] Woodrow Wilson, the U.S. president during World War I, thought that the balance of power was an evil principle because it encouraged statesmen to treat countries like cheeses to be cut up for political convenience regardless of the concerns of their peoples.

Wilson also disliked the balance of power because he believed that it caused wars. Defenders of balance-of-power policies argue that they produce stability, but peace and stability are not the same thing. Over the five centuries of the European state system, the great powers were involved in 119 wars. Peace was rare; during three-fourths of the time, there was war involving at least one of the great powers. Ten of those wars were large general wars with many of the great powers involved. Thus if we ask whether the balance of power preserved peace very well over the five centuries of the modern state system, the answer is no.

That answer is not surprising, because states balance power not to preserve peace but to preserve their independence. The balance of power helps preserve the anarchic system of separate states. Not every state is preserved. For example, at the end of the eighteenth century, Poland was, indeed, cut up like a cheese, with Poland's neighbors—Austria, Prussia, and Russia—all helping themselves to a large slice. In 1939, Josef Stalin and Adolf Hitler made a deal in which they carved up Poland again and gave the Baltic states to the Soviet Union. Thus Lithuania, Latvia, and Estonia spent half a century, until 1991, as Soviet republics. The balance of power has not preserved peace and has not always preserved the independence of each state, but it has preserved the anarchic state system.

The difficulty of measuring changing power resources (which we discussed in Chapter 2) is a major problem for leaders trying to assess the balance of power. For analysts of international politics, additional confusion ensues when the same word is used for different things. We must try to separate and clarify the underlying concepts covered by the loose use of the same words. The term *balance of power* commonly refers to at least four different things.

Balances as Distributions of Power

The term *balance of power* can be used, first, simply to describe a distribution of power. If you hear the phrase "the current balance of power," you are probably hearing someone use the term in this purely descriptive sense. In the 1980s, it was common to hear some Americans argue that if Nicaragua became a communist state, the Cold War balance of power would change. That might have been true, but it would have done so only marginally, so in the grand scheme of things, it was not a very interesting or important insight. This purely descriptive use of the term can be powerful rhetorically, but it is often of limited use analytically.

A special (and rare) use of the phrase in this sense is to describe a situation in which power is distributed equally. This usage conjures up the image of a set of scales in equilibrium. Although some realists argue that the international system is most stable when there is an equal balance of power, others argue that the system is most stable when one side has a preponderance of power so the others dare not attack it. That is the view held by proponents of *hegemonic stability theory*. In this view, a strong dominant power is the best guarantee of stability. But according to hegemonic stability theory's first cousin, *hegemonic transition theory*, when the strongest power begins to slip, as it inevitably will, or as a new aspirant for hegemony arises, war is particularly likely. A declining hegemon or states fearing a rising power will take desperate measures to protect their position, whereas a rising power will gamble to attain hegemony. As we will see later in this chapter, hegemonic transition theory sheds light on the outbreak of World War I. It also helps us make sense of Thucydides' account of the origins of the Peloponnesian War. Recall that, according to Thucydides, Sparta's fear of the allegedly growing power of Athens led it to take the bold and risky gamble of supporting Corinth.

We must be cautious about such theories because they tend to overpredict conflict. In the 1880s, the United States passed Britain as the largest economy in the world. In 1895, the United States and Britain disagreed over borders in South America, and it looked as if war might result. There was a rising challenger, a declining hegemon, and a cause of conflict, but you do not read about the great British-American War of 1895 because it did not occur. As Sherlock Holmes pointed out, we can get important clues from dogs that do not bark. In this case, the absence of war leads us to look for other causes. Realists point to the rise of Germany as a more proximate threat to Britain. Liberals point to the increasingly democratic nature of the two English-speaking countries and to transnational cultural ties between the old leader and the new challenger. To some extent, we can attribute it to sensible British policy makers who, aware of Britain's declining power position both vis-à-vis the United States across the Atlantic and Germany in Europe, cleverly cultivated the United States over time (in part through a policy of appeasement).[5] The best we can conclude about the balance of power in the first sense of the term is that changes in the distribution of power among leading states may be one factor that helps explain war and instability, but such changes are clearly not the whole story.

Balance of Power as Policy

The second use of the term *balance of power* refers to a deliberate policy of balancing. Lord Palmerston's dictum that states have no permanent friends or permanent enemies, merely permanent interests, is a view that any strong proponent of balance-of-power politics would hold. Indeed, as British foreign secretary in the mid-1800s, Palmerston pursued balance-of-power politics consistently. When Hitler invaded the Soviet Union in 1941, Prime Minister Winston Churchill (1874–1965) embraced balance-of-power politics as well. Churchill was a strong anticommunist who disliked Soviet leader Stalin, but an alliance with Stalin was vital to prevent Nazi Germany from dominating Europe. "If Hitler invaded Hell," Churchill famously said, "I would make at least a favourable reference to the Devil in the House of Commons."[6]

Leaders who embrace a balance-of-power policy are almost certainly also likely to hold an essentially realist view of international politics. For this reason, the consistent pursuit of a balance-of-power policy is often referred to by the German word *realpolitik*.

A key instrument for attempting to maintain a balance of power is *alliance*. Alliances are agreements that sovereign states enter into with each other to ensure their mutual security. As was the case with Britain's alliance with the Soviet Union in World War II, they can be motivated by purely military concerns: Two medium-sized states might decide they will be more secure against threats from a larger state by forming an alliance. Traditionally, military alliances have been one of the focal points of international politics. But states might also ally for nonmilitary reasons. From time to time, two or more states may be drawn together into an alliance for economic reasons or because of ideological or cultural affinity. That is particularly true in those parts of the modern world where purely military concerns are receding, such as in Western Europe and North America today.

Alliances collapse for as many reasons as they form; in general, though, states cease to ally when they come to see each other as irrelevant or as threats to their security. That might occur because the regime in one state changes. Before, the two states might have shared a common ideology; now they are opposed. Thus China and the United States were allies when the Nationalists were in power in China before 1949 and enemies after the Communists came to power in 1949. Of course, there may be other reasons for an alliance to end. One state may grow more powerful than the other. It might view the other state as a rival, whereas the other state might view it as a threat and look for alliances elsewhere to balance that threat.

Balance of Power as Theory

A third use of the term *balance of power* is to describe a more or less automatic equilibration of power in the international system, called balance-of-power *theory*. This theory predicts that states will act to prevent any one state from developing a preponderance of power. Put another way, it predicts that leaders will, as a matter of course, embrace a balance-of-power policy simply because they cannot afford not to. Recall that realists see the Westphalian system as a Hobbesian anarchy in which fear is endemic and trust is in short supply. They see it as a "self-help" system in which the only way to be sure of surviving is to do what one can to prevent any other state or group of states from attaining a preponderance of power. That can be done through internal adjustment (e.g., spending more on the military), external collaboration (e.g., allying with other countries), or both.

In domestic politics, we often see *bandwagoning* instead of balancing: Politicians often flock to a likely winner. Balance-of-power theory, however, predicts that a state will join whoever seems *weaker*, because states will act to keep any one state from becoming preponderant. Bandwagoning in international politics risks one's independence. In 1939 and 1940, the Italian dictator Benito Mussolini joined Hitler's attack on France as a way to get some of the spoils, but Italy became more and more dependent on Germany. That is why a balance-of-power policy says, "Join the weaker side." Balance of power is a policy of helping the underdog because if you help the top dog, it may eventually turn around and eat you.

Balance-of-power theory does not predict that states will make common cause with states that share ideological or cultural characteristics. As we will see in Chapter 7, when Iran and Iraq went to war in the early 1980s, some observers thought that all Arab states would support Saddam Hussein's Iraq, a largely Arab state dominated politically by Sunni Muslims (a minority in Iraq, but dominant in most Arab countries) and ruled by a secular Ba'ath Party, against Ayatollah Khomeini's Iran, an overwhelmingly Persian theocracy dominated by Shi'ite Muslims. But Syria, despite also being a largely Sunni Arab state ruled by a secular Ba'athist party, supported Iran. Why? Because Syria was worried about the growing regional power of its neighbor Iraq. Syria chose to balance Iraqi power regardless of its ideological preferences. Efforts to use ideology to predict state behavior are often wrong, whereas counterintuitive predictions based on balancing power are often correct.

Of course, there are exceptions. Human behavior is not fully determined. Human beings have choices, and they do not always act as predicted. Certain situations predispose people toward a certain type of behavior, but we cannot always predict the details. If someone shouts "Fire!" in a crowded lecture hall, we could predict that students would run for exits, but not *which* exits. If all choose one exit, the stampede may prevent many from getting out. Theories in international politics often have large exceptions. Even though balance-of-power theory provides a clear way of making predictions in international politics, its record is far from perfect.

Why do countries sometimes eschew balance of power and join the stronger rather than the weaker side, or stand aloof, thus ignoring the risks to their independence? Some countries may see no alternatives or believe that they cannot affect the balance. If so, a small country may decide that it has to fall within the sphere of influence of a great power while hoping that neutrality will preserve some freedom of action. For example, after World War II, Finland was defeated by the Soviet Union and was far from the center of Europe. The Finns believed that neutrality was safer than trying to become part of the European balance of power. They were in the Soviet sphere of influence, and the best they could do was bargain away independence in foreign policy for a large degree of control over their domestic affairs.

Another reason that balance-of-power predictions are sometimes wrong has to do with perceptions of threat. For example, a mechanical accounting of the power resources of countries in 1917 would have predicted that the United States would join World War I on the side of Germany because Britain, France, and Russia had 30 percent of the industrial world's resources and Germany and Austria had only 19 percent. That did not happen, though, in part because the Americans perceived the Germans as militarily stronger and the aggressor in the war.

Perceptions of threat are often influenced by *proximity*. A neighbor may be weak on some absolute global scale, but threatening in its region or local area. Consider Britain and the United States in the 1890s: Britain could have fought, but instead chose to appease the United States. It conceded to the United States on many issues, including the building of the Panama Canal, which allowed the United States to improve its naval position. One reason is that Britain was more worried about its neighbor Germany than it was about the distant Americans. The United States was larger than Germany, but proximity affected which threat loomed larger in British eyes. Proximity also helps explain the alliances after 1945. The United States was stronger than the Soviet Union, so why didn't Europe and Japan ally with the Soviet Union against the United States? The answer lies partly in the proximity of the threat. From the point of view of Europe and Japan, the Soviets were an immediate threat, and the United States was far away. The Europeans and the Japanese called in the distant power to rebalance the situation in their immediate neighborhood. That proximity often affects how threats are perceived qualifies any predictions based on a simple mechanical toting up of power resources.

Another exception to balance-of-power predictions relates to the growing role of economic interdependence in world affairs. According to a balance-of-power policy, France should not wish to see Germany grow, but because of economic integration, German growth stimulates French growth. French politicians are more likely to be reelected when the French economy is growing. Therefore, a policy of trying to hold back German economic growth would be foolish because the French and German economies are so interdependent. In economic considerations, joint gains would often be lost by following too simple a balance-of-power policy.

Finally—contrary to the predictions of balance-of-power theory—ideology sometimes does cause countries to join the top dog rather than the underdog.

Even in Thucydides' day, democratic city-states were more likely to align with Athens and oligarchies with Sparta. Britain's appeasement of the United States in the 1890s or the Europeans joining with the Americans in an alliance of democracies after 1945 owed something to the influence of ideology as well as to the proximity of a threat. But it is easy—and can be dangerous—to overestimate the relevance of ideology. Many Europeans believed that Stalin and Hitler could not come together in 1939 because they were at opposite ends of the ideological spectrum, and yet they did. Likewise, in the 1960s, the United States mistakenly assumed that all communist countries represented a united, monolithic threat. A policy based on balance of power would have predicted that China, the Soviet Union, Vietnam, and Cambodia would balance one another, as they eventually did. Had American leaders foreseen that, no doubt they would have found a far less expensive way to pursue stability in East Asia than by committing more than half a million troops to the war in Vietnam.

Balances of Power as Historical Multipolar Systems

The fourth way in which the term *balance of power* is sometimes used is to describe historical cases of multipolarity. The historian Edward Vose Gulick, for example, used the wording "the classical balance of power" to refer to eighteenth-century Europe's multipolar system. We often use the phrase "the nineteenth-century balance of power" to refer to the European system between the Napoleonic Wars and World War I. In this sense, a balance of power requires a number of countries that follow a set of rules of the game that are generally understood. Because this use of the term *balance of power* refers to historical systems, we look at the two dimensions of systems, structure and process, that were introduced in Chapter 2.

Follow Up

- Edward Vose Gulick, *Europe's Classical Balance of Power* (New York: Norton, 1967).
- William C. Wohlforth, Stuart J. Kaufman, and Richard Little, eds., *The Balance of Power in World History* (New York: Palgrave Macmillan, 2007).

The Nineteenth-Century Balance-of-Power System

3.2 Understand the structures and processes of different phases of the nineteenth-century balance of power.

The nineteenth-century balance-of-power system produced the longest interval without a general large-scale war in the modern state system: from 1815 to 1914. But it was a dynamic system that was far from entirely peaceful. Changes in its structure and processes were instrumental in bringing about two cataclysmic world wars in 1914 and 1939. We must therefore be careful not to romanticize or oversimplify a complex story. The concepts and distinctions we have discussed to this point can help us navigate the complexity and better understand the nineteenth-century origins of the great twentieth-century conflicts.

Structure

If we look at the structure of the nineteenth-century balance-of-power system as understood by neorealists—that is, as a simple distribution of power—we can identify three distinct periods (Table 3.1). The first began with the defeat of Napoleon at Waterloo. Napoleon had tried to establish French hegemony over Europe. His efforts united the other great powers in a coalition that eventually defeated France. Had he succeeded, the European system would have been unipolar. But after Napoleon's defeat in 1815, the Congress of Vienna restored the old multipolar order, with five major powers balancing one another: Britain, Russia, France, Prussia, and Austria. These five powers often shifted alliances to prevent any one of them from dominating the continent. From 1815 to 1870, the European system could be characterized as a "loose multipolarity."

When Germany and Italy unified, Europe now had six major powers. The big change came with the unification of Germany in 1871. Prior to that time, "Germany" had consisted of 37 states and had been an arena of international politics in which others intervened. After 1871, Germany became a united actor. Furthermore, it was located directly in the center of Europe, which had tremendous geopolitical consequences. From a structural perspective, a united Germany could be a problem if it were either too strong or too weak. If Germany were strong enough to defend itself against both Russia and France at the same time, it would also be strong enough to defeat either Russia or France alone; but if Germany were not strong enough to defeat Russia and France simultaneously, it might suffer the same fate as Poland did at the hands of its neighboring great powers: invasion, dismemberment, or domination.

During this second structural phase, German power steadily rose. For a while, Otto von Bismarck's brilliant diplomacy prevented a newly unified, rapidly growing German state in the center of Europe from destabilizing the system. But a combination of the growing wariness of Germany in the other capitals of Europe and a series of missteps by Bismarck's successors ushered in the third structural phase. By 1907, the European balance of power had lost all flexibility. Two sets of alliances developed and rigidified: the Triple Entente (Great Britain,

Table 3.1 Structural Changes in the Pre–World War I Balance of Power

1815–1871	Loose Multipolarity
1871–1907	Rise of Germany
1907–1914	Bipolarity of Alliances

France, and Russia) and the Triple Alliance (Germany, Austria-Hungary, and Italy). The polarization of the European balance of power into two tight blocs resulted in an inability to maintain balance, which, as we shall see below, contributed significantly to the outbreak of World War I.

Process

We cannot explain structural changes in the European system by looking solely at changes in the distribution of power. *Process*, which classical realists and constructivists emphasize, was crucially important. If we look at the ways in which the system worked and we take into account the changes in European culture and ideas that influenced patterns of relations among states, we can distinguish five different phases (Table 3.2).

Following Napoleon, European great powers sought to maintain order in part by holding periodic congresses in which they deliberated jointly and attempted to strike agreements that would both preserve the balance of power and stem the revolutionary tide of liberal nationalism. This system came to be known as the *Concert of Europe*. The Concert came into effect at the *Congress of Vienna*, at which the victors of Waterloo brought France back into the fold and agreed on certain rules of the game to equalize the players. From 1815 to 1822, the Concert was active and effective. European states met frequently to deal with disputes and to maintain an equilibrium. They accepted certain interventions to keep governments in power domestically when their replacements might lead to a destabilizing reorientation of policy. From 1822 to 1854, the Concert was less active and somewhat less effective. Ultimately, liberal nationalist revolutions challenged the practices of providing territorial compensation or restoring governments to maintain equilibrium, and the Concert ceased to function. As constructivists point out, the ideas of nationalism became too strong to allow such an easy cutting up of cheeses.

The third period in the nineteenth-century balance-of-power system, from 1854 to 1871, was far less moderate and was marked by five wars. One, the Crimean War, was to some extent a classic balance-of-power war in which France and Britain sought to prevent Russia from gaining at the expense of a declining Ottoman Empire. The other conflicts, however, were related to the unification of Italy and Germany. Political leaders abandoned old rules and began to use nationalism instrumentally. Bismarck, for example, was not an ideological

Table 3.2 Processes of the Pre–World War I Balance of Power

1815–1822	Concert of Europe
1822–1854	Loose Concert
1854–1871	Nationalism and the Unification of Germany and Italy
1871–1890	Bismarck's Revived Concert
1890–1914	The Loss of Flexibility

German nationalist. He was, in fact, a deeply conservative man who wanted Germany united under the Prussian monarchy. But he was quite prepared to use nationalist appeals and to engineer nationalist wars against Denmark and France to bring this about. He returned to a more conservative style once he had accomplished his goals.

The fourth period, 1871 to 1890, was the Bismarckian balance of power in which the new Prussian-led Germany played the key role. Bismarck played flexibly with a variety of alliance partners and tried to divert France into imperialistic adventures overseas so as to distract its attention from the provinces of Alsace and Lorraine that it lost to Germany at the conclusion of the Franco-Prussian War. To keep the balancing act in Europe centered on Berlin, he limited German imperialism. The hallmarks of Bismarck's alliance system were its flexibility and its complexity. The former made the resulting balance-of-power system stable because it allowed for occasional crises or conflicts without causing the whole edifice to crumble. But its complexity was its weakness. Its smooth operation required an expert juggler such as Bismarck who was able to keep several balls in the air at once. Bismarck's successors were not as gifted. They failed to renew his treaty with Russia, and they mistakenly allowed Britain, France, and Russia to gradually come together. They also failed to put the brakes on Austrian confrontations with Russia over the Balkans. Finally, Germany became involved in overseas imperialism and attempted to challenge Britain's naval supremacy. These policies exacerbated fears of rising German power and further polarized the system.

Although each of these five phases has distinct characteristics, the characteristics themselves and the changes from one phase to another were driven by a number of powerful trends that proceeded more or less unabated throughout the entire period, affecting states' goals, the instruments at their disposal for pursuing them, and their incentives for cooperation. The most important of these trends were the growth of liberalism and the growth of nationalism. Because of them, the state and the ruler gradually ceased being the same. More than a century before Waterloo, Louis XIV had famously said, *"L'état, c'est moi"* ("I am the state"), and no one had contradicted him. By the early nineteenth century, such a claim would have triggered an uproar. Napoleon may have failed to change the *structure* of European politics by failing to establish French hegemony, but he succeeded in changing the *process* by spreading revolutionary ideas across Europe. The Congress of Vienna held these ideas at bay for a while, but the volcanic forces of nationalism and liberalism erupted in the revolutions of 1848, signaling the beginning of the end of monarchical rule.

As the century progressed, both peoples and leaders began to see themselves differently. The nationalist challenge to the legitimacy of dynastic rulers led to some strange alliances that defied the classical balance of power. For example, in 1866, France failed to support Austria when it was attacked by Prussia, a major error from a structural realist point of view. France was opposed to Austrian repression of nationalism in the part of Italy that Austria occupied.

Structure and Process

> Statesmen regularly judged the European balance to be satisfactory or unsatisfactory on the basis of factors that had little or nothing directly to do with power and its distribution—e.g., the rank and status a state enjoyed, its honor and prestige, whether it was considered worthy of alliance, whether it was allowed a voice in international questions, etc. It helps explain how crises could and did arise when the balance of power was not affected or threatened, but the balance of satisfactions was. It shows how devices other than power-political ones—international laws, Concert practices, alliances used as devices for restraining one's ally—were more common and more useful in promoting and preserving the European equilibrium than power-political ones such as rival alliances or blocking coalitions.
>
> *—Paul Schroeder, "The Nineteenth Century System"*[7]

Bismarck played on the nationalistic views of other German states in unifying Germany under Prussian leadership, but nationalism became a restraint on what could be done later. When Bismarck took Alsace-Lorraine from France in 1871, he created nationalist resentment in France that prevented France and Germany from becoming potential alliance partners in the future. As constructivist approaches point out, the new ideologies changed states' goals and made the process of international politics less moderate over the course of the nineteenth century.

There were also changes in the means. The application of new industrial technology to military purposes produced massively powerful yet inflexible instruments of war. The development of railways made possible moving large numbers of troops from one place to another very quickly; doing so, however, required precise scheduling, which reduced crisis stability by reducing mobilization options and giving first-movers a crucial advantage in the first few days of war. The development of machine guns, heavy artillery, and trench warfare made a mockery of the idea of short, sharp, limited wars that Bismarck had used so successfully in the 1860s. Changes in technology, just like changes in ideas, altered leaders' perceptions of what was possible and what was desirable. Thus we need to look at both structure and process if we want to understand the changes in the nineteenth-century balance-of-power system that led to World War I.

Follow Up

- Henry A. Kissinger, *A World Restored: Metternich, Castlereagh and the Problems of Peace, 1812–1822* (New York: Grosset & Dunlap, 1964).

- John Lowe, *The Great Powers, Imperialism and the German Problem, 1865–1925* (London and New York: Routledge, 1994), pp. 202–239.

A Modern Sequel

The so-called German problem from the nineteenth century reemerged in debates when East Germany and West Germany were reunified in 1990. At first, Foreign Minister Eduard Shevardnadze of the Soviet Union argued that the reunification of Germany would profoundly destabilize the balance of power in Europe. Leaders once again asked, "How many German-speaking states are consistent with stability in Europe?" Over time, that question has had different answers. The Congress of Vienna in 1815 included thirty-seven German-speaking states. Bismarck believed that there should be two, not one. He did not want the Austrians included in his new German empire because he feared that they would dilute Prussian control of the new state. Hitler had a different answer: one, which would be the center of a world empire, thus leading to World War II. In 1945, the victorious Allies eventually decided on three: East Germany, West Germany, and Austria. When asked how many Germanys there should be, François Mauriac, a French author and winner of the 1952 Nobel Prize for Literature, quipped shortly after World War II, "I love Germany so much I'm glad there are two of them."

The decline of Soviet power in Eastern Europe in the late 1980s ended the bipolar structure of postwar politics and made possible Germany's reunification. But reunification created new anxieties about the union of 80 million people with Europe's largest economy located in the heart of the continent. Would Germans search for a new role? Would they again cast about, turn eastward, and then westward? Would they be drawn into the countries to their east where German influence had always been strong? Political scientist John Mearsheimer said the answer was "back to the future."[8] He relied on structural realist analysis to reach pessimistic conclusions that the future will be like the past because the structure of the situation is similar to the past.

But things have changed in three ways. At the structural level, the United States is involved in Europe, and the United States is roughly four times the size of the reunified Germany. Structuralists worry that the United States will not stay involved. With the Cold War over, at some point the Americans may turn isolationist and go home. But there are important nonstructural changes as well. The process of international politics in Europe has been transformed by the development of new institutions that liberals emphasize. The European Union unites Germany and other European states in a way in which they were never tied together before. A third change is not at the system level, but at the domestic level. Constructivists point out that Germany's domestic politics represent a half century of democracy, and changes in popular values have transformed a warfare state into a welfare state. The Germany that caused trouble in the heart of Europe in 1870, 1914, and 1939 was not democratic. Which of these approaches, structural or process or domestic, will best predict the future of Europe? We should pay attention to all three, but thus far predictions based on process and domestic change seem to have fared best.

Chronologies: Europe

The Seventeenth Century

1618–1648	Thirty Years' War: conflict between Catholic and Protestant Europe; last of the great religious wars; Germany devastated
1643–1715	Louis XIV king of France
1648	Peace of Westphalia; end of Thirty Years' War
1649–1660	English king Charles I beheaded; Commonwealth under Oliver Cromwell
1652–1678	Series of Anglo-French and Anglo-Dutch wars for supremacy of the seas
1660	Stuart restoration in England; accession of Charles II
1682–1725	Peter the Great begins "westernization" of Russia
1683	Turkish siege of Vienna repulsed
1685	Louis XIV revokes Edict of Nantes; persecution of French Protestants
1688–1689	Glorious Revolution in England
1688–1697	War of the League of Augsburg; general war against Louis XIV

The Eighteenth Century

1700–1721	Great Northern War: Russia, Poland, and Denmark oppose Swedish supremacy in the Baltic; Russia emerges as a European power
1701–1714	War of the Spanish Succession and the Treaty of Utrecht, which result in the permanent separation of French and Spanish thrones; further decline of French power
1707	Great Britain formed by union of England and Scotland
1740–1748	War of the Austrian Succession
1756–1763	Seven Years' War: Britain and France in colonial wars; France ejected from Canada and India; Britain emerges as world's major colonial power
1775–1783	War of the American Revolution
1789–1799	French Revolution
1799	Coup d'état by Napoleon Bonaparte in France
1799–1815	Napoleonic Wars make France preeminent power on European continent

The Nineteenth Century

1801	United Kingdom formed by union of Great Britain and Ireland
1804–1814	Napoleon I emperor of France
1806	End of Holy Roman Empire; imperial title renounced by Francis II
1810	Kingdom of Holland incorporated in French Empire
1812	French invasion of Russia; destruction of Napoleon's army
1814–1815	Congress of Vienna: monarchies reestablished in Europe
1815	Napoleon escapes from Elba but is defeated by British and Prussian armies in the Battle of Waterloo
1833–1871	Unification of Germany
1837–1901	Victoria queen of England: period of great industrial expansion and prosperity
1848	Revolutions in France, Germany, Hungary, and Bohemia; publication of Karl Marx's *Communist Manifesto*
1848–1916	Franz Joseph emperor of Austria; becomes ruler of the Austro-Hungarian Empire in 1867
1852–1870	Napoleon III emperor of Second French Empire
1853–1856	Crimean War: Britain and France support Ottomans in war with Russia
1855–1881	Alexander II tsar of Russia
1859–1870	Italian political unification, led by Giuseppe Garibaldi
1861	Emancipation of Russian serfs by Tsar Alexander II
1862–1890	Otto von Bismarck, premier and chancellor of Germany, forges German Empire
1864–1905	Russian expansion in Poland, Balkans, and central Asia
1867	Austro-Hungarian Empire founded
1870–1871	Franco-Prussian War: German invasion of France; Third French Republic created
1870–1914	European imperialism at peak; industrial growth; rise of labor movements and Marxism
1871	Paris Commune: Paris, a revolutionary center, establishes own government and wars with national government
1878	Congress of Berlin: division of much of Ottoman Empire among Austria, Russia, and Britain

(continued)

1881	Alexander II of Russia assassinated
1882	Triple Alliance of Germany, Austria-Hungary, and Italy; renewed in 1907
1899–1902	Boer War in South Africa

The First Decade of the Twentieth Century

1904	Dual Entente between Britain and France
1904–1905	Russo-Japanese War; Russia defeated; Japan emerges as world power
1907	Russia joins Britain and France in Triple Entente

The Origins of World War I

3.3 **Identify deep, intermediate, and proximate causes of World War I at various levels of analysis and assess whether the war was inevitable.**

World War I killed nearly 20 million people. In one battle, the Somme, 1.3 million were killed and wounded. Compare that with 36,000 casualties when Bismarck defeated Austria in 1866. The United States lost about 55,000 troops in both Korea and Vietnam. World War I was a horrifying war of trenches, barbed wire, machine guns, and artillery that ground up a generation of Europe's youth. It not only destroyed people, it destroyed three European empires: German, Austro-Hungarian, and Russian. Until World War I, the global balance of power was centered in Europe. After World War I, Europe still mattered, but the United States and Japan emerged as major players. World War I also ushered in the Russian Revolution in 1917 and the beginning of the ideological battles that racked the twentieth century.

How could such an event happen? Prince Bernhard von Bülow, the German chancellor from 1900 to 1909, met with his successor, Theobald von Bethmann Hollweg, in the chancellor's palace in Berlin shortly after the war broke out. Here is how von Bülow described what he remembered:

> Bethmann stood in the center of the room; shall I ever forget his face, the look in his eyes? There is a picture by some celebrated English painter, which shows the wretched scapegoat with a look of ineffable anguish in its eyes, such pain as I now saw in Bethmann's. For an instant we neither of us spoke. At last I said to him, "Well, tell me, at least, how it all happened." He raised his long, thin arms to heaven and answered in a dull, exhausted voice: "Oh, if I only knew!" In many later polemics on war guilt I have often wished it had been possible to produce a snapshot of Bethmann Hollweg standing there at the moment he said those words. Such a photograph would have been the best proof that this wretched man had never wanted war.[9]

Generations of historians have examined the origins of World War I and tried to explain why war came. As we will see, it is impossible to isolate one cause, but it is possible to break the question down into distinct levels. At each of these levels, the balance of power—as a *multipolar system* and as the *policy* of separate states and individual leaders—is essential to an understanding of the war's outbreak. As the alliance system became less flexible, the balance of power became less multipolar, and the likelihood of war increased.

Three Levels of Analysis

Parts of the answer lie at each of the three levels of analysis. Parsimony suggests we start with the simplest causes, see how much they explain, and go on to more complexity as needed. Thus we look first at the system-level explanations, both the structure and the process; then at the domestic societal level; and finally at the individuals. Then we will use counterfactual thought experiments to see how the pieces fit together to explain World War I.

At the structural level, there were two key elements: the rise of German power and the increased rigidity in the alliance systems. The rise of German power was truly impressive. German heavy industry surpassed that of Great Britain in the 1890s, and the growth rate of Germany's gross national product at the beginning of the twentieth century was twice that of Great Britain's. In the 1860s, Britain had 25 percent of the world's industrial production, but by 1913, its share had shrunk to 10 percent while Germany's share had risen to 15 percent. Germany transformed some of its industrial strength into military capability, including a massive naval armaments program. A strategic aim of Germany's "Tirpitz Plan" of 1911 was to build the second largest navy in the world, thereby advancing itself as a world power. This expansion alarmed Churchill, then Britain's first lord of the admiralty. Britain began to fear becoming isolated and worried about how it would defend its far-flung empire. These fears were increased during the Boer War due to German sympathy for the Boers, the Dutch settlers in South Africa, against whom Britain was fighting at the end of the century.

In 1907, Sir Eyre Crowe, permanent secretary of the British Foreign Office, wrote a document famous in the history of British foreign policy, a long memorandum in which he tried to interpret German foreign policy. He concluded that although German policy was vague and confused, Britain clearly could not allow one country to dominate the continent of Europe. Crowe argued that the British response was nearly a law of nature.

Britain's response to Germany's rising power contributed to the second structural cause of the war: the increasing rigidity in the alliance systems in Europe. In 1904, parting from its geographically semi-isolated position as a balancer off the coast of Europe, Britain moved toward an alliance with France. In 1907, the Anglo-French partnership broadened to include Russia (already allied with France) and became known as the Triple Entente. Germany, seeing itself encircled, tightened its relations with Austria-Hungary. As the alliances became

Photo: World History Archive/Alamy

Serbian nationalist Gavrilo Princip kills Austrian archduke
Franz Ferdinand and his wife, Sophie, Duchess of Hohenberg, in
Sarajevo, June 28, 1914

more rigid, diplomatic flexibility was lost. The balance of power could no longer
operate through the shifting alignments that characterized the balance of power
during Bismarck's day. Instead, the major powers wrapped themselves around
two poles. The tightening of alliances accentuated the security dilemma that defensive realists emphasize in their analyses. As the historian Christopher Clark
observed, "The bifurcation into two alliances blocs did not cause the war ... yet
without the two blocs, the war could not have broken out in the way it did."[10]

What about changes in the process? One was the continued rise of nationalism. In Eastern Europe, there was a movement calling for all Slavic-speaking peoples to come together. Pan-Slavism threatened both the Ottoman and
Austro-Hungarian empires, which each had large Slavic populations. A nationalistic hatred of Slavs arose in Germany. German authors wrote about the inevitability of the Teutonic-Slavic battles, and schoolbooks inflamed nationalist
passions. Nationalism proved to be stronger than socialism when it came to bonding working classes together and stronger than the capitalism that bound bankers together. Indeed, it proved stronger than family ties among the monarchs. Just
before the war broke out, the kaiser wrote to Russian tsar Nicholas II (1868–1918)
and appealed to him to avoid war. He addressed his cousin as "Dear Nicky"

and signed it "Yours, Willie." The kaiser hoped that because war was impending over the assassination of a fellow royal family member, the Austrian archduke Franz Ferdinand, the tsar would see things the same way he did. But by then nationalism had overcome any sense of aristocratic or monarchical solidarity, and that family telegram did nothing to prevent war.

A second cause for the loss of moderation in the early twentieth-century balance of power was a rise in complacency about peace. It is an example of the importance of changing ideas that constructivists emphasize. The great powers had not been involved in a war in Europe for 40 years. There had been crises—in Morocco in 1905–1906, in Bosnia in 1908, in Morocco again in 1911, and the Balkan wars in 1912—but they had all been manageable. The diplomatic compromises that resolved these conflicts caused frustration, however. Afterward, there was a tendency to ask, "Why should my side back down? Why didn't we make the other side give up more?" Additionally, there was growing acceptance of social Darwinism. Charles Darwin's ideas of survival of the fittest made good sense as a way of explaining why some genetic traits arise and others disappear in natural species over the course of many generations, but they were misapplied to human society and to unique events. Darwin's ideas were used to justify the view that "the strong *should* prevail," and if the strong should prevail, why worry about peace? Long wars seemed unlikely, and many leaders believed that short, decisive wars won by the strong would be a welcome change.

A third contributing factor to the loss of flexibility in the early twentieth-century balance of power was German policy. As Crowe said, it was vague and confusing. There was a terrible clumsiness about the kaiser's policy of seeking greater power that offensive realists focus on. The Germans were no different from other colonial powers in having "world ambitions," but they managed to press them forward in a way that antagonized everybody at the same time; it was just the opposite of the way that Bismarck played the system in the 1870s and 1880s. The kaiser and his advisors focused too much on hard power and neglected soft power. The Germans antagonized the British by starting a naval arms race (Figure 3.1). They antagonized the Russians over issues in Turkey and the Balkans. They antagonized the French over a protectorate in Morocco. The kaiser tried to shock Britain into a friendship, believing that if he scared Britain enough, it would realize how important Germany was and pursue improved relations. Instead, he scared the British first into the arms of the French and then into the arms of the Russians. So, by 1914, the Germans thought that they had to break out of this encirclement and thereby deliberately accepted the risk of war. Thus the rise of nationalism, increased complacency, social Darwinism, and German policy all contributed to the loss of moderation in the international system and helped contribute to the onset of World War I.

The second level of analysis allows us to examine what was happening in domestic society, politics, and government prior to World War I. We can safely reject one explanation at that level: Russian revolutionary Vladimir Lenin's argument that the war was caused by capitalism. In Lenin's view, World War I was

Figure 3.1 The European Balance of Military Power in 1914

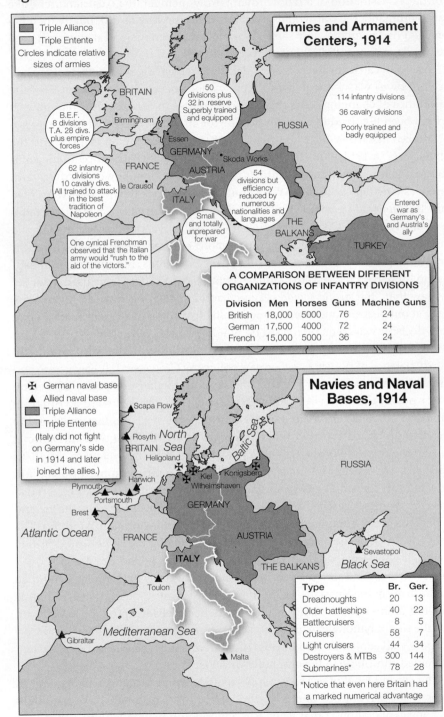

simply the final stage of capitalist imperialism. But the war did not arise out of imperialist conflicts on the colonial peripheries, as Lenin had expected. In 1898, Britain and France confronted each other at Fashoda in the Sudan as the British tried to complete a north-south line from South Africa to Egypt while the French tried to create an east-west line of colonies in Africa. If war had occurred then, it might have fit Lenin's explanation, but in fact the war broke out 16 years later in Europe, and even then bankers and businessmen strongly resisted it. Bankers believed that the war would be bad for business. Sir Edward Grey, the British foreign minister, thought that he had to follow Eyre Crowe's advice and that Britain had to prevent Germany from gaining mastery of the European balance of power. But Grey also worried about getting the London bankers to go along with declaring war. We can therefore reject the Leninist explanation. But two other domestic causes need to be taken more seriously: the internal crises of the declining Austro-Hungarian and Ottoman empires and the domestic political situation in Germany.

Both Austria-Hungary and Ottoman Turkey were multinational empires and were therefore threatened by the rise of nationalism. In addition, the Ottoman government was very weak, very corrupt, and an easy target for nationalist groups in the Balkans that wanted to free themselves from centuries of Turkish rule. The Balkan wars of 1912 pushed the Turks out, but in the next year, the Balkan states fell to war among themselves while dividing the spoils. These conflicts whetted the appetite of some Balkan states to fight Austria; if the Turks could be pushed out, why not the Austrians, too?

Serbia took the lead among the Balkan states. Austria feared disintegration from this nationalistic pressure and worried about the loss of status that would result. In the end, Austria went to war against Serbia not because a Serb assassinated its archduke, Franz Ferdinand (1863–1914), but because Austria wanted to weaken Serbia and prevent it from becoming a magnet for nationalism among the Balkan Slavs. General Conrad von Hötzendorf, the Austrian chief of staff in 1914, laid bare his motives very clearly: "For this reason, and not as vengeance for the assassination, Austria-Hungary must draw the sword against Serbia. . . .

The Kaiser's Reaction to Britain's Declaration of War

Edward VII [the kaiser's uncle and king of England, 1901–1910] in the grave is still stronger than I, who am alive! And to think there have been people who believed England could be won over or pacified with this or that petty measure!!! ... Now this whole trickery must be ruthlessly exposed and the mask of Christian pacifism roughly and publicly torn from the face [of Britain], and the pharisaical sham peace put in the pillory!! And our consuls in Turkey and India, agents and so forth, must fire the whole Mohammedan world to fierce revolt against this hateful, lying, unprincipled nation of shopkeepers; for if we are to bleed to death, England will at least lose India.

—Kaiser Wilhelm II[11]

The monarchy had been seized by the throat and had to choose between allowing itself to be strangled, and making a last effort to prevent its destruction."[12]
Disintegration of an empire because of nationalism was a more profound cause
of war than the assassination of Franz Ferdinand.

Another important domestic-level explanation of World War I lay in the
politics of Germany. German historian Fritz Fischer and his followers argue that
Germany's social problems were a key cause of the war. According to Fischer,
Germany's efforts toward world hegemony were an attempt by German elites
to distract attention from the poor domestic integration of German society. He
notes that Germany was ruled by a domestic coalition of landed aristocrats and
some very large industrial capitalists called the Coalition of Rye and Iron.[13] This
ruling coalition used expansionist policies to provide foreign adventures instead
of domestic reform—circuses in place of bread—and viewed expansionism as an
alternative to social democracy. Many historians now believe that Fischer and
his followers overstated Germany's social problems as a key cause. Internal economic and social tensions are not sufficient to explain World War I, but they do
help explain one source of the pressure that Germany put on the international
system after 1890.

A final domestic-level explanation appeals to the crisis instability of the
situation in the summer of 1914. Military leaders in all countries shared a "cult
of the offensive" favoring rapid mobilization and deployment, dramatic strategies involving sudden flanking movements of armies or breakthrough assaults,
and freewheeling tactics of maneuver. In fact, as we saw above, the prevailing
military technology of the day did not favor the offense, but European leaders
believed that it did (a phenomenon we can explain at the individual level of
analysis by noting that generals frequently expect the next war to look like the
last, and the most recent large-scale European war—the Franco-Prussian War of
1870–1871—was indeed a freewheeling affair). Once the July crisis hit, leaders
were under enormous pressure to get in the first blow. Of course, this particular
explanation does not help us understand why Europe sat on a powder keg. It
does, however, help us understand why the spark in the Balkans traveled so
quickly along the fuse.

What about the first level of analysis, the role of individuals? What distinguished the leadership on the eve of World War I was its mediocrity. The Austro-
Hungarian emperor, Franz Joseph (1830–1916), was a tired old man who was
putty in the hands of General von Hötzendorf Count Leopold von Berchtold,
his duplicitous foreign minister. Ironically, Franz Ferdinand, the crown prince
who was assassinated at Sarajevo, would have been a restraining force; the potential heir had liberal political views. In Russia, Tsar Nicholas II was an isolated
autocrat who spent most of his time resisting change at home. He was served
by incompetent foreign and defense ministers and was strongly influenced by
his sickly and neurotic wife. As historian Margaret MacMillan put it, "It was
Russia's misfortune, and the world's, that its leadership was so inadequate as
it was about to head into a major international storm."[14] In Germany, Kaiser

Wilhelm II (1859–1941) did not control policy, but his position gave him great influence. The kaiser had a great sense of inferiority. He was a blusterer, a weak man who was extremely emotional. He led Germany into a risky policy without any skill or consistency. As political scientist Richard Ned Lebow puts it:

> [Wilhelm] II did not want war, if only because he did not trust his nerves not to give way under the strain of any really critical situation. The moment there was danger, his majesty would become uncomfortably conscious that he could never lead an army into battle. He was well aware that he was neurasthenic. His more menacing jingo speeches were intended to give the foreigner the impression that here was another Frederick the Great or Napoleon.[15]

In addition, sycophantic German diplomats were filing overly rosy reports from most other great power capitals to please their vindictive superiors in the foreign ministry, which did not help the kaiser make sound decisions. Personality did make a difference. There was something about the leaders that made them significant contributory causes of the war. The relationships among some of the systemic, societal, and individual causes are illustrated in Figure 3.2.

Was War Inevitable?

When several causes exist, each of which is sufficient, we call a situation *overdetermined*. If World War I was overdetermined, does that mean that it was inevitable? The answer is no; war was not inevitable until it actually broke out in August 1914. And even then it was not inevitable that four years of carnage had to follow.

Let us distinguish three types of causes in terms of their proximity in time to the event we are studying. The most remote are *deep causes*, then come

Figure 3.2 Causes of World War I

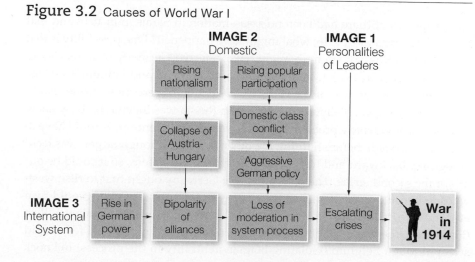

intermediate causes, and those immediately before the event are *precipitating causes*. By analogy, ask how the lights came to be on in your room. The precipitating cause is that you flicked the switch, an intermediate cause is that someone wired the building, and a deep cause is that Thomas Edison discovered how to distribute electricity. Another analogy is building a fire: The logs are the deep cause, the kindling and paper are the intermediate cause, and the actual striking of the match is the precipitating cause.

In World War I, the deep causes were changes in the balance of power and certain aspects of the domestic political systems. Especially important reasons were the rise of German strength, the development of a bipolar alliance system, the rise of nationalism and the resultant destruction of two declining empires, and German politics. The intermediate causes were German policy, the rise in complacency about peace, and the personal idiosyncrasies of the leaders. The precipitating cause was the assassination of Franz Ferdinand at Sarajevo by a Serbian terrorist and its rapid escalation owing to acute crisis-instability.

Looking back, things always look inevitable. Indeed, we might say that if the assassination had not occurred, some other precipitating incident would have caused the war. Some say precipitating events are like buses in that they come along at regular intervals. Thus the specific event at Sarajevo was not all that important; some incident would probably have occurred sooner or later. This type of argument can be tested by counterfactual history. We can ask, "What if?" and "What might have been?" as we look carefully at the history of the period. What if there had been no assassination in Sarajevo? What if the Social Democrats had come to power in Germany? There is also the issue of probability. The deep and intermediate causes suggested a high probability of war, but a high probability is not the same as inevitability. Using the metaphor of the fire again, logs and kindling may sit for a long time and never be lit. Indeed, if it rains before somebody comes along with a match, they may not catch fire even when a Sarajevo occurs.

Suppose that there had been no assassination in Sarajevo in 1914 and that no crisis occurred until 1916; what might have happened? One possibility is that the growth in Russian strength might have deterred Germany from recklessly backing Austria. In 1914, General Helmuth von Moltke and Foreign Secretary Gottlieb von Jagow, two of the German leaders who were most influential in precipitating the war, believed that war with Russia was inevitable. They knew Germany would have a problem fighting a war on two fronts and would have to knock out one side before fighting the other. Russia, although larger, was technologically backward and had a poor transportation system, so it could be put off for the second strike. They reasoned that Germany ought first to rush westward to knock out the French. After victory in the west, Germany could turn east and take its time to defeat the Russians. Indeed, that was the Schlieffen Plan (Figure 3.3), the war plan of the German general staff, which called for a rapid sweep through Belgium (violating Belgian neutrality in the process) to knock out France quickly and then to turn east.

Figure 3.3 Flawed Thinking on the Eve of War

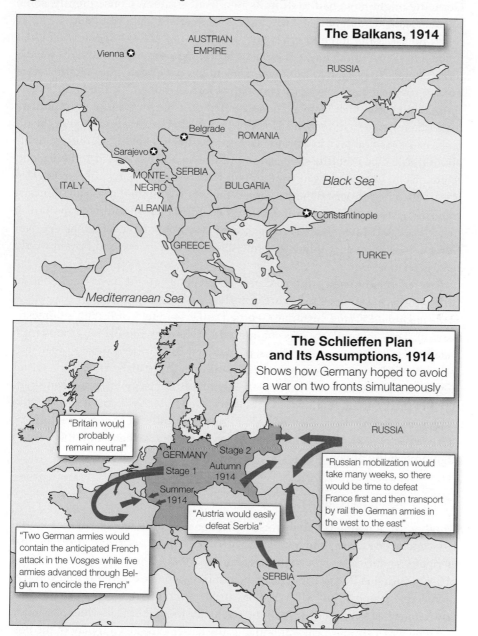

SOURCE: Brian Catchpole, A Map History of the Modern World (Oxford: Heinemann Publishers, 1982), reprinted with adjustments by permission.

But this strategy might have become obsolete by 1916 because Russia was using French money to build railroads. In the 1890s, it would have taken the Russians two or three months before they could have transported all their troops to the German front, giving Germany ample time to fight France first. By 1910, that time had shrunk to 18 days, and the German planners knew they no longer had a large margin of safety. By 1916, the margin would have been gone and Germany might have had to drop its two-front strategy. Consequently, some German leaders thought that a war in 1914 was better than a war later.

If no assassination and crisis had occurred in 1914 and if the world had made it to 1916 without a war, it is possible that the Germans might have felt deterred, unable to risk a two-front war. They might have been more careful before giving Austria a blank check to deal with Serbia as it liked. Or they might have dropped the Schlieffen Plan and concentrated on a war in the east only. Or they might have come to terms with Great Britain or changed their view that the offense had the advantage in warfare. Britain was already having second thoughts about its alliance with Russia because of Russian actions related to Persia and Afghanistan. In summary, in another two years, a variety of changes related to Russian strength might have prevented the war. Without war, German industrial strength would have continued to grow. Ironically, without war, the British historian A. J. P. Taylor has speculated, Germany might have won mastery over Europe.[16] Germany might have become so strong that France and Britain would have been deterred.

We can also raise counterfactuals about what might have happened in Britain's internal affairs if two more years had passed without war. In *The Strange Death of Liberal England*, historian George Dangerfield tells of Britain's domestic turmoil. The Liberal Party was committed to withdrawing British troops from Ireland, whereas the Conservatives, particularly in Northern Ireland, were bitterly opposed. There was a prospect of mutiny in the British army. If the Ulster Revolt had developed, it is quite plausible that Britain would have been so internally preoccupied that it would not have been able to join the coalition with France and Russia. Certainly many historically significant changes could have occurred in two more years of peace. In terms of the fire metaphor, there was a high probability of rain.

What Kind of War?

Another set of counterfactuals raises questions about what *kind* of war would have occurred rather than *whether* a war would have occurred. It is true that Germany's policies frightened its neighbors and that Germany in turn was afraid of being encircled by the Triple Entente, so it is reasonable to assume that war was more likely than not. But what kind of war? The war did not have to be what we now remember as World War I. Counterfactually, four other wars were possible.

One was a simple local war. Initially, the kaiser expected a replay of the Bosnian crisis of 1908–1909 when the Germans backed the Austrians, and Austria was therefore able to make Russia stand down in the Balkans. On July 5, 1914, the kaiser promised full support to Austria-Hungary. And with that, he went on vacation. They were not planning a preventive war. When the kaiser returned from his cruise, he found that the Austrians had filled in the blank check he left them by issuing an ultimatum to Serbia. When he realized that, the kaiser made efforts to keep the war from escalating (hence the Willie-Nicky telegrams referred to earlier). If his efforts had been successful, we might today recall not World War I, but merely a relatively minor Austro-Serbian War of August 1914.

A second counterfactual possibility was a one-front war. When the Russians mobilized their troops, the Germans also mobilized. The kaiser asked General von Moltke whether he could limit the preparations to just the eastern front. Moltke replied that it was impossible, because any change in the timetables for assembling the troops and supplies would create a logistical nightmare. He told the kaiser that if he tried to change the plans, he would have a disorganized mass instead of an army. After the war, however, General Hermann von Staab of the railway division of the German army admitted that it might have been possible, after all, to alter the mobilization schedules successfully. Had the kaiser known that and insisted, there might have been a one-front war.

A third counterfactual is to imagine a two-front war without Britain: Germany and Austria versus France and Russia. If the British had not been there to make the difference, Germany might well have won. It is possible that Britain might not have joined if Germany had not invaded Belgium, although Belgium was not the main cause of Britain entering the war. For some people, like Grey and the

Photo: Design Pics/Newscom

Britain's King George V visits his cousin Kaiser Wilhelm II at Potsdam for a wedding a little more than a year before the outbreak of World War I

Foreign Office, the main reason for entering the war was the danger of German control of the Continent. But Britain was a democracy, and the Liberal Party in the Cabinet was split. The left Liberals opposed war, but when Germany swept through Belgium and violated Belgian neutrality, it allowed the prowar Liberals to overcome the reluctance of the antiwar Liberals and to repair the split in the British Cabinet.

Finally, a fourth counterfactual is a war without the United States. By early 1918, Germany might have won the war if the United States had not tipped the military balance by its entry in 1917. In 1916, Woodrow Wilson won reelection on a platform of staying out of the war. One reason the United States became involved was the decision of the German military to resume an unrestricted submarine campaign against Allied and American shipping in hope of starving Britain into submission. There was also some German clumsiness: Germany sent a message, now known as the Zimmermann telegram, instructing its embassy in Mexico to approach the Mexican government regarding an alliance against the United States, which regarded these intercepted instructions as a hostile act. These factors ensured that the United States would enter the war, but even then it is worth noting that one of the options Wilson considered was "armed neutrality."

Our counterfactual analysis suggests ways in which the war might not have occurred in 1914 and ways in which the war that did occur did not have to become four years of carnage, which destroyed Europe as the heart of the global balance of power. It suggests that World War I was probable, but not inevitable. Human choices mattered.

The Funnel of Choices

History is path dependent. Events close in over time, degrees of freedom are lost, and the probability of war increases. But the funnel of choices available to leaders might open up again, and degrees of freedom could be regained (Figure 3.4). If we start in 1898 and ask what was the most likely war in Europe, the answer would have been war between France and Britain, which were eyeball to eyeball in a colonial dispute in Africa. But after the British and French formed the Entente in 1904, a Franco-British war looked less likely. The first Moroccan crisis in 1905 and the Bosnian crisis in 1908 made war with Germany look more likely. But some interesting events occurred in 1910. Bethmann Hollweg, the German chancellor, sought détente with Britain. Britain implied that it would remain neutral in any European war if Germany would limit its navy. At that same time, it looked as if renewed colonial friction between Britain and Russia in Asia and between the British and the French threatened a collapse or erosion of the Triple Entente. In other words, in 1910, the funnel of choices started to widen again.

But the funnel closed once more in 1911 with the second Moroccan crisis. When France sent troops to help the sultan of Morocco, Germany demanded

Figure 3.4 The Narrowing Funnel of Choices

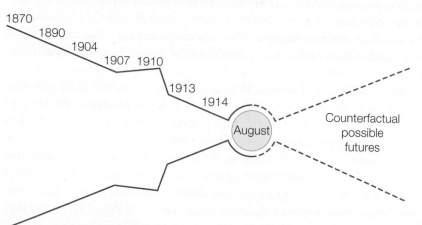

compensation in the French Congo and sent a gunboat to Agadir on the coast of Morocco. Britain prepared its fleet. French and German bankers lobbied against war, and the kaiser pulled back. But these events deeply affected public opinion and raised fears about German intentions.

Although the Balkan wars in 1912 and 1913 and the increased pressure on Austria set the scene for 1914, there was also a renewed effort at détente in 1912. Britain sent Lord Haldane, a prominent Liberal politician, to Berlin, and the British and Germans resolved a number of the issues. Also, it was clear by this time that Britain had won the naval arms race. Perhaps the funnel would open up again.

In June 1914, the feeling that relations were improving was strong enough for Britain to send four of its great dreadnought battleships to Kiel, Germany, for a state visit. If Britain had thought that war was about to occur, the last thing it would have done was put four of its prime battleships in an enemy harbor. Clearly, the British were not thinking about war at that point. In fact, on June 28, British and German sailors were walking together along the quay in Kiel when they heard the news that a Serbian terrorist had shot an Austrian archduke in a faraway place called Sarajevo. History has its surprises, and once again, *probable* is not the same as *inevitable*.

Lessons of History Again

Can we draw any lessons from this history? We must be careful about lessons. Analogies can mislead, and many myths have been created about World War I. For example, some say World War I was an accidental war. World War I was not purely accidental. Austria went to war deliberately. And if there was to be a war, Germany preferred a war in 1914 to a war later. There were miscalculations over the length and depth of the war, but that is not the same as an accidental war.

It is also said that the war was caused by the arms race in Europe. By 1912, however, the naval arms race was over, and Britain had won. Although there was concern in Europe about the growing strength of the armies, the view that the war was precipitated directly by the arms race is too simple.

On the other hand, we can draw some valid warnings from the long slide into World War I. One lesson is to pay attention to the process of a balance-of-power system as well as to its structure or distribution of power. Here the constructivists make an important point that some realists miss. Moderation evolves from the process. Stability is not assured by the distribution of power alone. Another useful lesson is to beware of complacency about peace or believing that the next crisis is going to fit the same pattern as the last crisis: The July crisis of 1914 was supposed to be a repeat of the Bosnian crisis of 1908, although clearly it was not. World War I was supposed to be a repeat of the Franco-Prussian War. In addition, the experience of World War I suggests that it is important to have military forces that are stable in crisis, without any feeling that one must use them or lose them. The railway timetables were not the major determinants of World War I, but they did make it more difficult for political leaders to buy time for diplomacy.

Today's world is different from the world of 1914 in two important ways. One is that nuclear weapons have made large-scale wars more dangerous; the other, as constructivists note, is that the ideology of war, the acceptance of war, is much weaker in many major societies. In 1914, war was thought to be inevitable, a fatalistic view compounded by the social Darwinist argument that war should be welcome because it would clear the air like a good summer storm. On the eve of World War I that was indeed the mood. As Margaret MacMillan describes it, "they accepted the coming of war with resignation and a sense of obligation, persuaded that their nations were the innocent parties . . . and the soldiers did indeed tell their families that they would be home for Christmas."[17] Winston Churchill's book *The World Crisis* captures this feeling as well:

> There was a strange temper in the air. Unsatisfied by material prosperity, the nations turned fiercely toward strife, internal or external. National passions, unduly exalted in the decline of religion, burned beneath the surface of nearly every land with fierce, if shrouded, fires. Almost one might think the world wished to suffer. Certainly men were everywhere eager to dare.[18]

They dared and they lost, and that is the lesson of 1914.

Follow Up

- Gordon Martel, *The Origins of the First World War* (New York: Pearson Longman, 2008).
- William Mulligan, *The Origins of the First World War* (Cambridge: Cambridge University Press, 2010).
- Kier A. Lieber, "The New History of World War I and What It Means for International Relations Theory," *International Security* 32:2 (Fall 2007), pp. 155–191.

Chronology: The Road to World War I

1905–1906	First Moroccan crisis: Kaiser visits Tangier as Germany attempts to supplant France; settled to France's satisfaction at the Algeciras Conference
1908	Austria proclaims annexation of Bosnia and Herzegovina, Slavic territories it had administered since 1878; Serbia threatens war but is powerless without Russian backing; Germany supports Austria-Hungary, deterring Russia
1911	Second Moroccan crisis: German gunboat *Panther* appears at Agadir in attempt to force France into colonial concessions in other areas in return for German recognition of French claims in Morocco
1912	First Balkan War: Bulgaria, Serbia, and Greece defeat Turkey and gain Thrace and Salonika; Austria-Hungary helps create Albania as check to Serbian power
1913	Second Balkan War: Serbia, Greece, and Romania defeat Bulgaria and gain territory at Bulgaria's expense
1914	
June 28	Assassination of Austrian archduke Franz Ferdinand and his wife at Sarajevo
July 5	Austria seeks and obtains German backing against Serbia
July 23	Austria sends harsh ultimatum to Serbia
July 25	Serbia rejects some terms of ultimatum; seeks Russian support
July 26	British foreign minister Sir Edward Grey proposes conference to resolve the crisis; Germany and Austria reject proposal
July 28	Austria declares war on Serbia
July 29	Austrian forces bombard Belgrade; Russia mobilizes against Austria
July 30	Russia and Austria order general mobilization; French troops withdraw ten kilometers from German border
July 31	Germany delivers ultimatum to Russia, demanding demobilization; Russia does not reply

August 1	Germany declares war on Russia; British fleet mobilizes; France mobilizes as German forces invade Luxembourg
August 2	Germany demands unimpeded passage through Belgium
August 3	Belgium rejects German ultimatum; Germany declares war on France
August 4	German troops march into Belgium; Britain declares war on Germany

Study Questions

1. Was World War I inevitable? If so, why and when? If not, when and how could it have been avoided?

2. How might you apply Kenneth Waltz's images to the origins of World War I?

3. Which of the following factors do you consider most significant in explaining the outbreak of World War I?

  a. alliance systems

  b. public opinion

  c. military doctrine or military leadership (specify countries)

  d. political leadership (specify countries)

  e. economic pressures or forces

  f. misperception

  g. other (specify)

4. Thucydides argued that the underlying cause of the Peloponnesian War was the growth of Athenian power and the fear that caused in Sparta. To what extent, if any, was World War I caused by the growth of German power and the fear that caused in Britain? Or the growth of Russian power and the fear this caused in Germany?

5. To what extent, if any, was World War I "accidental"? Does it make sense to talk about "accidental" wars? What about "unintended" ones? What kind of war was intended in World War I? By whom?

6. What do realist, liberal, and constructivist approaches add to our understanding of the origins of World War I?

7. What are some "lessons" from 1914 that might help policy makers avoid war today?

Notes

1. The Treaty of the Pyrenees (1659), which ended the war between France and Spain that began in 1635, is often considered part of the overall settlement.
2. Kalevi J. Holsti, *Peace and War: Armed Conflicts and International Order, 1648–1989* (Cambridge: Cambridge University Press, 1991), p. 39.
3. Charles Tilly, "War Making and State Making as Organized Crime," in Peter B. Evans, Dietrich Rueschemeyer, and Theda Skocpol, eds., *Bringing the State Back In* (Cambridge: Cambridge University Press, 1985), pp. 169–191.
4. Richard Cobden, *The Political Writings of Richard Cobden* (London: Unwin, 1903; New York: Kraus Reprint, 1969).

5. Aaron L. Friedberg, *The Weary Titan: Britain and the Experience of Relative Decline, 1895–1905* (Princeton, NJ: Princeton University Press, 1988).

6. Winston Churchill, June 22, 1941, to his private secretary, Sir John Colville, quoted in Robert Rhodes James, ed., *Churchill Speaks: Winston Churchill in Peace and War: Collected Speeches 1897–1963* (New York: Chelsea, 1980).

7. Paul Schroeder, "The Nineteenth Century System: Balance of Power or Political Equilibrium?," *Swords & Ploughshares* 4:1 (October 1989), p. 4.

8. John J. Mearsheimer, "Back to the Future: Instability in Europe after the Cold War," *International Security*, Vol. 15, No. 1 (Summer 1990), pp. 5–56.

9. Bernhard von Bülow, *Memoirs of Prince von Bülow 1909–1919* (Boston: Little, Brown, 1932), pp. 165–166.

10. Christopher Clark, *The Sleepwalkers: How Europe Went to War in 1914* (New York: HarperCollins, 2013), p. 123.

11. Kaiser Wilhelm II, quoted in Richard Ned Lebow, *Between Peace and War: The Nature of International Crisis* (Baltimore: Johns Hopkins University Press, 1981), p. 139.

12. Lebow, *Between Peace and War*, p. 144.

13. Fritz Fischer, *Germany's Aims in the First World War* (New York: W. W. Norton, 1967).

14. Margaret MacMillan, *The War That Ended Peace: The Road to 1914* (New York: Random House, 2013), p. 584.

15. Lebow, *Between Peace and War*, p. 144.

16. A. J. P. Taylor, *The Struggle for Mastery in Europe, 1848–1918* (Oxford: Clarendon Press, 1971).

17. MacMillan, *The War That Ended Peace*, p. 63.

18. Winston Churchill, *The World Crisis* (New York: Scribner's, 1923), p. 188.

Chapter 4
The Failure of Collective Security and World War II

Photo: Newscom

Victorious Allied leaders Georges Clemenceau, Woodrow Wilson, and David Lloyd George shortly before the signing of the Treaty of Versailles, 1919

⌄ Learning Objectives

4.1 Contrast collective security with balance of power and assess the relative role of each in great power relations between the two world wars.

4.2 Identify deep, intermediate, and proximate causes of World War II at various levels of analysis and assess whether the war was inevitable.

The Rise and Fall of Collective Security

4.1 Contrast collective security with balance of power and assess the relative role of each in great power relations between the two world wars.

World War I caused enormous social disruption and shock waves of revulsion at the senseless slaughter (Figure 4.1). Balance-of-power politics was widely blamed for the war. Woodrow Wilson, the U.S. president during World War I, was a classic nineteenth-century liberal who regarded balance-of-power policies as immoral because they violated democratic principles and national self-determination. He argued, "The balance of power is the great game now forever discredited. It's the old and evil order that prevailed before this war. The balance of power is a thing that we can do without in the future."[1]

Wilson had a point, because balance-of-power policies do not give priority to democracy or peace. As we saw in Chapter 3, the balance of power is a way to preserve the sovereign state system. States act to prevent any state from becoming preponderant. The resulting balance of power allows for war or violations of self-determination if that is the only way to preserve independence. World War I

Figure 4.1 Soldiers Mobilized in World War I (millions)

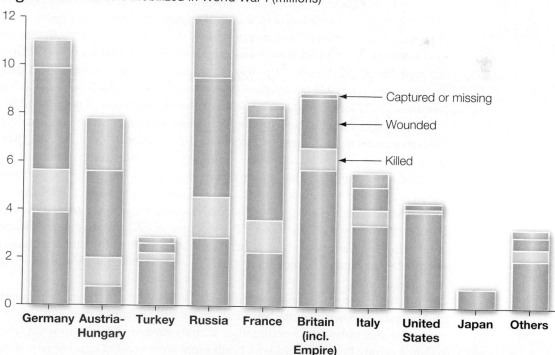

was so devastating, chaotic, and brutal, however, that many people began to think that war to preserve the balance of power was no longer tolerable. But if the world could not afford a balance-of-power system, what new system would take its place?

Sovereign states could not be abolished, Wilson admitted, but force could be tamed by law and institutions as it was at the domestic level. The liberal solution was to develop international institutions analogous to domestic legislatures and courts so that democratic procedures could be applied at the international level. Some liberals of the day thought that not only was World War I fought to make the world safe for democracy, but in turn democracy could make the world more peaceful. In January 1918, Wilson issued a *fourteen-point* statement of the United States' reasons for entering the war. The fourteenth point was the most important. It called for "a general association of nations [he meant states] to be formed under specific covenants for the purpose of affording mutual guarantees of political independence and territorial integrity to great and small states alike." In effect, Wilson wanted to change the international system from one based on balance-of-power politics to another based on collective security.

The League of Nations

Although critics called Wilson a utopian, he believed that organizing international security could be a practical approach to world politics. He knew that mere paper agreements and treaties would not be sufficient; organizations and rules were needed to implement the agreements and enforce the rules. That is why Wilson put so much faith in the idea of a *League of Nations*. Moral force was important, but a military force was necessary to back it up. Security had to be a collective responsibility. If all nonaggressive states banded together, Wilson believed, the preponderance of power would be on the side of the Good. International security would be a collective responsibility in which nonaggressive countries would form a coalition against aggressors. Peace would be indivisible.

How could the states bring about such a new system of collective security? First, they could make aggression illegal and outlaw offensive war. Second, they could deter aggression by forming a coalition of all nonaggressive states. If all pledged to aid any state that was a victim anywhere in the world, a preponderance of power would exist on the side of the nonaggressive forces. Third, if deterrence failed and aggression occurred, all states would agree to punish the state that committed aggression. This doctrine of *collective security* bore some similarities to balance-of-power policies in that states tried to deter aggression by developing a powerful coalition, and if deterrence failed, they were willing to use force.

But there were three important differences between the collective-security and balance-of-power approaches. First, in collective security, the focus was on the aggressive policies of a state rather than its capacity. That contrasted with balance-of-power politics, in which alliances were created against any state that was becoming too strong; that is, the focus was on the capacity of states. Second, unlike in a balance-of-power system in which coalitions were formed in advance, coalitions in a collective-security system could not be predetermined because it was not known which states would be aggressors. Once aggression occurred, however, all states would band against the aggressor. Third, collective security was designed to be global and universal, with no neutrals or free riders. If too many countries were neutral, the coalition of the Good might appear weak and diminish the coalition's ability to deter or punish the aggressor.

The doctrine of collective security was embodied in the Covenant of the League of Nations, which, in turn, was part of the treaties that ended World War I. Several of the articles of the League of Nations Covenant were especially noteworthy. In Article 10, states pledged to protect all members against aggression. In Article 11, any war or threat of war was declared to be of concern to all states. In Articles 12 and 15, states agreed to submit their disputes to arbitration and not to go to war until three months after arbitration failed. Article 16, the critical article, said any war disregarding League of Nations procedures would be regarded as a declaration of war against all the members of the League. The state that started a war would be immediately subject to economic sanctions, and the Council of the League might recommend further military measures.

This sounds straightforward, but there were ambiguities. All members had to agree to apply collective security. Each state had a veto. When states signed the Covenant, they agreed to abide by Article 16, but in practice it was up to each state to decide what kinds of sanctions to apply and how to implement them; they were not bound by any higher authority. Thus the League of Nations was not a move toward world government in which a higher authority could commit the member states to certain policies. It was not the end of the anarchic system of states, but rather an effort to make the states collectively discipline unruly members.

Collective security implicates two related concepts: *sovereignty* and *international law*. The definition of sovereignty, as we saw in Chapter 2, is very simple: legal supremacy within a given territory. As championed by state moralists and as recognized by the League of Nations, the sovereignty of the state is absolute and inviolable; a state government has full authority within its borders. It can limit that authority only with its own consent, that is, only if a government signs a treaty allowing another government to have some influence in its domains or agreeing to be bound by the decisions of others. They are agreed limitations rather than an infringement of sovereignty. Thus, by signing on to the League of Nations, states would voluntarily give up some sovereignty to the international community in return for the guarantees of collective security and the protections of international law.

As understood by Wilson and implied in the League of Nations charter, international law transcended national law and hence sovereignty in particular situations. Ever since the Peace of Westphalia in 1648, a central tenet of international law has been that states are sovereign except when they violate international law, in which case they are subject to punishment. Collective security was to international law what the police are to domestic law. International law enjoyed far less acceptance among states than domestic law, however. Many states refused to be constrained by international law and saw compliance as voluntary rather than mandatory.

The United States and the League of Nations

The unwillingness of some states to relinquish a degree of decision-making autonomy in exchange for collective security lay at the heart of one of the League's most notable weaknesses: the failure of the United States to join its own creation. The U.S. Senate refused to ratify the Treaty of Versailles, which contained language endorsing the creation of the League of Nations. As a result, the collective-security system had to function without what would have been its biggest player.

Why did the United States hold back when, to a large extent, the League was an American liberal plan to reorder world politics? After World War I, most Americans wanted to return to "normalcy." Many defined "normal" as avoiding international entanglements. Opponents of U.S. involvement in world affairs claimed that the Monroe Doctrine of 1823 limited U.S. interests to the Western Hemisphere and noted George Washington's warning that the United States should avoid open-ended foreign commitments. The leader of this opposition to the League of Nations, Senator Henry Cabot Lodge of Massachusetts, feared that Article 16 of the Covenant would dilute both U.S. sovereignty and the constitutional power of the Senate to declare war. Lodge suspected that the United States might be drawn into distant wars on the basis of the League's decisions to enforce collective security rather than by the Senate's decision or the will of the American people.

The debate between Wilson and his opponents is sometimes portrayed as a clash between idealism and realism, but it can also be seen as a debate between different forms of American moralism. Wilson's obdurate refusal to negotiate terms with Lodge—in part because of two of Wilson's more notable character traits, self-righteousness and inflexibility, as Alexander George and Juliette George point out in their fascinating psychobiography[2]—was part of the problem. But the Senate's resistance reflected a long-standing American attitude toward the balance of power in Europe. Opponents of the League believed that European states pursued immoral policies in the name of the balance of power and that the United States should not become an active player in such games. In fact, however, the United States was able to ignore the balance of power in the nineteenth century because Americans were enjoying a free ride behind the protection of Britain's fleet. Other European countries could not penetrate the Western Hemisphere to threaten Americans. And although the United States was isolationist toward Europe, it was not at all isolationist when it came to interfering in the affairs of its weak neighbors in Central America, Mexico, or Cuba. At the end of World War I, Americans were torn between two forms of moralism, and the isolationist impulse toward the European balance of power won. The result was that the country that had tipped the balance of power in World War I refused to accept responsibility for the postwar order.

The Early Days of the League

What France wanted more than anything else at the end of World War I was a set of military guarantees ensuring that Germany could not rise again. Because the United States would not join the League of Nations, France pressed Britain for a security guarantee and military preparations in case Germany recovered. Britain resisted on the grounds that such an alliance would be against the spirit of collective security, because it would identify the aggressor in advance. Moreover, Britain saw France as stronger than Germany and argued there was no need for an alliance, even on traditional balance-of-power terms. Britain said that it was important to reintegrate Germany into the international system, just as the Congress of Vienna had brought France back into the Concert of Europe at the end of the Napoleonic Wars in 1815. War passions had abated more quickly in Britain than in France, and the British believed that it was time to appease the Germans by bringing them back into the process.

Unmoved by these arguments, France formed alliances with Poland, which had been reborn at the end of World War I, and with the "Little Entente," the new states of Yugoslavia, Czechoslovakia, and Romania, which had emerged out of the former Austro-Hungarian Empire. The French policy fell between two stools: Not only were these alliances against the spirit of collective security, but they did not do very much for France in terms of the balance of power. Poland was on bad terms with its neighbors and, as France's ally, acted as a poor substitute for Russia, which had been ostracized because of the Bolshevik Revolution. The Little Entente states were destabilized by ethnic problems and domestic divisions and as a result were also feeble allies.

Germany emerged from World War I enormously weakened (Figure 4.2). It lost 25,000 square miles of territory that had been home to seven million people. Signed in June 1919, the Treaty of Versailles forced Germany to reduce its army to only 100,000 men and prohibited it from having an air force. The treaty contained the famous "war guilt clause," placing the blame for war solely on Germany. Because the victors believed that Germany was responsible, they argued that Germany should pay for its costs. The reparations bill was $33 billion, a sum

A Liberal Vision

My conception of the League of Nations is just this, that it shall operate as the organized moral force of men throughout the world, and that whenever or wherever wrong and aggression are planned or contemplated, this searching light of conscience shall be turned upon them.

—Woodrow Wilson[3]

Figure 4.2 Germany's Losses

The Price of Defeat
Germany's territorial losses by the 1919 Treaty of Versailles

Northern Schleswig to Denmark

Germany lost all of her colonies; many displaced Germans returned to Germany

Danzig (free city)

Memel

EAST PRUSSIA

Communist Rebellion 1918–1919

R. Oder

WEST PRUSSIA

HOLLAND

Berlin

POSEN

POLAND

Eupen & Malmedy to Belgium

New government met here because of the rebellion in Berlin: hence Germany became known as the Weimar Republic

R. Elbe

To Poland

BELGIUM

R. Rhine

Weimar

Silesia

Saar coalfields placed under French control for 5 years

• Paris
• Versailles

CZECHOSLOVAKIA

ALSACE & LORRAINE

Germany was forbidden to unite with Austria

AUSTRIA

R. Danube

To France (which lost this territory to Germany in 1871)

FRANCE

Demilitarized Zone

The Other Peace Treaties:
All were signed in French palaces a few miles from Paris
Treaty of St. Germain — 1919—with defeated Austria
Treaty of Neuilly — 1919—with defeated Bulgaria
Treaty of Sèvres — 1920—with defeated Turkey; however, this treaty was not adopted and a new one was signed at Lausanne in 1923
Treaty of Trianon — 1920—with defeated Hungary

☐ Territory lost by Germany to other countries
▨ Territory lost by Germany to the League
■▶ Displaced Germans

Germans thought impossibly high given their damaged economic position. When they initially failed to pay, France sent troops to occupy Germany's Ruhr industrial area until they did. After engaging in passive resistance, Germany suffered enormous inflation that wiped out the savings of its middle class. That, in turn, removed one of the sources of internal stability as the Weimar Republic struggled to create democracy.

Italy had never been keen on the Paris peace treaties or the League of Nations. Italy had originally been allied with Germany and Austria-Hungary, but at the beginning of the war, the Italians decided that they would get a better payoff from the Allies and switched sides. In the secret Treaty of London signed in 1915, Italy was promised compensation at the expense of the part of the Austro-Hungarian Empire that became postwar Yugoslavia. The Italians expected that these promises would be honored, but Wilson objected to such old-fashioned spoils-of-war behavior. In addition, after Benito Mussolini and the fascists took power in 1922, one of their foreign policy aims was to gain glory and finally fulfill the destiny of a new Roman Empire. These goals were inconsistent with the new vision of collective security.

With such a start, it is remarkable the League was able to achieve anything at all, yet 1924–1930 was a period of relative successes. Plans were made to scale down the reparations Germany had to pay. In 1924, governments signed a protocol on the peaceful settlement of disputes in which they promised to arbitrate their differences. Perhaps most important, in 1925, the Treaty of Locarno allowed Germany to enter the League of Nations and gave Germany a seat on its council.

The Treaty of Locarno had two aspects. In the west, Germany guaranteed that its borders with France and Belgium would be inviolable. Alsace-Lorraine, taken by Otto von Bismarck in the Franco-Prussian War (1870–1871), had been returned to France by the Treaty of Versailles, and Germany promised to demilitarize a zone along the Rhine. Locarno reaffirmed those results. In the east, Germany promised to arbitrate before pursuing changes in its eastern borders with Poland and Czechoslovakia. This second clause should have set off a warning bell, however, for there were now two kinds of borders around Germany: an inviolable part in the west and a negotiable part in the east. At that time, though, these agreements looked like progress.

The League managed to settle some minor disputes, such as one between Greece and Bulgaria, and it began a process of disarmament negotiations. Following up on the 1921 Washington Conference, in which the United States, Britain, France, Italy, and Japan had agreed to a measure of naval disarmament, the League organized a preparatory commission for broader disarmament talks, setting the scene for a worldwide conference that finally met (too late) in 1932. In addition, in 1928, states agreed to outlaw war in the Kellogg-Briand Pact, named after the U.S. and French foreign ministers. Most important, the League became a center of diplomatic activity. Although not members, the Americans and the Russians began to send observers to the League meetings in Geneva. The world financial collapse in October 1929 and the success of the National Socialist (or Nazi) Party in the 1930 German elections were harbingers of problems to come, yet there was still a sense of progress at the September 1930 annual assembly of the League of Nations. That optimism about the collective-security system, however, was dispelled by two crises in the 1930s over Manchuria and Ethiopia.

The Manchurian Failure

To understand the Manchurian case, we must understand the situation in Japan. Japan had transformed itself from a potential victim of imperialist aggression in the mid-nineteenth century to a very successful imperialist power by the century's end. Japan defeated Russia in the Russo-Japanese War (1904–1905), colonized Korea in 1910, and joined the Allies in World War I. After the war, Japan sought recognition as a major power. Europeans and Americans resisted. At the Paris peace talks in 1919, the Western governments rejected a Japanese proposal that the Covenant of the League affirm the principle of racial equality. This decision mirrored the domestic political sentiment in the U.S. Congress, which, in the 1920s, passed racist laws excluding Japanese immigrants. Simultaneously, Britain ended its bilateral treaty with Japan. Many Japanese thought that the rules were changed just as they were about to enter the club of the great powers.[4]

China was the other actor in the Manchurian crisis. The 1911 revolution led to the fall of the Manchu or Qing dynasty that had ruled China since 1644 and established a republic. But the country quickly fell into chaos as regional civil wars broke out among contending warlords. Manchuria, although part of China, was under the sway of one of these warlords and maintained a quasi-independent status. With Chiang Kai-shek (1887–1975) as chief military advisor to the republic, the Chinese Nationalist movement tried to unify the country and bitterly criticized the unequal treaties that had humiliated and exploited China ever since the end of the imperialist Opium Wars of the nineteenth century. As the Nationalists gained strength in the 1920s, friction with Japan increased, and China declared a boycott against Japanese goods.

Meanwhile, in Japan, military and civilian factions contended for dominance. The global economic crisis that began in the late 1920s left Japan, an island nation, extremely vulnerable. The military cliques gained the upper hand. In September 1931, the Japanese army staged an incident along the Manchurian Railway, where they had had a right to station troops since the Russo-Japanese War. This act of sabotage on the Manchurian Railway provided Japan with a pretext to take over all of Manchuria. Although Japan said that its actions were intended to protect the Manchurian Railway, it went further and set up a Japanese-controlled puppet state called Manchukuo, installing China's last Manchu emperor, Pu Yi, as its ruler. China appealed to the League of Nations to condemn Japan's aggression, but Japan prevented passage of a resolution asking it to withdraw its troops. In December 1931, the League agreed to send a committee under the British statesman Lord Lytton to investigate the events in Manchuria. Lord Lytton finally reported to the League in October 1932. His report identified Japan as the aggressor and rejected Japan's pretext as an unjustified intervention. Although his report recommended that the members of the League of Nations not recognize the state of Manchukuo, it did not call for applying Article 16 sanctions against Japan. In February 1933, the Assembly of the League of Nations voted 42 to 1 to accept Lytton's report on the Japanese invasion of Manchuria. The one opposing vote was Japan, which then announced its intention to withdraw from the League of Nations. Overall, the Manchurian case showed the procedures of the League of Nations to be slow, cautious, and totally ineffective. The Manchurian episode tested the League, and it failed.

The Ethiopian Debacle

The last great test of the League of Nations' collective-security system came in Ethiopia in 1935. This time, sanctions were applied, but the outcome was again failure. Italy had long planned to annex Ethiopia; not only was it near Italy's colonies in Eritrea on the Red Sea, but the ruling Italian fascists were affronted that the Ethiopians had defeated an Italian effort to colonize them during the imperialist era in the nineteenth century. Fascist ideologists argued that this historic "wrong" should be rectified. Between 1934 and 1935, Italy provoked incidents on the border between Ethiopia and Eritrea. It did so despite the existence of a peace treaty between Ethiopia and Italy, despite that Italy had signed the Kellogg-Briand Pact outlawing war, and despite its commitment as a member of the League of Nations to arbitrate for three months before doing anything.

In October 1935, Italy invaded Ethiopia. The invasion was a clear-cut case of aggression, and the Council of the League avoided an Italian veto by the procedural device of calling for a special conference to decide what sanctions to impose against Italy. Fifty states attended, and eight days after the invasion, the conference recommended to member states that they impose four sanctions: an embargo on the sale of all military goods to Italy; a prohibition against loans to Italy; cessation of imports from Italy; and refusal to sell certain goods that could not be easily bought elsewhere, such as rubber and tin. But three things were missing: Italy was still allowed to buy steel, coal, and oil; diplomatic relations were not broken; and Britain did not close the Suez Canal to Italian ships, allowing Italy to continue shipment of materials to Eritrea.

Why didn't the members of the League of Nations do more? There was general optimism that the recommended sanctions would force Italy to withdraw from Ethiopia. Sanctions certainly had an effect on the Italian economy: Italian exports declined by about one-third during the following year, the value of the Italian lira declined, and there were estimates that Italy's gold reserves would be exhausted in nine months. But aside from inflicting economic damage, sanctions did not cause Mussolini to change his policies toward Ethiopia. The anger of Britain and France over Ethiopia was more than offset by their concern for the European balance of power. Britain and France wanted to avoid alienating Italy because Germany, now under Adolf Hitler's leadership, was regaining its strength, and Britain and France thought that it would be useful to have Italy in a coalition to balance Germany. In 1934, when it looked as though Hitler would annex Austria, Mussolini moved Italian troops to the Austrian border, and Hitler backed down. The British and French therefore hoped that Mussolini could be persuaded to join a coalition against Germany.

Traditional diplomats did not fight the League of Nations' collective-security system; they reinterpreted it according to the old balance-of-power approach. From a balance-of-power perspective, the last thing they wanted was to become involved in a distant conflict in Africa when there were pressing problems in the heart of Europe. Distant aggression in Africa, said the traditional realists, was not a threat to European security. Conciliation and negotiation were needed to bring the Italians back into the coalition to balance Germany. Not surprisingly, the British and French began to get cold feet about sanctions. Sir Samuel Hoare and Pierre Laval, the British and French foreign ministers, respectively, met in December 1935 and drew up a plan that divided Ethiopia into two parts, one Italian and the other a League of Nations zone. When someone leaked this plan to the press, there was outrage in Britain. Accused of having sold out the League of Nations and collective security, Hoare was forced to resign.

But within three months, British opinion turned again. In March 1936, Hitler denounced the Locarno treaties and marched German troops into the demilitarized Rhineland. Britain and France immediately stopped worrying about Ethiopia. They met with Italy to consult about how to restore the balance of power in Europe. Consequently, the balance of power in Europe prevailed over the application of the collective-security doctrine in Africa. In May 1936, the Italians completed their military victory, and by July, the sanctions were removed.

The best line in this tragedy was spoken by the Haitian delegate to the League of Nations: "Great or small, strong or weak, near or far, white or colored, let us never forget that one day we may be somebody's Ethiopia."[5] Within a few years, most European nations fell prey to Hitler's aggression in World War II. The world's first efforts at collective security were a dismal failure.

Follow Up

- George Scott, *The Rise and Fall of the League of Nations* (New York: Macmillan, 1974).
- Graham Ross, *The Great Powers and the Decline of the European States System, 1919–1945* (London: Longman, 1983), pp. 109–126.

The Origins of World War II

4.2 Identify deep, intermediate, and proximate causes of World War II at various levels of analysis and assess whether the war was inevitable.

World War II overshadows all other wars in terms of its human costs, estimated to be between 35 million and 50 million people. The war was noted for advances in weaponry. Tanks and planes that had just been introduced and played an insignificant role in World War I dominated World War II. Radar played a significant role, for example, in the Battle of Britain, one of the turning points in World War II. And at the end of the war, of course, the atomic bomb ushered in the dawn of the nuclear age.

World War II ended with unconditional surrender. Unlike World War I, the Allies occupied Germany and Japan and transformed their societies during the occupation. The "German problem" was solved for half a century by dividing

Germany. World War II also created a *bipolar* world in which the United States and the Soviet Union emerged from the conflict much stronger than the world's former great powers. The war represented the end of Europe as the arbiter of the balance of power. Now Europe became an arena where outsiders contended, somewhat like Germany before 1870. The end of World War II in 1945 created the framework for world order until 1989.

Hitler's War?

World War II (1939–1945) is often called "Hitler's war." Although true, this label is too simple. World War II was also old business, act 2 of the Great War that ended Europe's hegemony in 1918; the interwar period was only an intermission. Hitler wanted war, but not the war we now know as World War II. He wanted a short, sharp war. Another reason it was not simply Hitler's war was the war in the Pacific. Hitler had continually, but unsuccessfully, urged the Japanese to attack the British colony of Singapore or to attack Siberia to divert Soviet troops away from Europe. Japan did neither; it surprised Hitler by attacking the U.S. naval base at Pearl Harbor instead. The war in the Pacific, although part of World War II, had different origins and was more a traditional imperial effort at regional hegemony.

Hitler greeted by the Reichstag in 1939

Photo: Bettmann/Corbis

On the other hand, we can go too far in emphasizing other causes. Some historians have nearly exonerated Hitler. A. J. P. Taylor argues that although Hitler was a terrible person and a very unpleasant adventurer, he was merely an opportunist stepping into the power vacuums created by the appeasement policies of the Western democracies.[6] But Taylor goes too far. For example, Hitler's 1924 book, *Mein Kampf*, set forth a vague plan that Taylor dismisses as Hitler's ranting in resentment of the French invasion of the Ruhr. But Hitler wrote another, secret book in 1928 that repeated many of the arguments in *Mein Kampf*. Even if it was not a detailed plan, it was a clear indication of what he wanted to do.

Taylor also deals too lightly with the "Hossbach memorandum." Colonel Friedrich Hossbach, an aide to Hitler, took notes at a meeting at Berchtesgaden in 1937 that detailed Hitler's plan to seize foreign territory by 1943, before Germany's adversaries had fully rearmed. Hitler knew that it was important to

> One Historian's View of Hitler
>
> Here, it seems to me, is the key to the problem whether Hitler deliberately aimed at war. He did not so much aim at war as expect it to happen, unless he could evade it by some ingenious trick, as he had evaded civil war at home. Those who have evil motives easily attribute them to others; and Hitler expected others to do what he would have done in their place.
>
> —A. J. P. Taylor, *The Origins of the Second World War*[7]

take opportunities when they arose in the east and that Austria and Czechoslovakia would be his first targets. Taylor dismisses the importance of this memo by saying that it was not an *official* memorandum. Since Taylor wrote, additional evidence has come to light. We now know that Hitler talked often of this timetable and of these objectives. The Hossbach memorandum generally predicted Hitler's actions.

Hitler's Strategy

Hitler had four options after he came to power in 1933, and he rejected three of them. He could have chosen *passivity*, accepting Germany's weakened international position. He could have tried *enrichment* through economic growth (like Japan after World War II) and led Germany to international influence through industrial expansion. He could have *limited his goals* to revision of the Treaty of Versailles and regained some of Germany's 1918 losses. This last option seemed likely even if some other leader had come to power in Germany. By the 1930s, the Western democracies were sensitive to the injustice of blaming Germany for *all* the events of World War I. But these three strategies were rejected by Hitler, who chose instead an *expansionist strategy* to break out from what he saw as Germany's containment. In his view, Germany, stuck in the middle of Europe, could not live forever encircled. It had to gain land. He would go east for living space, expand his base, and at a later stage go for a larger world role.

Hitler followed this fourth option through four phases. First, he set out to destroy the Versailles framework through a very clever set of diplomatic maneuvers. In October 1933, Germany withdrew from the League of Nations and from the disarmament conference that the League had convened. Hitler blamed the withdrawal on the French, who he said were not willing to cut their forces, thereby making it impossible for Germany to continue in the League or the conference. In January 1934, he signed a treaty with Poland, disrupting the arrangements that France had been trying to make with Poland and the smaller Eastern European states through the Little Entente. In March 1935, Hitler denounced the military clauses of the Versailles treaty, saying that Germany would no longer be restricted to an army of 100,000. Instead, he announced plans to triple the army and build an air force.

The British, French, and Italians met at Stresa (in Italy) to respond to Hitler's activities, but before they could reach a consensus, Hitler invited Britain to enter negotiations on a naval treaty. Britain leaped at the opportunity, thereby disrupting any coordinated response from the Stresa meeting. In March 1936, when events in Ethiopia diverted attention from central Europe, Hitler moved his troops into the Rhineland, which had been demilitarized by the Locarno Pact. He blamed France for forcing him to do so, claiming that France had destroyed the Locarno treaty by developing an arrangement with the Soviet Union. He dropped hints that he might return to the League of Nations after the other states in Europe accepted his views about the revisions of the Versailles treaty, a clever maneuver that played on guilt and uncertainty in many Western capitals.

The second phase (1936–1940) was Hitler's expansion into the small countries neighboring Germany. In 1936, Hitler outlined a four-year economic plan for a military buildup so as to be ready for war by 1940. He signed the Axis Pact with Italy and an Anti-Comintern Pact with Japan. (Founded by Vladimir Lenin in 1919 to foment worldwide Bolshevik-style revolution, the Communist International, or Comintern, changed its policy in 1935 under Josef Stalin to support so-called Popular Front governments, antifascist coalitions comprising socialists, anarchists, and "bourgeois parties.") Hitler also intervened on the side of the fascists in their war against a left-wing, democratically elected, popular-front government in Spain. Hitler justified sending troops and bombers to support the fascist general Francisco Franco in the Spanish Civil War (1936–1939) as part of the protection of the West against the threat of Bolshevism. In 1937, Spain became a testing ground for Germany's military muscle when Hitler's pilots bombed defenseless civilian populations and annihilated the Basque city of Guernica, a savage attack immortalized in what many regard as Pablo Picasso's best and most disturbing painting. Despite widespread international outcry, France, Great Britain, and the United States did little or nothing to defend the Spanish Republic. The following year, Chancellor Kurt von Schuschnigg of Austria called for a plebiscite on whether Austria should reunite with Germany, hoping that the Austrian people would vote against it before Hitler forced it upon them. But Hitler intervened. In the 1938 *anschluss* ("coming together"), German troops marched into Vienna, ending Austrian independence.

Czechoslovakia was next. Hitler pressured Czechoslovakia by pushing the issue of national self-determination for the three million Germans in the Sudetenland section of Czechoslovakia. This area where Czechoslovakia borders Germany was militarily important because it included the Bohemian mountains, the natural line of defense for Czechoslovakia and the logical place for it to resist a potential German attack. Hitler argued that the post–World War I settlement that put these German-speaking people in Czechoslovakian territory was a violation of their self-determination and another example of the perfidy of the Western countries. He demanded that the German-speaking territory be permitted to leave Czechoslovakia to join the German homeland. The Czechs became worried and mobilized portions of their reserves. That move infuriated Hitler, who vowed to crush Czechoslovakia.

These events also alarmed Britain, which did not want war to break out in Europe. Neville Chamberlain, the British prime minister from 1937 to 1940, made three trips to Germany to try to stave off war. Chamberlain believed that it was not possible for Britain to defend Czechoslovakia because of the distance and because Britain had no troops on the European continent. More important, he did not think that Czechoslovakia was worth war, and he knew that Britain was not ready for war. As the bombing of Guernica had shown, air power was becoming more significant, and fear of bombing campaigns was growing. Chamberlain realized that the British air defense and radar systems were not ready for an air war. (Some British officials also thought that Sudeten Germans had a valid complaint about being forcibly detached from Germany and given to Czechoslovakia after World War I.) For this combination of reasons, Chamberlain met with Hitler at Munich in September 1938 and agreed to the partition of Czechoslovakia, giving the Sudetenland to Germany if Hitler would promise to leave the rest of Czechoslovakia alone. Hitler promised, and Chamberlain returned to Britain claiming that he had saved Czechoslovakia and achieved "peace for our time."

Only six months later, in March 1939, German troops rolled into the rest of Czechoslovakia and took the capital city, Prague. A shocked Britain realized that Hitler might seek further conquests and that his next target might be Poland. Divided in the eighteenth century, Poland was re-created as a state after World War I and given a corridor to the port of Danzig on the Baltic Sea, although the area included German-speaking people. Again, Hitler used the same tactics. He claimed that having German-speaking people inside Polish territory was a violation of self-determination, another example of the perfidy of the Versailles treaty. This time, Britain and France tried to deter Hitler by issuing a guarantee to defend Poland.

Hitler then pulled off a brilliant diplomatic coup. Despite having said that he would protect the West against Bolshevism, Hitler suddenly signed a treaty with Stalin in August 1939. The pact gave Hitler a free hand to do what he wanted in the West. It also included a secret protocol for another partition of Poland. Stalin and Hitler each agreed to take a part. Hitler seized his part by starting a war against Poland on September 1, 1939. This time, he was not looking for another Munich agreement in which the British would step in and give him part of Poland in return for promises of moderation.

Phase three of Hitler's strategy was short. Germany achieved military mastery on the European continent in 1940 (Figure 4.3). After Hitler took Poland, things were temporarily quiet; this period was called the "phony war." Hitler expected Britain to sue for peace. In the spring of 1940, however, Hitler feared that Britain would move troops to Norway. He preempted a British landing in Norway by sending his troops there first. Then he launched his blitzkrieg into Holland, Belgium, and France. Sending his tanks through the supposedly

Figure 4.3 Early Stages of World War II

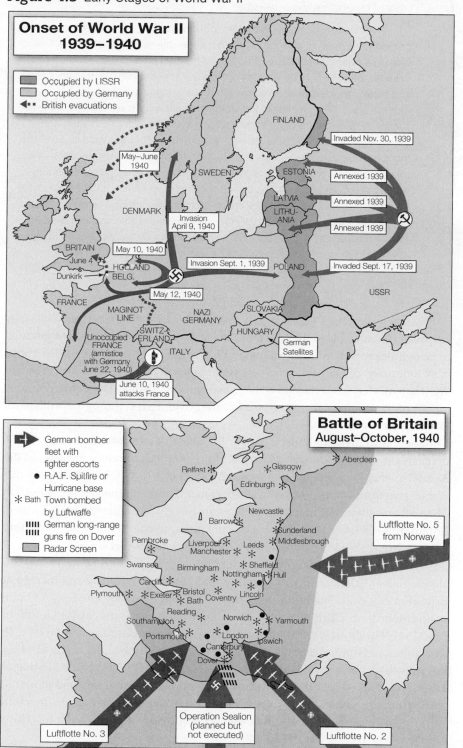

Onset of World War II 1939–1940

- Occupied by USSR
- Occupied by Germany
- ◀▪▪ British evacuations

FINLAND

Invaded Nov. 30, 1939

SWEDEN

ESTONIA
Annexed 1939

LATVIA
Annexed 1939

LITHU-ANIA
Annexed 1939

May–June 1940

DENMARK

Invasion April 9, 1940

BRITAIN
June 4
May 10, 1940
HOLLAND
BELG.
Dunkirk

Invasion Sept. 1, 1939

POLAND

Invaded Sept. 17, 1939

USSR

FRANCE

MAGINOT LINE

May 12, 1940

SWITZ-ERLAND

NAZI GERMANY

SLOVAKIA

HUNGARY

German Satellites

Unoccupied FRANCE (armistice with Germany June 22, 1940)

ITALY

June 10, 1940 attacks France

Battle of Britain
August–October, 1940

- ➡ German bomber fleet with fighter escorts
- ● R.A.F. Spitfire or Hurricane base
- ✳ Bath Town bombed by Luftwaffe
- ⦀⦀ German long-range guns fire on Dover
- Radar Screen

Aberdeen
Belfast
Glasgow
Edinburgh
Newcastle
Barrow
Sunderland
Middlesbrough
Pembroke
Liverpool
Leeds
Manchester
Sheffield
Swansea
Birmingham
Nottingham
Hull
Cardiff
Lincoln
Plymouth
Exeter
Bristol
Coventry
Bath
Reading
Norwich
Yarmouth
Southampton
London
Ipswich
Portsmouth
Canterbury
Dover

Luftflotte No. 5 from Norway

Luftflotte No. 3

Operation Sealion (planned but not executed)

Luftflotte No. 2

Another Historian's View of Hitler

The charismatic nature of Hitler's position as Fuhrer—a quasi-messianic personalized form of rule that arose from the desire for national rebirth and unity in a country traumatized by national humiliation and paralyzed by political collapse—could of its essence not settle into "normality" or routine, or sag into more conservative authoritarianism. Visionary goals of national redemption through European domination and racial purification were at the heart of the regime. These meant constant dynamism and self-perpetuating, intensifying radicalism. The longer the regime lasted, the more megalomaniac were its aims, the more boundless its destructiveness. Its gamble for world supremacy meant an alliance against extremely powerful allies. It was a gamble against the odds, in which the regime asked its own destruction and that of Germany itself. This was Nazism's essential irrationality. Hitler's charismatic leadership implied, therefore, not just an unprecedented capacity for destruction, but also an inbuilt tendency for self-destruction. In this sense the suicide of the German dictator on 30 April 1945 was not merely a welcome but also a logical end to the Third Reich.

—Ian Kershaw, "Hitler and the Nazi Dictatorship"[8]

impenetrable Ardennes Forest in May 1940, Hitler took the French and British by surprise. He had skirted the Maginot Line of French fortifications that guarded most of the French border with Germany. German forces drove the British troops back to the port of Dunkirk, where they had to leave their equipment and evacuate what was left of the troops across the English Channel. Thus Hitler became master of the European continent west of the Soviet Union through a brilliant set of moves in 1940.

The fourth phase of Hitler's plans, "the phase of overreaching" (1941–1945), unleashed the full-scale war. Hitler had long wanted to move east against the Soviet Union, but he wanted to dispose of Britain first to avoid the possibility of a war on two fronts. If he could gain air supremacy, he could then cross the English Channel and invade Britain. But Hitler's air force was defeated in the Battle of Britain (July–October 1940). Unable to gain air supremacy, Hitler was faced with a conundrum: Should he put off his plans to attack the Soviet Union?

Hitler decided to attack the Soviet Union even though he had been unable to defeat Britain, thinking that he could beat Stalin quickly and then go at Britain once again. Furthermore, he believed that attacking the Soviet Union would deprive the British of any potential alliance with the Soviet Union. In June 1941, Hitler attacked the Soviet Union, which was a massive mistake. In December 1941, after the Japanese attacked Pearl Harbor, he made another huge mistake: He declared war on the United States. Hitler probably did that to keep Japan locked into the war because he had been urging Japan to join him, and he took the occasion to unleash his U-boat campaign against American shipping. In doing so, he also unleashed the global war that ended his Third Reich.

The Role of the Individual

What role did Hitler's personality play in causing World War II? It was probably not the crucial factor in the first phase. The Western democracies were so guilt-ridden, weak, and internally divided that any clever German nationalist probably would have been able to revise the Versailles system. But the second and third phases that brought mastery over Europe depended on Hitler's skill, audacity, and bellicose nature. He often overruled his conservative generals and staff. Hitler wanted war and was willing to take risks. The fourth phase, which brought on global war and failure, is also attributable to two aspects of Hitler's personality. First, Hitler's appetite grew with the eating. He was convinced of his own genius, but that conviction led him to two crucial mistakes: invading the Soviet Union before he finished off Britain and declaring war on the United States, which gave Franklin Roosevelt, the U.S. president from 1933 to 1945, a pretext to become engaged in a war in Europe as well as in the Pacific (Roosevelt had been eager to join Britain in war against Hitler, but was unable to bring along a wary Congress until after Pearl Harbor).

Hitler's other great flaw was his racist ideology. Promoting the myth of a superior Aryan master race deprived him of critical assets. For example, when Germany first invaded the Soviet Union, many Ukrainians and others revolted against Stalin's brutality. But Hitler regarded the Slavs as an inferior people, unworthy of an alliance with him against Stalin. He also thought that the United States was weak because of its population of blacks and Jews. He used to joke about Roosevelt having a Jewish ancestor. He failed to understand that American pluralism could be a source of strength. Moreover, his anti-Semitism led him to expel some of the scientists crucial to developing the atomic bomb. In short, his individual leadership was a crucial factor in World War II. The kind of war it was and its outcome depended very much on Hitler's monomaniacal personality.[9]

Systemic and Domestic Causes

Of course, there were also other causes. World War II was more than just Hitler's war, and that is the value of A. J. P. Taylor's interpretation. There were systemic causes, both structural and procedural. At the structural level, World War I did not solve the German problem. The Versailles treaty was harsh enough to stir up German nationalism, but not harsh enough to leave the Germans incapable of doing something about it. Furthermore, the absence of the United States and the Soviet Union from the balance of power until very late in the game meant that Germany was undeterred from pursuing its expansionist policies. In addition, the processes of the international system were immoderate. Germany was a revisionist state bent on destroying the Versailles treaty system. In addition, the growth of ideologies—the great "isms" of fascism and communism—engendered hatred and hindered communication in the 1930s.

Three domestic-level changes were also particularly important. First, the Western democracies were torn apart by class cleavages and ideological disputes. Coordinated foreign policy making was nearly impossible. For example, when Léon Blum, a French socialist, came to power after 1936, French conservatives used the slogan, "Better Hitler than Blum." In 1939, the British conservative government sent a mission to Moscow to see whether it could sign a treaty with Stalin, but both the mission and the government were internally divided. Before the British could make up their minds, Hitler had beaten them to it. One reason for the delay was the British upper-class reluctance to deal with communists.

A second domestic-level cause of the war was economic collapse. The Great Depression was systemic in the sense that it affected all countries and grew out of the inability of the major capitalist states to establish effective international economic coordination to deal with imbalances in transnational trade and financial flows. But the Depression had powerful effects on domestic politics and class conflict. The enormous amount of unemployment had the political effect of pouring gasoline on a fire: It contributed to the Nazi takeover in Germany and weakened the governments of the Western democracies.

The third domestic cause was the U.S. policy of isolationism. The United States came out of World War I with the world's strongest economy, but it refused to fully accept the responsibilities of that position. In the 1930s, the Great Depression increased internal preoccupation and significantly deepened isolationism. In his first term as president, Roosevelt, along with other Americans, paid little attention to Europe. After his reelection in 1936, Roosevelt began to realize that if Hitler became too strong, he might dominate Europe and eventually threaten the United States. In 1937, Roosevelt began to speak about events in Europe, but the American public did not want to get involved. In 1940, Roosevelt traded destroyers to the British in return for military basing rights in British territories in the Western Hemisphere. In 1941, he persuaded Congress to approve "lend-lease" war supplies to Britain to prevent it from being defeated by Hitler. He was, however, limited by domestic opinion on how far he could go in resisting Hitler. Only Japan's attack on Pearl Harbor and Hitler's subsequent declaration of war ended America's isolationism.

How do these domestic, personal, and systemic causes fit together? We could say that the deep causes of World War II were systemic: the unfinished business of World War I. The intermediate causes were largely domestic: the social and ideological disruptions that produced Hitler in Germany and the

---

Hitler's View of Hitler

Now Poland is in the position in which I wanted her. . . . I am only afraid that at the last moment some swine or other will submit to me a plan for mediation.

—*Adolf Hitler, August 27, 1939*[10]

Figure 4.4 Causes of World War II

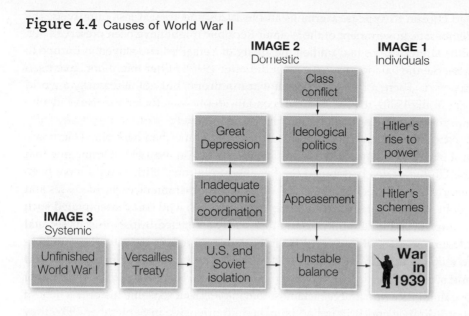

political and economic weaknesses in the democracies. The precipitating cause was Adolf Hitler's strategy for domination (Figure 4.4).

Was War Inevitable?

Was a second world war inevitable? No, but it became increasingly likely as time passed. In 1926 (after the Locarno treaties), the likelihood diminished, but after the Great Depression in 1929 and Hitler's ascent to power in 1933, the funnel of choices narrowed until the war became global in 1941 (Figure 4.5).

The failure of World War I to solve "the German problem" meant that there was already in 1918 some probability of a second war. If the Western democracies

Figure 4.5 Was War Inevitable?

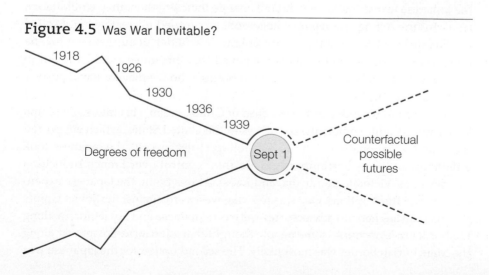

had chosen to appease Germany in the 1920s and treat it less punitively, the democratic government of the Weimar Republic might have been preserved. Or, if the United States had ratified the Treaty of Versailles and stayed in Europe to preserve the balance of power (as it did after 1945), Hitler might not have risen to power. There might have been a war in Europe, but not necessarily a world war. In the 1930s, the shock of the economic depression fueled the rise of ideologies that glorified aggression, making war more likely.

Counterfactually, suppose that Britain and France had confronted Germany and made an alliance with the Soviet Union early in the 1930s. Or imagine that the United States had joined the League of Nations. Hitler might have been deterred or delayed. He might not have had such dramatic early successes and might have been overthrown by his own generals, who had contemplated such a coup several times and who had repeatedly contacted British officials secretly to warn them of Hitler's warlike intentions and to beg them to do something to stop him.[11] But because these things did not happen, Hitler's personality and strategy became the key precipitating causes. By the late 1930s, once Hitler began to plan war, it became almost inevitable. Even so, some historians believe that if France and Britain had launched an offensive in September 1939, they might have defeated Germany.

The Pacific War

The war in the Pacific had separate origins. Japan's attention was focused on East Asia, and it was not deeply involved in European events. In the 1920s, Japan was far from being a perfect democracy, but it did have a parliamentary system. In the 1930s, however, the military and extreme nationalists gained control of the government. Their policy of imperialist expansion was widely popular. Japan had always worried about maintaining access to the raw materials it had to import to sustain its economy. When the Great Depression cut Japan's trade, the Japanese feared that if they did not change their situation, they would face a bleak future. Acting as a regional hegemon, Japan tried to create what it called the Greater East Asia Co-Prosperity Sphere (a wonderful euphemism for the conquest of one's neighbors). Japan believed that this move would allow it to resist threats from Britain and the United States, who were major naval powers in the Pacific.

Japan first expanded at the expense of China. Japan's brutal war in China brought Japan into diplomatic conflict with the United States, which supported the Chinese Nationalists. After France fell to Hitler in 1940, the Japanese took advantage of the opportunity to extend their control over French Indochina (modern-day Vietnam, Cambodia, and Laos). At this point, the Japanese expansionists had three options. One was to strike westward against the Soviet Union. Because clashes had already occurred between Japanese and Soviet forces along the border in Manchuria, some people thought that a Japanese-Soviet war along the Manchurian border was most likely. The second option for the Japanese was

Photo: Newscom

The attack on Pearl Harbor, December 7, 1941

to strike south and seize the Dutch East Indies (today's Indonesia), which had the oil Japan needed. Option three was to strike east against the United States, by far the riskiest of the three options.

The Japanese eventually chose both options two and three. On December 7, 1941, they struck east against the United States and south toward Indonesia and the Philippines. Although the move south was for raw materials, the attack on the United States is more difficult to explain. Given the disparity in power resources, the Japanese knew that they could not ultimately win a war against the United States, but they hoped that the surprise attack on Pearl Harbor would so demoralize the United States that full-scale war would never erupt. It was a gross miscalculation on the part of the Japanese, but from the perspective of the Japanese government, it seemed a better risk than the sure defeat they believed would ensue if they did nothing.

By the fall of 1941, Japanese expansionists no longer considered the Soviet Union a viable target. Hitler's attack on the Soviet Union had removed the Soviet threat to Japan. At the same time, the United States tried to deter the Japanese from striking south by placing an embargo on oil shipments to Japan. As Roosevelt put it, "The United States would slip a noose around Japan's neck and give it a jerk now and then." Assistant Secretary of State Dean Acheson was quoted at the time as saying this embargo would not lead to war because "no rational Japanese could believe that an attack on us could result in anything but disaster for his country."[12] But the Japanese believed that if they did not go to war with the United States, they would eventually suffer defeat in any case. With 90 percent of their oil imported, they calculated that their navy could not last for even a year if that supply were cut off; therefore, they concluded that it was better to go to war than to be slowly strangled.

In addition to restricting Japan's oil supplies, the United States demanded that Japan withdraw from China. The Japanese believed that doing so would cut them off from the area they viewed as their economic hinterland. As a Japanese military officer explained to Emperor Hirohito, the situation was like that of a patient with a serious illness: "An operation, although it might be extremely dangerous, would still offer some hope of saving his life."[13] From their point of view, it was *not* totally irrational for Japan to go to war because it was the least bad of the alternatives they saw. If Germany defeated Britain and if American opinion was discouraged by the suddenness of the attack, a negotiated peace might result. A poorly reasoned form of the Japanese leaders' mood was expressed by Vice Army Chief of Staff Ko Tsukada:

> In general, the prospects if we go to war are not bright. We all wonder if there isn't some way to proceed peacefully. There is no one who is willing to say, "Don't worry, even if the war is prolonged, I will assume all responsibility." On the other hand, it is not possible to maintain the status quo. Hence, one unavoidably reaches the conclusion that we must go to war.[14]

Of course, Japan had the option of reversing its aggression in China and Southeast Asia, but that was unthinkable for the military leaders with their expansionist and bellicose outlook. Thus on December 7, 1941, the Japanese attacked Pearl Harbor (Figure 4.6).

What about the three levels of analysis as applied to the Pacific war? The *role of the individual* is certainly less pronounced than it was with Hitler in Europe, but individual policy makers nonetheless influenced the trajectory of events. In Japan, expansionist generals and admirals wanted to increase Japan's regional dominance and actively sought an expanded war: west to China; south to Singapore, Indonesia, and the Philippines; and east to U.S. possessions in the Pacific. Military leaders such as General Hideki Tojo played a leading role in determining government policy. Tojo, however, supported policies identical to those of many other high-ranking military and political leaders. Although Hitler had military and industrial support in Germany, he made decisions largely on his own. In Japan, there was a greater diffusion of power at the top, and decisions were more the result of consensus among the political and military elite.

The role of the individual was also important for determining U.S. policy. Roosevelt was willing to impose punitive sanctions in response to Japanese aggression in Southeast Asia, but many in Congress and throughout the United States were uneasy with his activist and confrontational foreign policy.

Figure 4.6 World War II in the Pacific

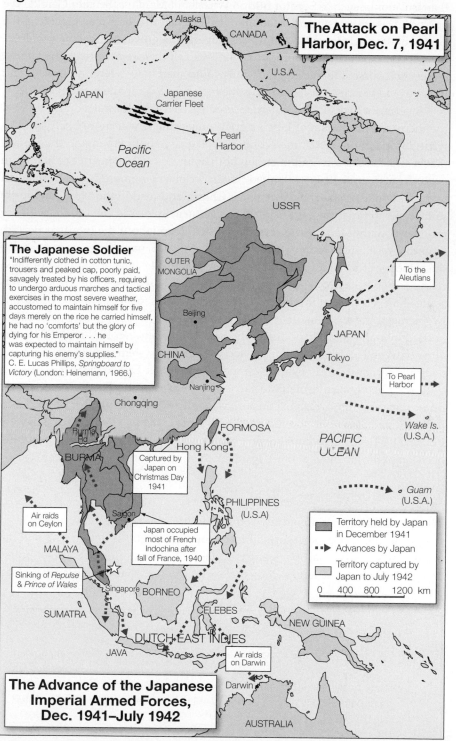

The Attack on Pearl Harbor, Dec. 7, 1941

The Japanese Soldier
"Indifferently clothed in cotton tunic, trousers and peaked cap, poorly paid, savagely treated by his officers, required to undergo arduous marches and tactical exercises in the most severe weather, accustomed to maintain himself for five days merely on the rice he carried himself, he had no 'comforts' but the glory of dying for his Emperor . . . he was expected to maintain himself by capturing his enemy's supplies."
C. E. Lucas Phillips, *Springboard to Victory* (London: Heinemann, 1966.)

The Advance of the Japanese Imperial Armed Forces, Dec. 1941–July 1942

There was still strong isolationist sentiment in the United States in 1940 and 1941. If an isolationist such as Senator Burton Wheeler of Montana, Senator Gerald Nye of North Dakota, or Senator Hiram Johnson of California had been president, the United States might have tried to appease Japanese aggression rather than confront it, and, consequently, Japan might never have felt the need to attack the United States. Of course, Japanese aggression would then have been unchecked, and Japan would have established itself as the regional power in the western Pacific.

In terms of *domestic* and *systemic causes*, we have seen how at a domestic level the increased militarism of Japan's government made war more likely. And as with Europe in the 1930s, the economic collapse in both Japan and the United States affected the foreign policies of both countries. While Japan became more expansionist, until 1940 the United States became even more isolated. In addition, the domestic chaos in Nationalist China continued in the 1930s, making it vulnerable to Japanese expansion. That, in turn, increased the influence of the militarists within Japanese domestic politics. Throughout the interwar period, lingering resentment among the Japanese for the U.S. unwillingness to enshrine the principle of racial equality in the Covenant of the League of Nations poisoned relations between Tokyo and Washington. At the system level, the Treaty of Versailles had left the ambitions of Japan in China unsatisfied, and the economic problems of the 1930s made it difficult for Japan to obtain the raw materials it needed by trade alone. In addition, the breakdown between 1931 and 1933 of the already weak League of Nations' collective-security system in Asia removed any institutional constraints on Japan's imperial ambitions. Unlike the war in Europe, both the deep and intermediate causes of the war in the Pacific were largely domestic: the shift toward expansion in Japan and toward greater isolationism in the United States and the chaos of 1930s China. The precipitating causes were Roosevelt's decision to implement a full embargo in July 1941 and the resulting decision of the Japanese military to attack the United States on December 7.

Appeasement and Two Types of War

What lessons can we now draw? Some say that the key lesson of the 1930s is that *appeasement* does not work; indeed, some say that it is downright evil. But appeasement is not bad per se; it is a classic tool of diplomacy. It is a policy choice to allow for changes in the balance of power that benefit a rival state.

Japan's Predicament, as Seen by Its Leaders

Even if we should make concessions to the United States by giving up part of our national policy for the sake of a temporary peace, the United States, its military position strengthened, is sure to demand more and more concessions on our part; and ultimately our empire will lie prostrate at the feet of the United States.

—Records of Japan's 1941 Policy Conferences

Rather than attempting to deter or contain the aggression of adversaries, a state might prefer to allow its adversaries modest gains. On the eve of the Peloponnesian War, Corinth tried to persuade Athens that it should be allowed to absorb Corcyra, but Athens refused to appease Corinth and chose instead to fight. Given subsequent events, it is possible that Athens would have done better to appease Corinthian ambitions than to challenge Corinth over Corcyra. Appeasement was used successfully in 1815 when the victorious powers appeased the defeated but still strong France. In the late nineteenth and early twentieth centuries, Britain very effectively appeased the rising United States.[15] We could even argue that appeasement might have been the right policy for the Western Allies to have taken toward Germany in the 1920s, particularly because the British were especially willing to try appeasement when it would satisfy "legitimate grievances" (many in Britain came to have serious moral qualms about the Treaty of Versailles' territorial dismemberment of Germany).[16] One of the great ironies of the interwar period is that the West confronted Germany in the 1920s when it should have been appeased and appeased Germany in the 1930s when it should have been confronted.

Appeasement was the wrong approach to Hitler, but Chamberlain, the British prime minister, was not such a coward as the Munich experience makes him out to be. He wanted to avoid another world war. In July 1938, he said,

> When I think of those four terrible years [1914–1918] and I think of the 7 million young men who were cut off in their prime and 13 million who were maimed and mutilated, the misery and suffering of the mothers and fathers, sons and daughters, I must say that there are no winners in a war, but all losers. It is those thoughts which make me feel that it is my prime duty to strain every nerve to avoid repetition of the Great War in Europe.[17]

Chamberlain's sins were not his intentions, but rather his ignorance and arrogance in failing to appraise the situation properly. In that failure, he was not alone.

World Wars I and II are often cast as two quite different models of war: accidental war versus planned aggression. World War I is sometimes portrayed as an unwanted spiral of hostility. To some extent, it might have been avoided with appeasement, although German demands might not have been easily accommodated. Political scientist David Calleo has argued that "the proper lesson is not so much the need for vigilance against aggressors, but the ruinous consequences of refusing reasonable accommodation of upstarts."[18] World War II, however, was definitely not an unwanted spiral of hostility; rather, it was a failure to deter Hitler's planned aggression. In that sense, the policies appropriate for preventing World Wars I and II were almost opposite. Accommodation of Germany might have helped delay or forestall World War I, and deterrence of Germany, if indeed Hitler could have been deterred, might have prevented World War II. But the policies were reversed. In trying to avoid a repetition of World War I, British leaders in the 1930s helped precipitate World War II. At the same time, the efforts of U.S. leaders to deter Japan helped bring on war in the Pacific. Deterrence failed because the Japanese felt cornered in a situation in which the alternative of peace looked worse than risking a war.

Of course, these two models of war are too simple. World War I was not purely accidental, and World War II was not merely the result of Hitler's planned aggression (certainly in the Pacific, it was not the result of Hitler's aggression at all). The ultimate lesson is to be wary of overly simple historical models. Always ask whether a model is true to the facts of history and whether it really fits the current reality. It helps to remember the story of Mark Twain's cat. As Twain pointed out, a cat that sits on a hot stove will not sit on a hot stove again, but neither will it sit on a cold one. It is necessary to know which stoves are cold and which are hot when using historical analogies or when using World Wars I and II as models for understanding later events.

Follow Up

- A. J. P. Taylor, *The Origins of the Second World War* (London: Hamilton, 1961).
- Alan Bullock, "Hitler and the Origins of the Second World War," in W. R. Louis, ed., *The Origins of the Second World War: A. J. P. Taylor and His Critics* (New York: Wiley, 1972), pp. 117–145.
- Scott Sagan, "The Origins of the Pacific War," *Journal of Interdisciplinary History* 18:4 (Spring 1988), pp. 893–922.

Chronology: Between the World Wars

1919	Peace Conference opens at Versailles; adoption of Weimar Constitution
1920	Creation of the League of Nations
1921–1922	Washington conference on naval armaments
1922	Permanent Court of Justice at The Hague established; Treaty of Rapallo between Germany and the Soviet Union; Benito Mussolini assumes power in Italy
1923	France and Belgium occupy the Ruhr in response to German default on coal deliveries; Nazi Beer Hall *Putsch* aborted
1924	Dawes Plan for reparations accepted; Geneva Protocol for the peaceful settlement of international disputes adopted
1925	Locarno Conference and treaties
1926	Germany admitted to the League of Nations
1928	Kellogg-Briand Pact signed

(*continued*)

1930	London Naval Conference
1931	Japanese invasion of Manchuria; failure of the Austrian Credit-Anstalt; Bank of England forced off the gold standard
1932	Disarmament conference; Lausanne Conference on German reparations
1933	Adolf Hitler becomes chancellor of Germany; Reichstag fire; Enabling Act passed establishing Nazi dictatorship; Germany withdraws from the disarmament conference and League of Nations
1934	Soviet Union joins the League of Nations
1935	Germany renounces the disarmament clauses of the Versailles treaty; Franco-Russian alliance formed; Anglo-German naval agreement reached; Italian invasion of Ethiopia; Hoare-Laval Pact
1936	Germany denounces Locarno pacts and reoccupies the Rhineland; Italy wins the war in Ethiopia; League of Nations discredited as a political instrument; Rome-Berlin axis formed; Anti-Comintern Pact formed
1936–1939	Civil war in Spain
1937	Japan launches attacks on Nanjing and other Chinese cities
1938	German invasion and annexation of Austria; Chamberlain meets Hitler at Berchtesgaden, Godesberg, and Munich to resolve the German-Czech crisis; Munich agreement signed
1939	Crisis in Czechoslovakia; Germany occupies all of Czechoslovakia; British and French pledges to Poland and guarantees to Greece and Romania; Italy invades Albania; Russian-German (Molotov–von Ribbentrop) Pact; Germany invades Poland; Britain and France declare war on Germany
1940	Hitler invades Denmark and Norway; Hitler invades the Netherlands, Belgium, Luxembourg, and France; Battle of Britain; Japan occupies French Indochina
1941	Hitler invades the Soviet Union; Japan attacks Pearl Harbor

Study Questions

1. What "lessons" of World War I did policy makers draw at the time? How did those lessons affect their behavior in the interwar period?

2. How did the concept of collective security differ from balance-of-power politics? Is the notion of collective security utopian? If not, how might collective security have worked better during the interwar period?

3. Was World War II inevitable? If so, why, and when? If not, when and how could it have been avoided?

4. To what extent can the outbreak of World War II be attributed to the personalities of the leaders involved?

5. What might be some lessons of the interwar period that might help policy makers avoid war today?

6. Was Japan irrational to attack the United States in 1941?

Notes

1. Woodrow Wilson, quoted in Ray S. Baker and William E. Dodd, eds., *The Public Papers of Woodrow Wilson: War and Peace*, vol. 1 (New York: Harper, 1927), pp. 182–183.

2. Alexander L. George and Juliette L. George, *Woodrow Wilson and Colonel House* (New York: John Day Co., 1956). See also John Milton Cooper, Jr., *Breaking the Heart of the World: Woodrow Wilson and the Fight for the League of Nations* (Cambridge: Cambridge University Press, 2001).

3. Woodrow Wilson, quoted in Inis L. Claude, *Power and International Relations* (New York: Random House, 1962), p. 104.

4. In fact, the treaty was superseded by agreements signed at the Washington, D.C., conference that recognized Japan's great-power status. Britain's decision to terminate the treaty was influenced heavily by the Canadian government's fear that renewal would alienate the United States. Phillips Payson O'Brien, "Britain and the End of the Anglo-Japanese Alliance," in Phillips Payson O'Brien, ed., *The Anglo-Japanese Alliance, 1902–1922* (London: Routledge Curzon, 2003), pp. 264–284.

5. Quoted in F. P. Walters, *A History of the League of Nations* (London: Oxford University Press, 1952), p. 653.

6. A. J. P. Taylor, *The Origins of the Second World War*, 2nd ed. (Greenwich, CT: Fawcett, 1961).

7. Ibid., p. xvi.

8. Ian Kershaw, "Hitler and the Nazi Dictatorship," in Mary Fulbrook, ed., *German History Since 1800* (London: Edward Arnold, 1997), p. 336.

9. Hitler has been the subject of numerous biographies and personality studies, and of course any history of World War II will discuss Hitler in detail. Particularly valuable for its insight, and also particularly well written, is a relatively old biography at this point: Alan Bullock, *Hitler: A Study in Tyranny*, abr. ed. (New York: Harper & Row, 1971). The best genuine psychobiography—carefully researched, yet appropriately cautious about the conclusions it draws—is Fritz Redlick, *Hitler: Diagnosis of a Destructive Prophet* (New York: Oxford University Press, 1999).

10. Adolf Hitler, quoted in Gordon Craig, *Germany, 1866–1945* (New York: Oxford University Press, 1978), p. 712.

11. Bullock, *Hitler*, p. 190; John Toland, *Adolf Hitler* (Garden City, NY: Doubleday, 1976), pp. 467–469; Sidney Aster, *1939: The Making of the Second World War* (New York: Simon and Schuster, 1973), p. 235.

12. Dean Acheson, quoted in Scott Sagan, "The Origins of the Pacific War," in Robert I. Rotberg and Theodore K. Rabb, eds., *The Origin and Prevention of Major Wars* (New York: Cambridge University Press, 1989), pp. 335–336.

13. Sagan, "The Origins of the Pacific War," p. 325.

14. Ko Tsukada, quoted in Scott Sagan, "Deterrence and Decision: An Historical Critique of Modern Deterrence Theory" (Ph.D. thesis, Harvard University, 1983), p. 280.

15. Stephen R. Rock, *Appeasement in International Politics* (Lexington: University Press of Kentucky, 2000), pp. 25–47.

16. Robert J. Caputi, *Neville Chamberlain and Appeasement* (Selinsgrove, PA: Susquehanna University Press, 2000), p. 39.

17. Neville Chamberlain, *In Search of Peace: Speeches 1937–38* (London: Hutchinson, n.d.), p. 59.

18. David P. Calleo, *The German Problem Reconsidered: Germany and the World Order, 1870 to the Present* (Cambridge: Cambridge University Press, 1978), p. 6.

Chapter 5
The Cold War

Winston Churchill, Franklin Roosevelt, and Josef Stalin at Yalta, 1945

Learning Objectives

5.1 Define deterrence and containment, and articulate the relationship between them.

5.2 Distinguish traditionalist, revisionist, and postrevisionist explanations of the Cold War.

5.3 Assess the U.S. war in Vietnam both from a pragmatic perspective (as an attempt at containment) as well as from a moral perspective.

5.4 Assess the role of personalities, ideas, economic trends, and nuclear weapons in ending the Cold War peacefully.

Given its violent first half, a most remarkable feature of the second half of the twentieth century was the absence of World War III. Instead, there was a *cold war*, a period of intense hostility without actual war. The hostility was so intense that many expected armed conflict between the superpowers. Fighting occurred, but it was on the peripheries and not directly between the United States and the Soviet Union. The Cold War lasted four decades, from 1947 to 1989. The height of the Cold War was from 1947 to 1963, when there were few serious negotiations between the United States and the Soviet Union. There were not even any summit meetings between 1945 and 1955. In 1952, George Kennan, the U.S. ambassador in Moscow, compared his isolation in the American embassy to his experience of being interned during World War II in Berlin. The later phases of the Cold War in the 1970s and 1980s were very different. The Americans and Soviets had many contacts, and they constantly negotiated arms control. The end of the Cold War was sudden and surprising, and quickly followed changes in Soviet policies after Mikhail Gorbachev came to power in 1985. Soviet hegemony over Eastern Europe collapsed in 1989, and the Soviet Union itself disintegrated in 1991.

Deterrence and Containment

5.1   Define deterrence and containment, and articulate the relationship between them.

Why did the Cold War not turn hot? There are several answers to that question, as we shall shortly see. Because of its unusual trajectory, the Cold War offers a unique perspective on international relations, and it illuminates the dynamics of two foreign policy choices that were made: the choice to *deter* and the choice to *contain*. To deter is to dissuade through fear. Although frequently associated with the Cold War, deterrence was not a new concept in international politics. Throughout history, countries built armies, formed alliances, and issued threats to deter other countries from attacking. During the Cold War and with the advent of nuclear weapons, the superpowers attempted to maintain peace more by dissuading an attack by threatening painful retaliation than by preparing to defend against an attack after it had occurred. Cold War deterrence depended on the maintenance of large nuclear arsenals, but it was also an extension of balance-of-power logic. Deterrence by nuclear threat was one way that each superpower tried to prevent the other from gaining advantage and hence upsetting the balance of power between them. As we shall see, deterrence often aggravated the tension between the United States and the Soviet Union, and it is not necessarily easy to demonstrate that deterrence worked. There is always the danger of spurious causation. If a professor said that her lectures kept elephants out of the classroom, it would be difficult to disprove her claim if no elephants ever came to class. We can test such claims by using counterfactuals: How likely is it that elephants would come to class if someone else had been lecturing? Similarly, what provides a better explanation for peace during the Cold War: nuclear deterrence or an absence of aggressive designs? We knew during the Cold War that the United States had no desire for military conquest, but Americans assumed that the Soviets did. Now that Soviet Cold War archives are open, it appears that Soviet leaders were just as uncertain of U.S. intentions as Americans were of theirs.

Fearing Soviet expansionism, the United States practiced *containment*, a specific policy of surrounding the Soviet Union with U.S. allies and U.S. bases and of promoting a liberal economic and political world order outside of the Soviet sphere of influence. But like deterrence, containment did not originate with the Cold War, even though the term did. Containment has been a tool of foreign policy for centuries. In the eighteenth century, the conservative monarchical states of Europe attempted to contain the ideology of liberty and equality espoused by the French Revolution, and even earlier, the Catholic Church in the Counter-Reformation attempted to contain the spread of the Reformation and the ideals of Martin Luther. There are different forms of containment. It can be offensive or defensive. It can use military power in the form of war or alliances, it can use economic power in the form of trading blocs or sanctions, and it can use soft power in the form of promoting ideas and values. During the Cold War, the United States wavered between an expansive policy of containing communism and a more limited policy of containing the Soviet Union; but throughout, it used a combination of hard and soft power resources.

Follow Up

- Alexander L. George and Richard Smoke, *Deterrence in American Foreign Policy* (New York: Columbia University Press, 1974).

- George F. Kennan, "The Sources of Soviet Conduct," *Foreign Affairs* 25:4 (July 1947), pp. 566–582.

Explaining the Cold War

5.2 Distinguish traditionalist, revisionist, and postrevisionist explanations of the Cold War.

Who or what caused the Cold War? Almost since it began, those questions have been the subject of fierce debate among scholars and policy makers. There are three main schools of opinion: *traditionalists*, *revisionists*, and *postrevisionists*.

The *traditionalists* argue that the answer to the question of who started the Cold War is quite simple: Josef Stalin and the Soviet Union. At the end of World War II, U.S. diplomacy was defensive, whereas the Soviets were aggressive and expansive. The Americans only slowly awoke to the nature of the Soviet threat.

What evidence do the traditionalists cite? Immediately after the war, the United States was proposing a universal world order and collective security through the United Nations. The Soviet Union did not take the United Nations very seriously because it wanted to expand and dominate its own sphere of influence in Eastern Europe. After the war, the United States demobilized its troops, whereas the Soviet Union left large armies in Eastern Europe. The United States recognized Soviet interests; for example, when Franklin Roosevelt, Stalin, and Winston Churchill met in February 1945 at Yalta, the Americans went out of their way to accommodate Soviet interests. Stalin, however, did not live up to his agreements, particularly by not allowing free elections in Poland.

Soviet expansionism was further confirmed in the eyes of traditionalists when the Soviet Union was slow to remove its troops from northern Iran after the war. Eventually, they were removed, but only under pressure. In 1948, the communists took over the Czechoslovakian government. The Soviet Union blockaded Berlin in 1948 and 1949, trying to squeeze the Western governments out. And in 1950, communist North Korea's armies invaded South Korea. According to the traditionalists, these events gradually awakened the United States to the threat of communist expansionism and launched the Cold War.

The *revisionists*, who wrote primarily in the 1960s and early 1970s, believe that the Cold War was caused by American rather than Soviet expansionism. Their evidence is that at the end of World War II the world was not really bipolar: The Soviets were much weaker than the United States, which was strengthened by the war and had nuclear weapons, whereas the Soviets did not. The Soviet Union lost up to 30 million people during World War II, and industrial production was only half its 1939 level. Stalin told U.S. ambassador Averell Harriman in October 1945 that the Soviets would turn inward to repair their domestic damage. What is more, say the revisionists, is that Stalin's external behavior early in the postwar period was quite moderate: In China, Stalin tried to restrain Mao Zedong's communists from taking power; in the Greek civil war, he tried to restrain the Greek communists; and he allowed noncommunist governments to exist in Hungary, Czechoslovakia, and Finland.

Revisionists come in two varieties that stress the first and second levels of analysis. Level one revisionists stress the importance of individuals and claim that Roosevelt's death in April 1945 was a critical event, because U.S. policy toward the Soviet Union became harsher after President Harry S. Truman took office. In May 1945, the United States so precipitously cut off the lend-lease program of wartime aid that some ships bound for Soviet ports had to turn around in midocean. At the Potsdam Conference near Berlin in July 1945, Truman tried to intimidate Stalin by mentioning the atomic bomb. In the United States, the Democratic Party gradually shifted from the left and center to the right. In 1948, Truman fired Henry Wallace, his secretary of agriculture, who urged better relations with the Soviets. At the same time, James Forrestal, Truman's new secretary of defense, was a strong anticommunist. These revisionists say that these personnel changes help explain why the United States became so anti-Soviet.

The level two revisionists have a different answer. They see the problem not in individuals, but in the nature of U.S. capitalism. Joyce and Gabriel Kolko, as well as William A. Williams, for example, argue that the U.S. economy required expansionism and that the United States planned to make the world safe not for democracy but for capitalism.[1] American economic hegemony could not tolerate any country that might try to organize an autonomous economic area. U.S. leaders feared a repeat of the 1930s, because without external trade, there would be another Great Depression. According to level two revisionists, the Marshall Plan of aid to Europe (discussed below) was simply a way to expand the U.S. economy. The Soviets were correct to reject it as a threat to their sphere of influence in Eastern Europe. In Williams's words, Americans always favored an open-door policy in the international economy because they expected to walk through it.

The *postrevisionists* of the late 1970s and 1980s, as exemplified by historian John Lewis Gaddis, have yet another explanation that focuses on the structural level.[2] They argue that the traditionalists and revisionists are both wrong because nobody was to blame for starting the Cold War. It was inevitable, or nearly so, because of the bipolar structure of the postwar balance of power. In 1939, there was a multipolar world with seven major powers, but after the destruction wrought by World War II, only two superpowers were left: the United States and the Soviet Union. Bipolarity plus the postwar weakness of the European states created a power vacuum into which the United States and the Soviet Union were drawn. They were bound to come into conflict; therefore, say the postrevisionists, it is pointless to look for blame.

Postrevisionists also note that the Soviets and the Americans had different kinds of goals at the end of the war. The Soviets were more concerned with securing control of territory—both home territory and a buffer sphere of influence—whereas the United States was primarily interested in setting up a liberal, rule-governed international order. American *milieu goals,* in other words, clashed with the Soviets' tangible possession goals. The United States promoted the global UN system; the Soviets worked to consolidate control of Eastern Europe. But these differences were no reason for Americans to feel sanctimonious, say the postrevisionists, because the United States benefited from the United Nations and, with a majority of allies voting, was not very constrained by it. The Soviets may have had a sphere of influence in Eastern Europe, but the United States also had a sphere of influence in the Western Hemisphere and Western Europe.

The United States and the Soviet Union were both bound to expand, say the postrevisionists, not because of the economic determinism that the revisionists stress, but because of the age-old security dilemma of states in an anarchic system. Neither could allow the other to dominate Europe any more than Athens could afford to let the Corinthians gain control of Corcyra's navy. As evidence, postrevisionists cite Stalin's comment to a Yugoslav leader, Milovan Djilas, in 1945: "This war is not as in the past; whoever occupies a territory also imposes on it his own social system. Everyone imposes his own system as far as his army can reach."[3] In other words, in an ideological bipolar world, a powerful state would use its military power within its sphere of influence to reshape other societies in its image to ensure its own security. As Roosevelt wrote in a letter to Stalin in the fall of 1944, "In this global war there is literally no question, political or military, in which the United States is not interested."[4] Given this bipolar structure, say the postrevisionists, a spiral of hostility set in: Hard lines in one country bred hard lines in the other. Both began to perceive the enemy as analogous to Hitler in the 1930s. As perceptions became more rigid, the Cold War deepened.

Since the end of the Cold War, a modest flow of documents from formerly inaccessible Soviet archives has given new vigor to the debate over which side started the confrontation. Gaddis, for example, has become increasingly convinced that the Soviet Union was primarily responsible for the onset and the nature of the superpower conflict. He cites the ideological rigidity of Stalin and other Soviet leaders as well as the Kremlin's equally rigid commitment to maintaining a formal empire in its sphere of influence. Gaddis's move back toward a traditionalist viewpoint has garnered a skeptical reception in some scholarly quarters, guaranteeing that the debate will continue into the foreseeable future.

Roosevelt's Policies

Franklin Roosevelt wanted to avoid the mistakes of World War I, so instead of a Versailles-like peace, he demanded Germany's unconditional surrender. He wanted a liberal trade system to avoid the protectionism that had damaged the world economy in the 1930s and contributed to the onset of war. The United States would avoid its tendency toward isolationism that had been so damaging in the 1930s. It would join a new and stronger League of Nations in the form of a United Nations with a powerful Security Council. Cordell Hull, U.S. secretary of state during most of the war, was a committed Wilsonian, and public opinion in the United States was strongly in favor of the United Nations.

To promote his great design, Roosevelt needed to maintain bipartisan domestic support for his international position. Externally, he needed to reassure Stalin that the Soviet Union's security needs would be met by joining the United Nations. Roosevelt has been accused of a naive approach to postwar planning. His design was not naive, but some of his tactics were. He placed too much faith in the United Nations, overestimated the likelihood of American isolationism, and, most importantly, misunderstood Stalin. Roosevelt thought that he could treat Stalin the way he would treat a fellow American politician, throwing his arm around him, bonding politician to politician.

Although Roosevelt misinterpreted Stalin, he did not sell out U.S. interests at the Yalta Conference in 1945, as some later claimed. Roosevelt was not naive in all aspects of his policy. He tried to tie economic aid to political concessions by the Soviets and refused to share the secrets of the atomic bomb with them. He was simply realistic about who would have troops in Eastern Europe at the end of the war and, therefore, who would have leverage in that region. Roosevelt's mistakes were in thinking that Stalin saw the world his way, that he understood domestic politics in the United States, and that the same American political skills in which a leader blurred differences and appealed to friendship would work in dealing with Stalin.

Stalin's Policies

Stalin's immediate postwar plans were to tighten domestic control. World War II did tremendous damage to the Soviet Union, not just the terrible losses of life and industry already described, but also to the ideology of communism. Many in the Soviet Union collaborated with the Germans because of their deep resentment over the harshness of communist rule. Germany's invasion seriously weakened Stalin's control. Indeed, Stalin had to increase his appeals to Russian nationalism during the war because the weakened communist ideology was insufficient to motivate his people. (In the Soviet Union at the time, and in Russia today, the war is called "The Great Patriotic War.") Stalin's isolationist policy at the end of the war was designed to cut off external influences from Europe and the United States. Stalin used the United States as an objective enemy as a way of cultivating mistrust of outsiders and increasing central control over the Soviet people. But it does not follow that Stalin wanted the Cold War that actually developed.

Stalin preferred some cooperation, especially if it helped him pursue his goals in Eastern Europe and brought him some economic assistance from the United States. As a good communist, he believed that the United States would have to give him economic assistance because the capitalist system had to export capital due to insufficient demand at home. Stalin also believed that in ten or fifteen years, the next crisis of the capitalist system would come along and that the Soviet Union would have recovered at that time and be ready to benefit in the inevitable conflict with the capitalists.

In foreign policy terms, Stalin wanted to protect himself at home as well as maintain the gains the Soviet Union had made in Eastern Europe from the 1939 pact with Hitler. Stalin also wanted to probe soft spots, something better done when there is no crisis. In 1941, Stalin told the British foreign minister, Anthony Eden, that he preferred arithmetic to algebra; in other words, he wanted a practical rather than a theoretical approach. When Churchill proposed a formula on the postwar division of influence in the Balkans—that is, some countries under British control, some under Soviet control, and others 50/50—Stalin was quite receptive to the idea. Some of Stalin's early caution in supporting communist governments right away in China, Czechoslovakia, and Hungary fit quite well with this arithmetic rather than algebraic approach to achieving his objectives. Stalin was a committed communist who, although he saw the world through the lens of communism, often used pragmatic tactics.

Phases of the Conflict

The early stages of the Cold War can be divided into three phases: 1945–1947, the prelude and slide into the Cold War; 1947–1949, the onset of the Cold War; and 1950–1963, the height of the Cold War.

Neither Stalin nor Truman was looking for a cold war. At the end of World War II, Truman sent Roosevelt's former aide Harry Hopkins to Moscow to see if some arrangements could be worked out. Even after the Potsdam Conference, Truman continued to see Stalin as a moderate. Indeed, as late as 1949, he compared Stalin to his old friend Boss Pendergast in Kansas City. In 1946, Kennan, writing from Moscow as the U.S. embassy's chargé d'affaires, was trying to warn American decision makers about Stalin's true nature and intentions, and Churchill gave a famous speech in Fulton, Missouri, warning that an "iron curtain" was descending across Europe. Although Secretary of State James Byrnes was still trying to negotiate a postwar treaty with the Soviets, Truman asked his aide Clark Clifford to prepare a report on what the Soviets were really planning. Clifford talked with a variety of people and concluded that Kennan was correct: The Soviets were going to expand whenever they found an inexpensive opportunity. When Truman received the report in December 1946, however, he told Clifford that he did not want its results widely known because he was still trying to follow Roosevelt's great design and had not yet developed a new strategy.

Six issues contributed to the eventual change of U.S. strategy and the onset of the Cold War. One was Soviet actions in Poland and Eastern Europe. Poland, of course, had been one of the precipitating causes of World War II, and the United States believed that Stalin broke a clear commitment to hold free elections in Poland after the war. It was not clear what Stalin had agreed to do, however. When Stalin and Roosevelt met at Tehran in 1943, Roosevelt raised the Polish issue, but he appealed to Stalin in the context of the looming 1944 American election: There were many Polish-American voters, and he needed to tell them that there would be elections in Poland after the war. Stalin, who never worried about elections in the Soviet Union, did not take Roosevelt's concerns seriously. The February 1945 Yalta agreement was also somewhat ambiguous, and Stalin stretched the meaning as far as he could by setting up a puppet government in Warsaw after Soviet troops had driven out the Germans. The Americans felt cheated, but Stalin believed that they would adjust to the reality that Soviet troops had liberated Poland.

Second, in May 1945, the lend-lease aid program was abruptly stopped, and the economic relationship between the United States and the Soviet Union became strained. The precipitous termination of lend-lease was to some extent a bureaucratic mistake, but the overall situation was not improved when in February 1946 the United States refused Soviet requests for loans. The Soviets interpreted both acts as hostile.

Germany was a third problem. At the Yalta meeting, the United States and the Soviet Union agreed that Germany should pay $20 billion in reparations, with half going to the Soviets. The details of how and when the payments would be made were not worked out at Yalta, although both sides agreed that they would be negotiated later. At the Potsdam meeting in July 1945, the Soviets demanded their $10 billion; furthermore, they wanted it from the western zones of Germany that the Americans, British, and French had occupied. Harry Truman, worried about how Germany would be reconstructed, said that if the Soviets wanted to take $10 billion out of Germany, they should take it out of the eastern zone they occupied; if there was anything left over after the reconstruction of the western side of Germany, he would let the Soviets know. Thus began a series of divisions between the United States and the Soviet Union about how to reconstruct Germany. The Americans, along with the British and French, created a single currency in the western zones (the deutsche mark), starting the process of West German integration, which in turn caused the Soviets to tighten control of the eastern zone of Germany.

East Asia was a fourth issue. The Soviets were neutral in the Pacific war until the very last week. Then the Soviets declared war and opportunistically seized from Japan Outer Manchuria, southern Sakhalin Island, and the entire Kurile Island chain. At Potsdam, the Soviets asked for an occupation zone in Japan, like the U.S. occupation zone in Germany. Truman's response was, in effect, that the Soviets had arrived at the party late, so they would get no zone. From an American point of view, this stance seemed perfectly reasonable, but the situation reminded the Soviets of Eastern Europe, where the Americans wanted free elections and influence, but the Soviet armies had arrived there first. So, the Soviets saw the Far Eastern situation as analogous to Eastern Europe, whereas the Americans saw it as one more example of the Soviets pressing for their own expansion.

A fifth issue was the atomic bomb. Roosevelt had decided not to share the secret of the atomic bomb with the Soviet Union. Most historians now agree that Truman dropped the bomb on Hiroshima and Nagasaki primarily to bring a quick end to the war with Japan, not to intimidate the Soviet Union, as some revisionists have claimed. But he did expect the bomb to have some political effects. At the Potsdam meeting, when Truman told Stalin that the United States had an atomic bomb, Stalin remained poker-faced and seemingly unimpressed. Of course, Stalin already knew about it from his own spies, but his equanimity was a bit of a jolt to the Americans. In 1946, when the United States set forth the Baruch Plan for UN control of nuclear weapons, Stalin rejected it because he wanted to build his own bomb. As he saw it, a bomb under international control would still be a U.S. bomb because only the Americans knew how to build it. Stalin believed that it would be far better for Soviet security to have their own, which they eventually developed in 1949.

The sixth issue concerned countries in the eastern Mediterranean and the Middle East, where the British had been influential before World War II. After the war, several things occurred. First, the Soviets refused to remove their troops from northern Iran in March 1946. The United States supported Iran in a debate within the United Nations. The Soviets eventually moved out, but not without a good deal of bitterness. The Soviet Union also began to put pressure on Turkey, its neighbor to the south, at the same time that the communists seemed to be winning the civil war in Greece. Once again, the West believed that the Soviets were attempting to expand.

These six issues were real, although some misperceptions were involved in almost all of them. Could they have been solved by negotiation and appeasement? Would appeasement have worked? Probably not. Kennan argued that Stalin was intent on probing any soft spots. Appeasement would have been interpreted as a soft spot and invited more probing. In June 1946, Maxim Litvinov, the former Soviet foreign minister, warned an American counterpart against any concessions, because the root cause of the tension was "the ideological conception prevailing here that conflict between Communist and capitalist worlds is inevitable." Concessions would merely lead "to the West's being faced, after a more or less short time, with the next series of demands."[5] Appeasement probably would not have worked, but harder bargaining might have limited some of the events that led to the onset of the Cold War. A tactical appeal to Stalin's pragmatism from a firmer U.S. position, plus a willingness to negotiate, might have worked out better in that early period, from 1945–1947.

The second phase, the onset of the Cold War from 1947–1949, followed from the problems in Greece and Turkey (Figure 5.1). Britain, severely weakened by World War II, believed that it could no longer provide security in the eastern Mediterranean. The United States had to decide whether to let a vacuum develop or to replace British power by providing assistance to Greece and Turkey. This latter option involved a considerable break from traditional U.S. foreign policy. Truman was not sure that American public opinion would support such a move. There was still fear that isolationism would be the mainstay of America's postwar foreign policy. Truman asked Senator Arthur Vandenberg, the Republican leader from Michigan, whether the Senate would go along with aiding Greece and Turkey. Vandenberg said that Truman would have to "scare the hell out of them" to get congressional support for this break with traditional U.S. policy. Thus, when Truman explained the policy change, he did not talk about the need to maintain a balance of power in the eastern Mediterranean by providing aid to Greece and Turkey. Instead, he talked about the need to protect free people everywhere. This moralistic, ideological explanation for U.S. assistance became known as the Truman Doctrine.

Kennan, by then back in the State Department, objected to this ideological approach to formulating foreign policy, arguing that it was too open-ended and would get the United States into trouble. Indeed, there were enormous ambiguities in the policy of containment that flowed from the Truman Doctrine. Was the United States interested in containing Soviet power or communist ideology? At the beginning, containing Soviet power and containing communist ideology seemed to be the same, but later in the Cold War when the communist movement split, the ambiguities became important.

Was Truman wrong to exaggerate the sense of threat and the ideological rationale for the policy change? Some observers believe that it is harder to change

Figure 5.1 The Early Days of the Cold War in Europe

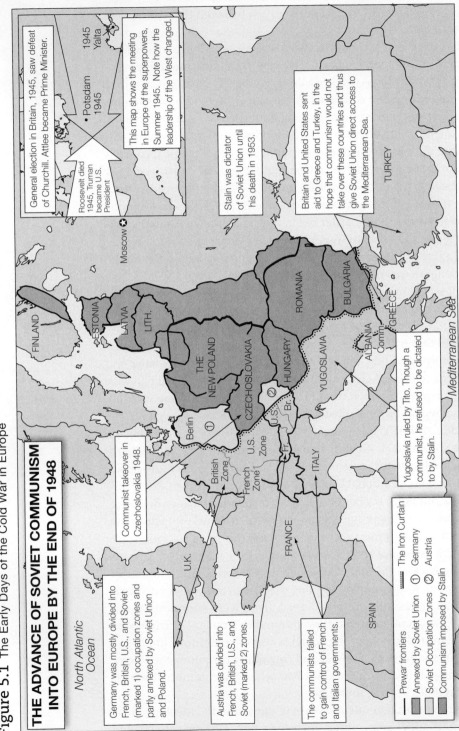

THE ADVANCE OF SOVIET COMMUNISM INTO EUROPE BY THE END OF 1948

General election in Britain, 1945, saw defeat of Churchill. Attlee became Prime Minister.

This map shows the meeting in Europe of the superpowers, Summer 1945. Note how the leadership of the West changed.

Roosevelt died 1945, Truman became U.S. President

Stalin was dictator of Soviet Union until his death in 1953.

Britain and United States sent aid to Greece and Turkey, in the hope that communism would not take over these countries and thus give Soviet Union direct access to the Mediterranean Sea.

Yugoslavia ruled by Tito. Though a communist, he refused to be dictated to by Stalin.

Germany was mostly divided into French, British, U.S., and Soviet (marked 1) occupation zones and partly annexed by Soviet Union and Poland.

Communist takeover in Czechoslovakia 1948.

Austria was divided into French, British, U.S., and Soviet (marked 2) zones.

The communists failed to gain control of French and Italian governments.

Prewar frontiers

- - - - - The Iron Curtain
① Germany
② Austria

Annexed by Soviet Union

Soviet Occupation Zones

Communism imposed by Stalin

public opinion in democracies than it is to change policies in totalitarian countries. They argue that exaggeration speeds up the process of change in democracies. It is necessary to tug harder on the reins when trying to turn an unruly team of horses. Regardless of whether the exaggeration was necessary, it helped change the nature of the Cold War.

In June 1947, Secretary of State George Marshall announced a plan for economic aid to Europe. The initial Marshall Plan proposal invited the Soviet Union and the Eastern Europeans to join if they wished, but Stalin put strong pressure on the Eastern Europeans not to do so. Stalin saw the Marshall Plan not as American generosity, but as an economic battering ram to destroy his security barrier in Eastern Europe. When Czechoslovakia indicated that it would like U.S. aid, Stalin tightened the screws in Eastern Europe, and the communists took full power in Czechoslovakia in February 1948.

Truman heard echoes of the 1930s in these events. He began to worry that Stalin would become another Hitler. The United States advanced plans for West German currency reform; Stalin replied by blockading the Western occupation zones in Berlin. The United States answered with an airlift and began plans for an anticommunist alliance, the North Atlantic Treaty Organization (NATO). Hostility began to escalate in a tit-for-tat fashion.

The most rigid phase of the Cold War occurred after two shocks in 1949: The Soviet Union exploded an atomic bomb, much sooner than some U.S. leaders thought they could; and the Chinese Communist Party took control of mainland China, forcing the Nationalists to retreat to the island of Taiwan. The alarm in Washington was illustrated by a secret government document, National Security Council Report 68 (NSC-68), which forecast a Soviet attack in four to five years as part of a plan for global domination. NSC-68 called for a vast increase in U.S. defense expenditures. Beset by budget problems, Truman resisted NSC-68 until June 1950, when North Korea's troops stormed into South Korea.

The effect of the Korean War was like pouring gasoline onto a modest fire (Figure 5.2). It confirmed all the worst Western suspicions about Stalin's expansionist ambitions and led to a huge increase in the U.S. defense budget. Why did Stalin permit North Korea to invade South Korea? Nikita Khrushchev gives an explanation in his memoirs: Kim Il Sung, the North Korean leader, pressed Stalin for the opportunity to unify the peninsula. The United States had said that Korea was outside its defense perimeter; Secretary of State Dean Acheson had articulated this position, and the Joint Chiefs of Staff had planned accordingly. To Stalin, Korea looked like a soft spot. But when North Korea actually attacked South Korea, Truman responded in a knee-jerk rather than a calculating way: Truman remembered Hitler moving into the Rhineland and recalled the maxim that aggression must be resisted everywhere. Calculated plans about defense perimeters were overshadowed by the historical analogies triggered by North Korea's invasion. The United States was able to mobilize the UN Security Council to endorse collective security (which was possible because the Soviet Union was then boycotting the Security Council over its failure at that point to give

Figure 5.2 The Korean War

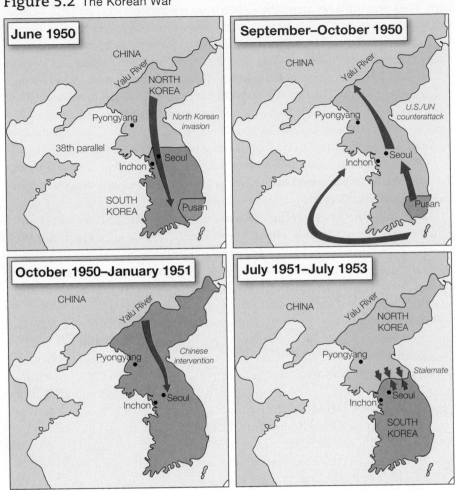

the communist government in Beijing, instead of the Nationalist government in Taiwan, the China seat) and sent troops to Korea under the UN flag to push the communists back above the thirty-eighth parallel that bisected the peninsula and had previously divided North and South.

Roosevelt and Stalin: Mutual Misunderstandings

The President acted as if genuine cooperation as the Americans understood the term were possible both during and after the war. Roosevelt apparently had forgotten, if indeed he ever knew, that in Stalin's eyes, he was not all that different from Hitler, both of them being heads of powerful capitalist states whose long-term ambitions clashed with those of the Kremlin.

—*William Taubman, Stalin's American Policy*[6]

At first, North Korea's armies swept down the peninsula almost to the tip. In September 1950, however, a U.S. amphibious landing at Inchon, halfway up the peninsula, routed the North Koreans. Had the United States stopped there, it could have claimed victory by restoring the preinvasion status quo, but Truman succumbed to domestic pressures to pursue the retreating communist troops north of the thirty-eighth parallel. As the Americans approached the Yalu River, which divides Korea from China, the Chinese communists intervened, pushing the UN troops back to the middle of the peninsula. There the battle stalemated bloodily for three years until a truce was signed in 1953. The United States had become embroiled with China, and communism appeared to be monolithic. At home, the frustrating war led to domestic division and the rise of McCarthyism, named after the harsh and poorly founded accusations of domestic communist subversion made by Senator Joseph McCarthy of Wisconsin. The Cold War blocs tightened and communication nearly ceased.

Inevitability?

Was the onset of the Cold War inevitable? The postrevisionists are correct if we relax the interpretation of inevitability to mean "highly probable." The bipolar structure made it likely that both sides would be sucked into a power vacuum in Europe and find it difficult to disengage. The intense ideological climate hampered the working of the United Nations, restricted clear communication, and contributed to the immoderate process of the international system. Under such systemic conditions, conflicts would have arisen over the six issues just identified, or some others, and proven difficult to resolve.

The postrevisionists rely too heavily, however, on systemic explanation. Perhaps some cold war was inevitable, but its depth was not. After all, there were different degrees of hostility in different phases, and because the bipolarity of the system did not change until 1989, neorealist structural explanations cannot account for the different phases or varying depth of the hostility. That is where individuals and domestic politics matter. Leaders' personalities and the domestic political contexts in which they operated have to be considered to fully understand the Cold War. The revisionists are right to focus on domestic questions, but they are wrong to focus so strongly on economic determinism. More

Korea and NSC-68

The purpose of NSC-68 was to so bludgeon the mass mind of "top government" that not only could the President make a decision but that the decision could be carried out. Even so, it is doubtful whether anything like what happened in the next few years could have been done had not the Russians been stupid enough to have instigated the attack against South Korea and opened the "hate America" campaign.

—Secretary of State Dean Acheson, Present at the Creation[7]

important was the role of ideology and exaggeration in domestic politics. Stalin used ideology because of Soviet domestic problems after the war, and Truman exaggerated the nature of the communist threat to rally support for changing U.S. foreign policy. The use of 1930s analogies helped reinforce rigidity on both sides. Ironically, alternative strategies at different times might have alleviated the depths of hostility. For example, if the United States had followed Kennan's advice and responded more firmly in 1945–1947 and had tried more pragmatic negotiation and communication from 1947–1950, Cold War tensions might not have risen to the extent they did in the early 1950s.

Levels of Analysis

The origins of the Cold War can be characterized in terms of the different images or levels of analysis as illustrated in Figure 5.3.

In the nineteenth century, Alexis de Tocqueville (1805–1859) predicted that Russia and the United States were bound to become two great continental-scale giants in the world. Realists might thus predict that these two would become locked in some form of conflict. And, of course, in 1917, the Bolshevik Revolution added an ideological layer to the conflict. When President Woodrow Wilson first heard of the Russian Revolution, he congratulated the Russian people for their democratic spirit. But it did not take long before the Americans were

Figure 5.3 Causes of the Cold War

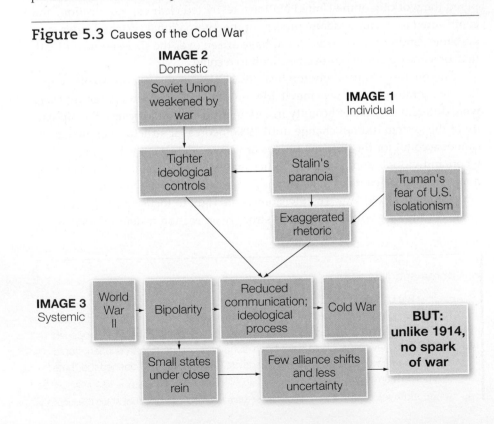

accusing the Bolsheviks of regicide, expropriation, and cooperation with Germany in World War I. The United States added a small contingent of troops to an Allied intervention, allegedly to keep the Russians in the war against Germany, but the Soviets saw it as an attempt to strangle communism in its cradle. Despite these differences, the United States and the Soviet Union avoided serious conflict in the interwar period and became allies in the early 1940s. The bipolarity that followed the collapse of all the other great powers in World War II and the resulting power vacuum changed the relationship. Earlier, there had been distrust between the two countries, but they distrusted each other at a distance. Before World War II, they could avoid each other, but after 1945, they were face to face, Europe was divided, and deep conflict began after 1947. Some people wonder whether the bipolar structure had to have this effect. After all, the Soviet Union was a land-based power, whereas the United States was a maritime power; why could there not have been a division of labor between the bear and the whale, each staying in its own domain?

The answer is that the key stakes in world politics, the countries that could tip the balance of power, were located on the peripheries of the Soviet Union, particularly Europe and Japan. As Kennan described the situation after the war, there were four great areas of technological and industrial creativity, which, if they were allied one way or the other, could tip the global balance of power: the United States, the Soviet Union, Europe, and Japan.[8] That Europe and Japan became allied with the United States against the Soviet Union was of profound importance.

Systemic explanations predicted conflict, not how deep it would go (see Figure 5.3). For that we need to go beyond systems explanations to look at the state and individual levels of analysis as well as at constructivist explanations. At the state level, the two countries were very different from each other. A thumbnail sketch of the Soviet Union's political culture and its expression in foreign policy would show two influences: Russian and communist. Constructivists point out that Russian political culture emphasized absolutism rather than democracy, a desire for a strong leader, fear of anarchy (Russia had been a large, unwieldy empire, and the fear that anarchy and dissent could lead to disintegration was very real), fear of invasion (Russia was a geographically vulnerable land-based power that had invaded and been invaded by its neighbors many times throughout the centuries), worry or shame about backwardness (ever since Peter the Great, Russians had been trying to prove their vitality in international competition), and secrecy (a desire to hide the seamy side of Russian life). In addition, the communist system treated class rather than individual rights as the basis for justice. The proper role for a person or for a society was to lead the proletariat or working class toward dominance, because that was supposed to be the course of history.

The ideological overlay gave an additional outward thrust to traditional Russian imperialism and resulted in a secret and tightly held foreign policy process. It is interesting to note the strengths and weaknesses of that process. The strengths were evident in 1939 when Stalin was able to sign his nonaggression pact with Hitler so quickly. Public opinion did not constrain him, and he did not have to worry about a bureaucracy holding him back. He was free to rush into the pact with Hitler while the British and French were still dithering about whether or not to deal with him. The opposite side of the same coin became evident in 1941, however, when Hitler attacked the Soviet Union. Stalin was unable to believe that Hitler would do such a thing and went into a deep depression for more than a week. None of his subordinates dared to fill the leadership vacuum, and the result was a delayed response that proved disastrous for Soviet defenses in the early phases of the war.

In contrast, the political culture of the United States emphasized liberal democracy, pluralism, and fragmentation of power. Instead of shame about backwardness, the United States took pride in its technology and expanding economy. For much of its history, it had no real fear of invasion because its neighbors were weak (and therefore vulnerable to American invasion), because it was separated from other great powers by two vast oceans, and because the British navy prevented others from projecting influence into the Western Hemisphere. In terms of secrecy, the United States was so open that government documents often reached the press within a matter of days and weeks. Instead of a class basis for conceptions of justice, there was a strong emphasis on individual justice. The foreign policy that resulted from this political culture was moralistic, was public, and tended to oscillate between inward and outward orientation. The result was that the U.S. foreign policy process often appeared inconsistent and incoherent. But there was an opposite side to this coin, too. The strengths of openness and pluralism often protected the United States from deeper mistakes.

Thus it is not surprising to constructivists that these two societies, so differently organized and with such different foreign policy processes, would confuse each other. We saw examples in the way that both Roosevelt and Truman dealt with Stalin in the 1940s. It was difficult for the Americans to understand the Soviet Union during the Cold War, because it was like a black box. U.S. leaders could see what went in and what came out of the box, but not what happened inside. The Americans confused the Soviets as well. The United States was like a machine that produced so much white noise that it was difficult to hear the true signals clearly. There were too many people saying too many things. Thus, the Soviets were often confused about what the Americans really wanted.

U.S. and Soviet Goals in the Cold War

The Soviets were often accused of being expansionist, of being a revolutionary power rather than a status quo power, but the postrevisionist view is both more subtle and more accurate: The Soviet Union was, in fact, more interested in tangible or possession goals, whereas the United States tended to want intangible or milieu goals. We can see this difference in the demands that Stalin, Churchill, and Roosevelt brought to the bargaining table at Yalta. Stalin had very clear objectives at Yalta: Germany and Poland. Roosevelt wanted the United Nations and an open international economic system. (Churchill wanted the restoration of France to help balance Soviet power in case the Americans went home!) In some ways, Stalin's postwar goals were classic Russian imperialist goals; he wanted to keep the gains he had made in the treaty with Hitler. His wish list would have been familiar to Peter the Great.

Some Americans thought that the Soviets were as expansionist as Hitler in desiring world domination. Others said that the Soviets were basically security oriented, that their expansion was defensive. There were at least two ways in which Soviet expansionism was not like Hitler's. First, it was not bellicist; the Soviets did not want war. When Hitler invaded Poland, he worried that he would be offered another Munich instead of the war he wanted. Another difference was that the Soviet Union was cautiously opportunistic, not recklessly adventuresome. Adventurism was seen as a sin against communism because it might disrupt the natural course of history, which would, in Soviet eyes, result in the inevitable defeat of capitalism. During the Cold War, the Soviet Union was never as bellicose or as reckless as Hitler was.

There are nonetheless problems in portraying Soviet behavior as purely defensive. It can be very hard in a bipolar world to distinguish offense from defense. Certain actions may have defensive motives but may look very threatening to the other side. Moreover, there is a long tradition of defensive expansion, or imperialism. For example, in the nineteenth century, Britain originally went into Egypt to protect the sea routes to India. After it took Egypt, it thought that it had to take the Sudan to protect Egypt and then that it had to take Uganda to protect the Sudan. After it took Uganda, Britain had to take Kenya to build a railway to protect Uganda. The appetite grows with the eating as the security dilemma is used to justify further and further expansion. Soviet communism added an ideological motive of freeing working classes in all areas of the world, which further legitimized expansion. In short, the Soviet Union was expansionist during the Cold War, but cautiously and opportunistically so.

What about U.S. goals? During the Cold War, the U.S. government wanted to contain the Soviet Union, yet the policy of containment involved two large ambiguities. One was the question of the ends: whether to contain Soviet power or to contain communism. The second was a question of means: whether to spend resources to prevent any expansion of Soviet power or just in certain key areas that seemed critical to the balance of power. Those two ambiguities in the ends and means of containment were hotly debated in the period before the Korean War. Kennan dissented from the rather expansive version of containment that Truman proclaimed. Kennan's idea of containment was akin to classical diplomacy. It involved fewer military means and was more selective. A good example was Yugoslavia, which had a communist totalitarian government under Josip Broz Tito. In 1948, Tito split with Stalin over Soviet efforts to control Yugoslavia's foreign policy, including Belgrade's support for the Greek communists. According to an ideologically driven containment policy, the United States should not have helped Yugoslavia, because Yugoslavia was communist. But in a containment policy driven by balance-of-power considerations, the United States should have helped Yugoslavia as a means of weakening Soviet power.

Kennan's View of Containment

> It would be an exaggeration to say that American behavior unassisted and alone could exercise a power of life and death over the Communist movement and bring about the early fall of Soviet power in Russia. But the United States has it in its power to increase enormously the strains under which Soviet policy must operate, to force upon the Kremlin a far greater degree of moderation and circumspection than it has had to observe in recent years, and in this way to promote tendencies which must eventually find their outlet in either the break-up or the gradual mellowing of Soviet power.
>
> —X (George Kennan), *"The Sources of Soviet Conduct"*[9]

That, in fact, is what the United States did. It provided military aid to a totalitarian communist government, even though the Truman Doctrine proclaimed the goal of defending free peoples everywhere. The United States did so for balance-of-power reasons, and the policy put a big dent in Soviet power in Europe.

After the Korean War, however, Kennan's approach to containment lost ground. Then it looked as though the NSC-68 predictions of Soviet expansionism had been justified. Communism seemed monolithic after the Chinese entered the Korean War, and the rhetoric of containment emphasized the ideological goal of preventing the spread of communism. In this context, the United States became involved in Vietnam's civil war.

Follow Up

- Robert J. McMahon, *The Cold War: A Very Short Introduction* (New York: Oxford University Press, 2003).

- John Lewis Gaddis, *The Cold War: A New History* (New York: Penguin, 2005).

Containment in Action: The Vietnam War

5.3 **Assess the U.S. war in Vietnam both from a pragmatic perspective (as an attempt at containment) as well as from a moral perspective.**

For nearly two decades (1955–1973), the United States tried to prevent communist control of Vietnam, at a cost of 58,000 American lives, somewhere between 2 million and 3 million Vietnamese lives, $600 billion, and domestic turmoil that undercut support for the policy of containment itself. In addition to containing communism in South Vietnam, the United States feared that a defeat might weaken the credibility of its global military commitments and thus containment in other parts of the world. Under the leadership of Ho Chi

Minh, Vietnam successfully fought French efforts to reassert colonial control after World War II, and in 1954, an international conference in Geneva partitioned the country into a communist North Vietnam with its capital in Hanoi and a noncommunist South Vietnam with its capital in Saigon (today, Ho Chi Minh City). The Vietnam War began as a civil war between these two governments, with the South Vietnamese government opposing the North's efforts to "unify the country." With the support of the United States, the South successfully blocked a referendum on reunification that had been agreed to at Geneva.

The United States saw the conflict in Cold War terms as aggression by a communist government against a noncommunist government. It feared that if South Vietnam fell, other noncommunist governments in Southeast Asia would topple like a row of dominoes. The North Vietnamese government and its southern allies (the National Liberation Front, or NLF, generally referred to by Americans as the "Viet Cong") viewed the war as a continuation of the struggle against the French for independence and self-determination. After 15 years of fighting, direct U.S. involvement ended with the signing of a peace treaty in Paris in 1973. The war between the North and South continued until Hanoi succeeded in uniting the country in 1975. But rather than toppling local dominoes, a unified Vietnam wound up fighting with its communist neighbors, Cambodia and China. If the United States had correctly interpreted the conflict as being more about nationalism and self-determination than communism, it might have seen the conflict in terms of the balance of power and used a metaphor of checkers rather than dominoes to guide its policy. Ironically, the communist government of Vietnam enjoys good relations with the United States today.

Motives, Means, and Consequences

Quite apart from the question of whether the Vietnam War was smart, in the light of U.S. objectives, is the question of whether it was moral. What principles can be used to judge the Vietnam War morally? Three dimensions of judgment are related to the just war tradition (which, you will recall, we examined in Chapter 1): motives, means, and consequences. All three are important because judging interventions by one dimension alone may yield an incomplete understanding of the conflict and an ethically problematic judgment.

Good intentions alone do not justify an intervention. The writer Norman Podhoretz argued that the United States was right to intervene in Vietnam because the Americans were trying to save the South Vietnamese from totalitarian rule.[10] Here is an analogy: Suppose that a friend offers to drive your child home one night. It is a rainy night; your friend drives too fast and skids off the road, and your daughter is killed. Your friend says, "My intentions were purely good. I wanted to get her home early for a good night's rest." You, however, would no doubt be much more concerned with the consequences of your friend's actions, which were clearly the fault of recklessness. Likewise, Podhoretz's argument that the U.S. action in Vietnam was what he called "imprudent but moral" fails to account either for consequences or means. By the same token, consequences alone would not justify intervention. President Lyndon Johnson's national security advisor, Walt Rostow, argued that the Vietnam War was justified because the evident willingness of the United States to pay enormous costs in terms of blood and treasure to meet its long-standing commitment to South Vietnam demonstrated American credibility and bolstered deterrence in Western Europe. Even if it were true that the Vietnam War had this effect (many foreign leaders were more puzzled than impressed by the U.S. commitment to South Vietnam), it would be a bit like your friend saying that he deserved nothing but praise for driving your daughter home safely even though the only reason he offered was to avoid his obligation to wash the dishes at home (motives) and even though he drove through every red light along the way (means). Finally, means alone do not do the trick. It would be no defense of the Vietnam War if it had been fought strictly legally (which, sadly, was not the case). If your friend killed three pedestrians en route yet he obeyed all speed limits and traffic signals, he would be no worthier of praise than if his goal in driving your daughter home was to avoid washing dishes. In evaluating interventions, we have to consider motives, means, *and* consequences.

In the Vietnam War, it was not enough that the United States tried to save South Vietnam from the horrors perpetrated by North Vietnamese communists. Even if the cause were just, the means used are a different proposition. Some questions to ask are: Were there alternatives? Was intervention a last resort? Were there efforts to protect innocent life? Was it proportional—did the punishment fit the crime, so to speak—or was it excessive? To what extent was there attention to international multilateral procedures that might have checked the human tendency to weight these considerations in one's own favor? What about the consequences? What about the prospects for success? What about the danger of unintended consequences because a local situation was not well enough understood, because of the difficulty of differentiating between civilians and guerrillas? As obvious as it seems, we must still emphasize the need to be careful about situations where there is enormous complexity and very long causal chains. Motives, means, and consequences must all be considered before judgments can be made.

Consider how the policy of containment led to intervention in Vietnam. As we saw above, in the early stages just after World War II, the issue was whether the United States should step into Britain's place in the eastern Mediterranean to defend Turkey and Greece against possible Soviet encroachment. U.S. policy makers struggled with how to frame this intervention to the American people. Marshall was quite cautious. Others, such as Acheson, then under Marshall, and

Vandenberg, the Republican senator, pushed for a moral argument to appeal to the American people's belief in a universal right to freedom. Consequently, when Truman explained his actions in the Truman Doctrine, he talked of protecting free people everywhere.

The diplomat Kennan, who had warned against Stalin's aggressive plans, became disillusioned as containment became highly ideological. He argued that the United States was trying to contain Soviet power and therefore that anything that balanced Soviet power without intervening directly with U.S. troops was for the good. But those who took the more ideological view said that the United States should contain communism directly, through more aggressive means. Over time, the argument for balancing Soviet power gave way to a broader view of containment as keeping the world free from communism. In Vietnam, this view caused leaders to underestimate national differences among communist states. The United States began to think that it had to contain Chinese and Soviet power and the spread of communist ideology. By the time the doctrine of containment moved from the eastern Mediterranean in 1947 to Southeast Asia in the 1950s, it had become a justification for an overly ambitious and ill-fated intervention.

Follow Up

- David A. Welch, *Painful Choices: A Theory of Foreign Policy Change* (Princeton, NJ: Princeton University Press, 2005), pp. 117–160.

- Richard J. Regan, *Just War: Principles and Cases* (Washington, DC: Catholic University of America Press, 1996), pp. 136–150.

Chronology: American Involvement in Vietnam

1954	In response to the French defeat at Dien Bien Phu, President Dwight D. Eisenhower articulates the "domino theory," warning that if Vietnam falls to the communists, other states in Southeast Asia will follow
1956	
Summer	Following French withdrawal, the U.S. Military Assistance Advisor Group begins training South Vietnamese military forces
July	Vietnam fails to hold elections, as required under the Geneva Convention Agreements of 1954

1961	*By year's end, U.S. assistance to the South exceeds $1 million a day*
January	Soviet premier Nikita Khrushchev announces Soviet support for "wars of national liberation"; North Vietnamese president Ho Chi Minh interprets it as a green light to escalate the communist assault on South Vietnam
May	President John F. Kennedy deploys 400 Green Berets to serve as "advisors" to the South Vietnamese military regarding counterinsurgency warfare
1963	*As of December 31, approximately 16,000 U.S. military advisors are stationed in Vietnam*
November 1	With the tacit approval of the United States, South Vietnamese troops surround the presidential palace in Saigon; on November 2, President Ngo Dinh Diem is assassinated
November 22–24	Following the assassination of Kennedy, Lyndon Johnson becomes president and says that the United States will "not lose" Vietnam during his administration
1964	*The cost of U.S. support to the Vietnamese Army exceeds $2 million per day; by December 31, approximately 23,000 U.S. military advisors are deployed to South Vietnam*
August 2	Three North Vietnamese patrol boats open fire on the USS *Maddox* in the Gulf of Tonkin
August 7	Congress overwhelmingly approves the Gulf of Tonkin resolution authorizing Johnson to "take all necessary steps, including the use of armed force, … to prevent further aggression"
1965	*As of January, public support for U.S. involvement in Vietnam is approximately 80 percent; by the end of the year, approximately 184,000 U.S. troops are deployed to Vietnam*
March	Johnson orders the start of Operation Rolling Thunder, a three-year bombing campaign, and authorizes ground combat patrols
December	U.S. Secretary of Defense Robert McNamara warns Johnson that time favors the North and that U.S. combat deaths could top 1,000 per month; late in the month, the second bombing pause begins

1966	*As of year's end, approximately 390,000 U.S. military personnel are deployed to Vietnam*
Late January	The U.S. military commences six weeks of "search and destroy" missions to root out the NLF; the U.S. bombing campaign restarts, and B-52 strategic bombers are introduced in April
1967	*U.S. troop levels reach approximately 463,000 by year's end, and combat deaths total roughly 16,000*
November 29	McNamara resigns as secretary of defense, in part because of his increasing discomfort with Johnson's war policies
1968	*U.S. troop levels rise to 495,000 by year's end; more than 1,000 U.S. troops are killed each month, and the total number of U.S. troops killed in Vietnam tops 30,000*
January	The NLF launches the Tet Offensive, a series of attacks against South Vietnamese cities, including Saigon; although U.S. forces defeat the communist insurgents, the size of their offensive causes the American press and public to question optimistic Pentagon claims about the progress of the war; subsequent polls show only 26 percent of Americans support Johnson's war policy
March 31	Johnson announces that he will not seek reelection; additionally, he calls for a partial halt to U.S. bombing and encourages the North Vietnamese to attend peace talks
May 10	The "Paris Peace Talks" begin with the United States represented by Averell Harriman and the North represented by Foreign Minister Xuan Thuy; negotiations between both sides continue on and off for the next five years
November	Richard Nixon elected president
1969	*Total U.S. combat deaths are approximately 40,000*
Late January	Paris Peace Talks resume
March 17	Nixon orders secret bombing campaign against North Vietnamese supply depots in Cambodia
April	U.S. troop levels reach their highest point: 543,400
June	Nixon and Secretary of Defense Melvin Laird announce a U.S. policy of "Vietnamization," by which the United States will begin withdrawing forces and handing over more responsibilities to South Vietnamese troops

1970	*U.S. troops drop to 280,000 by December 31*
February	Secretary of State Henry Kissinger begins two years of secret talks with North Vietnamese envoy Le Duc Tho
April 30	Nixon announces an expansion of the U.S. war effort into Cambodia
June 24	U.S. Senate votes to repeal the Gulf of Tonkin resolution
December 22	Congress passes the Cooper-Church Amendment, banning the use of defense spending for U.S. military operations in Laos or Cambodia
1971	*U.S. troop levels decrease to approximately 156,000 by year's end; total combat deaths exceed 45,000*
June 18–22	The U.S. Senate passes a nonbinding resolution calling for the withdrawal of all U.S. forces from Vietnam by year's end
1972	
April	Nixon orders B-52s to bomb Hanoi and Haiphong, with the intent of pressuring the North to make further concessions at the peace talks
July	Paris Talks resume
October	Kissinger announces that "peace is at hand" after reaching a broad agreement with Tho; South Vietnamese president Nguyen Van Thieu, however, rejects the U.S. proposal that communist forces be permitted to remain in South Vietnam
December	Peace talks collapse after the North balks at dozens of amendments submitted by Thieu; Nixon orders a series of "Christmas bombings" to force the North back to the negotiation table
1973	*By year's end, all U.S. troops are withdrawn from Vietnam; the combat death toll is 47,424 U.S. military personnel*
January	Kissinger and Tho reach a revised agreement, which the U.S. forces Thieu to accept; Thieu calls the agreement "tantamount to surrender"
March 29	The United States completes its military withdrawal from Vietnam

1974

December   North Vietnam launches a new offensive against the
                    South, taking the Mekong Delta region; the United
                    States responds diplomatically

1975

April 30   As North Vietnamese troops enter Saigon, the last
                    U.S. government personnel evacuate the embassy;
                    within hours, the North declares the end of the
                    Vietnam War

The Rest of the Cold War

**5.4   Assess the role of personalities, ideas, economic trends, and nuclear
weapons in ending the Cold War peacefully.**

In 1952, Dwight D. Eisenhower was elected president of the United States on a
campaign pledge to end the Korean War and roll back communism. His Republican Party argued that containment was a cowardly accommodation to communism: The right approach was to roll it back. Within six months, however, it
became clear that rolling back communism would carry too great a risk of nuclear war. After Stalin died in 1953, the frozen relations of the Cold War thawed
slightly. In 1955, there was a U.S-Soviet summit in Geneva at which both sides
agreed to the establishment of Austria as a neutral state. In 1956, Khrushchev,
now first secretary of the Communist Party of the Soviet Union, gave a secret
speech exposing Stalin's crimes to the Twentieth Party Congress. The secret
leaked out and contributed to a period of disarray in the Soviet sphere in Eastern
Europe. Hungary attempted to revolt, but Khrushchev intervened militarily to
keep it in the communist camp.

Khrushchev decided that he needed to get the Americans out of Berlin
and reach a final settlement of World War II so that he could consolidate the
Soviet hold on Eastern Europe and begin to take advantage of the decolonization occurring in the Third World. But his style and efforts to negotiate
with the United States were reminiscent of the kaiser's style in trying to force
the British to bargain before 1914: full of bluster and deception. Efforts to
make the United States come to terms had the opposite effect. Khrushchev
failed in the Berlin crisis of 1958–1961 and again in the Cuban missile crisis
in 1962.

As we will see later, the Soviet Union and the United States came so
close to the nuclear brink during the Cuban missile crisis that they scared
each other into a new phase in their relationship. From 1963 to 1978, there
was a gradual détente, or relaxation of tensions. In the aftermath of the
Cuban missile crisis, arms control negotiations produced the Limited Test

Ban Treaty that restricted atmospheric nuclear tests in 1963 and the Nuclear Non-Proliferation Treaty in 1968. Trade began to grow gradually, and détente seemed to be expanding. The Vietnam War diverted U.S. attention more to the threat from Chinese communism and away from Soviet tensions.

From 1969 to 1974, the Nixon administration used détente as a means to pursue the goals of containment. After the Cuban missile crisis, the Soviets launched a major military buildup and gained parity in nuclear weapons. The Vietnam War led to the American public's disillusionment with Cold War interventions. Nixon's strategy was (1) to negotiate a strategic arms control treaty with the Soviet Union to cap each country's nuclear arsenal at relative parity, (2) to open diplomatic relations with China and thus create a three-way balance of power in Asia (rather than pushing the Soviets and the Chinese together), (3) to increase trade so there would be carrots as well as sticks in the U.S.-Soviet relationship, and (4) to use "linkage" to tie the various parts of the policy together. The high point of détente occurred in 1972 and 1973, but it did not last very long.

The Middle East War of 1973 and Soviet assistance to anti-Western movements in Africa led to bad feelings about who misled whom. U.S. domestic politics contributed to the decline of détente when U.S. legislators such as Senator Henry M. ("Scoop") Jackson tried to link trade with the Soviet Union to human rights issues, such as the treatment of Soviet Jews, rather than to the Soviet Union's international behavior. In 1975, when Portugal decolonized Angola and Mozambique, the Soviet Union provided transport for Cuban troops dispatched by Fidel Castro to help keep communist-oriented governments in power there. In the 1976 presidential campaign, President Gerald Ford never used the word "détente." His successor, Jimmy Carter, tried to continue détente with the Soviet Union during his first two years in office, but the Soviet Union and Cuba became involved in the Ethiopian civil war. The Soviets continued their military buildup, and in December 1979, the Soviet Union delivered the coup de grâce to détente by invading Afghanistan.

Why was there a resurgence in the level of hostility? One argument is that détente was always oversold: Too much was expected of it. More to the point, there were three trends in the 1970s that undercut it. One was the Soviet military buildup in which the Soviets increased their defense spending by nearly 4 percent annually and introduced new heavy missiles that particularly worried American defense planners. The second was Soviet intervention in Angola, Ethiopia, and Afghanistan. The Soviets thought that these military actions were justified by what they called the changing "correlation of forces" between capitalism and socialism; it was their belief, in other words, that history was moving in the direction that Marxism-Leninism predicted. Third were changes in U.S. domestic politics: a rightward trend that tore apart the coalition supporting the Democratic Party. The result of the interaction of Soviet acts and U.S. political trends reaffirmed the view that the Cold War persisted and that détente could not last. The renewed hostility in the 1980s was *not* a return to the Cold War of the 1950s, however. There was a return to the rhetoric of the 1950s, but actions were quite different. Even though President Ronald Reagan talked about the Soviet Union as an "evil empire," he pursued arms control agreements. There was increased trade, particularly in grain, and there were constant contacts between U.S. and Soviet officials. The superpowers even evolved certain rules of prudence in their behavior toward each other: no direct wars, no nuclear use, and discussions of arms and the control of nuclear weapons. It was a different kind of cold war in the 1980s than in the 1950s.

The End of the Cold War

When did the Cold War end? Because the origins of the Cold War were very heavily related to the division of Europe by the United States and the Soviet Union, the end of the Cold War might be dated by when the division ended in 1989. When the Soviet Union did not use force to support the communist government in East Germany and the Berlin Wall was breached by jubilant crowds in November 1989, the Cold War could be said to be over.

But why did it end? One argument is that containment worked. Kennan argued immediately after World War II that if the United States could prevent the Soviet Union from expanding, there would be no successes to feed the ideology, and gradually Soviet communism would mellow. New ideas would arise, people would realize that communism was not the wave of the future and that history was not on its side. In some larger respect, Kennan was correct. Although the opening of Soviet archives after the Cold War demonstrated that American fears of Soviet expansionism had been overblown, there is little doubt that U.S. military power kept the Soviet Union on its heels and that the soft power of American culture, values, and ideas eroded communist ideology. But the puzzle of timing remains: Why did the Cold War end in 1989? Why did it last four decades? Why did it take the Soviet Union so long to mellow? Alternatively, why didn't it last another ten years?

Another possible explanation is "imperial overstretch." Historian Paul Kennedy has argued that empires expand until overexpansion saps their internal strength.[11] With more than a fourth of its economy devoted to defense and foreign affairs (compared with 6 percent for the United States in the 1980s), the Soviet Union was overstretched. But Kennedy went on to say that none of the overexpanded multinational empires in history ever retreated to their own ethnic base until they had been defeated or weakened in a great power war, and the Soviet Union had not.

A third explanation is that the U.S. military buildup in the 1980s forced the Soviets to surrender in the Cold War, quite simply because they could not keep up. It is certainly true that the Soviet economy had difficulty supporting an expensive arms race, particularly when, in the early days of what at the time people called the "revolution in military affairs," the Soviet Union was falling further and further behind the United States technologically. But with very few (and short-lived) exceptions, the United States had always been ahead of the Soviet Union technologically, its economy generally outperformed that of the Soviets, and arms races had been the norm rather than the exception throughout the Cold War. Why would this particular arms race have this particular effect at this particular time? Why had the Soviet Union not given up earlier?

To explain why the Cold War ended when it did, we need to look at our three types of causes: precipitating, intermediate, and deep. The most important precipitating cause of the end of the Cold War was an individual, Mikhail Gorbachev. He wanted to reform communism, not replace it. The reform, however, snowballed into a revolution driven from below rather than controlled from above. In both his domestic and foreign policy, Gorbachev launched a number of actions that accelerated the existing Soviet decline and hastened the end of the Cold War. When he first came to power in 1985, Gorbachev tried to discipline the Soviet people as a way to overcome economic stagnation. When discipline was not enough to solve the problem, he launched the idea of *perestroika*, or "restructuring," but he was unable to restructure from the top because the Soviet bureaucrats kept thwarting his orders. To light a fire under the bureaucrats, he used a strategy of *glasnost*, or open discussion and democratization. Gorbachev

Photo: Cliff Owen/Bettmann/Corbis

George H. W. Bush, Ronald Reagan, and Mikhail Gorbachev in New York, 1987 believed that airing people's discontent with the way the system was working would put pressure on the bureaucrats and help perestroika work. But once glasnost and democratization let people say what they were thinking and vote on it, many people said, "We want out. There is no new form of Soviet citizen. This is an imperial dynasty, and we do not belong in this empire." Gorbachev unleashed the disintegration of the Soviet Union, which became increasingly evident after a failed coup by hard-liners in August 1991. By December 1991, the Soviet Union ceased to exist.

Gorbachev's foreign policy, which he called "new thinking," also contributed to the end of the Cold War. This policy had two very important elements. One was changing ideas that constructivists emphasize, such as the concept of common security, in which the classical security dilemma is escaped by joining together to provide security. Gorbachev and the people around him said that in a world of increasing interdependence, security was a non-zero-sum game, and all could benefit through cooperation. The existence of the nuclear threat meant that all could perish together if the competition got out of hand. Rather than try to build as many nuclear weapons as possible, Gorbachev proclaimed a doctrine of "sufficiency," holding a minimal number for protection. The other dimension of Gorbachev's foreign policy change was his view that expansionism is usually more costly than beneficial. Soviet control over an empire in Eastern Europe, and its expensive subsidies to faraway client states such as Cuba, was costing too much and providing too little benefit. The invasion of Afghanistan proved to be a particularly costly disaster. Gorbachev believed that there had to be some way to provide for Soviet security other than to impose and maintain "friendly" communist states on Soviet borders or elsewhere.

Thus, by the summer of 1989, Eastern Europeans were allowed a greater degree of freedom. Hungary permitted East Germans to escape through its territory into Austria. This exodus of East Germans put enormous pressure on the East German government. Additionally, Eastern European governments no longer had the nerve (or Soviet backing) to put down demonstrations. In November, the Berlin Wall was pierced in a dramatic conclusion to a crescendo of events occurring over a very short period. We can argue that these events stemmed from Gorbachev's miscalculations. He thought that communism could be repaired, but in fact, in trying to repair it, he punched a hole in it. And as if through a hole in a dam, the pent-up pressures began to escape, rapidly increasing the opening and causing the entire system to collapse.

That still leaves the question, why 1989? Why under this leader? To some extent, Gorbachev was an accident of history. In the early 1980s, three old Soviet leaders died, one after another. It was not until 1985 that the younger generation—the people who had come up under Khrushchev, the so-called generation of 1956—had their chance. But if the members of the Communist Party Politburo had chosen one of Gorbachev's hard-line competitors in 1985, it is quite plausible that the declining Soviet Union could have held on for another decade. It did not have to collapse so quickly. Gorbachev's personality explains much of the timing.

As for the intermediate causes, Kennan and Kennedy were both on target. Two important intermediate causes were the soft power of liberal ideas, emphasized in constructivist explanations, and imperial overstretch, emphasized by realists. The ideas of openness, democracy, and new thinking that Gorbachev used were Western ideas that had been adopted by the generation of 1956. One of the key architects of perestroika and glasnost, Aleksandr Yakovlev, had been an exchange student in the United States for a year and ambassador to Canada for a decade. He was attracted to Western theories of pluralism. The growth of transnational communications and contacts pierced the Iron Curtain and helped spread Western popular culture and liberal ideas. The demonstrated effect of Western economic success gave them additional appeal. Although hard military power would have prevented Soviet expansionism, soft power ate away the belief in communism behind the Iron Curtain. When the Berlin Wall finally fell in 1989, it did not succumb to an artillery barrage, but to an onslaught of civilian hammers and bulldozers.

As for imperial overstretch, the enormous Soviet defense budget began to affect other aspects of Soviet society. In the Soviet Union, health care declined, and the mortality rate increased (the only developed country in which that occurred). Without funds for upkeep, the country's infrastructure began to crumble. Eventually, even the military became aware of the tremendous burden caused by imperial overstretch. In 1984, Marshal Nikolai Ogarkov, the Soviet chief of staff, realized that the Soviet Union needed a better civilian economic base and more access to Western trade and technology. But during the period of stagnation, the old leaders were unwilling to listen, and Ogarkov was removed from his post.

Thus the intermediate causes of soft power and imperial overstretch are important; ultimately, though, we must deal with the deep causes, which were the decline of communist ideology (a constructivist explanation) and the failure of the Soviet economy (a realist explanation). Communism's loss of legitimacy over the postwar period was quite dramatic. In the early period, immediately after 1945, communism was widely attractive. Many communists had led the resistance against fascism in Europe, and many people believed that communism was the wave of the future. The Soviet Union gained a great deal of soft power from its communist ideology, but squandered it. Soviet soft power was progressively undercut by de-Stalinization in 1956, which exposed his horrendous crimes; by Soviet repression of political reforms in Hungary in 1956 and Czechoslovakia in 1968; and by the growing transnational communication of liberal ideas. Although in theory communism aimed to instill a system of class justice, Vladimir Lenin's heirs maintained domestic power through a brutal state security system involving reform camps, gulags, broad censorship, and the widespread use of informants. The net effect of these repressive measures on the Russian people was a general loss of faith in the system as voiced in the underground protest literature and the rising tide of dissent advanced by human rights activists.

Behind this scene, there was also decline in the Soviet economy, reflecting the diminished ability of the Soviet central planning system to respond to change in the world economy. Stalin had created a system of centralized economic direction that emphasized heavy smokestack industries. It was very inflexible—all thumbs and no fingers—and tended to stockpile labor rather than transfer it to growing service industries. As the economist Joseph Schumpeter pointed out, capitalism is creative destruction, a way of responding flexibly to major waves of technological change.[12] There was a great deal of turmoil in the world economy at the end of the twentieth century, but the Western economies using market systems were able to transfer labor to services, to reorganize their heavy industries, and to switch to computers. The Soviet Union could not keep up with the changes. For instance, when Gorbachev came to power in 1985, there were 50,000 personal computers in the Soviet Union and 30 million in the United States. Four years later, there were about 400,000 personal computers in the Soviet Union and 40 million in the United States. Market-oriented economies and democracies proved more flexible in responding to technological change than the centralized Soviet system that Stalin created for the smokestack era of the 1930s. Soviet goods and services could not keep up to world standards. According to one Soviet economist, by the late 1980s, only 8 percent of Soviet industry was competitive at world standards. It is difficult to remain a superpower when 92 percent of your industry is subpar.

At the end of the twentieth century, the major technological change of the third industrial revolution was the growing economic role of information. The Soviet system was particularly inept at handling information. The deep secrecy of its political system meant that the flow of information was slow and cumbersome. The situation was so bad that Soviet officials took to using Central Intelligence Agency estimates of Soviet economic performance in their own planning and forecasting exercises. Reagan's defense buildup added pressure on an already economically stressed political regime.

Explaining the Cold War from Inside and Out

In contrast to the way most history is written, Cold War historians through the end of the 1980s were working within rather than after the event they were trying to describe. We had no way of knowing the final outcome, and we could determine the motivations of only some—by no means all—of the major players. . . . We know now, to coin a phrase. Or, at least, we know a good deal more than we once did. We will never have the full story: we don't have that for any historical event, no matter how far back in the past. Historians can no more reconstruct what actually happened than maps can replicate what is really there. But we can represent the past, just as cartographers approximate terrain. And with the end of the Cold War and at least the partial opening of documents from the former Soviet Union, Eastern Europe, and China, the fit between our representations and the reality they describe has become a lot closer than it once was.

—*John L. Gaddis, "The New Cold War History"*[13]

The end of the Cold War was one of the great transformative events of the twentieth century. It was equivalent to World War II in its effects on the structure of the international system, but it occurred without war. In the next chapters, we turn to what that may mean for international politics in the future.

Since the breakup of the Soviet Union, Russia has undergone a significant transformation. Renouncing the planned economy of the Soviet state, post–Cold War Russia tentatively embarked on a path of democratization and economic liberalization. That road has been fraught with peril, however. Following the advice of the International Monetary Fund, the Russian government at first embraced economic "shock therapy" as a way of making the transition from economic autocracy to liberal democracy, yet it so disrupted Russian society that it was quickly shelved in favor of a more gradualist approach. As the economic situation in Russia has deteriorated, Russian nationalism has become rejuvenated. Although Russia is formally democratic today, it has lapsed back into old authoritarian patterns. President Vladimir Putin enjoys a degree of personal control in Russia today not seen since Gorbachev first came to power in 1985. Theorists such as Michael Doyle, hypothesizing that liberal democracies do not fight wars with one another, have suggested that if Russia does eventually succeed in transitioning to genuine democracy, it will bode well for international peace.[14] At the moment, things seem to be heading in quite the opposite direction.

Regardless of what the future holds, one major puzzle remains. Just as important as the question of why the Cold War ended is the question of why it did not turn hot. Why did the Cold War last so long without a "hot war" erupting between the two superpowers? Why did it not result in World War III?

The Role of Nuclear Weapons: Physics and Politics

Some analysts believe that advanced developed societies learned from the lessons of World War I and World War II and simply outgrew war. Others believe that the "long peace" in the second half of the twentieth century stemmed from the limited expansionist goals of the superpowers. Still others credit what they consider the inherent stability of pure bipolarity in which two states (not two tight alliances) are dominant. But for most analysts, the largest part of the answer lies in the special nature of nuclear weapons and nuclear deterrence.

The enormous destructive power of nuclear weapons is almost beyond comprehension. A 1-megaton nuclear explosion can create temperatures of 100 million degrees Celsius, or four to five times the temperature in the center of the sun. The bomb dropped on Hiroshima in 1945 was relatively small, about the equivalent of 15,000 tons of TNT. Today's missiles can carry 100 times that explosive power or more. In fact, all the explosive power used in World War II could fit in one 3-megaton bomb, and that one bomb could fit in the nose cone of one large intercontinental missile. By the 1980s, the United States and the Soviet Union together had thousands of nuclear weapons (Figure 5.4).

Figure 5.4 U.S. and Soviet Strategic Nuclear Weapons

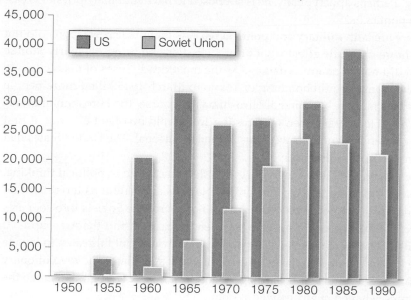

Some physical effects of nuclear explosions are uncertain. For example, the theory of nuclear winter holds that a nuclear war would kick so much dust and ash into the atmosphere that it would block sunlight, preventing most plants from photosynthesizing and leading to mass extinctions and the destruction of human civilization. A National Academy of Sciences study reported that nuclear winter is possible, but highly uncertain.[15] Much would depend on whether the weapons were aimed at cities rather than at other weapons. Burning cities would generate an enormous amount of smoke that would block a great deal of sunlight, but it is uncertain how long the smoke would stay aloft. If the bombs exploded in the Northern Hemisphere, would the smoke travel to the Southern Hemisphere? Some skeptics argue that the worst result would not be nuclear winter, but nuclear autumn, which is a faint consolation. The certainty is that a large-scale nuclear war would destroy civilization as we know it, at least in the Northern Hemisphere. In their 1983 report on nuclear weapons, the American Catholic bishops engaged in only slight hyperbole when they said, "We are the first generation since Genesis with the capability of destroying God's creation."[16]

Nuclear weapons changed the nature of warfare, but they did not change the basic way in which the world is organized. The world of anarchic states with no higher government above them continued in the nuclear age. In 1946, when the United States proposed the Baruch Plan to establish international control of nuclear weapons, the Soviet Union viewed it as just another American plot.

After this failure, Albert Einstein lamented that everything changed except our thinking. Perhaps apocryphally, he is supposed to have said that "physics is easier than politics."

There are both military and political reasons that nuclear weapons did not have a more dramatic effect right after 1945. For one thing, the early atomic weapon did not do as much damage as the most deadly uses of mass conventional weapons. The firebombing of Tokyo in March 1945 killed more people than did the nuclear bombing of Hiroshima. Of course, the Hiroshima raid involved a single B-29 bomber, whereas the Tokyo raid involved 279. But at first there were very few nuclear weapons in the U.S. arsenal. The United States had only two in 1947, but fifty in 1948.

The emerging U.S.-Soviet rivalry also slowed change in political thinking. The Soviet Union mistrusted the United Nations and saw it as too reliant on the United States. The United States could not coerce the Soviets into cooperation because Europe was a hostage between the Soviets and the Americans. If the United States threatened nuclear attack, the Soviets could threaten to invade Europe with conventional forces. The result was a stalemate. The revolutionary physical effects of nuclear technology were initially not enough to change the ways states behaved in an anarchic system.

The second stage of the nuclear revolution occurred in 1952 when the hydrogen bomb was first tested. Hydrogen bombs rely on the energy released when two atoms are fused into one, instead of split apart as in the early fission bombs. The H-bomb vastly increased the amount of destruction possible with a single weapon. The largest human-made explosion on Earth's surface occurred in 1961 when the Soviet Union conducted a 60-megaton nuclear test; that particular weapon had 20 times the explosive power used in total in World War II, and it was tested at half strength.

Ironically, the more important change that accompanied the development of the H-bomb was miniaturization. Fusion made it possible to deliver enormous amounts of destructive power in very small packages. The systems built to deliver the early atomic bombs got bigger and bigger and required more space as the bombs increased in size. The B-36 bomber, which served with the U.S. Air Force from 1948 to 1958, was a huge eight-engine airplane with one big cavity to hold one bomb. An H-bomb, on the other hand, could put the same potential destruction in a much smaller space. Once that destructive power was mounted in the nose cone of a ballistic missile, an intercontinental nuclear war could occur with only thirty minutes' warning, compared with the eight hours it took a B-36 to fly the same distance.

The increased destructiveness of hydrogen bombs also dramatized the consequences of nuclear war. No longer could warfare be considered merely an extension of politics by other means. Karl von Clausewitz (1780–1831), a nineteenth-century Prussian general and military theorist, said that war is a political act, and therefore absolute war is an absurdity. The enormous destructive power of nuclear weapons meant that there was now a disproportion

Photo: Air Force Historical Research Agency

The Convair B-36 (right) and the Boeing B-29 (left), which dropped atomic bombs on Hiroshima and Nagasaki

between the military means and virtually all the political ends a country might seek. This disjunction between ends and means caused a paralysis in the use of the ultimate force in most situations. Nuclear weapons have not been used since 1945. Nuclear weaponry is muscle-bound. It is too powerful and thus disproportionate to any meaningful political goal.

The H-bomb had five significant political effects, even though it did not reorganize the anarchic way in which the world goes about its business. First, it revived the concept of limited war. The first half of the twentieth century saw a change from the limited wars of the nineteenth century to the two world wars, which took tens of millions of lives. At midcentury, analysts were referring to the twentieth century as "the century of total war." But war in the second half of the century was more like the old wars of the eighteenth and nineteenth centuries. For instance, although the Korean and Vietnam wars each cost more than 55,000 American deaths (combat and noncombat), they remained limited in scope and scale. In Vietnam and Afghanistan, the United States and the Soviet Union each accepted defeat rather than use their ultimate weapon.

Second, crises replaced wars as moments of truth. In the past, war was the time when all the cards were face up on the table, but in the nuclear age, war is too devastating and the old moments of truth too dangerous. The Berlin crises, the Cuban missile crisis, and the Middle East crises of the early 1970s played the functional equivalent of war in this sense, providing glimpses into the true correlation of forces in military power.

Third, nuclear weapons made deterrence (dissuasion through fear) the key strategy. It was now critical to organize military might to produce fear in advance so that an attack would be deterred. In World War II, the United States relied on its ability to mobilize and gradually build a war machine after the war started, but that mobilization approach no longer worked when a nuclear war could be over in a matter of hours.

A fourth political effect was the development of a de facto regime of superpower prudence. The two superpowers, despite their bitter ideological differences, developed one key common interest: avoiding nuclear war. During the Cold War, the United States and the Soviet Union engaged in proxy or indirect peripheral wars, but in no case did the two countries go head to head. In addition, the two sides developed spheres of influence. Although the Americans talked about rolling back communism in Eastern Europe in the 1950s, in practice, when the Hungarians revolted against their Soviet rulers in 1956, the United States did not rush in to help them, fearing nuclear war. Similarly, with the exception of Cuba, the Soviets were relatively careful about incursions into the Western Hemisphere. Both countries adhered to a developing norm of nonuse of nuclear weapons. Finally, the superpowers learned to communicate. After the Cuban missile crisis, Washington and Moscow developed a "hotline" (initially a teletype connection) to allow virtually instantaneous communication between Soviet and American leaders. Simultaneously, the codification of a number of arms control treaties, starting with the Limited Test Ban Treaty in 1963, and frequent arms control negotiations became a way to discuss stability.

Fifth, nuclear weapons in general, and the H-bomb in particular, were seen by most officials as unusable in time of war. It was not purely a matter of the destructive potential of the H-bomb. A stigma gradually came to be attached to the use of nuclear weaponry that did not similarly apply to conventional weaponry. By the late 1960s, in fact, engineers and scientists had managed to shrink the size and "yield" (destructive blast) of nuclear weapons so greatly that some—nuclear mines and nuclear demolition charges, for example—could have been used by the United States in Vietnam and the Gulf War or by the Soviet Union in Afghanistan without causing much more destruction than conventional weapons. Both Americans and Soviets, however, refrained from using smaller-yield nuclear weapons in favor of conventional ones. In part, they feared that using any nuclear weapon, no matter how small, would open the window to using other nuclear weapons, and that risk was simply unacceptable.

There was yet another dimension to the reluctance to use nuclear weapons. Ever since the first bomb was dropped by the United States on Hiroshima, there was a lingering sense that nuclear weapons were immoral, that they went beyond the realm of what was acceptable in war. Although that normative restraint is hard to measure, it clearly suffused the debates over nuclear weapons and was one reason for the unwillingness of states to use them.

Balance of Terror

Nuclear weapons produced a peculiar form of the balance of power that was sometimes called the "balance of terror." Tests of nuclear strength were more psychological than physical. Both sides followed a policy of preventing preponderance by the other, but the result was different from previous systems. Unlike the nineteenth-century balance-of-power system in which five great powers shifted alliances, the Cold War balance was very clearly organized around two very large states, each capable of destroying the other in a matter of minutes.

The problems raised by the classical security dilemma were not ended by the terror of nuclear weapons, but the superpowers acted prudently despite their ideological differences. Their prudence was similar to the effects of the constant communications that occurred in managing the multipolar nineteenth-century balance of power. At the same time, the superpowers tried to calculate balances of force, just as in the days when statesmen compared provinces, infantry, and artillery.

The nuclear balance of terror coincided with a period of bipolarity. Recall that some neorealists, such as Kenneth Waltz, define bipolarity as a situation in which two large states have nearly all the power.[17] That type of pure bipolarity is rare. More often, bipolarity has occurred in history when alliances tighten so much that flexibility is lost, as happened in the Peloponnesian War. Even though they were independent city-states, the alliances around Athens and around Sparta coalesced tightly into a bipolar situation. Similarly, on the eve of World War I, the alliance systems became tightly bound into bipolarity.

Waltz argued that bipolarity can be stable because it simplifies communication and calculations: When you only have one other great power to pay particularly close attention to, you can monitor the balance very closely. On the other hand, bipolar systems lack flexibility and magnify the importance of marginal conflicts such as the Vietnam War, and without other significant countries to throw their weight into the balance on the weaker side if one side begins to outstrip the other, the balance can break down entirely. As we have seen, the conventional wisdom in the past was that bipolarity either erodes or explodes. If so, why did bipolarity not explode after World War II?

Perhaps the prudence produced by nuclear weapons provided the answer, and the stability that Waltz attributed to pure bipolarity was really the result of the bomb. The very terror of nuclear weapons may have helped produce stability through the "crystal ball effect." Imagine that in August 1914 the kaiser, the tsar, and the emperor of Austria-Hungary looked into a crystal ball and saw a picture of 1918. They would have seen that war would cost them their thrones, that their empires would be dismembered, and that millions of their people would be killed. Would they still have gone to war? Probably not. Knowledge of the physical effects of nuclear weapons may be similar to the effect of giving leaders in the post-1945 period a crystal ball. Because few or no political goals would be proportionate to such destruction, they would not want to take great risks. Of course, crystal balls can be shattered by accidents and by miscalculations, but the analogy suggests why the combination of bipolarity and nuclear weapons produced the longest period without a significant great power war since the beginning of the modern state system. (The previous record was 1871–1914.)

Problems of Nuclear Deterrence

Nuclear deterrence is a subset of general deterrence, but the peculiar qualities of nuclear weapons changed how the superpowers approached international relations during the Cold War. Nuclear deterrence encourages the reasoning, "If you attack me, I may not be able to prevent your attack, but I can retaliate so powerfully that you will not want to attack in the first place." Nuclear weapons thus put a new twist on an old concept.

One way to assess the efficacy of nuclear deterrence is by counterfactual analysis. How likely was it that the Cold War would have turned hot in the absence of nuclear weapons? The political scientist John Mueller argues that nuclear weapons were irrelevant.[18] He argues that the peoples of Europe had been turning away from war as a policy instrument ever since the horrors of World War I. The cause of peace was the increased recognition of the horror of war, at least in the developed world. According to Mueller, Hitler was an aberration, a rare person who had not learned the lessons of World War I and was still willing to go to war. After World War II, the new revulsion toward war returned more strongly than before. Most analysts, however, believe that nuclear weapons had a lot to do with avoiding World War III. Crises over Berlin, Cuba, and perhaps the Middle East might have spiraled out of control without the prudence instilled by the crystal ball effect of nuclear weapons.

That assessment raises a number of questions. One is, what deters? Effective deterrence requires both the capability to do damage and a credible threat that the weapons will be used. Credibility depends on the stakes involved in a conflict. For example, a U.S. threat to bomb Moscow in retaliation for a nuclear

---

Nuclear Weapons and the Vietnam War

When President Kennedy made the first decision to increase significantly the American military presence in 1962–63, . . . he had in mind two things: What would have happened if Khrushchev had not believed him in the Berlin crisis of 1961–62, and what would have happened if Khrushchev [had not believed him] in the Cuban Missile Crisis of 1962?

I think we made a mistake in concluding that the Chinese would probably not intervene in the Korean War in 1950, and that influenced the American decision not to invade North Vietnam. The military said they did not think China would come in, but if it did, it would lead to nuclear war, and that decided that.

—*Secretary of State Dean Rusk*[19]

attack was probably credible. But suppose the United States had threatened to bomb Moscow in 1980 if the Soviets did not withdraw their troops from Afghanistan. The United States certainly had the capability, but the threat would not have been credible because the stakes were too low, and the Soviets could easily have threatened in return to bomb Washington. So deterrence is related not just to capability, but also to credibility.

The problem of credibility leads to a distinction between deterring threats against one's homeland and extending deterrence to cover an ally. For example, the United States could not stop the Soviet Union from invading Afghanistan by nuclear deterrence, but for the four decades of the Cold War, it threatened to use nuclear weapons if the Soviet Union invaded the NATO countries of Western Europe. Thus, to look for the effects of nuclear weapons in extending deterrence and averting war, we must look at major crises in which the stakes were high.

Can history answer these questions about the effect of nuclear weapons? Not completely, but it can help. From 1945 to 1949, the United States alone had nuclear weapons but did not use them. So, there was some self-restraint even before mutual nuclear deterrence. It was due in part to the small size of U.S. arsenals, a lack of understanding of these new weapons, and the American fear that the Soviets would capture all Europe with their massive conventional forces. By the 1950s, both the United States and the Soviet Union had nuclear weapons, and U.S. leaders considered their use in several crises. Nuclear weapons were not used in the Korean War or in 1954 and 1958 when the Chinese communists mobilized forces and threatened to invade territory held by the Nationalists based in Taiwan. Both Truman and Eisenhower vetoed the use of nuclear weapons for several reasons. In the Korean War, it was not clear that dropping a nuclear weapon would stop the Chinese, and the United States was concerned about the Soviet response. There was always the danger that the threats might escalate and the Soviets might use a nuclear weapon to help their Chinese ally. So, even though the Americans had a larger nuclear arsenal, there was the danger of escalating to a wider war involving more than just Korea and China.

In addition, ethics and public opinion played a role. In the 1950s, U.S. government estimates of the number of citizens who would be killed by a nuclear attack were so high that the idea was put aside. When asked about using nuclear weapons, Eisenhower said, "We can't use those awful things against Asians for the second time in less than ten years. My God!"[20] Even though the United States had more nuclear weapons than the Soviet Union in the 1950s, a combination of factors persuaded the Americans not to use them.

The Cuban Missile Crisis

The key case in nuclear deterrence in the Cold War was the Cuban missile crisis of October 1962, triggered by Khrushchev's attempt to sneak strategic nuclear missiles into Cuba. This 13-day period was the closest the world has ever come to nuclear war. If a total outsider, a "man from Mars," had looked at the situation, he would have seen that the United States had a massive superiority in nuclear weaponry. The Soviets had a mere handful of strategic missiles that could have reached the United States.[21] If Kennedy considered Khrushchev's gambit so utterly unacceptable, why didn't the president order an attack on the Soviet missile sites in Cuba, most of which were still under construction when discovered, and all of which were relatively vulnerable? The answer was that Kennedy was not willing to run the risk of even one or two of the Soviet missiles escaping destruction and being fired at a U.S. city. In addition, as the crisis unfolded, both Kennedy and Khrushchev learned how little they could actually control the potentially disastrous actions of their own military organizations, which were on high alert and ready to fight at a moment's notice. What they did not know would have frightened them even more.[22] Khrushchev expressed the fear very powerfully in a letter to Kennedy near the climax of the crisis: "We and you ought not now to pull on the ends of the rope in which you have tied the knot of war," he wrote, "because the more the two of us pull, the tighter that knot will be tied. And a moment may come when that knot will be tied so tight that even he who tied it will not have the strength to untie it, and then it will be necessary to cut that knot. And what that would mean is not for me to explain to you, because you yourself understand perfectly of what terrible forces our countries dispose."[23]

The "Gravest Issues"

By mid-October 1962, the Cold War had intensified in unforeseen ways. Cuba, which had long been a virtual colony of the United States, had recently moved into the Soviet orbit. In late September, U.S. newspapers had begun reporting shipments of Soviet weapons to Cuba. President John F. Kennedy told the American public that, to the best of his understanding, these weapons were defensive, not offensive. Soviet Premier Nikita Khrushchev had given him absolute assurances that this was the case. "Were it to be otherwise," Kennedy said, "the gravest issues would arise."

Shortly before 9:00 A.M. on Tuesday, October 16, Kennedy's Assistant for National Security Affairs, McGeorge Bundy, brought to his bedroom photographs showing that the "gravest issues" had indeed arisen. Taken from very high altitude by a U-2 reconnaissance plane, these photographs showed the Soviets in Cuba setting up nuclear-armed ballistic missiles targeted on cities in the continental United States.

For Kennedy, the presence of these missiles was intolerable. So was the fact that Khrushchev had lied to him. For the next 13 days, Kennedy and a circle of advisers debated how to cope with the challenge. They knew that one possible outcome was nuclear war, and during their discussions Kennedy's civil defense expert offered the chilling information that the U.S. population was frighteningly vulnerable.

—*Ernest May and Philip Zelikow, The Kennedy Tapes*[24]

Twenty-five years after the event, a group of Harvard scholars organized a conference with Americans who had been members of Kennedy's Executive Committee of the National Security Council, the first of six such meetings that ultimately included both Soviets and Cubans. One of the most striking differences among the participants was their willingness to take risks. That in turn depended on how likely each thought were the prospects of nuclear war. Robert McNamara, Kennedy's secretary of defense, became more cautious as the crisis unfolded. At the time, he thought that the probability of nuclear war in the Cuban missile crisis might be one chance out of fifty (although later he rated the risks much higher after he learned in the 1990s that the Soviets had delivered both strategic and tactical nuclear weapons to Cuba). Douglas Dillon, who was the secretary of the treasury, said he thought that the risks of nuclear war were about zero. He did not see how the situation could possibly progress to nuclear war and as a result was willing to push the Soviets harder and to take more risks than was McNamara. General Maxwell Taylor, the chairman of the Joint Chiefs of Staff, also thought that the risk of nuclear war was low, and he complained that the United States let the Soviet Union off too easily. He argued that Kennedy could have pushed much harder and should have demanded the removal of Castro, Cuba's president. General Taylor said, "I was so sure we had 'em over a barrel, I never worried much about the final outcome."[25] But the risks of losing control weighed heavily on Kennedy, who took a very cautious position; indeed, he was more prudent than some of his advisors would have liked. The moral of the story is that a little nuclear deterrence can go a long way. It has been called *finite* or *existential deterrence*. It is clear that such nuclear deterrence made a difference in the Cuban missile crisis.

At the end of the day, Khrushchev backed down. There are at least three possible reasons for this move. One possibility is that he backed down because the United States had more nuclear weapons than the Soviet Union did. A second possible explanation adds the importance of the relative stakes of the two superpowers in the crisis; Cuba was in the United States' vital sphere of interest, but far from the Soviet Union. A third possible explanation is that Cuba's proximity to the United States meant that the Americans could bring overwhelming conventional forces to bear if the crisis were to escalated to a shooting war; the Soviets had no hope of actually defending Cuba in the face of a full-scale U.S. invasion to rid Cuba of Soviet nuclear missiles (and, probably, of Castro as well). The psychological burden was on the Soviets because higher stakes and readily available conventional forces bolstered the credibility of the U.S. threat.

In fact, although the Cuban missile crisis was widely considered a U.S. victory at the time—because Khrushchev publicly agreed to reverse his nuclear deployment—it was something of a compromise. The Americans had three options in the Cuban missile crisis. One was a shoot-out, that is, to bomb the missile sites; the second was a squeeze-out by blockading Cuba to persuade the Soviets

Photo: Bettmann/CORBIS

Kennedy and Khrushchev meeting in Vienna in 1961

to take the missiles out; the third was a buyout by offering to trade something the Soviets wanted, such as removal of U.S. missiles from Turkey. For a long time, the participants did not say much about the buyout aspects of the solution, but it came to light many years after the crisis that Kennedy had made a quiet promise to remove obsolete U.S. missiles from Turkey in return for the withdrawal of Soviet missiles from Cuba. The available evidence suggests not only that the fear of escalation to nuclear war deterred Khrushchev from hanging tough, but that it also deterred Kennedy from trying to push American advantages too far. The absolute number of nuclear weapons each side possessed proved to be less important than the fear that even a few nuclear weapons could wreak horrific devastation if either side miscalculated or misstepped.

Moral Issues

After the Cuban missile crisis, there was a relative easing of the tension in the Cold War. It was almost as if the United States and the Soviet Union had had a near-death experience, stumbling to the brink of a cliff, peering over, and pulling themselves back. In 1963, they agreed to create a hotline allowing fast direct communication between Washington and Moscow, and they signed an arms control treaty limiting atmospheric nuclear tests. Kennedy announced that the United States would be willing to trade more with the Soviet Union, and there was some relaxation of tension. Through the late 1960s, the United States was preoccupied with the Vietnam War, yet there were still arms control efforts. Intense fear of nuclear war returned after the Soviet Union invaded Afghanistan in 1979. During "the little cold war" from 1980 to 1985, strategic arms limitation talks stalled, rhetoric became particularly harsh, and military budgets and the number of nuclear weapons increased on both sides. Reagan talked about fighting and "winning" a nuclear war, and peace groups pressed for first a freeze, and then ultimately the abolition, of nuclear weapons.

In this climate of heightened anxiety about nuclear war, many people asked a basic question: Is nuclear deterrence moral? As we saw in Chapter 1, just war theory offers a number of common-sense principles for making moral judgments about a potential use of force. Self-defense is usually regarded as a just cause, but the means and consequences by which a war is fought are equally important. In terms of the means, civilians must be distinguished from combatants; in terms of consequences, there has to be some proportionality—some relationship—between the importance of the ends and the cost of the means.

Could nuclear war possibly fit the just war model? Technically, it could. Low-yield nuclear artillery shells or depth charges might be used against radar systems, submarines, ships at sea, or deep underground command bunkers without being dramatically different in their effects from similar conventional weapons. In that case, a "small" nuclear war might pass a just war theory test. But would fighting stop there, or would it escalate? As Clausewitz argued in the nineteenth century, there is a natural tendency for war to escalate. Generals always prefer to err on the side of using too much force rather than on the side of using too little.

Learning from History

In 1962 President Kennedy insisted that each member of the National Security Council read Barbara Tuchman's *The Guns of August*. The book is the story of how the nations of Europe inadvertently blundered into World War I. The author begins by quoting Bismarck's comment that "some damned foolish thing in the Balkans" would ignite the next war. She then related the series of steps—following the assassination on June 28, 1914, of the Austrian heir apparent,

> Archduke Franz Ferdinand, by Serbian nationalists—each small and insignificant in itself, that led to the most appalling military conflict in the history of the world. Time and again, at the brink of hostilities, the chiefs of state tried to pull back, but the momentum of events dragged them forward.
>
> President Kennedy reminded us of the 1914 conversation between two German chancellors on the origins of that war. One asked, "How did it happen?" and his successor replied, "Ah, if we only knew." It was Kennedy's way of stressing the constant danger of miscalculation.
>
> —Robert McNamara, *Blundering into Disaster*[26]

Once states cross the threshold of nuclear combat, the dangers of escalation become truly chilling, for what could be worth hundreds of millions of lives or the fate of the planet?

During the Cold War, some people answered, "It's better to be Red than dead." But that may have been the wrong way to pose the question. Instead, we might ask, is it ever justifiable to run a small risk of a large calamity? During the Cuban missile crisis, Kennedy was reputed to have said he thought the chances of war were "between one out of three and even."[27] And there was a risk of nuclear escalation as well. Was he justified in taking such a risk? We can ask the counterfactual: If Kennedy had not been willing to take the risk in Cuba, would Khrushchev have tried something even more dangerous? What if a Soviet success had led to a later nuclear crisis or an even larger conventional war, such as over Berlin?

Nuclear weapons probably played a significant role in preventing the Cold War from turning hot. During the 1980s, the American Association of Catholic Bishops said that nuclear deterrence could be justified on a conditional basis as a tolerable interim measure until something better was developed.[28] But how long is the interim? As long as nuclear knowledge exists, some degree of nuclear deterrence will exist. Although the weapons induced prudence during the Cold War, complacency is a danger. It took the United States and the Soviet Union some time to learn how to control nuclear weapons, and it is far from clear that such control systems will exist among new nuclear states such as North Korea and possibly Iran. Moreover, terrorist groups might have no use for controls.

Concern about the proliferation of nuclear weapons continues. Although 190 states have signed the Nuclear Non-Proliferation Treaty, India and Pakistan exploded weapons in 1998, followed by North Korea in 2006. Countries such as Iraq, Iran, and Libya also had nuclear weapons programs despite having signed the treaty. Also of concern is the spread of unconventional arsenals such as biological and chemical weapons. Libya, Iraq, and Syria, for example, constructed chemical weapons facilities. Iraq used them in its war with Iran (1980–1988), and Syria used them against its own people in 2013. UN inspectors uncovered and destroyed major Iraqi nuclear, biological, and chemical weapons programs after the Gulf War in 1991, but the fear that such programs could be reconstituted was one of the causes of the Iraq War in 2003. Under international pressure, the Syrian government agreed to the destruction of its chemical weapons in 2014.

States are not the only actors of concern when it comes to the proliferation of nuclear, chemical, or biological weapons. In 2004, it was disclosed that a Pakistani nuclear scientist, A. Q. Khan, had sold nuclear secrets to a number of countries, including Libya, Iran, and North Korea. Terrorist groups such as the Japanese Aum Shinrikyo cult and Osama bin Laden's al-Qaeda network are known to have been seeking nuclear, chemical, and biological weapons. One fear is that if nonstate actors of this kind acquire such weapons, they cannot be deterred from using them. How do you deter by threatening someone with destruction of their homeland if they have no homeland or if they happily embrace the concept of martyrdom?

The continued international worry about weapons of mass destruction has both a moral and a realist dimension. The moral opprobrium against nuclear weapons is shared not just by states that do not have the capacity or desire to make such weapons, but even by states that continue to have them, such as the United States, Britain, France, and Russia. Chemical and biological weapons have been condemned since World War I, when the use of mustard gas led to a widespread outcry. The realist dimension is simple: Weapons of mass destruction carry great risk of escalation and enormous potential for devastation. Whenever these weapons are present, the dynamics of conflict change. Weak states with nuclear or unconventional weapons are better able to threaten strong states, whereas strong states with these weapons can more effectively threaten and deter adversaries. At the same time, the risk that these devices will be used if a crisis spins out of control raises the level of tension, whether between the United States and North Korea, India and Pakistan, or Israel and Iran. And the threat of use by terrorists adds a chilling dimension in which deterrence is not a sufficient response, as we shall see in Chapters 9 and 10. The Cold War may be over, but the era of weapons of mass destruction is not.

Follow Up

- Richard Ned Lebow and Thomas Risse-Kappen, eds., *International Relations Theory and the End of the Cold War* (New York: Columbia University Press, 1995).

- T. V. Paul, *The Tradition of Non-Use of Nuclear Weapons* (Stanford, CA: Stanford University Press, 2009), pp. 1–123.

- Don Munton and David A. Welch, *The Cuban Missile Crisis: A Concise History* (New York: Oxford University Press, 2011).

- Joseph S. Nye, Jr., *Nuclear Ethics* (New York: Free Press, 1986).

Chronology: The Cold War Years

1943	Tehran meeting among Josef Stalin, Winston Churchill, and Franklin Roosevelt
1944	
July	Bretton Woods Conference: Creation of International Monetary Fund and World Bank
August	Dumbarton Oaks Conference: Creation of United Nations
October	Moscow meeting between Churchill and Stalin: Spheres of influence plan for the Balkans
1945	
February	Yalta Conference among Stalin, Churchill, and Roosevelt
April	Roosevelt dies
May	Germany surrenders
April–June	San Francisco Conference; UN Charter drafted
July	First test of atomic bomb; Potsdam Conference: Harry S. Truman, Churchill and Stalin
August	Hiroshima and Nagasaki destroyed by atomic bombs; the Soviet Union enters war in Asia; Japan surrenders
1946	Churchill's Iron Curtain speech; resumption of Greek civil war
1947	
March	Truman Doctrine announced
June	Marshall Plan announced
October	Creation of Cominform by Moscow
1948	
February	Coup by Czech Communist Party
March	Partial blockade of Berlin begins
June	Berlin airlift begins; Yugoslavia ousted from Cominform
November	Truman reelected president
1949	
April	North Atlantic Treaty signed in Washington
May	End of the Berlin blockade
August	Soviet Union explodes first atomic bomb
September	Federal Republic of Germany (West Germany) created
October	People's Republic of China proclaimed; German Democratic Republic (East Germany) proclaimed

1950

February	Sino-Soviet pact signed in Moscow
April	National Security Council Report 68 drafted
June	Beginning of Korean War
1952	First U.S. hydrogen bomb exploded; Dwight D. Eisenhower elected president

1953

March	Death of Stalin
June	East Berlin uprising
July	Armistice in Korea
August	First Soviet H-bomb test
September	Nikita Khrushchev becomes first secretary of Soviet Communist Party
1954	Chinese bombardment of Quemoy and Matsu
1955	West Germany admitted to NATO; Warsaw Pact signed; Austrian State Treaty signed; Austria neutralized

1956

February	Khrushchev denounces Stalin at Twentieth Party Congress
June	Poznan uprising in Poland
October	Start of Hungarian uprising
November	Soviet Union intervenes in Hungary

1957

August	Launching of first Soviet intercontinental ballistic missile (ICBM)
October	Sputnik satellite launched

1958

February	Launching of first U.S. satellite
August	China threatens Taiwan

1959

January	Victory of Fidel Castro in Cuba
September	Khrushchev visits United States

1960

February	First French atomic bomb test
May	U.S. U-2 reconnaissance plane shot down over Soviet Union; Paris summit fails

1961

April	Failure of Bay of Pigs landing in Cuba
June	Khrushchev and John F. Kennedy meet in Vienna
August	Building of the Berlin Wall
October	Incidents at Checkpoint Charlie in Berlin; tensions increase

1962

October	Cuban missile crisis

1963

June	Kennedy visits Berlin, declares *"Ich bin ein Berliner"* ("I am a Berliner") as a gesture of solidarity
October	Kennedy signs Limited Test Ban Treaty; Soviet Union, United States, and Britain outlaw tests in the atmosphere, underwater, and in space
November	Kennedy assassinated; Lyndon Johnson sworn into office

1964

August	Tonkin Gulf Resolution passes Congress, escalating U.S. involvement in Vietnam
October	Khrushchev ousted, replaced by Leonid Brezhnev and Alexei Kosygin
November	China detonates first atomic bomb

1966

March	Anti–Vietnam War rallies held in United States and Europe
April	Beginning of Chinese Cultural Revolution

1967

January	United States, Soviet Union, and 60 other countries agree to Outer Space Treaty limiting military uses of space
June	China explodes first H-bomb

1968

January	Prague Spring reforms begin in Czechoslovakia; Tet Offensive in Vietnam
July	Treaty on the Non-Proliferation of Nuclear Weapons by United States, Soviet Union, and 58 other countries
August	Soviet invasion of Czechoslovakia
November	Richard Nixon elected president
December	U.S. forces reach peak of 543,400 in Vietnam

1969	Strategic Arms Limitation Talks (SALT) begin between United States and Soviet Union
1970	
February	Paris Peace Talks begin between United States and North Vietnam
April	U.S. troops invade Cambodia; four U.S. college students killed by National Guard at Kent State University at antiwar rally
1971	People's Republic of China joins United Nations
1972	
February	Nixon visits China
May	SALT I signed, freezing number of ICBMs and submarine-launched ballistic missiles in place for five years
1973	
January	Paris Accords establish cease-fire and political settlement of Vietnam War
May	East Germany and West Germany establish formal diplomatic relations
September	Chilean socialist government of Salvador Allende overthrown in U.S.-backed military coup
October	Yom Kippur War between Israel and Arab states; United States and Soviet Union nearly drawn into conflict; Arab oil embargo against the United States that lasts until March 1974
1974	Nixon resigns over Watergate; Gerald Ford sworn in as president
1975	
April	United States leaves Vietnam after fall of Saigon
July	U.S. and Soviet astronauts link up in space; United States and Soviet Union sign Helsinki Accords, pledging acceptance of European borders and protection for human rights
1976	Jimmy Carter elected president
1979	
January	United States and People's Republic of China establish full diplomatic relations
June	SALT II agreement limiting long-range missiles and bombers signed by Carter and Brezhnev

July	Sandinista forces overthrow dictatorship in Nicaragua
December	Soviet Union invades Afghanistan; United States imposes sanctions and announces intention to boycott Moscow Olympics
1980	Carter Doctrine states that Persian Gulf is a vital U.S. interest
1981	
January	Lech Walesa leads Polish Solidarity union in illegal strike; Ronald Reagan inaugurated
December	Martial law imposed in Poland
1982	Reagan outlines Strategic Arms Reduction Treaty (START) to reduce ICBMs and number of strategic nuclear weapons on both sides
1983	
March	Reagan proposes Strategic Defense Initiative (SDI), popularly called "Star Wars," to develop missile defense technology
November	United States begins deployment of intermediate-range nuclear Pershing II missiles in West Germany
1985	Mikhail Gorbachev becomes Soviet general secretary; Nuclear and Space Talks open in Geneva, based on START model
1986	
October	At Reykjavik Summit, Reagan refuses Gorbachev's proposal to make significant arms reductions if United States gives up SDI
November	Secret funding of Nicaraguan contras through arms sales to Iran becomes public
1987	At Washington Summit, Reagan and Gorbachev agree to eliminate intermediate-range nuclear forces and work toward completing a START agreement
1988	
April	Soviet Union agrees to withdraw from Afghanistan by February 1989
June	Gorbachev tells Communist Party leaders that elements of communist doctrine must change
August	Cuba withdraws troops from Angola
November	George H. W. Bush elected president

1989

| June | Chinese army assaults prodemocracy demonstrators in Tiananmen Square |
| November | Berlin Wall falls; thousands of East Germans cross to Western side |

1990

May–June	Washington Summit between Bush and Gorbachev
October	Germany reunifies
November	Treaty of Conventional Armed Forces in Europe cuts size of land armies
December	Walesa elected president of Poland

1991

July	Bush and Gorbachev sign START, pledge to destroy thousands of nuclear weapons
August	Coup against Gorbachev fails, but power flows to Russian president Boris Yeltsin
September	All Strategic Air Command bombers, tankers, and Minuteman II ICBMs taken off alert
December	Soviet Union dissolves; United States recognizes Armenia, Belarus, Kazakhstan, Kyrgyzstan, Russia, and Ukraine

Study Questions

1. When did the Cold War begin? Why? What do realist, liberal, and constructivist approaches contribute to your answers?

2. Was the Cold War inevitable? If so, why and when? If not, when and how could it have been avoided?

3. Why were leaders unable to restore a nineteenth-century-style Concert system after World War II? What sort of system evolved?

4. How important were first- and second-image considerations in the development of the Cold War? What were the views of U.S. and European leaders on the Soviet Union and its international ambitions? What were Soviet views of the United States and the rest of the West?

5. Some historians argue that the real question is not why the Cold War occurred, but why it did not escalate into a "hot" war. Do you agree? Why didn't a hot war begin?

6. What is "containment"? How did this U.S. policy emerge, and how was it implemented? What were Soviet responses?

7. How are nuclear weapons different from conventional weapons? Has the advent of nuclear weapons fundamentally changed the way that countries behave?

8. Is Mueller correct that nuclear weapons are not the cause of the obsolescence of major wars among developed states? What other factors does he consider?

9. Is nuclear deterrence morally defensible? Or, in the words of one theorist, is it morally analogous to tying infants to the front bumpers of automobiles to prevent traffic accidents on Memorial Day? Might some strategies of deterrence be more ethical than others?

10. What is the significance of nuclear weapons to international relations apart from nuclear deterrence? How useful are they?

11. Why did the Cold War end? What do realist, liberal, and constructivist approaches contribute to your answers? What roles did hard power and soft power play?

Notes

1. Joyce Kolko and Gabriel Kolko, *The Limits of Power: The World and United States Foreign Policy, 1945–1954* (New York: Harper & Row, 1972); William Appleman Williams, *The Tragedy of American Diplomacy* ([New York,: Dell Pub. Co., 1972).

2. John Lewis Gaddis, *The Cold War: A New History* (New York: Penguin, 2005); *We Now Know: Rethinking Cold War History* (Oxford: Clarendon Press, 1997).

3. Milovan Djilas, *Conversations with Stalin*, trans. Michael B. Petrovich (San Diego: Harcourt Brace Jovanovich, 1962), p. 114.

4. Roosevelt to Stalin, October 4, 1944; in Susan Butler, ed., *My Dear Mr. Stalin: The Complete Correspondence between Franklin D. Roosevelt and Joseph V. Stalin* (New Haven, CT: Yale University Press, 2005), p. 260.

5. William Taubman, *Stalin's American Policy* (New York: Norton, 1982), p. 133.

6. Ibid., p. 36.

7. Dean Acheson, *Present at the Creation* (New York: Norton, 1969), p. 375.

8. X (George F. Kennan), "The Sources of Soviet Conduct," *Foreign Affairs*, Vol. 25, No. 4 (July 1947), pp. 566–582. Republished with permission of Foreign Affairs from George Kennan, "The Sources of Soviet Conduct." Permission conveyed through Copyright Clearance Center, Inc.

9. Ibid., p. 582.

10. Norman Podhoretz, *Why We Were in Vietnam* (New York: Simon and Schuster, 1982).

11. Paul M. Kennedy, *The Rise and Fall of the Great Powers: Economic Change and Military Conflict from 1500–2000* (London: Fontana press, 1989).

12. Joseph A. Schumpeter, *Capitalism, Socialism and Democracy* (Milton Park, Abingdon, Oxon: Routledge, 2010).

13. John L. Gaddis, "The New Cold War History," *Foreign Policy Research Institute Footnotes* 5:5 (June 1998).

14. Michael Doyle, "Liberalism and World Politics," *American Political Science Review*, Vol. 80, No. 4 (December 1986), pp. 1151–1169.

15. Committee on the Atmospheric Effects of Nuclear Explosions, National Research Council, *The Effects on the Atmosphere of a Major Nuclear Exchange* (Washington, D.C.: National Academy Press, 1985).

16. United States Catholic Conference, "The Challenge of Peace: God's Promise and Our Response," *Origins* 13:1 (May 19, 1983), p. 1.

17. Kenneth N. Waltz, *Theory of International Politics* (New York: Random House, 1979).

18. John Mueller, "The Essential Irrelevance of Nuclear Weapons: Stability in the Postwar World," *International Security*, Vol. 13, No. 2 (Autumn 1988), pp. 55–79.

19. Quoted in *The New York Times*, April 30, 1985, p. 6.

20. Stephen E. Ambrose, *Eisenhower* (New York: Simon & Schuster, 1983), p. 184.

21. The intelligence available to the Central Intelligence Agency in September 1961 suggested that the Soviets had somewhere between 10 and 25 intercontinental ballistic missile (ICBM) launchers. Jeffrey Richelson, *The Wizards of Langley: Inside the CIA's Directorate of Science and Technology* (Boulder, CO: Westview Press, 2001), p. 28.

22. Among the sobering events at the height of the crisis were, on the U.S. side, a reconnaissance plane accidentally straying into Soviet airspace, a Titan ICBM being launched from California according to its preplanned flight-test schedule, a Minuteman ICBM crew in Montana hot-wiring their launch control system, and a training tape mistakenly feeding into radar monitors in New Jersey indicating a Soviet nuclear missile attack. On the Soviet side, a submarine commander, mistakenly thinking war had already broken out, ordered his nuclear torpedo armed and fired (an order countermanded by the submarine's cooler-headed political officer); and the shooting down of a U.S. reconnaissance plane over Cuba in violation of standing orders. Don Munton and David A. Welch, *The Cuban Missile Crisis: A Concise History*, 2nd ed. (New York: Oxford University Press, 2011), pp. 99–100. See also Michael Dobbs, *One Minute to Midnight: Kennedy, Khrushchev, and Castro on the Brink of Nuclear War* (New York: Knopf, 2008).

23. Khrushchev to Kennedy, October 26, 1962, http://microsites.jfklibrary.org/cmc/oct26/doc4.html.

24. Ernest R. May and Philip D. Zelikow, eds., *The Kennedy Tapes: Inside the White House During the Cuban Missile Crisis* (Cambridge, MA: Belknap & Harvard University Press, 1997), p. 1.

25. James Blight and David Welch, *On the Brink: Americans and Soviets Reexamine the Cuban Missile Crisis* (New York: Hill & Wang, 1989), p. 80.

26. Robert McNamara, *Blundering into Disaster: Surviving the First Century of the Nuclear Age* (New York: Pantheon, 1986), p. 14.

27. Theodore C. Sorensen, *Kennedy* (New York: Harper & Row, 1965), p. 705.

28. National Conference of Catholic Bishops, *The Challenge of Peace: God's Promise and Our Response: A Pastoral Letter on War and Peace* (Washington, D.C.: U.S. Catholic Conference, 1983).

Chapter 6

Conflict and Cooperation in the Post–Cold War World

Photo: Shi Jindong/Xinhua/Landov

Chinese UN peacekeeper helping African children

∨ Learning Objectives

6.1 Identify the distinctive features of cooperation problems and explain how managing international conflict differs from managing domestic conflict.

6.2 Articulate the complexity and changing nature of armed conflict today and identify relevant moral criteria for international intervention.

Managing Conflict on the World Stage

6.1 Identify the distinctive features of cooperation problems and explain how managing international conflict differs from managing domestic conflict.

Conflict marks all aspects of our social lives. Anytime two or more people have different preferences, there is a potential conflict. If you want to watch *Game of Thrones* and your sister wants to watch *The Vampire Diaries* and there is only one television set, you have a conflict. The overwhelming majority of conflicts in life are resolved peacefully. Very few escalate to violence. In some cases, conflicts are resolved by one party winning and another losing. If your parents tell you that you must let your sister watch *The Vampire Diaries*, she has won and you have lost. You may not be happy about it, but you are unlikely to fetch a gun and start shooting.

Another way of resolving conflict is a compromise in which you get some—but not all—of what you want. If you and your sister both want the last piece of cake, one solution is to cut it in half. This method may work with cake, but it does not work very well with television dramas. You and your sister are both likely to think that half a piece of cake is better than none, but half an episode of *Game of Thrones* is completely unsatisfying.

When your parents tell you to let your sister watch *The Vampire Diaries*, they may soften the blow by promising that you will get your way next time. If so, they would be managing the conflict by invoking a norm of turn-taking, a form of reciprocity. This move effectively embeds a single instance of winner/loser conflict resolution into a broader pattern of compromise. Over time, you and your sister will share the television. If you are like most people, that will soothe the sting of defeat. It will also make you more likely to respect your parents' authority, because they are being reasonable and fair.

A third way of resolving conflict is for someone to persuade either party or both to change their preferences. Your father may inform you that tonight's episode of *Game of Thrones* is a rerun that you have already seen. Your mother may offer to pay if you both go out for ice cream instead of watching TV.

Notice the variety in these scenarios not only in the solutions, but also in the conflict management strategies. By simply ordering you to defer to your sister, you parents leveraged their authority, which, as you will recall from Chapter 2, is a right to rule. By proposing a norm of turn-taking, they leveraged your sense of fairness and promoted a norm. By telling you about the rerun, your father wielded soft power by altering your preferences by providing new information. By offering to buy you ice cream, your mother wielded hard power in the form of a material incentive.

Peaceful conflict management of this kind requires mutual *cooperation*, which the dictionary defines simply as "working or acting together" but which in political science, economics, or game theory has one additional key component:

namely, resisting a temptation to cheat, defect, or "free ride." Cooperation does not normally come naturally. Someone, or something, must usually arrange it. Take, for example, defense spending in the context of a military alliance. If you are confident that the other members of the alliance will protect you, you have a strong incentive to spend little on defense and let them carry the burden. But if everyone does that, the alliance will not be strong enough to protect anyone. So, alliances typically negotiate burden-sharing arrangements.

Harmony is a situation in which people share the same preference and everyone can be happy at once. Harmony is nice, and most people experience it at least some of the time; often, though, we do not even notice it because it does not present us with a problem to solve. At most, harmony requires simple *coordination*. The orchestra conductor's job is to make sure that everyone plays their instrument at just the right time; if they don't, the music sounds terrible. Because everybody has a strong interest in the music sounding beautiful, no one is giving anything up, or resisting a temptation to defect, by playing in time with the conductor.

Not all solutions or strategies of conflict management are available at all times or are effective in all cases. Much depends on the nature of the "good" at stake. Economists distinguish between four main types of goods:

1. "Private goods" are *excludable*: It is possible to prevent others from getting them. There is also *rivalry* for private goods. If you have a private good, it means that no one else can have it. Your car is a private good. If you have the keys (and a decent antitheft system), you can prevent others from driving it, and if you are driving it, others cannot.

2. "Public goods" are nonexcludable and nonrivalrous: There is no way of preventing others from enjoying them, and if you have some, it does not effectively diminish what is available for the benefit of others. Clean air is a public good: It is virtually impossible to prevent people from breathing, and your breathing does not reduce the ability of others to breathe as well.

3. "Club goods" are excludable and nonrivalrous. They include such things as satellite television signals. In contrast to conventional radio signals, satellite TV broadcasts are encrypted, and you can prevent people from watching by controlling access to the set-top boxes that decrypt them. Anyone with a decoder can watch, however. Your decoding the signal does not weaken it for others.

4. "Common goods" are nonexcludable and rivalrous. They include such things as wild fish and game. You cannot stop people from fishing, but if you catch a fish, no one else can catch it. The exception is if you are fishing purely for sport and throw it back, in which case you have turned that particular fish into a public good!

Different kinds of goods pose different problems for cooperation. As the defense spending illustration shows, a classic problem of cooperation concerning public goods is underprovision: Because everyone can benefit from a public good, no one has a strong incentive to shoulder the cost of providing it. Roads are another example of a public good. Most drivers would be willing in principle to chip in voluntarily for the cost of building and maintaining roads, but there would always be people who sought a free ride. Studies show that the amount of money that would be available for roads if the entire budget came from voluntary donations would be nowhere near what was needed, so governments resort to taxes, tolls, or some combination of the two.

A classic cooperation problem involving common goods is called the "tragedy of the commons." The North Atlantic cod fishing industry, for example, collapsed in the 1990s in part because every individual trawler captain had a financial incentive to catch as many fish as possible, and as a result, fishing fleets caught cod faster than the fish could reproduce.

Cooperation is required to decide how to allocate and safeguard the use of private goods and club goods as well. Your car is only really *your* car against the backdrop of a complex social, legal, and economic system that makes possible things such as financing, licensing, registration, and law enforcement (to defend your right to ownership). Someone had to mark out a particular part of the electromagnetic spectrum for the use of satellite TV and prevent someone else from trying to broadcast at that frequency. The same can be said of radio signals in a sense. The signals may be public goods, but the radio spectrum is not: It is a private good. You can prevent people from using it at all, and if someone broadcasts at a particular frequency, no one else within range can broadcast at that frequency at the same time.

As we can see, cooperation is often essential to ensure that people can benefit from goods of any kind. The above examples demonstrate that many of the most effective solutions to cooperation problems involve rules and norms, often created and enforced by governments (or other authorities, such as parents, associations, and clubs). In fact, governments sometimes use their powers to ensure that goods do not migrate from one category to another. MP3 music files, for example, are in a certain sense natural public goods: With online file sharing, it is almost impossible to prevent people from getting them, and one person downloading an MP3 file does not prevent another person from downloading it also. But if music were a true public good, performers and composers would be unable to earn a living from music because of the free-rider problem. So, governments try to enforce intellectual property rights by passing laws against file sharing, and increasingly they go after people who illegally share files. In the summer of 2009, a Boston University graduate student was ordered to pay four record labels $675,000 for downloading and sharing music by groups such as Green Day and Nirvana.

One of the great differences between international politics and domestic politics is precisely that there is no higher authority than states, which means that a large number of mechanisms for solving problems of international cooperation are simply not available. That does not make international cooperation impossible, but it does complicate it. Green Day and Nirvana can get the U.S. government to prosecute people in the United States who illegally share music, but Washington cannot arrest, try, and punish someone who shares files from his home computer in Shanghai. Instead, U.S. officials must try to persuade the government of China to pass and enforce intellectual property rights laws. As a sovereign state, China has a perfect right to decide whether or not to do so, although it must consider the political or economic costs of annoying other countries if it refuses.

Interestingly, even though international cooperation is generally more difficult than domestic cooperation, the overwhelming majority of international conflicts are resolved peacefully. Relatively few escalate to violence. That is true for almost any kind of conflict over any kind of good: trade disputes, macroeconomic policy disputes, burden-sharing disputes, environmental disputes, and even territorial disputes. When attempts to resolve them fail, the most common outcome is either a standoff or further efforts to find agreeable solutions. Rarely does war break out. During the Cold War, most people did not notice that cooperation was so common, because the Cold War itself was such a preoccupation. Even so, as we saw in Chapter 5, there was remarkably little Cold War violence, at least when seen against the background of the levels of destruction of which the superpowers were capable. Most Cold War violence took place on the so-called periphery and involved Cold War "proxies" (Soviet or U.S. client regimes, liberation movements, and militias or irregular forces of various kinds). Even though there were many unresolved East-West conflicts, most of them were nothing more than standoffs that gradually came to be managed through broader and deeper cooperative agreements, either formal (such as arms control treaties) or informal (various "security regimes").

International Law and International Organization

Two of the primary vehicles for managing conflict and promoting cooperation in world politics are international law and international organization. We have already encountered them many times in the course of our exploration thus far, but it is worth examining them more closely here because many people heralded the end of the Cold War as an opportunity at last to realize the Wilsonian dream of a world governed more effectively and more reliably by means of both. One could say that new Wilsonians expected constructivist processes of socialization and norm-promotion to overcome realist obstacles to liberal ideals. Arguably, the world is a more orderly place today precisely because of progress in international governance and the deepening and thickening of norms of peaceful conflict resolution. But the most optimistic neo-Wilsonians have been disappointed thus far; the world is not as peaceful, not as stable, and not as safe as they had hoped it would be by now. At the same time, however, the pessimists who confidently predicted that the enduring logic of realism would simply give rise to some new dominant axis of enmity that would frustrate any progress whatsoever have been proven wrong as well.

People sometimes have problems understanding international law and organization because they use a misleading domestic analogy. International organizations are not exactly like domestic government agencies or ministries, and international law is not exactly like domestic law. International organizations do not act as an incipient world government for two reasons. First, the sovereignty of member states is protected in the charters of most international organizations. The United Nations is the closest thing we have to a world government, because of its near-universal membership and its exceptionally broad mandate and agenda, but Article 2.7 of the UN Charter says: "Nothing in the Charter shall authorize the United Nations to intervene in matters within domestic jurisdiction." In other words, the organization is not an effort to replace states. Similarly, the *World Trade Organization* (WTO) does a good job of resolving trade disputes, but not because it has authority over and above its member states. Its effectiveness depends entirely on its member states' realization that obeying a global set of trade rules is in their long-term self-interest, even if it means having to be willing to lose a particular trade dispute case every now and then. (Although the WTO does a good job of promoting *cooperation* in trade, the International Civil Aviation Organization, or ICAO, does an excellent job of *coordinating* rules and procedures for air travel. Aviation, unlike trade, is a case of harmony, not conflict, because everyone shares the same set of interests and has no short-term incentive to defect. But neither the WTO nor the ICAO has authority comparable to that of the Commerce Department or the Federal Aviation Administration in the United States, both of whose decisions can be backed up by U.S. courts and the full weight of U.S. law.)

The other reason that international organization is not incipient world government is because of its weakness. There is an international judiciary in the form of the *International Court of Justice* (ICJ), which consists of fifteen judges elected for nine-year terms by the United Nations, but the ICJ is not a world supreme court. States may refuse its jurisdiction, and a state may refuse to accept the court's judgments even if it has accepted the court's jurisdiction. In the 1980s, for example, the Reagan administration refused to accept an ICJ ruling that the United States had acted illegally in mining the harbors of Nicaragua.

If we imagine the UN General Assembly as the equivalent of Congress, it is a very strange kind of legislature. It is based on the principle of one state, one vote, but that principle reflects neither democracy nor power relations in the world. Democracy rests on the principle of one person, one vote. In the UN General Assembly, the Maldive Islands in the southern Indian Ocean with a population of only 350,000 has one vote, and Brazil, a country with 200 million people, has one vote. That means that a Maldive Islander has roughly 570 times the voting power of a Brazilian in the UN General Assembly, which does not fit well with the democratic criteria for legislatures. It is not a very good reflection of power either, because the Maldive Islands has the same vote in the General Assembly as the United States or India or China. So there is an oddity about the General Assembly that makes states unwilling to have it pass binding legislation. UN General Assembly resolutions are just that: resolutions, not laws.

Finally, we might imagine that the secretary-general of the United Nations is the incipient new president of the world, but that is also misleading. The secretary-general is a weak executive, more secretary than general. If the secretary-general has power, it is more like the soft power of a pope than the combination of hard power and soft power that a president possesses. Trying to understand international organizations by analogy to domestic government is a sure way to get the wrong set of answers. They are better understood as frameworks by which states arrange cooperation or coordination.

International law is not like domestic law in various important ways. Domestic law is the product of legislatures and customs, sometimes called common law. Domestic law involves provisions for enforcement, adjudication, and orderly revision. Public international law is similar in the sense that it consists of treaties—which are agreements among states—and customs—which are the generally accepted practices of states—but it differs dramatically in enforcement and adjudication. On enforcement, there is no executive to make a state accept a court decision. International politics is a self-help system. In the classic ways of international law, enforcement was sometimes provided by the great powers. For example, in the law of the sea, a custom developed that a state could claim a three-mile jurisdiction out into the oceans. In the nineteenth century, when Uruguay claimed broader territorial seas to protect the fisheries off its coasts, Britain, the greatest naval power of the day, sent gunboats within three miles of the coast. In the 1980s, when Libya attempted to claim the Gulf of Sidra as territorial water, the United States, then and still the greatest naval power in the world, sent in the Sixth Fleet. You might ask, "Who enforced the law against Britain or the United States if they violated the law?" The answer is that enforcement in a self-help system is a one-way street.

Unlike domestic legal systems, in which individuals can bring cases before courts, many international courts, including the ICJ, only take cases brought by states. (The European Union's General Court in Luxembourg is a regional exception.) The ICJ has had relatively few cases, in part because states often prefer to try to negotiate solutions to disputes and in part because states frequently do not like to run the risk of losing. In the 1990s, special tribunals were established to try war criminals from the Bosnian and Rwandan conflicts. In 2002, a large number of states established an *International Criminal Court* (ICC) to try war criminals and genocidaires if their national governments failed to try them, but many significant states, including the United States and China, refused to ratify the treaty because they believed that it infringed on their sovereignty. In addition, there are problems about how customary rules should be interpreted even when a principle is agreed on. Take the principle of expropriation. It is accepted that a state can nationalize a corporation from another country that operates on its territory, but it must pay compensation for what the corporation is worth. But who is to say what is just compensation? Many of the less developed countries that have nationalized properties owned by foreign firms have argued that low compensation is adequate; rich countries that are commonly home to those firms usually want higher levels.

Finally, even when the UN General Assembly has passed resolutions, there is a good deal of ambiguity about what they mean. They are not binding legislation. The only area in the UN Charter in which a state must legally accept a decision is Chapter VII, which deals with threats to peace, breaches of the peace, and acts of aggression. If the Security Council (not the General Assembly) finds that there has been an act of aggression or threats to peace warranting sanctions, member states are bound to apply the sanctions. That is what happened in 1990 when Iraq invaded Kuwait and in 2001 after the United States was the target of the 9/11 transnational terrorist attacks.

The other way in which new law is sometimes created is through intergovernmental conferences that negotiate draft treaties for governments to sign. Such conferences are often very large and unwieldy. For example, in the 1970s the Law of the Sea Conference involved more than 100 participating states trying to draft principles for a 12-mile territorial sea, an exclusive economic zone for fisheries out to 200 miles, and designating the minerals on the bottom of the ocean as the common heritage of all. The trouble was that some states agreed to only parts of the text, leaving the outcome unclear in international law. In 1995, when the United States wanted to resist possible Chinese claims to the seas around the Spratly Islands, it nonetheless appealed to the United Nations Convention on the Law of the Sea, as it continues to do today even though the U.S. Senate has not yet ratified it.

International law reflects the fragmented nature of international politics. The weak sense of community means that there is less willingness to obey or restrain oneself out of a sense of obligation or acceptance of authority. The absence of a common executive with a monopoly on the legitimate use of force means that sovereign states are in the realms of self-help, force, and survival. And when matters of survival come up, law usually takes second place.

Predictability and Legitimacy

International law and organization are nonetheless an important part of political reality because they affect the way states behave. States have an interest in international law for two reasons: predictability and legitimacy.

States, like people, are involved in conflicts with one another all the time. The vast range of international transactions, both public and private, includes trade, tourism, diplomatic missions, and contacts among peoples across national boundaries. As interdependence grows, those contacts grow, and there are increasing opportunities for friction. International law allows governments to avoid conflict at a high level when such friction arises. For example, if an American tourist is arrested for smuggling drugs in Mexico, if a British ship collides with a Norwegian ship in the North Sea, or if a Japanese firm claims that an Indian company has infringed its patents, the governments may not want to spoil their other relations over these private conflicts. Handling such issues by international law and agreed principles depoliticizes them and makes them predictable. Predictability is necessary for transactions to flourish and for the orderly handling of the conflicts that inevitably accompany them.

Legitimacy is a second reason governments have an interest in international law. Politics is not merely a struggle for physical power, but also a contest over legitimacy. As we saw in Chapter 2, power and legitimacy are not antithetical, but complementary. Humans are neither purely moral nor totally cynical. It is a political fact that the belief in right and wrong helps move people to act; therefore, legitimacy is a source of power. If a state's acts are perceived as illegitimate, the costs of a policy will be higher because compliance will be lower. States appeal to international law and organization to legitimize their own policies or delegitimize others, and that often shapes their tactics and outcomes. Legitimacy enhances a state's soft power.

In major conflicts of interest, international law may not always restrain states, but it often helps shape the flow of policy. Law is part of the power struggle. Cynics may say that law is just made up of games lawyers play; governments nonetheless find it important to make legal arguments or to take the resolutions of international organizations into account, which shows that laws are not completely insignificant. To put it in an aphorism: "When claims to virtue are made by vice, then at least we know virtue has a price." Simply put, governments may be trapped by their own legal excuses.

An example is UN Security Council Resolution 242. Passed at the end of the 1967 Middle East War, it called for a return to prewar boundaries. Over the years, it had the effect of denying the legitimacy of the Israeli occupation of the territories that it captured during that war. That put Israel on the defensive in the United Nations. The Arab states lost the war, but they were nonetheless able to put pressure on Israel. In 1976, when the Arab coalition tried to expel Israel from the United Nations, the United States spent a good deal of political capital lobbying before the General Assembly to prevent Israel's expulsion, another indication that symbols of legitimacy in international organizations are part of a power struggle.

When vital issues of survival are at stake, a state will use its most effective form of power, which is military force, which may explain the limited success of efforts of international law and organization to deal with the use of force. It is one thing to handle drug smuggling, collision of ships at sea, or patent infringement by international law; it is another to put the survival of one's country at risk by obeying international law. That was the problem with collective security in the 1930s, but a modified form of collective security was re-created in the UN charter.

The United Nations: Collective Security, Peacekeeping, and Peacebuilding

The classical balance of power did not make war illegal. The use of military force was accepted, and it often ensured the stability of the system. During the nineteenth century, with changes in technology making war more destructive and with the rise of democracy and peace movements, there were several efforts to organize states against war. Twenty-six states held a peace conference at The Hague in 1899. In 1907, another Hague conference was attended by 44 states. The approach taken in these conferences was very legalistic. The conferees tried to persuade all states to sign treaties of arbitration so that disputes would be handled by arbitration rather than force. They also tried to codify rules of war in case arbitration did not work.

As we saw in Chapter 4, the League of Nations was an attempt after World War I to develop a coalition of states that would deter and punish aggressors. In the eyes of Woodrow Wilson and those who thought as he did, World War I had been largely an accidental and unnecessary war caused by the balance of power, and such wars could be prevented by an alliance of all states for collective security. If the League of Nations was designed to prevent another World War I, the United Nations was designed in 1943–1945 to prevent a repeat of World War II. Forty-nine states met in San Francisco in 1945 to sign a charter that included innovations to repair the deficiencies of the League. Unlike the balance-of-power system of the nineteenth century, the use of force was now illegal for any state that signed the UN charter, with exceptions only for self-defense, collective self-defense, and collective security.

The designers of the United Nations also created a Security Council composed of five permanent members and a rotating pool of nonpermanent members. The Security Council can be seen as a nineteenth-century balance-of-power mechanism integrated into the collective security framework of the United Nations. The Security Council can pass binding resolutions under Chapter VII of the charter. If the five great power police officers do not agree, they each have a veto, which is like a fuse box in a house lighting system. The United Nations' founders believed that it was preferable to allow the great powers each to have a veto that makes the lights go out rather than have the house burn down in the form of a war against one or two recalcitrant great powers.

During the Cold War, the UN collective security system only worked once, in the Korean War, and it only worked then because the Soviet Union was boycotting the Security Council over the issue of the Nationalist government in Taiwan, rather than the Communist government in Beijing, occupying the China seat. For most of the Cold War, the great powers could not agree on what counted as a legitimate use of force. They also experienced great difficulty trying to define aggression. For example, how should one weigh covert infiltration against forces crossing a border first? In 1956, Israel suffered from covert attacks by Egyptian-backed guerrillas, yet Israeli conventional forces crossed the border into Egypt first. Depending on which side you favored, you took a different view regarding who was the aggressor in this case. For two decades during the Cold War, UN committees tried to define aggression. They came up with a vague and generally ineffective rule: A list of acts of aggression was followed by the proviso that the Security Council could determine that other acts also constituted aggression. Even when armed force had been used, the Security Council could choose not to declare that there had been any aggression. So, as far as the United Nations was concerned, aggression was committed when the Security Council said it was. Everything depended on a consensus in the Security Council, and that was rare during the Cold War.

The impasse over collective security gave rise to the concept of UN preventive diplomacy and *peacekeeping* forces. Rather than identifying and punishing the aggressor, which is the basic concept of collective security, the United Nations would assemble independent forces and interpose them between the warring powers. The model was developed during the Suez Canal crisis of 1956.

In July 1956, President Gamal Abdel Nasser of Egypt nationalized the Suez Canal (Figure 6.1). Sir Anthony Eden, the British prime minister, saw this move as a major threat to Britain. He regarded Nasser as a new Adolf Hitler, and he drew analogies to the 1930s. He worried about Nasser having accepted Soviet arms. Britain worked up a secret plan with France and Israel: Israel would attack Egypt, which had been sending guerrillas across the Israeli border, whereupon France and Britain would "intervene" to restore peace, occupying the Suez Canal in the process. The UN Security Council debated a resolution calling for a cease-fire, which Britain and France vetoed. They wanted their intervention to continue long enough to destabilize Nasser.

Dag Hammarskjöld, the UN secretary-general, working with Lester Pearson, Canadian secretary of state for external affairs, devised a plan to separate the Israelis and the Egyptians by inserting a UN peacekeeping force. A resolution in the General Assembly, where there was no veto, authorized a UN force in the Sinai region. The United States did not support its European allies, worrying that their intervention would antagonize Arab nationalists and increase the opportunities for the Soviet Union in the Middle East. On November 15, the first United Nations Emergency Force (UNEF) deployed into the Sinai between Egyptian and Israeli forces, and later in December, the United Nations took on the task of clearing the ships that had been sunk in the canal.

UNEF served as a model for dozens of "blue helmet" peacekeeping missions, and in 1992, the United Nations created a Department of Peacekeeping Operations to oversee them. The total number of UN peacekeeping operations to date is 69, and at present, there are 16 missions on four continents. Nearly 100,000 troops from 120 countries participate, with a 2014–2015 budget of just over $7 billion. Peacekeeping is an excellent example of a useful function that the United Nations invented for itself. The founders of the United Nations in 1945 never imagined it. They did imagine collective security operations, of course, but thus far there have been only two (Korea in 1950 and Kuwait in 1991).

Thus, even though the Cold War prevented the United Nations from implementing the formal doctrine of collective security, it did not prevent the innovation of using international forces to keep two sides apart. In collective security, if a state crosses a line, all the others are to unite against it and push it back. In peacekeeping, if a state crosses a line, the United Nations steps in and holds the parties apart without judging who is right or wrong. During the Cold War, one

Figure 6.1 The Suez Crisis and the Birth of Peacekeeping

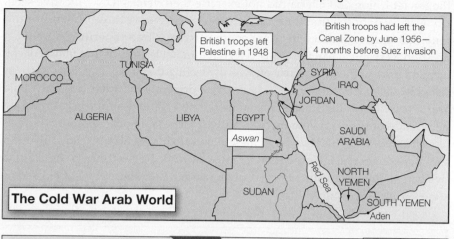

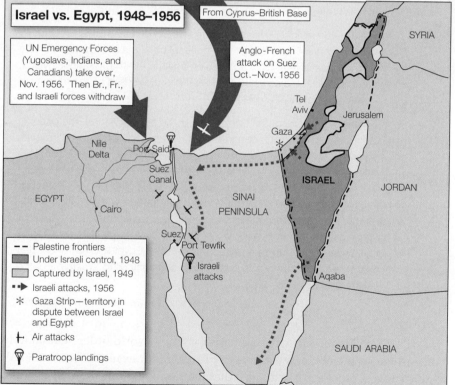

SOURCE: Brian Catchpole, A Map History of the Modern World (Oxford: Heinemann Publishers, 1982), reprinted with adjustments by permission.

of the basic principles of UN peacekeeping was that the forces always came from small states, not from the Soviet Union or the United States, so that the great powers would be kept out of direct conflict. Preventive diplomacy and peace-keeping were important innovations that still play significant roles in regulating international conflicts. But they are not collective security, and today many peacekeepers are trying to separate parties in internal conflicts.

Iraq's 1990 invasion of Kuwait was the first post–Cold War crisis. Because the Soviet Union and China did not exercise their vetoes, UN collective security was used for the first time in forty years. There were three reasons for this remarkable resurrection. First, Iraq committed an extraordinarily clear-cut aggression, very much like the 1930s, which reminded leaders of that failure of collective security. The second reason was the feeling that if UN collective security failed in such a clear case, it would not be a principle for order in a post–Cold War world. Third, the small states in the United Nations supported the action because most of them were fragile and had disputable postcolonial boundaries. The arguments that Saddam Hussein used to justify his invasion of Kuwait threatened most of the other small states as well. To paraphrase the Haitian delegate to the League of Nations quoted earlier, they did not want to become someone else's Kuwait.

A Letter to President Dwight D. Eisenhower

In the nineteen-thirties Hitler established his position by a series of carefully planned movements. These began with occupation of the Rhineland and were followed by successive acts of aggression against Austria, Czechoslovakia, Poland and the West. His actions were tolerated and excused by the majority of the population of Western Europe . . . .

Similarly the seizure of the Suez Canal is, we are convinced, the opening gambit in a planned campaign designed by Nasser to expel all Western influence and interests from Arab countries. He believes that if he can get away with this, and if he can successfully defy eighteen nations, his prestige in Arabia will be so great that he will be able to mount revolutions of young officers in Saudi Arabia, Jordan, Syria and Iraq. (We know that he is already preparing a revolution in Iraq, which is most stable and progressive.) These new Governments will in effect be Egyptian satellites if not Russian ones. They will have to place their united oil resources under the control of a United Arabia led by Egypt and under Russian influence. When that moment comes Nasser can deny oil to Western Europe and we here shall be at his mercy.

—British Prime Minister Anthony Eden, 1956[1]

Will UN collective security be a basis for a new world order? Only rarely. The permanent members of the Security Council, for example, were not able to agree on resolutions to authorize either the Kosovo or Iraq wars in 1999 and 2003. There are important problems. First, the UN system works best when there is clear-cut aggression; it is much more difficult to apply in civil wars. Second, collective security will work if there is no veto, but if the United States, Russia, China, Britain, and France cannot reach agreement, collective security will be hamstrung once more. Moreover, in 1945, UN collective security was not designed to be applicable against the five great powers with vetoes in the Security Council. Third, collective security works when UN member states provide the necessary financial and military resources, but it is difficult to imagine collective security working if the states with large military forces do not contribute. Collective security was a miserable failure in the 1930s, was put on ice during the Cold War, and then, like Lazarus, rose from the dead in the Persian Gulf in 1991. But it was only a minor miracle, because, as we shall see in Chapter 10, collective security is only part of what will be needed for world order in the future.

The United Nations has political effects, even when collective security cannot be applied, because the presumption against force written into the UN charter places the burden of proof on those who want to use force. As constructivists note, such changes in normative ideas about the use of force affect states' soft power. In addition, the Security Council provides an important forum for the discussion of international violence, dramatizing the practice of collective concern and directing attention to important matters in times of crisis. It sometimes crystallizes viewpoints, raising the costs of aggressive uses of force, and acts as a safety valve for diplomacy. Finally, the role of the UN peacekeeping forces is limited but useful. These trip wires and buffer zones are devices that states have found to be in their interests again and again.

With the end of the Cold War came more opportunities for the United Nations. In addition to overseeing peacekeeping forces, it played a role in the decolonization of Namibia, in monitoring human rights in El Salvador, in the elections in Nicaragua, and in the administration in Cambodia. Its recent peacekeeping record is mixed. UN peacekeepers helped in Haiti and Cambodia in the 1990s, but failed to prevent genocide in Rwanda and Sudan or to stop civil war in Angola, and in Bosnia had to be replaced by a stronger North Atlantic Treaty Organization (NATO) force. Sometimes it is difficult even to assess success or failure. UN peacekeepers have certainly helped prevent bloodshed between Greek and Turkish Cypriots, but critics of the Cyprus mission argue that the seemingly open-ended commitment (blue helmets have been on the ground since 1964) has actually impeded progress toward a negotiated reunification of the country. It seems that neutral interposition of troops does not always work well in ethnic conflicts. Indeed, some political scientists argue that neutral interventions may lengthen the duration of civil wars, causing greater bloodshed and loss of life. On the other hand, the United Nations still plays an important legitimizing role. The failure of the United States and Britain to obtain a Security Council resolution explicitly authorizing their use of force in 2003, for example, greatly increased the cost of their occupation of Iraq.[2]

The United Nations continues to invent new roles for itself. One good example is *peacebuilding*, illustrated by the United Nations Assistance Mission for Iraq (UNAMI). Established by UN Security Council Resolution 2110 in July 2013, UNAMI is charged with advising, supporting, and assisting the government of Iraq in promoting such things as political dialogue, national reconciliation, electoral and constitutional revision, legal reform, internal boundary dispute resolution, border security, energy security, the social and political reintegration of former members of illegal armed groups, humanitarian assistance, social service delivery, reconstruction, economic reform, training, human rights, and the rule of law. It is a much more ambitious agenda than just separating warring factions. "Peace support operations" of this kind were never envisaged by the drafters of the UN Charter in San Francisco, but are an increasingly important component of the United Nations' contribution to managing conflict. Peace support operations come in different shapes and sizes and can have narrower or broader sets of tasks. UNAMI is at the broader and more ambitious end of the spectrum; the United Nations Electoral Observation Mission in Burundi, in contrast, sits at the narrower end. At present, there are four peacebuilding missions led by the UN Department of Political Affairs, which maintains an additional nine offices in recent conflict zones.

Even though the original doctrines of collective security do not fit as neatly as once thought, it would be a mistake to dismiss international law and the United Nations. They are part of the political reality of the anarchic state system. It is a mistake to be too cynical or too naive about international law and organization. States do not live by law alone, but they do not live completely without it.

Many observers have called for the reform of UN institutions. The 15 members of the Security Council have the legal power to authorize the use of force, and 5 permanent members (China, the United States, Russia, Britain, and France) have had veto power since 1945. In 2005, a "High-Level Panel" appointed by Secretary-General Kofi Annan suggested enlarging the Security Council to 24 members and adding India, Brazil, Japan, and Germany as permanent members. The plan failed, however, when China objected to Japan's inclusion, regional rivals raised objections, and African states demanded more seats. The panel made a number of other useful suggestions for reform, including a Peacebuilding Commission to oversee the reconstruction of failed states, revision of the Human Rights Commission to exclude states that violate human rights, clearer criteria for preemptive use of force and humanitarian intervention, and an agreed definition of terrorism. Except for a small Peacebuilding Commission and a modest new Human Rights Council, the member states were reluctant to implement these recommendations.

The United Nations is clearly not the "parliament of humankind" that some of its founders hoped for when it was created in 1945. With an annual regular budget of $2.7 billion a year and a central staff of 17,000 members, the organization has fewer resources than many cities (just one-third, for example, of the annual budget for the City of Los Angeles). Even when the special budget for peacekeeping operations (roughly $7 billion) and the annual budgets of all the specialized agencies and development funds are added together, the total comes to around $12 billion, or just over 2 percent of what the United States spends on defense. The budget for human rights activities is smaller than that of the Zurich

Opera House, and the budget of the United Nations' World Health Organization is similar to that of one large university hospital system.

The United Nations remains an assembly of 193 sovereign states trying through diplomacy to find a common denominator for dealing with international problems while protecting their national interests. It also represents a central point for focusing on issues of security, international development, humanitarian assistance, environmental degradation, drugs, transnational crime, health and diseases, and global common spaces that require international collaboration. Despite its flaws, it remains the only universal organization that creates a focal point for international diplomacy. It is sometimes said that if the United Nations did not exist, it would have to be invented. Given the diversity of cultures and national interests in the world today, it is not clear that it could be.

Follow Up

- Anne L. Herbert, "Cooperation in International Relations: A Comparison of Keohane, Haas and Franck," *Berkeley Journal of International Law* 14:1 (1996), pp. 222–238.

- Linda M. Fasulo, *An Insider's Guide to the UN*, 3rd ed. (New Haven: Yale University Press, 2015), pp. 1–22, 236–253.

Post–Cold War Armed Conflict: Patterns and Trends

6.2   Articulate the complexity and changing nature of armed conflict today and identify relevant moral criteria for international intervention.

There is good news and bad news when it comes to conflicts that have turned violent since the end of the Cold War. The good news is that interstate clashes so far have been rare, have been mostly minor, and have never involved one great power fighting another (Table 6.1). Although it would be wrong to believe that wars between great powers are now unthinkable, as we will see in Chapter 7, most observers would also say that a major war involving great powers is less likely now than at any time in history because of economic interdependence, the horrific lessons of the two world wars, deepening and strengthening norms against the use of force, the increased availability of alternative modes of dispute resolution, and, not least importantly, the nuclear crystal ball.

Table 6.1 Post–Cold War interstate armed conflicts

1989	U.S. invasion of Panama*
1990–1991	Gulf War† (Iraq vs. Kuwait, United States, and coalition partners)
1995	Cenepa War* (Ecuador vs. Peru)
1994–1996	Bakassi Peninsula dispute* (Nigeria vs. Cameroon)
1998–2000	Eritrean-Ethiopian War†
2003	Iraq War† (Iraq vs. United States and coalition partners)
2008	Djibouti-Eritrea border conflict*
2012	Heglig crisis* (Sudan vs. South Sudan)

*Fewer than 1,000 casualties
†More than 1,000 casualties

The bad news is that regional and domestic conflicts persist (Figures 6.2 and 6.3). Of the 71 conflicts that have occurred since the end of the Cold War, 52 were purely intrastate (civil wars), and another 11 were intrastate with foreign intervention.[3] All are "globalized" in the sense that they involve state actors, international organizations, nongovernmental organizations, diasporas, and other nonstate actors (such as corporations or black marketeers, usually arms dealers or drug dealers) in various combinations playing various formal or informal roles.[4] Many of these intrastate conflicts are *ethnic* or *communal wars*; they are wars in which belligerents define themselves in part along cultural lines such as language, religion, or similar characteristics. Others are revolutionary wars in which the combatants divide along ideological lines. Some of the worst conflicts are deliberately fueled by governments; in other cases, governments find themselves powerless to stop them. The carnage can be extreme. Since the end of the Cold War, more than 100,000 people have died in countries such as Afghanistan, the Democratic Republic of the Congo, Iraq, Liberia, Rwanda, Sierra Leone, Somalia, Sudan, Syria, and Yugoslavia.

Most intrastate wars occur when established mechanisms for mediating conflicts break down. The inability of governments to mediate conflict frequently occurs in the aftermath of collapsed empires, such as the European colonial empires in Africa or the Soviet Empire in the Caucasus and Central Asia. Such "failed states" either never had a strong government or their governments were undermined by economic conditions, loss of legitimacy, or outside intervention. Thus, even though the end of the bipolar Cold War conflict led to the withdrawal of foreign troops from Afghanistan, Cambodia, Angola, and Somalia, intrastate war continued. And in the former Yugoslavia, which held together to preserve its independence in a bipolar world, the death of leader Marshal Tito and the end of the Cold War weakened the ability of the central government to mediate ethnic conflicts.

Constructivists point out that ethnicity is not an immutable fact that inevitably leads to war. It is socially constructed in the sense that symbols, myths, and memories can be altered over time.[5] For example, in Rwanda, which suffered a genocide in 1994, people spoke the same language and had the same skin color,

Figure 6.2 Annual Armed Conflicts by Type

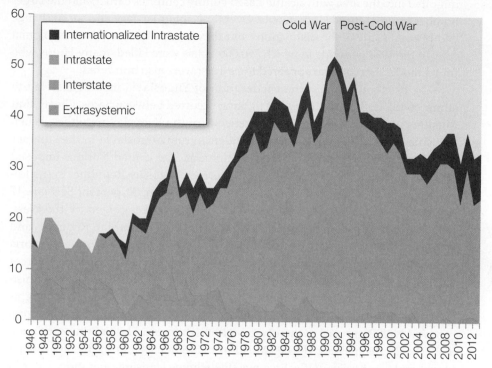

Figure 6.3 Annual Armed Conflicts by Intensity

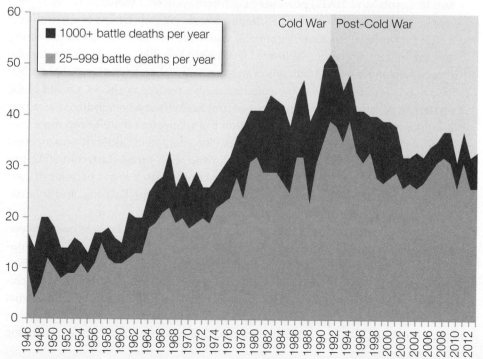

but there were economic class differences between the Tutsi people, who had migrated into the area with a cattle-based culture centuries earlier, and the larger number of agricultural Hutu people. Over time, intermarriage and social change had blurred some of the distinctions, but they were reinforced during colonial rule. In the 1994 genocide in which 750,000 Tutsis were killed, many Hutus who urged moderation or who appeared to be Tutsi were also murdered.

The breakup of the former federation of Yugoslavia in 1991 also led to ethnic conflicts. Some of the worst fighting occurred between Serbs, Croats, and Muslims in Bosnia, the most heterogeneous of the Yugoslav republics. When Slovenia and Croatia declared independence from Yugoslavia in the summer of 1991, ethnic Serbs and Croats began fighting. The United Nations imposed an arms embargo on all members of the former Yugoslav Republic. In the following year, Bosnia-Herzegovina (44 percent Muslim, 31 percent Serbian, 17 percent Croatian) declared independence and was recognized by the West. Within Bosnia, Bosnian Serbs declared an independent Serbian Republic, and war erupted as ethnic tensions exploded. In 1992 and 1993, there were reports of "ethnic cleansing" or expulsions of Muslims in Bosnia. Moreover, Serb forces blocked UN humanitarian convoys intended to protect Muslims. The Serbs also rejected a division of Bosnia along ethnic lines as Croatians switched from fighting against the Serbs to fighting Muslims. In 1994, Bosnian government forces received NATO support in their battle with Serb forces. The fighting continued in 1995 as Serbs massacred 6,000 Muslims in Srebrenica and the Croatian army forced Serbs in Krajina to flee in a massive ethnic-cleansing operation. Later in the year, Bosnia, Serbia, and Croatia signed the Dayton Peace Accord to end the war in Bosnia, and NATO peacekeeping forces were sent there.

In 1998, Serbian president Slobodan Milošević sent troops to quell unrest in the province of Kosovo. A guerrilla war with the Kosovo Liberation Army ensued, and in September, Milošević faced a NATO ultimatum to either stop the crackdown on Kosovar Albanians or to expect airstrikes. In 1999, NATO bombed Yugoslavia for 78 days, which created a massive refugee crisis. As a result of the airstrikes, Milošević withdrew troops from Kosovo and was indicted as a war criminal by a special UN tribunal. Following an election in 2000 and huge protests against Milošević, he stepped down. One year later, Milošević was arrested and handed over to The Hague tribunal. Milošević's trial started in 2002, but was never concluded because he died of natural causes in his prison cell four years later. Final status issues remain unresolved in the Balkans, and international peacekeepers continue to be deployed there.

But one can also regard the conflict in the former Yugoslavia as one between rural areas, where old identities and myths were strongest, and urban communities, where many people had intermarried and come to identify themselves as "Yugoslavs" rather than as Croats, Serbs, or Muslims. Once Yugoslavia collapsed and fighting broke out, some of these people had new identities thrust upon them. As one man said in 1993, "All my life I considered myself a Yugoslav, not a Muslim. Now I am a Muslim because that has been forced upon me." Some theorists attribute ethnic conflicts to deep and ancient hatreds or grand clashes of civilizations, but, as Michael Ignatieff argues, the ethnic distinctions are better described by Sigmund Freud's term "the narcissism of minor differences."[6]

> ## Mobilizing Identity Differences
>
> When I asked a Bosnian Croat military commander during a battle in Mostar how he knew whom to shoot, since people on the street looked so similar, his reply was that before the war, you would have to know their name, but now uniforms made it easy.
>
> —*Joseph S. Nye, Jr.*

Why do people kill over minor differences? Most often they do not. Humans always differentiate themselves into groups, and sometimes the differences are accompanied by prejudice and hatred. But such differences rarely lead to large-scale violence. Although no two conflicts are exactly the same, a common dynamic is that ethnic symbols and myths create divisions; economic rivalries or the weakening of state authority create fears for group survival. Elites or leaders then mobilize support by appealing to ethnic symbols, and any number of events (such as Bosnia's declaration of independence in 1992 or the death of Rwanda's president in an April 1993 plane crash) can spark the fighting.

Political scientist John Mueller stresses the role of violent groups who achieve their ends by manipulating ethnic myths and fears. In his view, the entire concept of "ethnic warfare" is misguided because it implies a Hobbesian war of all against all, whereas so-called ethnic conflicts are "waged by small groups of combatants, groups that purport to fight and kill in the name of some larger entity."[7] Mueller argues that the minority that resorts to violence destroys the space for the moderate middle, and pathological and criminal elements thrive in the resulting chaos. Stuart Kaufman emphasizes the role of symbolic politics. Political entrepreneurs and extremist groups use the emotional power of ethnic symbols to reconstruct the larger group's preferences. The classic security dilemma that we described in Chapter 1 arises among rational actors when lack of trust and inability to enforce agreements under anarchic conditions cause serious conflicts to erupt. But in Kaufman's view, many ethnic conflicts "erupted because one or both sides preferred conflict to cooperation."[8] In a failed state such as Sierra Leone, Liberia, or Somalia, uneducated and unemployed young men developed a vested economic interest in looting and plundering. In addition to the problem that rational actors face in the structural conditions of anarchy, the security dilemmas involved in the early stages of ethnic conflict often grow out of the manipulation of emotional symbols by those who prefer and profit from violence.

Intervention and Sovereignty

Where failed states exist or genocide is threatened, some analysts believe that outsiders should ignore sovereignty and intervene for humanitarian purposes.

In 2005, the UN High-Level Panel on Threats, Challenges and Changes endorsed the "norm that there is a collective international responsibility to protect . . . civilians from the effects of war and human rights abuses." According to the UN panel, this responsibility is "exercisable by the Security Council, authorizing military intervention as a last resort, in the event of genocide and other large-scale killing, ethnic cleansing or serious violations of humanitarian law which sovereign Governments have proved powerless or unwilling to prevent."

Intervention is a confusing concept, partly because the word is both descriptive and normative. It not only describes what is happening, but it also casts value judgments. Thus discussions of intervention often involve moral issues. Nonintervention in the internal affairs of sovereign states is a basic norm of international law. Nonintervention is a powerful norm because it affects both order and justice. Order sets a limit on chaos. International anarchy—the absence of a higher government—is not the same as chaos if basic principles are observed. Sovereignty and nonintervention are two principles that provide order in an anarchic world system. At the same time, nonintervention affects justice. States are communities of people who deserve the right to develop a common life within their own boundaries. Outsiders should respect their sovereignty and territorial integrity. But not all recognized states fit this ideal. Sovereignty is a concept that has been applied to many states where it fits poorly. For example, group and clan fighting meant that no government was effectively in control in Sierra Leone, Liberia, or Somalia at the beginning of the twenty-first century. Even children were pressed into battle. Thus there is often a tension between justice and order that leads to inconsistencies about whether to intervene.

Defining Intervention

In its broadest definition, *intervention* refers to external actions that influence the domestic affairs of another sovereign state. Some analysts use the term more narrowly to refer to *forcible* interference in the domestic affairs of another state. The narrow definition is merely one end of a spectrum of influences ranging from low coercion to high coercion (Figure 6.4). At the low end of the scale, intervention may be simply a speech designed to influence domestic politics in

Figure 6.4 Defining Intervention

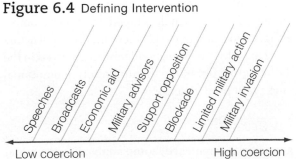

another state. For example, in 1990, President George H. W. Bush appealed to the Iraqi people to overthrow Saddam Hussein, and in 1999, Saddam appealed to the peoples of several Arab states to overthrow their leaders. Such speeches are designed to interfere in the domestic politics of another state, almost always without much effect. In the 1980s, the U.S. government established Radio Martí to broadcast its messages against Fidel Castro in Cuba, but Castro remained in power until 2008, when age and infirmity prompted him to hand the reins of government to his brother Raúl.

Economic assistance can also influence the domestic affairs of another country. For example, during the Cold War, U.S. economic aid to El Salvador and Soviet aid to Cuba were designed to influence domestic affairs in those states. Although a form of illegal economic assistance, bribing high-level foreign officials can induce them to pursue a third party's preferred policies. During the Cold War, U.S. and Soviet intelligence agencies often poured resources into foreign elections in an attempt to engineer a favorable outcome. Similarly, in the 1970s, the government of South Korea spent a great deal of money to help elect U.S. politicians who were more favorable to its interests.

A little further along the spectrum of coercion is the provision of military advisors. In the late 1950s, during the early days of the Vietnam War, the United States began its intervention first with economic and later with military assistance. Similarly, the Soviet Union and Cuba provided military aid and advisors to Nicaragua and other "client" states. Another form of intervention is support for the opposition. For example, in the early 1970s, the United States channeled money to the opponents of Salvador Allende, the democratically elected president of Chile, and at various times, the Soviet Union channeled money to peace groups in Western European countries. More recently, the United States has provided financial assistance to nascent democratic movements in several former Soviet bloc countries, including Ukraine; Syria has been heavily involved in Lebanon; and Venezuela has used its oil wealth to influence elections in Latin American countries.

Toward the coercive end of the spectrum is limited military action. For example, in the 1980s, the United States bombed Libya in response to its support of terrorism. In 1998, the United States launched cruise missile attacks into Sudan and Afghanistan in reprisal for terrorist attacks against U.S. embassies in East Africa. It also used air and ground support for local forces to overthrow the Taliban government in Afghanistan after 9/11. In 2011, during the civil war that erupted in Libya in the course of the "Arab Awakening" (which we will discuss in Chapter 9), 18 UN members contributed military forces to enforce a no-fly zone. Full-scale military invasion or occupation is at the upper end of the spectrum of coerciveness. Examples include U.S. actions in the Dominican Republic in 1965, Grenada in 1983, Panama in 1989, and Iraq in 2003; and the Soviet Union's actions in Hungary in 1956, Czechoslovakia in 1968, and Afghanistan in 1979. It is not merely great powers that intervene with force. For example, in 1979, Tanzania sent troops into Uganda, and Vietnam invaded Cambodia. In

1997, tiny Rwanda intervened militarily in the affairs of its troubled larger neighbor, the Democratic Republic of the Congo; and in 2007, Ethiopia sent troops into Somalia. Some interventions are multilateral, but often one state takes the lead. For example, the United States led the 1995 UN intervention in Haiti and NATO's 1999 intervention in Kosovo, and Nigeria led a group of West African states that intervened in Liberia and Sierra Leone in the 1990s.

The broad definition of intervention therefore includes the whole range of behavior, from not very coercive to highly coercive. The degree of coercion involved in intervention is important because it relates to the degree of choice that the local people have and thus the degree of outside curtailment of local autonomy.

Judging Intervention

For skeptics, moral judgments do not matter, but realists, cosmopolitans, and state moralists have different views of intervention. For realists, the key values in international politics are order and peace, and the key institution is the balance of power; they believe that intervention can be justified when it is necessary to maintain the balance of power and to maintain order. This approach to intervention was used throughout the Cold War by both superpowers to maintain their two respective spheres of influence: the U.S. sphere in the Western Hemisphere and the Soviet sphere in Eastern Europe. For example, the United States intervened in the Dominican Republic in 1965 and in Central America in the 1980s on the grounds that there should be no more communist governments in the Western Hemisphere, and the Soviet Union intervened to preserve communist governments in Eastern Europe. The Soviets articulated a right to intervention in 1968 with the Brezhnev Doctrine, which claimed that they had a right to intervene to preserve socialism in their sphere of influence. Realists might justify such interventions on the grounds that they preserved order and prevented the possibility of misunderstandings and miscalculations that might escalate to war, particularly nuclear war.

In contrast, cosmopolitans value justice. For them, the key international institution is a society of individuals. Therefore, intervention can be justified if it promotes individual justice and human rights; it is permissible to intervene on the side of the "good." But how is "good" to be defined? During the Cold War, liberal cosmopolitans argued that intervention was justified against right-wing regimes such as the dictatorship of Ferdinand Marcos in the Philippines (1965–1986) or the apartheid regime in South Africa (1948–1990), whereas conservative cosmopolitans said that intervention was justified against left-wing governments. In the 1980s, some Americans proclaimed a Reagan Doctrine when defending the United States' right to intervene against the Sandinista government in Nicaragua and against the communist governments in Angola and Mozambique because of their violation of democratic rights. In the 1990s, with the end of the Cold War, cosmopolitans urged humanitarian intervention in Somalia (1992) to halt widespread starvation, in Haiti (1994) to restore a democratically elected leader to power, in Bosnia (1995) to stop a civil war, and in Kosovo (1999) to stop "ethnic cleansing" triggered by the government of Milošević in Serbia. Similarly, they called for U.S. intervention in conflicts in Liberia (2003) and the Darfur region of Sudan (2008). What cosmopolitans, left and right, share is the view that intervention is justified if it promotes individual justice and human rights.

For state moralists, the key value in international politics is the autonomy of the state and its people. The key institution is a society of states with certain rules and international law. Of these precepts, the most important is nonintervention in the sovereign territory of another state. Consequently, state moralists believe that intervention is justified only to defend a state's territorial integrity or to defend its sovereignty against external aggression. The real world is sometimes more complicated, however. External aggression is often ambiguous. For example, in June 1967, Israel preemptively attacked Egypt in response to its decision to deny Israel access to vital shipping lanes and mass troops along its border. Who was the aggressor, the Egyptians who massed their forces on the border and appeared to be preparing an attack on Israel or the Israelis who struck just before the Egyptians could attack?

Exceptions to the Rule of Nonintervention

In *Just and Unjust Wars*, Michael Walzer, a political scientist who presents the state moralist position, discusses four situations that could morally justify war or military intervention in the absence of overt aggression. The first exception to a strict rule is preemptive intervention, exemplified by the Israeli attack in 1967. If there is a clear and serious threat to a state's territorial integrity and political sovereignty, it must act right away because if it does not, it will have no chance to act later. But the threat must be imminent. Such an argument would not justify, for example, the 1979 Soviet intervention in Afghanistan or the 2003 U.S.-led war on Iraq. There is a distinction between preemptive wars and preventive wars. A *preemptive strike* occurs when war is imminent. A *preventive war* occurs when leaders believe merely that war is better now than later. As we saw in Chapter 3, views regarding preventive war influenced the German general staff in 1914, which feared that if Germany waited until 1916 to fight, Russia would be too strong for the Schlieffen Plan to work. Walzer's first exception to nonintervention would not have allowed a preventive war because there was no clear and present danger to Germany. And as we saw earlier with our counterfactual examples, many other things might have changed the situation between 1914 and 1916. During the buildup to the 2003 Iraq War, U.S. officials blurred this classic distinction by claiming that a preventive strike against Iraq was preemptive even though the threat of an Iraqi attack against the United States or its allies was not imminent.

The second exception to the strict rule against intervention occurs when intervention is needed to balance a prior intervention. This rule goes back to John Stuart Mill and the nineteenth-century liberal view that a "people" has the right to determine its own fate. If an intervention prevents local people from determining their own fate, a counterintervention nullifying the first intervention can be justified because it restores the people's right to decide. Mill's argument permits intervention only as far as it counterbalances a prior intervention; more than that is not justifiable. The overriding principle is to allow the local people to solve their own problems. The United States sometimes used this principle as a justification for its involvement in Vietnam. In 1979, China intervened in Vietnam by crossing the border, but China pulled its troops back within a few weeks. China argued that it was countering Vietnam's intervention in Cambodia.

The third exception to the rule against intervention is when it is necessary to rescue people who are threatened with massacre. If such people are not saved from total destruction, there is no point to nonintervention as a sign of respect for their autonomy or rights. In 2015, Nigerian forces proved impotent against Boko Haram militants who were terrorizing innocent civilians in the northeastern part of the country, so without Nigeria's permission, Chad and Niger sent in their own troops instead. In 1979, Tanzania invaded Uganda when a dictatorial leader was slaughtering large numbers of people, and it justified its intervention as rescuing people threatened by massacre. Vietnam used a similar justification for its invasion of Cambodia in 1978. Still, massacres or genocide do not necessarily lead states or the international community to intervene. Note the reluctance of the United States to send troops to Rwanda in 1994, to Bosnia between 1992 and 1995, to Liberia in 1996, to Sierra Leone in 1999, and to the Democratic Republic of the Congo in 2003. In 2005, the UN General Assembly passed a resolution accepting a responsibility to protect people suffering from avoidable catastrophe, but humanitarian intervention remains contentious. In the troubled Darfur region of Sudan, for example, support for a military intervention to stop the killing of various ethnic groups was limited to a modest peacekeeping operation.

The fourth exception to nonintervention is the right to assist secessionist movements when they have demonstrated their representative character. In other words, if a group of people within a country has clearly demonstrated that it wants to be a separate country, it is legitimate to assist its secession because doing so helps the group pool its rights and develop its autonomy. But when does a secessionist movement become worthy of assistance? Is their success the way to judge their worthiness? Part of Mill's argument was that to have a legitimate claim, a people must be able to seek its own salvation and fight for its own freedom. Such a view is consistent, at least, with the principle of nonintervention and a society of states, but it is deficient as a moral principle because it suggests that might makes right.

Problems of Self-Determination

A major problem of intervention on behalf of secessionist movements is defining a "people." Who shares a common life? How do outsiders know whether a people really agreed to pool their rights in a single community or state?

Self-determination is the right of a group of people to decide their own political fate, and most commonly it expresses itself in the desire to form a state. This principle is important, but there is always the question of who determines. Consider Somalia, whose people, unlike many other African states, have roughly the same linguistic and ethnic background. Neighboring Kenya was formed by colonial rule from dozens of different peoples or tribes, with different linguistic backgrounds and customs. Part of northern Kenya was inhabited by Somalis. Somalia said that the principle of national self-determination should allow the Somalis in the northeastern part of Kenya and the southern part of Ethiopia to secede because they were all part of one Somali nation. Kenya and Ethiopia refused, saying that they were still in the process of building multinational states. The result was a number of wars in northeast Africa over the Somali nationalist question. The ironic sequel was that Somalia itself later fragmented in a civil war among its clans and warlord leaders.

Voting does not always solve problems of self-determination. First, there is the question of where one votes. Slightly more than 17 percent of the population of Ukraine, for example, is ethnically Russian. In the aftermath of the 2014 Maidan uprising that led to the ouster of pro-Russian president Viktor Yanukovych, however, only in Crimea, where Russians are in the majority (60 percent), did officials hold what was in effect a referendum on secession from Ukraine and union with Russia. Had the other largely Russian-speaking parts of Ukraine been included, the referendum would almost certainly have failed.[9] That the Crimean referendum was held under the watchful eyes of occupying Russian forces—coupled with what were clearly inflated official results and the emergence after the fact that Russian president Vladimir Putin had preplanned the annexation of Crimea—undermines the legitimacy of the vote and helps explain why almost the entire international community has rejected it, continues to recognize Crimea as an integral part of Ukraine, and considers Russian involvement an unjustified instance of foreign intervention.

The history of secession movements raises a host of additional problematic issues. Does secession harm those left behind? What about the resources the secessionists take with them or the disruption they create in the country they leave? For example, after the dismantlement of the Austrian Empire in 1918, the Sudetenland was incorporated into Czechoslovakia even though the people spoke German. After the Munich Agreement in 1938, the Sudeten Germans seceded from Czechoslovakia and joined Germany, but that meant that the mountainous frontier went under German control, which was a terrible loss for Czech defenses. Was it right to allow self-determination for the Sudeten Germans, even if it meant stripping Czechoslovakia of its military defenses? When eastern Nigeria decided that it wanted to secede and form the state of Biafra in the 1960s, other Nigerians resisted in part because Biafra had most of Nigeria's oil. They argued that the oil belonged to all the people of Nigeria, not just the eastern area. Indonesia has made the same argument about secessionist demands in its oil-rich province of Aceh.

After 1989, the issue of self-determination became acute in Eastern Europe and the former Soviet Union. Throughout the former Soviet Union, different ethnic groups claimed the right of self-determination, just as many of them had done between 1917 and 1920. In the Caucasus region, Azerbaijanis, Armenians, Georgians, Abkhazians, and Chechens all demanded states on the basis of self-determination.

As we saw above, in the former state of Yugoslavia, different ethnic and religious groups seceded and claimed self-determination. The Slovenes, Serbs, and Croats managed to carve out independent republics in the early 1990s, but the Muslims in Bosnia-Herzegovina were less successful. The war in Bosnia was devastating for the civilian population, and war-crimes tribunals were convened in The Hague, starting in 1996, to convict those responsible for the massacres. For much of the conflict, however, the United Nations, NATO, and the European Union were divided over how to respond. Part of what made the war in Bosnia so complicated for the international community was the problem of assessing how much of the fighting could be attributed to tensions among Bosnian Croats, Serbs, and Muslims and how much of the violence was caused by Serbia's intervention. If it was not simple aggression by Serbia, the only grounds for intervention would be to prevent a massacre. As with Rwanda, the international community was united in its condemnation of the Balkan violence, but was unable to agree on effective joint action until late in the conflict, in 1995, when a NATO peacekeeping force was sent to the troubled area.

Self-determination turns out to be an ambiguous moral principle. Wilson thought that it would solve problems in central Europe in 1919, but it created as many as it solved. Hitler used the principle to undermine fragile states in the 1930s. With less than 10 percent of the world's states being relatively homogeneous, it is clear that treating self-determination as a primary rather than secondary moral principle could have disastrous consequences for many parts of the world.

The best hope for the future is to ask *what* is being determined as well as *who* determines it. In situations in which groups have difficulties living together, it may be possible to allow a degree of autonomy in the determination of internal affairs. Internal self-determination could allow degrees of cultural, economic, and political autonomy similar to that which exists in countries such as Switzerland or Belgium. Where such loosening of the bonds is still not enough, it may be possible in some cases to arrange an amicable divorce, as happened when Czechoslovakia peacefully divided into two sovereign countries—the Czech Republic and Slovakia—on January 1, 1993. But absolute demands for self-determination are more likely to become a source of violence unless handled extremely carefully. No doubt the civil war currently raging in Eastern Ukraine only got worse because ethnic Russian separatists in Donetsk and Luhansk were encouraged by the "secession" of Crimea.

In sum, although there are circumstances in which intervention can be justified, the norm of nonintervention remains important. The burden of moral proof lies with the intervenor, because it is so easy for intervention to do more harm than good. Exceptions to nonintervention must be judged on a case-by-case basis by looking at the motives, means, and consequences.

Genocide and the "Responsibility to Protect"

In Chapter 2, we noted that sovereign statehood requires the recognition of others. In this respect, the Westphalian system of sovereign states resembles a club: You can only be a member if other members of the club agree to your membership. Since the seventeenth century, membership criteria have evolved. Sovereignty used to represent more of a barrier to outside interference than it does today. Increasingly, members of the international community require that governments meet certain standards of behavior within their borders before they will agree to respect the principle of nonintervention. As the Report of the International Commission on Intervention and State Sovereignty put it, "State sovereignty implies responsibility, and the primary responsibility for the protection of its people lies with the state itself." In practical terms, "Where a population is suffering serious harm, as a result of internal war, insurgency, repression or state failure, and the state in question is unwilling or unable to halt or avert it, the principle of nonintervention yields to the international responsibility to protect."[10]

As so often happens with major normative shifts in world politics, the Responsibility to Protect (R2P) was in large part a reaction to prior failure. That the international community stood idly by while genocide unfolded in Rwanda and intervened only belatedly in Yugoslavia prompted a genuine sense of shame. In this respect, the doctrine of R2P resembled the Convention on the Prevention and Punishment of the Crime of Genocide (colloquially known as the "Genocide Convention"), adopted by the UN General Assembly in December 1948 as a sincere reaction to the world's failure to stand up to Hitler and prevent the Holocaust. But although the doctrine of R2P is relatively young, it and the Genocide Convention have had eerily similar fates. Indeed, arguably, all such well-meaning attempts to internationalize responsibility for peace, justice, and security—the League of Nations and the 1928 Kellogg-Briand Treaty outlawing war both come to mind—have run into a powerful set of obstacles: power politics, self-interest, and free rider problems. States are generally reluctant to take on stronger states. Sometimes powerful states see an overriding interest in preventing the international community from interfering in the domestic affairs of allies, clients, or satellites. Often states are wary of setting a precedent that could be used against themselves by too readily agreeing to authorize intervention elsewhere. And peace, justice, and security are, in a sense, public goods: Because they benefit everyone, every state has an incentive to let other states shoulder the cost of providing them.

The Convention on the Prevention and Punishment of the Crime of Genocide illustrates all these problems and more. Article 2 of the Convention counts as genocide "any of the following acts committed with intent to destroy, in whole or in part, a national, ethnical, racial or religious group, as such: (a) Killing members of the group; (b) Causing serious bodily or mental harm to members of the group; (c) Deliberately inflicting on the group conditions of life calculated to bring about its physical destruction in whole or in part; (d) Imposing measures intended to prevent births within the group; (e) Forcibly transferring children of the group to another group."[11] The definition itself provides ample opportunity for the international community to justify inaction in the face of atrocity. For example, perpetrators and their apologists can argue that victims are targeted for political reasons, not for their national, ethnic, racial, or religious identities. They can argue that the dead and displaced are "collateral damage" rather than victims of intentional efforts to destroy the groups to which they belong. They can argue that "in whole or in part" means all or virtually all members of a group, not just a portion of it, even if that portion numbers in the hundreds of thousands. Even when a case fits a highly restrictive interpretation of the definition, the international community may consider intervention impractical or premature in the light of ongoing diplomatic efforts. The result is that more than 40 years passed between the adoption of the Convention and the first prosecutions under it, and all international prosecutions have taken place in the context of ad hoc tribunals. That the tribunals have brought charges of genocide at all is certainly an important marker of progress, as is that the judgments themselves have broadened and refined the definition of genocide; rape, for example, is now legally considered a form of genocide under certain circumstances. But progress has been painfully slow.

R2P was a deliberate attempt to address some of these flaws. It asserts a positive and proactive obligation to intervene to deal with "mass atrocity" (including, but not limited to, genocide as understood by the Convention). Despite early enthusiasm for the doctrine, however, it has had very little effect on intrastate violence thus far.

The conflict in Darfur was an early acid test of R2P, and it was not a very encouraging one. Since its outbreak in 2003, as many as 450,000 civilians may have been killed in ethnic conflict in this westernmost province of Sudan (estimates vary widely; official Sudanese government figures put the number at fewer than 20,000). Most of the deaths have been at the hands of the Janjaweed militia, which operates on behalf of the government of Sudan, despite the government's claims to the contrary. So far, the United States is the only permanent member of the UN Security Council that has been willing to call the conflict a genocide (many states are reluctant to do so precisely because doing so triggers an obligation to act). The international community's only muscular response was to dispatch an African Union peacekeeping force that was inadequately manned, armed, trained, and led and that even lacked a mandate to protect civilians. Contrary to popular belief, R2P always envisaged military intervention as a last resort, but critics argued that if Darfur did not galvanize decisive international action, it is difficult to know what might.

More encouraging was the international intervention in the 2011 Libyan civil war, which broke out when frustration with the autocratic regime of Muammar Gaddafi boiled over into armed revolt. Opponents of the regime secured control of much of the eastern part of the country, as well as pockets in the west, prompting the Gaddafi regime to go on the offensive. With unchallenged air supremacy, superior armor, and evident willingness to target civilians supporting the opposition, Gaddafi's onslaught seemed to herald a bloodbath. In an unusual display of swiftness and solidarity, the UN Security Council passed Resolution 1973, imposing a no-fly zone for the purpose of protecting civilians. It was the first decisive implementation of the doctrine of R2P.

Whether Resolution 1973 represented a sea change in the international community's willingness to put muscle behind R2P remains to be seen. In the short term, the answer would appear to be no. Although it did justify foreign military intervention in the form of aerial combat missions and although these missions did succeed in largely destroying Gaddafi's air force, it explicitly prohibited the deployment of foreign soldiers on the ground and in that sense represented a half measure. By some accounts, too, the speed with which the Security Council passed Resolution 1973 did not reflect enthusiasm for R2P as much as the fear of certain members (primarily China and Russia) that if they did not agree to a no-fly zone, further bloodshed would result in calls for more robust forms of intervention, including "boots on the ground," measures that they would prefer not to be seen vetoing but that their own sensitivities about foreign intervention would not allow them easily to approve. Indeed, Russia and China both later expressed concerns about "mission creep"—the use of ground-attack aircraft to strike armored columns, logistical facilities, command and control sites, and even Gaddafi's compound—which seemed to go well beyond the mandate to impose a no-fly zone. But perhaps the single greatest reason Resolution 1973 may not have the legacy that its proponents hoped is that it did not have the effect that its proponents hoped. Libya today remains mired in civil strife. Gaddafi may have been an autocrat, but under his rule Libya was not the failed state that it is today. That R2P did not work out as hoped in Libya is probably a major reason it was never seriously considered in what has proven to be an even bigger humanitarian disaster: the civil war in Syria, about which we will have more to say in Chapter 7.

Follow Up

- Michael Walzer, *Just and Unjust Wars: A Moral Argument with Historical Illustrations* (New York: Basic Books, 2006), pp. 86–108.

- Gareth J. Evans, *The Responsibility to Protect: Ending Mass Atrocity Crimes Once and for All* (Washington, D.C.: Brookings Institution Press, 2008).

Study Questions

1. What is the difference between cooperation and coordination?

2. How do international organizations differ from domestic governmental agencies, ministries, or departments?

3. How does international law differ from domestic law? In what respects are they the same?

4. Why would fully sovereign states comply with international rulings or international laws when it would be to their short-term advantage not to comply?

5. How do collective security, peacekeeping, and peacebuilding differ from one another?

6. Why are interstate wars so rare nowadays?

7. What is ethnic conflict? When is it likely to occur?

8. When is intervention justified? Is self-determination always a justification? What are the limits of humanitarian intervention?

9. How would you assess international intervention in Libya on the basis of Responsibility to Protect doctrine from the perspective of motives, means, and consequences?

Notes

1. Anthony Eden, quoted in Robert R. Bowie, *Suez 1956* (New York: Oxford University Press, 1974), p. 124.

2. "Binding the Colossus," *The Economist*, November 22, 2003, pp. 25–26.

3. Calculated from UCDP/PRIO Armed Conflict Dataset v.4-2014a, 1946–2013. See also Nils Petter Gleditsch, Peter Wallensteen, Mikael Eriksson, Margareta Sollenberg, and Håvard Strand, "Armed Conflict 1946–2001: A New Dataset," *Journal of Peace Research* 39:5 (September 2002), pp. 615–637; and Lotta Themnér and Peter Wallensteen, "Armed Conflict, 1946–2012," *Journal of Peace Research* 50:4 (July 2013), pp. 509–521.

4. Chester A. Crocker, Fen Osler Hampson, and Pamela R. Aall, eds., *Managing Conflict in a World Adrift* (Washington, DC: United States Institute of Peace Press, 2014).

5. Steven J. Mock, *Symbols of Defeat in the Construction of National Identity* (Cambridge: Cambridge University Press, 2011).

6. Michael Ignatieff, *Blood and Belonging: Journeys into the New Nationalism* (New York: Farrar, Straus and Giroux, 1994).

7. John Mueller, "The Banality of Ethnic War," *International Security* 25:1 (Summer 2000), p. 42.

8. Stuart Kaufman, *Modern Hatreds* (Ithaca, NY: Cornell University Press, 2001), p. 220.

9. Pew Research Center, "Despite Concerns about Governance, Ukrainians Want to Remain One Country," May 8, 2014, http://www.pewglobal.org/files/2014/05/Pew-Global-Attitudes-Ukraine-Russia-Report-FINAL-May-8-2014.pdf.

10. International Commission on Intervention and State Sovereignty, *The Responsibility to Protect: Report of the International Commission on Intervention and State Sovereignty* (Ottawa: International Development Research Centre, 2001), p. xi.

11. Convention on the Prevention and Punishment of the Crime of Genocide, 1948; available at http://www.hrweb.org/legal/genocide.html.

Chapter 7
Current Flashpoints

Photo: Handout/Alamy

Learning Objectives

7.1 Articulate and evaluate realist, liberal, and constructivist accounts of post–Cold War tensions between Russia and the West.

7.2 Assess the relative importance of identity and material interests in various conflicts in the Near East and Middle East.

7.3 Assess the stability of nuclear deterrence in India-Pakistan relations.

7.4 Identify the main threats to China's "peaceful rise" in East Asia and Southeast Asia.

7.5 Explain how North Korea threatens regional stability.

As we saw in Chapter 6, intrastate war has caused more death, destruction, and displacement than has interstate war since World War II, and this imbalance has only increased in the post–Cold War period. Even before the Cold War ended, the apparent decline of interstate war prompted political scientist John Mueller to argue that major interstate war had become "obsolescent."[1] If that means that it is increasingly difficult to imagine a cost-benefit calculation justifying a major interstate war, Mueller is probably correct. The states that are capable of waging major wars are all either developed countries with enormous stakes in a peaceful, well-regulated international order that have at their disposal a wide array of conflict management tools or rapidly developing countries (such as China) that eagerly seek to take their place among this select group. But history shows that wars sometimes break out for reasons that are difficult to explain in traditional cost-benefit terms. Accidents, misperceptions, and inadvertent actions have played important roles in triggering wars from time to time. History also shows that states sometimes wage war for reasons that do not seem entirely rational but that reflect powerful commitments to symbols, ideals, or other intangible, emotionally laden considerations. So, although we should take heart that the world has done a relatively good job of wrestling the problem of interstate war to the ground, we should be wary of declaring victory over the problem, particularly because a number of countries that have ongoing serious disputes have nuclear weapons.

Interstate war is not equally likely everywhere. Many would consider it virtually impossible in the "islands of peace" known as security communities that we discussed in Chapter 2: Western Europe, Scandinavia, North America, and Australia/New Zealand/Japan. In still other parts of the world, such as parts of sub-Saharan Africa, states are so weak, fractured, or racked with intrastate violence already that interstate war is hardly a pressing problem. Interstate war remains acutely dangerous in the various "flashpoints" where well-armed states with longstanding grievances confront each other and where international crises have the potential to escalate to nuclear war. For reasons that are not entirely clear, these flashpoints are concentrated along a giant arc sweeping from western Russia to the Indian subcontinent and up to Northeast Asia. How dangerous are these flashpoints? Is each one unique, or do they share important characteristics? How can theory and history help us answer these questions?

Eastern Europe: A New Cold War?

7.1 Articulate and evaluate realist, liberal, and constructivist accounts of post–Cold War tensions between Russia and the West.

The end of the Cold War and the breakup of the Soviet Union gave Russia and the West an opportunity to end their historic rivalry and embark on a new era of mutual prosperity and security. The collapse of communism meant that the Cold War's defining ideological division ceased to exist. Democracy began to take root in Russia and Eastern Europe. Command economies began transitioning to liberal capitalist economies. The adversary of the North Atlantic Treaty Organization (NATO) members, the Warsaw Pact, disbanded. The Iron Curtain gave way to an increasingly thick web of trade, investment, and personal contacts. Almost miraculously, newly independent former Soviet republics such as Ukraine and Kazakhstan negotiated the peaceful transfer back to Russia of Soviet nuclear weapons deployed or stored on their soil, and the United States helped secure them through an ambitious program of nuclear safety technology transfer. Before long, the United States and the Soviet Union began reducing their nuclear arsenals. Fissile material from dismantled Soviet nuclear weapons even found its way into U.S. civilian nuclear power plants, where today, coupled with material recovered from decommissioned U.S. nuclear weapons, it accounts for roughly 10 percent of the electricity generated in the United States.

The honeymoon, however, was short-lived. Within a few years, goodwill on both sides began to erode, and hostility and suspicion began to reemerge. Today, relations between Washington and Moscow are in a virtual deep-freeze, thanks to Russian actions in Crimea and eastern Ukraine (which we will discuss below) and the painful Western economic sanctions they triggered. Arms control has stalled. Both sides are bolstering their defenses through modernization, procurement, and redeployment. In scenes reminiscent of the height of the Cold War, Russian and NATO aircraft are once again playing cat and mouse over international waters. What went wrong?

Arguably, both sides oversold an optimistic vision of the future. All countries have conflicts of interest, and it was unrealistic to herald a golden age of universal understanding. Russia had always had tense relations with many of its neighbors, too, including (perhaps primarily!) with some of its former Warsaw Pact allies who all too easily remembered Russia's tendency to dominate and feared a future relapse (Figure 7.1). Democratic and capitalist transitions in Russia and Eastern Europe were bound to be somewhat painful with occasional steps backward as well as forward, but was the deterioration in relations that we have witnessed inevitable?

Recall the four competing paradigms we discussed in Chapter 2: realism, liberalism, Marxism, and constructivism (see Table 2.1). We can rule out Marxism as a potential source of insight in this case, because the tensions we have witnessed are not class tensions. The worrying turn in the direction of a new Cold War has not pitted workers against capitalists, but Russians against Americans and East Europeans. It is very hard to tell a story that makes sense of post–Cold War years in terms of concepts that Marxism emphasizes, such as greed and exploitation.

The liberal paradigm has somewhat better conceptual tools with which to make sense of what has happened, but to the extent that a liberal explanation works, it works by highlighting the potential value of what might have been. A liberal would say that if Russia had become more fully integrated with the West institutionally, if true democracy had taken root in Russia (rather than the faux democracy we witness under Vladimir Putin's authoritarian rule), and if economic ties with Russia had been thicker and deeper, cooperation would have been easier and relations more positive. That may all be true, but what liberalism cannot do is explain why none of that happened.

Figure 7.1 Eastern Europe

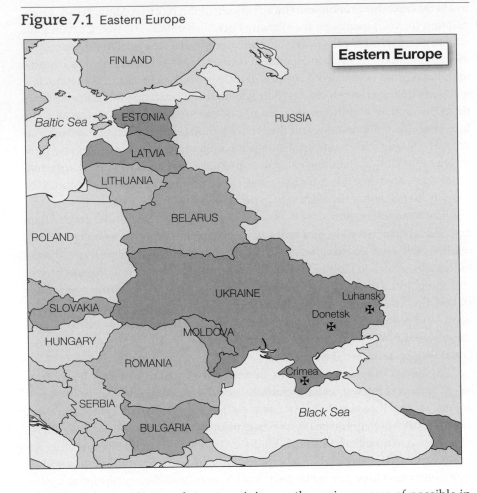

This leaves realism and constructivism as the main sources of possible insight into the causes of what is increasingly looking like a new, if milder, "Cold War." Recall that for realists, the dominant drive is fear, and in a Hobbesian anarchy such as the Westphalian system of sovereign states, self-help tends to lead to balancing behavior. (According to realism, weak states might sometimes bandwagon, but great powers tend to balance.) In this view, a new Cold War of sorts might well have been inevitable. As great powers, Russia and the United States were bound to view each other with suspicion and to err on the side of caution when providing for their own security. Trust would be hard to come by. This stance would lead to competition not only in arms, but in allies and influence. Perhaps what we have seen of relations between Russia and the West since the end of the Cold War is simply the result of realist dynamics at work.

Constructivism, in contrast, draws our attention to the ways in which identities and interests evolve through interaction. A constructivist would say not that a new Cold War between Russia and the West was inevitable, but that once old animosities resurfaced, and in the absence of any serious efforts to overcome them, it is not surprising that an adversarial dynamic developed and snow-balled. Which explanation fits the facts better?

To assess the power of a realist explanation, one has to have a sense of the relevant power trends. After all, Thucydides claimed, it was the growing power of Athens and the fear that it inspired in Sparta that led to the second Pelopon-nesian War.[2] One key measure of power, as we saw in Chapter 2, is the size of a country's economy, typically measured by gross domestic product (GDP), which for comparison purposes we usually adjust to reflect price differentials (purchasing power parity GDP, or PPP GDP).[3] Figure 7.2 shows post–Cold War PPP GDP for the world's six largest economies. You will notice that it has essentially been a two-horse race between the United States and China. Economically, Russia is the weakest of the six. Classical balance-of-power theory, using GDP as the key indicator, would certainly predict rivalry between China and the United States, but would it predict rivalry between Russia and the United States?

One way of making realism fit is to argue that Russia has bandwagoned with China against the United States. Superficially, there are indications of in-creased cooperation between China and Russia on important matters such as energy and military security. In particular, Russia and China are increas-ingly actively promoting regional security cooperation through the Shanghai

Figure 7.2 Purchasing Power Parity GDP (Constant 2011 International $Trillion)

SOURCE: World Bank, retrieved at http://data.worldbank.org/indicator/NY.GDP.MKTP.CD

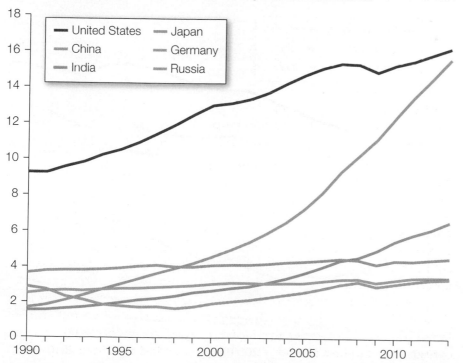

Cooperation Organization and through bilateral security cooperation, as illustrated by joint naval exercises in the Mediterranean and the Pacific in 2015. But no formal alliance binds China and Russia, and the timing of Chinese-Russian cooperation suggests that it was a response to Russia's deteriorating relations with the West rather than a cause of it. Something else was driving that deterioration in the first place.

The sheer size of a country's economy, of course, does not give a clear indication of how sophisticated it is or how well it functions. These measures can be very important considerations when attempting to assess a state's power because they tell us how effectively a country can mobilize its resources or innovate to address security challenges. Per capita GDP and life expectancy at birth are more relevant indicators here. Per capita GDP gives us an indication of how much surplus wealth is in the system and how far along the development/modernization curve a country is at any given time. Life expectancy at birth gives us an indication of the ability of a state to deliver key goods such as public health, a clean environment, and workplace safety. As Figures 7.3 and 7.4 indicate, neither Russia nor China fares particularly well on these measures, only further casting doubt on a realist balance-of-power interpretation.

Figure 7.3 Purchasing Power Parity GDP per capita (Constant 2011 International $Thousand)

SOURCE: World Bank, retrieved at http://data.worldbank.org/indicator/NY.GDP.PCAP.PP.KD

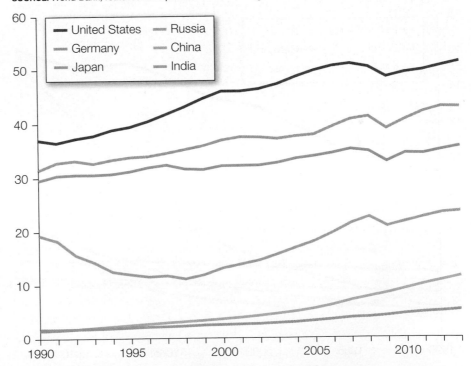

Figure 7.4 Life Expectancy at Birth (Years)

SOURCE: World Bank, retrieved at http://data.worldbank.org/indicator/SP.DYN.LE00.IN

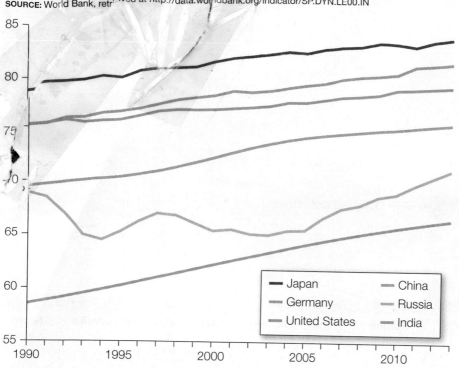

The one hard-power measure on which Russia fares extremely well is nuclear weapons (Figure 7.5). Seen through this lens, the world is indeed very bipolar, and Russia and the United States are clearly at the poles. But it cuts two ways. On the one hand, although the nuclear balance can explain why Russia and the United States might see each other as their primary security threat, they have always had the lion's share of nuclear weaponry, which from a realist point of view would make it hard to explain how it was that they had any post–Cold War "honeymoon" at all. On the other hand, as we saw in Chapter 2, nuclear weapons are hopelessly muscle-bound. It is hard to imagine the foreign policy goal that would ever justify their use. That undermines their utility as a hard-power resource and makes nuclear weapons a threat not only to others but to the very states that possess them. One could argue that U.S. and Russian leaders today would do well to heed the lessons learned by John F. Kennedy and Nikita Khrushchev during the Cuban missile crisis: that nuclear weapons are a problem, not a solution, and that there is little more important in great power politics than cooperating to reduce the danger of their use.

A constructivist account of the deterioration in relations between Russia and the West would put identities front and center, and the story would go roughly as follows. When the Cold War ended and the Soviet Union collapsed, Russia

Figure 7.5 Number of Nuclear Weapons by Country (2015)

SOURCES: Based on Nuclear Threat Initiative; Arms Control Association

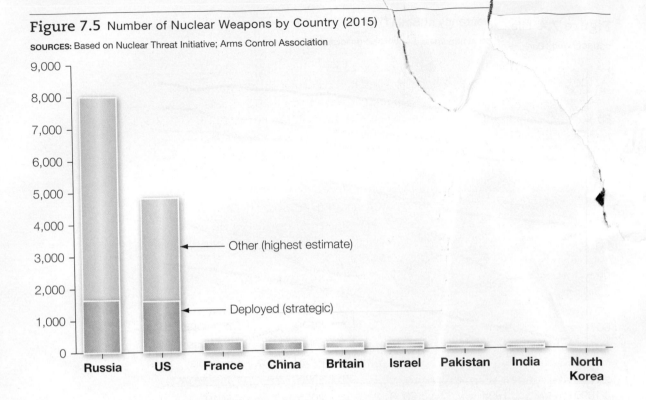

sought to shed its communist past but retained its sense of national pride and, in particular, its understanding of itself as a great power. Post-Soviet elites in Russia, including key players such as President Boris Yeltsin and Foreign Minister Andrei Kozyrev, looked westward for opportunity, inspiration, and even a degree of help as the country reengineered its politics and its economy. They were willing, as Sanjoy Banerjee puts it, to accept for a time "a structure of cooperative but asymmetric interaction."[4] But they expected Russia to be treated as an equal and with the respect they believed that it deserved. Moreover, they did not think that they had "lost" the Cold War. They believed that they had transcended it.

A key element of being treated with respect, from the Russian perspective, was that the West keep its commitments and take Russia's basic security interests into account. Memories of NATO's hostility were still fresh in Russian minds, and although the Warsaw Pact disbanded in 1991, NATO did not. According to Soviet officials involved in negotiations concerning the reunification of Germany in 1990 (i.e., after the fall of the Berlin Wall but before the collapse of the Soviet Union), Western officials made clear commitments that if the Soviet Union did not object to reunification, NATO would agree not to expand eastward. The last thing the Soviet Union (and, shortly thereafter, Russia) wanted was NATO right on its border. Some Western officials insist that no such formal commitment was made, but in any case, the damage was done when Hungary, Poland, and the Czech Republic joined NATO in 1999 and when Bulgaria, Romania, Slovakia, Slovenia, Estonia, Latvia, and Lithuania joined in 2009. That the last three countries joined—former Soviet republics, no less—added insult to injury. Russia believed that it was misled, betrayed, and disrespected. To Russian eyes, NATO enlargement unambiguously demonstrated the West's hostility to Russia, as did many other things; examples are NATO's "humanitarian" air campaign in support of Kosovo separatists against Russia's traditional Balkan client Serbia in 1998 and U.S. plans in 2002 to establish missile-defense bases in Poland and the Czech Republic, ostensibly to defend against Iranian missiles, but seen by Moscow as a threat to Russia's nuclear deterrent.[5]

Important events in international politics often resemble the plot in Akira Kurosawa's famous film *Rashomon*, in which eyewitnesses give entirely different accounts of what has happened. The end of the Cold War is no exception. Western leaders had little or no overt hostility toward Russia, and they genuinely sought to move forward in a true spirit of cooperation, but they believed that the West *had* won the Cold War and had earned the right to take the lead in shaping the post–Cold War era. Russia's insistence on being treated as a full equal seemed both unrealistic and undeserved. Not least importantly, it was profoundly irritating. Initiatives such as the Partnership for Peace (1994), the Euro-Atlantic Partnership Council (1997), and the Russia-NATO Council (2002) were sincere attempts to engage Russia in cooperative security and address Russian concerns that seemed increasingly unappreciated and unreciprocated as Russia's anti-NATO rhetoric ramped up. Russia seemed increasingly to reject the West's hand of friendship and to retreat into a bombastic nationalistic shell. As Europhiles left office in Russia or were thrown out in favor of nationalists and Eurasianists, relations cooled, and Western governments began to lose hope or interest in turning things around.

Matters came to a head in the fall of 2013 as a result of events in Ukraine, a former Soviet republic with a significant Russian-speaking minority, particularly in the east and in Crimea. As we mentioned earlier, Ukraine-Russian relations were in some ways a model of cooperation in the immediate post–Cold War period. Not only did the government of newly independent Ukraine readily agree to the withdrawal of Soviet nuclear weapons from its soil, it even permitted the Russian Black Sea Fleet to operate from bases on Ukrainian territory. But the big unanswered question about Ukraine was whether its future lay east or west. Those who spoke Russian and ethnic Russians (primarily in eastern Ukraine) valued their ties to Russia and feared a potential drift toward Europe. Far from fearing this scenario, ethnic Ukrainians, who were in the majority, increasingly desired it, for both economic and security reasons. When pro-Russian president Viktor Yanukovych reneged on a promise to sign an association agreement with the European Union (EU) and instead signed a treaty with (and accepted a multibillion-dollar loan from) Russia, outraged Ukrainian citizens flooded Maidan Square in central Kiev. After weeks of violence on both sides, the protests forced Yanukovych from office. The new president, Petro Poroshenko, signed the EU-Ukraine Association Agreement on June 27, 2014.

Here again, dominant narratives conflict. The Russian story is that the West opportunistically engineered an illegal coup d'état against a duly elected president, with the help, and effectively doing the bidding, of fascists such as the far-right group Svoboda. The Western story is that Vladimir Putin strong-armed Yanukovych into betraying the democratic will of the people of Ukraine so as to keep the country in Russia's orbit and under Russia's thumb. At any rate, the result was civil war in the eastern Donbass region between ethnic Russian separatists, heavily armed and supported (covertly) by regular Russian forces, and the ill-equipped and ill-trained Ukrainian army, openly but only modestly supported by Western governments. Several ceasefires and de-escalation agreements have been negotiated and ignored, and at present, matters have settled into an uncertain stalemate. The precise human cost to date is unknown, but the United Nations Office for the Coordination of Humanitarian Affairs puts the number at more than 6,000, with nearly 2 million either internally displaced or having fled the country. Among the great tragedies of the conflict was the accidental shooting down of a civilian airliner, Malaysian Airlines flight MH17 bound for Kuala Lumpur from Amsterdam, over Donetsk on July 17, 2014, killing all 298 people aboard. Although the precise details of the tragedy remain unclear, there is little doubt that the plane was brought down by a mobile Russian surface-to-air missile. The only question is whether Russian separatists or regular Russian forces pulled the trigger.

Perhaps the most disturbing feature of the Ukraine crisis, from a larger international politics perspective, is Russia's opportunistic annexation of Crimea and Sevastopol—sovereign Ukrainian territory—following a hastily arranged sham referendum on March 16, 2014. It is now known that the annexation was planned in Moscow and preceded by a well-executed infiltration by Russian forces. Most countries of the world have refused to recognize it. By a vote of 100 to 11, the United Nations General Assembly proclaimed it illegal and declared that Crimea and Sevastopol remain sovereign Ukrainian territory. What is particularly disturbing about the annexation is not merely that it violated Russia's own commitment to recognize and defend Ukrainian territorial integrity under the terms of the 1994 Budapest Memorandum, but that it violated one of the most important and hitherto most robust norms of the postwar order: namely, the norm against unilaterally attempting to change international borders.

These events, and that there are two conflicting narratives about virtually every aspect of them, demonstrate the power of constructivism in this case. The end of the Cold War truly did represent an opportunity for Russia and the West to embark on a new path, one that potentially stood to benefit both. But fundamental disagreements on whether the Cold War had a "winner" and a "loser" and on whether Russia was being treated with the respect and consideration it deserved, coupled with latent (and quickly activated) oppositional national identities, resulted in a vicious spiral of misunderstanding, mistrust, and ultimately hostility. Just as constructivists would expect, here we see interests and identities evolving through interaction over time. Liberals are probably correct in thinking that it would not have happened if Russia had been more quickly and more completely integrated institutionally and economically and if its nascent democracy not been hijacked by oligarchs, kleptocrats, and authoritarians; realists are surely correct to describe relations between Russia and the West today as characterized by fear, mistrust, and old-fashioned power politics, but only constructivists can tell a compelling story about why that is so. One can only hope that enlightened leaders on both sides will find a way of halting any further slide into hostility. The last thing the world needs is another long Cold War, with all of the attendant risks of turning hot.

Chronology: Russia and the West since 1990

1991	Soviet Union is formally dissolved; the Russian Federation declares itself to be the successor state to the Soviet Union
1993	Russian President Boris Yeltsin and U.S. President Bill Clinton meet in Vancouver, Canada, to discuss an expanded aid package, including food and medical assistance and loans to Russian entrepreneurs
1994	The first joint U.S.-Russian space shuttle mission launches in February; the United States and Russia end the practice of aiming their nuclear missiles at each other
1995	U.S. space shuttle *Atlantis* successfully docks with Russian space station *Mir*; Russia joins the NATO-led Implementation Force in Bosnia
1998	Russia invited to join the Group of Seven (G7), which becomes known as the G8
1999	Yeltsin resigns; Prime Minister Vladimir Putin succeeds Yeltsin as acting president; Russia introduces a UN Security Council resolution opposing the NATO-led intervention in Kosovo; Hungary, Poland, and the Czech Republic join NATO
2000	Putin wins the presidential election
2002	United States begins talks with Poland and other European countries to establish bases to intercept long-range missiles, drawing criticism from Russia

(continued)

2004	Putin is reelected president
2007	United States begins formal negotiations with Poland and the Czech Republic to establish missile defense bases, prompting Russia to threaten deploying short-range nuclear missiles on its Western border
2008	Putin says that the expansion of NATO to Russia's borders would be interpreted as a direct threat to Russian security; Putin is ineligible for reelection due to term limits; Dmitry Medvedev wins the election and appoints Putin as prime minister; Russia launches an invasion of Georgia under the guise of protecting South Ossetia and Abkhazia from a Georgian offensive, which the United States and other countries call an unwarranted invasion and send humanitarian and military aid to Georgia; Russia deploys a naval fleet to Venezuela for joint exercises; United States claims that this act is a provocation
2009	United States cancels the missile defense project in Poland and the Czech Republic; Bulgaria, Romania, Slovakia, Slovenia, Estonia, Latvia, and Lithuania join NATO
2010	Russia and the United States sign the New Strategic Arms Reduction Treaty; United States says that it will support Russia's accession to the World Trade Organization; Ukraine's governing coalition signals that it will not join NATO; Medvedev signals support by visiting Ukraine
2011	A new law extends the Russian presidential term from four to six years; Putin announces that he will seek a third term as president; Economist Intelligence Unit declares that Russia is in the process of regressing into authoritarianism
2012	Putin elected president for a third term
2013	Russia grants political asylum to Edward Snowden, a former National Security Agency contractor sought by the United States for espionage; President Barack Obama cancels a scheduled meeting with Putin; Ukraine President Viktor Yanukovych reneges on a promise to sign a partnership agreement with the European Union; protests erupt in Maidan Square, Kiev

| 2014 | Yanukovych ousted; Russia annexes Crimea; United States and European Union impose sanctions on Russia, accusing Putin of encouraging separatists; Malaysian Airlines Flight MH17 shot down over eastern Ukraine by Russian-supplied rebels |

Fragmentation and Ferment in the Near East and Middle East

7.2   Assess the relative importance of identity and material interests in various conflicts in the Near East and Middle East.

Moving south and east, the next set of flashpoints we encounter are in the Near East and Middle East. These terms have an imprecise geographic denotation, but Figure 7.6 indicates the countries we include under these labels for present purposes.

The Near East and Middle East have been the scenes for some of the world's most notorious regional conflicts. In contrast to post–Cold War relations between Russia and the West, in which constructivism holds the key to explaining what has happened, much of what has happened in the Near East and Middle East can understood fairly well through a realist lens (although

---

Figure 7.6 The Near East and Middle East

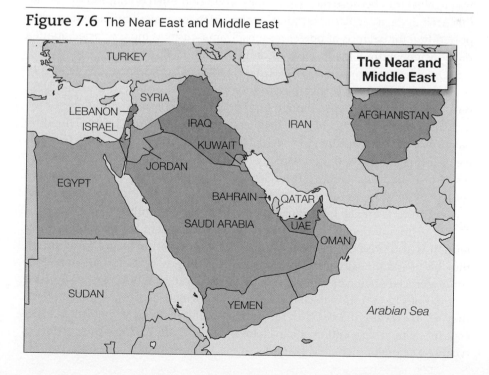

nationalism and religion also play an important role, as do international law and organization). The Iran-Iraq War (1980–1988) offers a good example. Why did Iraq invade its larger neighbor? One reason was the Islamic revolution that overthrew Mohammad Reza Pahlavi, the shah of Iran. Under the shah, Iran had claimed the whole Shatt al-Arab waterway between Iran and Iraq. But after the 1979 Iranian Revolution deposed the shah, Iran was torn apart by domestic strife, and Iraq's president, Saddam Hussein, saw an opportune time to attack. Moreover, revolutionary Iran was causing problems inside Iraq. Iraqi Muslims were divided between Sunnis and Shi'ites, and Saddam was a secular head of state. The Shi'ite fundamentalists in Iran urged the Iraqi Shi'ites to rise up against Saddam. This transnational religious appeal failed when Saddam killed many Iraqi Shi'ite leaders. But Iraq also miscalculated. Iranians are not Arabs, and there was a large Arabic-speaking minority in the part of Iran adjacent to Iraq. Iraqis thought that they would be welcomed as liberators in the Arabic-speaking part of Iran, but that was not the case. Instead, Iraq's attack helped unite the Iranians.

After this pair of miscalculations, the war bogged down into a long, drawn-out affair instead of the short, profitable war that Saddam had intended. Iraq decided that it wanted to withdraw, but Iran refused to let go. Having been attacked, it was not going to let Iraq decide when to quit. Ayatollah Ruhollah Khomeini, the spiritual leader of Iran, said that Iran would not end the war until the downfall of Saddam. For most of the decade, the rest of the world looked on. Conservative Arab countries such as Saudi Arabia and Jordan supported Iraq against Iran because they were more afraid of Iranian revolutionary power. But Arab Syria, a secular and radical regime in many ways similar to Iraq, supported Iran for balance-of-power reasons. Damascus was more worried about a rising neighbor, Iraq, than a more distant Iran.

Outsiders also took sides. The United States, worried about the growth of Iranian power, provided covert assistance to Iraq. Israel secretly shipped U.S.-built weapons to Iran, even though fundamentalists in Iran were calling for the destruction of Israel. Israel's covert weapons assistance can be explained by balance-of-power considerations. Israel feared both Iraq and Iran, but Iraq was a closer threat, and on the principle of "the enemy of my enemy is my friend," Israel provided assistance to Iran. So a war that started from miscalculations rooted in religion, nationalism, and ambition was expanded by balance-of-power concerns into an intractable, nearly decade-long conflict.

How does nationalism cause war? Nationalism is not merely a descriptive term, it is also prescriptive. When words are both descriptive and prescriptive, they become political words used in struggles for power. Nationalism has become a crucial source of state legitimacy in the modern world on the principle that nations have a right to self-determination, which, as we saw in Chapter 2, they often express in a demand for statehood. If a people can get others to accept its claim to be a nation, it can claim national rights and use such claims as weapons against others. For example, in the 1970s, the Arab states successfully lobbied in the UN General Assembly to pass a resolution that labeled Zionism—the belief that Jews were entitled to a state of their own in the biblical lands—as racism. Their intent was to deprive Israel of legitimacy by undermining Jewish nationalism. To be a nation is good; to be a racist is bad. The analytic problem with the argument was that religion can be a basis of national identity. It is also true that a religious basis can make it more difficult for minorities outside the religion to share the national identity. Life can be more difficult for Muslims in Israel than for Jews, just as daily life can be more trying for Hindus in Pakistan than for Muslims. But there is nothing inherently racist about a people using religion as a basis for national self-determination. The UN General Assembly finally annulled the resolution by a second vote in 1991.

In the eighteenth century, nationalism was not all that important. Why have claims to nationalism become so important now? After all, as constructivists showed, humans are capable of multiple crosscutting loyalties—above and below the state level—and these loyalties can change. Loyalties tend to change when the usual patterns of life are disrupted. The idea of the nation often starts among the most disrupted, with people who are marginal figures in their own cultures and less certain about their identity. They are often people who are jolted out of normal patterns, who start to ask questions. National claims often start with intellectuals or with deviant religious groups. For example, the early Arab nationalists in the nineteenth century were often Christians rather than Muslims. Gradually, their concern about a new identity developed broader support as industry and urbanization disrupted the traditional patterns and loyalties of rural societies.

The disruptions that mobilize people for new identities can come from internal or external forces. Modern nationalism was greatly stimulated by the French Revolution. The rise of the middle class disrupted traditional political and social patterns. Rising political groups no longer wanted the state of France to be defined by the king but instead to be defined in terms of the nation, all the people. And externally, as Napoleon's armies marched across Europe, they disrupted society and mobilized nationalist feelings among German-speaking peoples and other groups. By the middle of the century, there was widening support for the idea that each nation should have a state. This ideal culminated in the unifications of Germany and Italy. Ironically, as we saw in Chapter 2, Otto von Bismarck was a conservative who did not try to unite all German speakers, only those he could control for the Prussian crown. He nonetheless harnessed nationalism for his purposes, and the unifications of Germany and Italy became models of success.

World War II weakened the European colonial empires, and decolonization was one of the major movements in Asia and Africa over the next three decades. The metropolitan societies had been weakened by the war itself, and elites in the colonized areas began to use the idea of nationalism against the crumbling European empires. But if the nineteenth-century model of states based on language and ethnicity had been used to organize the postcolonial world, it would have led to thousands of ministates in Africa and many parts of Asia. Instead, the postcolonial elites asserted the right of the state to make a nation, just the opposite of the nineteenth-century pattern. The local leaders argued that they needed to use the state machinery that the colonists had established—the budget, the police, the civil service—to shape a nation out of smaller tribal groups. The same ideology of nationalism came to be used to justify two things that are almost the opposite of each other—nation makes state or state makes nation—because *nationalism* is a political word with an instrumental use. In that sense, national identities are socially constructed. (Even in the seemingly classic "nation makes state" case of France, the state used education and police to bring laggard regions such as Brittany into line.)

In the early romantic days of colonial liberation movements, there was often a successful blurring of these differences in "pan" movements. Europe in the nineteenth and early twentieth centuries saw the rise of pan-Slavism, claiming a common identity of all Slavic-speaking peoples. The modern Middle East saw pan-Arabism, and Africa, pan-Africanism. Early opponents of alien rule argued that because colonized people all suffered alike from the external colonizers, they should form pan-African or pan-Arab nations. But when it came to the actual business of governing, as opposed to liberating or resisting colonialism, the business of government required the instruments of state such as budgets, police, and civil service, and those instruments existed not on a "pan" basis, but on the basis of the artificial boundaries created by colonial rule. So, as the romanticism gradually wore away, identity based on the state began to replace that of the "pan" movements. The romanticism of the "pan" movements nonetheless often lingered on as a disruptive force.

The Middle East has often seen appeals to pan-Arabism and odd situations in which countries suddenly announce that they are forming a union, as Egypt and Syria did in forming the United Arab Republic in 1958. Over time, however, the forces of the state have prevailed over these pan-nationalist movements. But the gradual process is far from complete. Much of the postcolonial world saw enormous disruption of the normal patterns of life because of economic change and modern communications. Political leaders tried to control this postcolonial discontent. Some used national appeals, some used pan-Arab appeals, and others used fundamentalist religious appeals, all contributing to the complexity of the forces that create conflict in regions such as the Near East and Middle East. The failure of states in the region to modernize effectively explains why some of their citizens turned toward fundamentalism or terrorism.

As you can see, the Near East and Middle East are politically complex places. That complexity, in combination with various other factors such as inequality, poverty, and population and resource pressures, no doubt contributes to its volatility. We will now have a look at some of the more significant theaters of conflict in these highly complex regions.

Israel

The Arab-Israeli conflict has produced five interstate wars and almost nonstop low-level conflict (occasionally leading to large-scale military operations) between two groups of people asserting different national identities, but claiming the same small piece of land. The Israeli claim dates to biblical times when the area was controlled by Jews before the Romans asserted their authority in the first century BCE. In modern historical times, Israelis have pointed to several events tied to World Wars I and II to justify the existence of Israel. During World War I, the British issued the Balfour Declaration, a letter written by the British government to Lord Rothschild of the British Zionist Federation promising that the British government would work for a Jewish homeland in Palestine. After World War II, Israelis argue, the horrors of Adolf Hitler's Holocaust proved the need for a Jewish state. In 1948, Jewish settlers were willing to accept a partition of Palestine, but the Arab people in the area were not. The United Nations recognized the new Jewish state, but the Israelis had to fight to preserve it from concerted Arab attack. That, the Israelis say, is the historical origin and justification of the state of Israel.

Toward a Partition of Palestine

His Majesty's Government views with favour the establishment in Palestine of a national home for the Jewish people, and will use their best endeavours to facilitate the achievement of this object, it being clearly understood that nothing shall be done which may prejudice the civil and religious rights of existing, non-Jewish communities in Palestine, or the rights and political status enjoyed by Jews in any other country.

—The Balfour Declaration, November 2, 1917

The Palestinian Arabs respond that they also have lived in the area for many centuries. At the time of World War I, when the Balfour Declaration was issued, 90 percent of the people living in Palestine were Arabs. Indeed, as late as 1932, 80 percent were Arabs. They argue that Britain had no right to make a promise to the Jews at the Arabs' expense. What is more, the Arabs continue, the Holocaust may have been one of history's greatest sins, but it was committed by Europeans. Why should Arabs have to pay for it?

Both sides have valid points. In World War I, the area that is now Palestine was ruled by the Turks, and the Ottoman Empire was allied with Germany. After Turkey's defeat, its empire was dismembered, and its Arab territories became mandates under the League of Nations. France governed Syria and Lebanon; Britain called the area it controlled between the Jordan River and the Mediterranean "Palestine," and it called the area it governed across the Jordan River "Trans-Jordan."

In the 1920s, Jewish immigration to Palestine increased slowly, but in the 1930s, after the rise of Hitler and intensified anti-Semitism in Europe, it began to increase rapidly. By 1936, nearly 40 percent of Palestine was Jewish, and the influx led the Arab residents to riot. The British established a royal commission that recommended partition into two states. In May 1939, with World War II looming, Britain needed Arab support against Hitler's Germany, so Britain promised the Arabs that it would restrict Jewish immigration. But restriction was hard to enforce after the war. Because of the Holocaust, many in Europe were sympathetic to the idea of a Jewish homeland, and there was a good deal of smuggling of Jewish refugees. In addition, some of the Jewish settlers in Palestine engaged in terrorist acts against their British rulers. Britain, meanwhile, was so financially and politically exhausted from World War II and the decolonization of India that it announced in the fall of 1947 that, come May 1948, it would turn Palestine over to the United Nations.

In 1947, the United Nations recommended a partition of Palestine. Ironically, it would have been better for the Arabs if they had accepted the UN partition plan, but instead they rejected it. That led to outbreaks of local fighting. In May 1948, Israel declared itself independent, and Israel's Arab neighbors attacked to try to reverse the partition. The first war lasted for eight months of on-and-off fighting. Even though the Arabs outnumbered the Israelis 40 to 1, they were poorly organized and hampered by disunity. After a cease-fire and UN mediation, Jordan controlled the area called the West Bank and Egypt controlled Gaza, but most of the rest of the Palestinian mandate was controlled by the Israelis, more than they would have had if the Arabs had accepted the 1947 UN plan.

The war produced a flood of Palestinian refugees, a sense of humiliation among many Arabs, and broad resistance to any idea of permanent peace. The Arabs did not want to accept the outcome of the war because they did not want to legitimize Israel. They believed time was on their side. Arab leaders fostered pan-Arab feelings and the belief that they could destroy Israel in another war. King Abdullah of Jordan was assassinated when he tried to sign a separate peace treaty with Israel in 1951, further decreasing the likelihood of a peaceful settlement between the Arab states and the new Israeli government.

The second Arab-Israeli war occurred in 1956. In 1952, Gamal Abdel Nasser and other young nationalist officers overthrew King Farouk of Egypt and seized power. They soon received arms from the Soviet Union and maneuvered to gain control of the Suez Canal, a vital commercial shipping channel linking Europe and Asia. Egypt harassed Israel with a series of guerrilla attacks. As mentioned in Chapter 6, Britain and France, angry about the canal and worried about Nasser dominating the Middle East, colluded with Israel to attack Egypt. The United States refused to help Britain, however, and the war was stopped by a UN resolution and peacekeeping force that was inserted to keep the sides apart. But there was still no peace treaty.

The third war, the Six-Day War of June 1967, was the most important because it resulted in the primary current territorial issue. Nasser and the Palestinians continued to harass the Israelis with guerrilla attacks, and Egypt closed
the Straits of Tiran, which cut off Israeli shipping from the Red Sea. Nasser was
not quite ready for war, but he saw the prospect of a Syrian-Israeli war looming
and thought that he would do well to join. Nasser asked the United Nations to
remove its peacekeeping forces from his border. Israel, watching Nasser prepare
for war, decided not to wait, but instead to preempt Egypt's likely attack. The
Israelis caught the Egyptian air force on the ground and went on to capture not
only the whole Sinai Peninsula, but also the Golan Heights from Syria and the
West Bank from Jordan (Figure 7.7).

At that point, the superpowers stepped in to press the two sides to accept
a cease-fire. In November 1967, the UN Security Council passed Resolution 242,
which said that Israel should withdraw from occupied lands in exchange for
peace and recognition. But Resolution 242 contained some deliberate ambiguities. Some of the several language versions of the resolution said just "territories," not *all* territories, implying that some land might not have to be returned.
It was also ambiguous about the status of the Palestinians, who were not

Figure 7.7 Israel's Borders Pre- and Post-1967

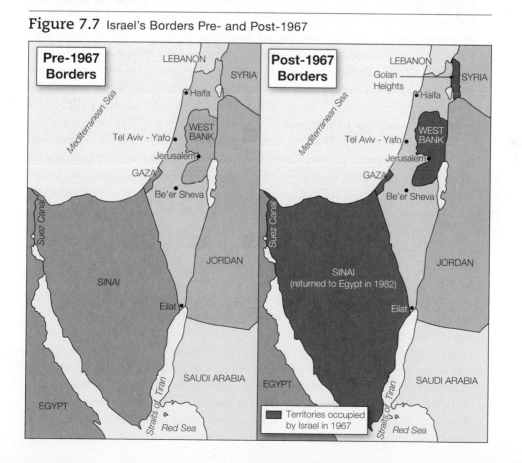

recognized as a nation but were described as refugees. Again, the basic issue was not settled.

The fourth war, the War of Attrition, was a more modest affair. In 1969–1970, Nasser, with support from the Soviet Union, organized crossings of the Suez Canal and other harassments. These moves provoked an air war in which Israeli and Egyptian pilots fought a number of air battles. Eventually, the air war tapered off into a stalemate.

The fifth war was the Yom Kippur War of October 1973. After Nasser died, he was succeeded by Anwar Sadat, who realized that Egypt could not destroy Israel. He decided that some psychological victory was necessary before he could make any conciliatory moves toward peace. Sadat decided to attack across the Suez Canal but not to try to recapture the entire Sinai Peninsula. Sadat colluded with the Syrians and achieved an effective surprise. In the first stages, the war went well for the Egyptians, but the Israelis vigorously counterattacked. Once again, the superpowers stepped in and called for a ceasefire. U.S. Secretary of State Henry Kissinger flew to Moscow, but while he was there, the Israelis surrounded the Egyptian armies. The Soviets thought that they had been cheated. They mobilized their forces in the southern part of the Soviet Union and sent the United States a letter suggesting that the superpowers introduce their own forces directly. The United States responded by raising its level of nuclear alert. Intended as a show of resolve, the alert, we now know, merely confused the Soviets, but in any case, the Soviets dropped their demand. The Israelis also backed down under U.S. pressure and released the noose around the Egyptian army. The war was followed by a series of diplomatic maneuvers in which the United States negotiated a partial pullback by Israel. UN observers were placed in the Sinai and on the Golan Heights. The most dramatic result of the war, however, was delayed. In 1977, Sadat went to Israel and announced that Egypt was ready to negotiate a separate peace. In 1978 and 1979, with President Jimmy Carter's mediation, Israel and Egypt negotiated the Camp David Accords, which returned the Sinai to Egypt and provided for talks about local autonomy in the West Bank. The Camp David Accords meant that the largest Arab state had quit the coalition confronting Israel. Egyptian nationalism had prevailed over pan-Arabism. Sadat broke the pan-Arab coalition, but he was assassinated a few years later by religious extremists who objected to his policy.

Israel's subsequent large-scale military operations have all been against nonstate actors, not sovereign states. The scene of the first was Lebanon. Once a well-functioning pluralist state, Lebanon's latent sectarian tensions finally flared into civil war in 1975, and the country became a sanctuary for groups dedicated to the destruction of Israel, such as the Palestine Liberation Organization (PLO) and Hezbollah ("Party of God"), backed by Syria and Iran. In 1982, Israel launched Operation Peace for Galilee to clear these sanctuaries, ultimately advancing all the way to Beirut. The Israeli Defense Forces (IDF) withdrew from most of Lebanon in 1985 and from a small buffer zone in the south in

2000. The PLO ultimately recognized Israel's right to exist in 1993, prompting Israel to recognize the PLO as the legitimate representative of the Palestinian people (which in turn led to the creation of the Palestinian Authority, which governs the West Bank today). But Hezbollah remained entrenched in Lebanon, from which it continued to harass Israel, firing rockets across the border into Israel and leading to another indecisive clash in 2007. Meanwhile, in Gaza, Hamas, or the "Islamic Resistance Movement," refused to recognize Israel's right to exist, challenged the PLO's authority, infiltrated fighters to mount attacks into Israel proper, and began launching rocket barrages just as Hezbollah had done in the north. Israel has responded militarily repeatedly, most notably in 2008 (Operation Cast Lead), 2012 (Operation Pillar of Defense), and 2014 (Operation Protective Edge).

The history of violence between Israel and its neighbors shows how regional conflicts based on ethnicity, religion, and nationalism can become embittered and difficult to resolve. Hard-liners reinforce one another. Arab governments were slow to make peace because they did not want to legitimize Israel, and in their rejection, they reinforced the domestic position of those Israelis who did not want to make peace with the Arabs. The extremists formed a de facto transnational coalition that made it very difficult for moderates who wanted to find a compromise. In 1973 and 1977, Sadat took risks, and he eventually paid for them with his life. A decade later, Israeli prime minister Yitzhak Rabin also took risks for peace and was assassinated by a Jewish religious extremist. In such a world of extremes, trust and cooperation are difficult, particularly when the conflict is over a private good such as territory, which, as you will recall from Chapter 6, is excludable and rivalrous.

During the bipolar Cold War era, the wars between Israel and its neighbors tended to be short, in part because the superpower role was so prominent. On the one hand, each superpower supported its clients, but when it looked as if the clients might pull the superpowers toward the nuclear brink, they pulled their clients back. The pressures for cease-fires came from outside. In 1956, the pressure came from the United States via the United Nations; in 1967, the United States and the Soviet Union used their hotline to arrange a cease-fire; in 1973, the United States and the Soviet Union stepped in; and in 1982, the United States pressed Israel to draw back from Lebanon. Although in many instances the Cold War exacerbated regional conflicts, it also placed a safety net underneath them.

In the Arab-Israeli conflict, we see the same pattern that we can observe on a global scale: a shift over time from interstate to intrastate war, from regular military combat to irregular (insurgency and counterinsurgency) combat. The last major war between the Israel armed forces and the armed forces of a neighboring state took place in 1973, but there has been no true peace since. In 2014 alone, 2,314 Palestinians and 87 Israelis were killed in the occupied Palestinian territories, mostly as a result of Operation Protective Edge in Gaza, which caused half a million Palestinians and 28,000 Israelis to flee their homes.[6]

Owing to the superior organization and firepower of the IDF, many more Palestinians than Israelis have died in ongoing violence, the Palestinians have suffered almost all the physical destruction of infrastructure, homes, and property. But both sides are vulnerable. The weaker side in an *asymmetrical* conflict often resorts to unconventional means of inflicting harm, and indeed Palestinians have often resorted to using tactics such as suicide bombings, particularly during the Second Intifada ("Uprising"). More than 500 people, mostly Israeli civilians, died in 140 suicide attacks between 2000 and 2007. The deadliest year was 2002, with 55 attacks killing 220 people, prompting calls to complete a physical barrier to prevent attackers from Palestinian-controlled areas from crossing into Israel proper and into Israeli settlements in the occupied territories. The barrier, which Israelis often refer to as "the security fence" and which Palestinians often refer to as "the Apartheid Wall," was effective in stemming suicide attacks, but it caused enormous hardship for Palestinians who travel back and forth between their homes on one side and their jobs on the other. The barrier is controversial as well because it does not always follow the 1949 armistice line, or "Green Line," considered by most of the international community to demarcate Israel's legitimate border: Roughly 12 percent of the West Bank falls on the Israeli side.

The intractability of the Arab-Israeli conflict is largely a function of it being a conflict over a private good: namely, territory. Sovereignty, you will recall from Chapter 2, is an absolute concept, and territoriality is an essential characteristic of a sovereign state. Although some states (and many nonstate actors, such as Hamas) do not recognize Israel's right to exist, most states do, and Israel is a full member of the United Nations. As of yet, however, there is no Palestinian equivalent, although on November 29, 2012, the UN General Assembly passed resolution 67/19 elevating Palestine from an "observer entity" to a "non-member observer state," and at present, more than two-thirds of full UN members have formally recognized Palestine as a state. As time goes by, more and more people arrive at the conclusion that the only prospect for lasting peace lies in a "two-state" solution.

What would it take to solve the Arab-Israeli conflict? Israel craves above all recognition of its right to exist behind secure borders as a Jewish state (de facto, if not de jure; Israel has no formal constitution, and its basic laws nowhere actually define Israel as a Jewish state). Exactly what borders would be acceptable is a matter of great internal debate. Israel also insists on retaining Jerusalem as its capital, with full control of the sites in the Old City that are holy to Judaism. Palestinians claim at a minimum a right of return for the descendants and remaining first-generation refugees forced to flee their homes and villages as a result of the 1948 and 1967 wars and insist that Jerusalem should be the capital of Palestine. They also insist on full control of the Old City's sites that are holy to Islam, some of which directly abut Jewish holy sites. Creative solutions may well be possible for issues such as Jerusalem and the holy sites, such as shared or overlapping sovereignty (in effect transforming private goods into jointly managed common goods), but only if moderates on both sides prevail.

For a genuinely durable peace, Israel would have to resolve its longstanding dispute with Syria over the Golan Heights, occupied by Israel since 1967; work out acceptable terms for Israeli settlers in the West Bank and Gaza; and negotiate long-term sharing and management of scarce water resources with Syria, Jordan, and the Palestinians. And it would have to do so all against the backdrop of decades of grievance and mistrust. It is a small wonder that the Arab-Israeli conflict has proven to be one of the world's least tractable!

Israeli Prime Minister Benjamin Netanyahu meets Palestinian President Mahmoud Abbas for talks in Washington with U.S. Secretary of State Hillary Clinton, September 2010.

Chronology: Israeli-Palestinian Conflict

1897	Publication of Theodor Herzl's *The Jewish State*; First World Zionist Congress meets
1917	Balfour Declaration stating that the British government favored "the establishment in Palestine of a national home for the Jewish people … it being understood that nothing shall be done which may prejudice the civil and religious rights of existing non-Jewish communities in Palestine"
1922	Great Britain given the Palestine Mandate by the League of Nations

(*continued*)

1937	Palestinian Arab revolt against British authority; Peel Commission report proposes partition into three states: one Arab, one Jewish, and one a British-administered territory; scheme adopted by the World Zionist Congress and rejected by the Pan-Arab Congress
1939	British White Paper calls for independent Palestine in ten years
1947	British government refers Palestine dispute to the United Nations; UN General Assembly votes for partition of Palestine into Jewish and Arab states with Jerusalem under UN trusteeship; UN partition plan accepted by Jews but rejected by Arabs
1948	Fighting between Arabs and Jews in Palestine; British mandate ends; Jewish provisional government under David Ben-Gurion proclaims the State of Israel; Israel recognized by the United States and the Soviet Union
1949	Israel admitted to the United Nations; signs armistice agreements with neighboring countries; former British territory of Palestine is divided between the State of Israel, Jordan (then Trans-Jordan), and the All-Palestine Government in the Egyptian-controlled Gaza Strip
1956	Suez Crisis; with covert assistance from France and Britain, the United Nations Emergency Force (UNEF I), the first international peacekeeping force, created to establish order in the region
1957	Israel withdraws from the Sinai Peninsula
1959	Yasser Arafat forms Fatah
1964	Formation of the Palestine Liberation Organization (PLO)
1967	Six-Day War: in response to Egyptian military activity, Israel seizes the Sinai, Gaza Strip, West Bank, and Golan Heights; adoption of UN Resolution 242 calling for Israeli withdrawal from occupied Arab lands in return for peace within negotiated permanent borders; Palestinian demands referred to only as the "refugee" problem
1973	Yom Kippur War; Egypt, Syria, and Jordan launch a surprise attack against Israel; despite the combined enemy forces, Israel successfully repels the attack and achieves victory

1974	The Arab League recognizes the PLO as the sole representative of the Palestinians.
1978	Camp David Accords signed between Israel and Egypt; Israel agrees to withdraw from the Sinai; Egypt cedes claim to Gaza in favor of the PLO
1982	Israel invades Lebanon
1987	Beginning of first Palestinian uprising (*intifada*) in Gaza Strip and West Bank; Hamas created from the Gaza wing of the Egyptian Muslim Brotherhood
1988	Jordan's King Hussein renounces Jordanian sovereignty over West Bank; PLO declares independent Palestinian state on West Bank and Gaza
1991–1992	Arab-Israeli peace talks in Madrid and Washington
1993	Oslo negotiations and Declaration of Principles between Israel and the PLO
1994	Jordanian-Israeli peace treaty signed in Washington; PLO-Israeli agreement for Palestinian control of Gaza and Jericho
1995	Yitzhak Rabin, Labor prime minister of Israel, assassinated in Tel Aviv
1996	Likud leader Benjamin Netanyahu elected prime minister after terrorist bombings in Israeli cities undermines support for Shimon Peres, Rabin's Labor successor
2000	Camp David Summit fails; Second Intifada begins; Israeli Prime Minister Ehud Barak resigns
2001	Talks between Israel and the Palestinian Authority (PA) attempt to settle the conflict, but pause pending the Israeli election; Ariel Sharon elected Israeli prime minister, refuses to continue the talks
2002	Israel reoccupies towns in West Bank and Gaza and begins construction of security barrier between the West Bank and Israel; UN Security Council demands Israel withdraw from Palestinian towns
2003	The United States, the European Union, Russia, and the United Nations release a three-phase "road map" calling for an independent Palestinian state and full peace by 2005; Arafat appoints Mahmoud Abbas (also known as Abu Mazen) prime minister; Abbas, Sharon, and President George W. Bush meet in Jordan for peace talks (June); Abbas resigns after cease-fire collapses and talks break down.

(continued)

2004	Death of Arafat; Abbas becomes president of the PA
2005	Israel withdraws from Gaza, retains control of airspace, borders, and ports
2006	Hamas wins Palestinian election; the Quartet (the United States, European Union, United Nations, and Russia) demands that Hamas renounce violence and recognize Israel's right to exist; Hamas refuses; international aid to the PA ceases
2007	Military conflict between Fatah and Hamas reaches climax, Hamas seizes complete control of Gaza; Fatah-Hamas unity government collapses; de facto separation of the Palestinian territories into two separate entities (West Bank, Gaza) begins
2008	Israel closes border crossings to Gaza; Israel and Hamas agree to six-month cease-fire; Israel reopens borders only to close them in retaliation for Islamic Jihad attacks; Israel launches massive air raid on Gaza eight days after cease-fire expires
2009	Israel launches ground incursion into Gaza; Israel and Hamas declare unilateral cease-fires and claim victory; Likud leader Netanyahu sworn in as prime minister; Netanyahu visits United States, where President Barack Obama publicly announces the need for Palestinian statehood and for a halt on settlement construction; Netanyahu conditionally accepts two-state solution
2010	Talks between Israel and PA collapse when Israel refuses to extend a moratorium on Israeli settlements in the West Bank
2011	Fatah-Hamas Reconciliation Agreement signed, with parties agreeing to a joint caretaker government, with presidential and legislative elections to be held in 2012; Netanyahu calls the agreement a "big prize for terror"; Hamas and Fatah fail to agree on who would become prime minister
2011	PA moves a UN resolution to recognize Palestinian statehood; PA given membership in UNESCO, whereas statehood vote delayed under threat of U.S. veto

2012	UN General Assembly votes to upgrade Palestine to nonmember observer state status; Israel responds by announcing new settlements in the West Bank; military conflict between Hamas in Gaza and Israeli forces results in a ceasefire
2014	Fatah and Hamas sign yet another reconciliation agreement; responding to Hamas rocket attacks, Israel launches Operation Protective Edge
2015	Palestine joins International Criminal Court; Netanyahu wins reelection

Iraq

We saw above that external powers were sometimes involved in the Arab-Israeli conflict, but most often participating not directly and officially. Although the United States backed Israel and the Soviet Union assisted Arab states during the Cold War, they stopped short of getting immediately entangled in the hostilities for two reasons. First, neither superpower was willing to get drawn into a conflict that might have ended in nuclear war. Second, the United States was reluctant to wage a major war abroad because memories of Vietnam had not yet faded. Similarly, the Soviet Union had already been fighting a costly war in Afghanistan since the late 1970s. With the end of the Cold War and the demise of the Soviet Union, however, major military involvement in the Middle East became a new pattern, and the main scene of action was Iraq.

The first Persian Gulf crisis started on August 2, 1990, when Saddam Hussein invaded Kuwait. Iraq had always claimed that Kuwait was an artificial creation of the colonial era and should not be a separate state. In 1961, it tried to take over Kuwait but was deterred by Britain. As we have seen above, the idea that colonial boundaries are meaningless promised to create enormous havoc in other regions of the postcolonial world, which may explain why so many countries in the United Nations rejected Iraq's reasoning.

In any case, there were deeper economic and political reasons. Iraq had been economically devastated by its eight-year war with Iran. It had an $80 billion debt, which was increasing at the rate of $10 billion every year. At the same time, Iraq sat next to a proverbial gold mine—Kuwait—with enormous oil surpluses and a small population. In addition, Iraq was angry with Kuwait over Kuwait's oil policy. Iraq argued that Kuwait ignored guidelines for oil production set by the Organization for Petroleum Exporting States, or OPEC, and that every dollar reduction in the price of a barrel of oil cost Iraq $1 billion per year. Moreover, Iraq believed that Kuwait was pumping too much oil from a particular field that straddled the border. Capturing Kuwait not only looked like a solution to Iraq's economic problems, but it would have gratified Saddam's sense of grievance.

Politically, Saddam was worried about the security of Iraq. He believed that everybody was out to undercut his country. After all, in 1981, the Israelis had bombed his nuclear research reactor, and with the decline of the Soviet Union, it looked as though the United States and Israel were becoming ever more powerful. In a speech in Amman, Jordan, in February 1990, Saddam said that the Soviet Union was in decline and could no longer counter the Americans and the Israelis. Saddam believed that he would have to do it himself. He undertook a number of actions designed to test the United States. Ironically, the United States was trying to appease Saddam, to bring him back into the community of responsible states, and to use Iraq as an effective balance to Iranian power in the region. The inconsistency of U.S. policy misled Saddam, and he believed that he could get away with the invasion of Kuwait without suffering serious reprisals.

Saddam was wrong. A series of UN resolutions applied the doctrine of collective security against Iraq. Why did the United States and others respond as they did? One argument is that it was all for oil. Oil exports to the United States and other leading Western industrialized nations made the Persian Gulf an abnormally important region, but there was more to the 1990 crisis than oil. For example, Britain was deeply involved in the war, but Britain did not import any Persian Gulf oil. There was also concern about collective security and echoes of the failure to stand up to German aggression in the 1930s. There was also a third dimension: preventive war. Saddam was building weapons of mass destruction. He had a nuclear weapons program with covertly imported materials, he had chemical weapons, and he was developing biological weapons. If in addition he were to have the revenues that came from Kuwait's oil, the world would face a larger, stronger, more devastating Iraq later in the decade. Some reasoned that if there were to be a war, it was better to have it now than later.

But others argued that the war was unnecessary because economic sanctions could force Iraq to withdraw its troops from Kuwait. The counterfactual is hard to prove, but historically, sanctions have rarely achieved their intended effect in a short time frame. As U.S. and coalition troops poured into the region, it looked more and more as though Iraq could not win. Why did Saddam not back down? Partly, it seems, as a result of a miscalculation. As he told the U.S. ambassador to Iraq in August 1990, he believed that the United States had no stomach for high casualties and would not commit itself to a long, drawn-out war. In that sense, he was a victim of the Vietnam analogy. Partly, too, Saddam was driven by pride and his unwillingness to accept the humiliating loss of face that withdrawal would have entailed.

The 1991 Gulf War was short and one-sided. Coalition air power pummeled Iraq's military infrastructure, and coalition ground forces pushed Iraqi troops out of Kuwait in less than a week. Desperate to avoid defeat, Saddam even ordered his troops to fire Scud missiles at Israel, hoping to trigger Israeli retaliation that would prompt the coalition's Arab partners to switch sides or stand down. But under intense diplomatic pressure from Washington, Israel weathered the barrage without responding, although it did covertly supply military hardware to at least one of its implacable foes: Saudi Arabia.

What did the Gulf War achieve? It briefly revived the doctrine of UN collective security, but one can reasonably question how typical this regional conflict was. The cease-fire set a precedent whereby UN inspectors visited Iraq and destroyed its known nuclear and chemical facilities, but it left Saddam Hussein in place. President George H. W. Bush decided not to occupy Baghdad because he thought that Saddam might be removed by his own people, and he was concerned that neither the American public nor the UN coalition would tolerate a costly occupation. Many believed that this restraint left unfinished business in view of Saddam's hegemonic regional ambitions, his demonstrated willingness to attack his neighbors, the eagerness with which he had sought weapons of mass destruction, and his obvious antipathy to Israel.

Among those who had this sense of unfinished business were Bush's son, George W. Bush, who became president in 2001, and key members of his administration who used the terrorist attacks of 9/11 as an excuse to focus the world's attention once again on Saddam. Convinced both that Saddam still posed a dire regional threat that would have to be dealt with sooner or later and that he had an underground weapons of mass destruction program that he was hiding from UN inspectors, they played up the implausible danger that Saddam would supply al-Qaeda with nuclear weapons. In 2002, they decided on war and began building up the necessary forces in the region.

The problem, however, was that both the moral case and the international-legal case for war were weak. Saddam did not pose the kind of imminent threat that would have satisfied the "just cause" requirement of *jus ad bellum* that we introduced in Chapter 1. The United States and its (few) coalition partners—most notably Britain, whose prime minister, Tony Blair, was just as keen to remove Saddam as was Bush ("But the man's uniquely evil, isn't he?" Blair said of Saddam to a group of Middle East experts assembled at 10 Downing Street in November 2002)—described military action against Iraq as "preemptive." Many countries, however, saw the United States' proposed invasion as a "preventive" war of choice because the threat posed by Iraq was not imminent. And while the UN Security Council passed a resolution demanding that Saddam cooperate fully with international inspectors to prove that he was complying with resolutions passed a decade earlier assuring that he had given up his nuclear, biological, and chemical weapons programs, all indications were that he finally was doing just that. He allowed inspectors to return to Iraq for the first time in four years and gave them unfettered access to any site of their choice, quite possibly because the United States and its coalition partners were pouring troops into the region.

As UN inspectors asked for more time to complete their work, Bush and Blair believed that time was running out. The weather was getting hot, and the forces they had deployed would have to be unleashed on Saddam or brought back home. After failing to obtain a second Security Council resolution authorizing an attack against Iraq, Bush and Blair insisted that earlier UN resolutions provided all the legal basis for action that they needed. The attack began just before dawn on March 20, 2003. Within three and a half weeks, Baghdad fell, and Saddam had fled.

Winning the war proved much easier than winning the peace. Although the occupation was initially welcomed in some of the Shi'a and Kurdish areas of the country, many of the former Sunni ruling groups and some Shi'a formed an insurgency against the occupation. They were aided by foreign terrorists, such as the Jordanian-born al-Qaeda operative Abu Musab al-Zarqawi, who crossed into Iraq and sought to continue their radical jihad against the United States. The Bush administration had not planned for enough troops to manage the looting that followed the collapse of Saddam's regime or for the insurgency that followed the invasion. The ensuing violence slowed reconstruction efforts that could have helped generate popular support and soft power. Additionally, the failure to obtain a second UN resolution meant that many countries believed that the invasion lacked legitimacy. As a result, their participation in the reconstruction effort was limited.

The costs of the war for U.S. soft power were compounded when inspectors failed to find any weapons of mass destruction afterward. Two of the three reasons given for the war before the invasion—Saddam's weapons of mass destruction and an alleged connection between Saddam and the events of 9/11—turned out to be based on false intelligence and political exaggeration. That left the third cause: the hope that removing Saddam's brutal dictatorship would lead to a democratic Iraq, which would begin a democratic transformation of the Middle East. Three rounds of national elections were successfully held in Iraq in 2005, but elections are not sufficient to produce a liberal democracy where societies are divided along ethnic and religious lines, institutions are weak, and there is little sense of overarching community that makes minorities willing to acquiesce in the rule of the majority. To this day, Iraq is still riven by sectarian violence, and the central government has limited reach and limited capacity to deliver basic public goods. The largely self-governing Kurdish region of northern Iraq is peaceful and prosperous for the most part, but large swaths of the country, particularly north and west of Baghdad and along Iraq's border with Syria, are either controlled by extremists or contested by rival militias, increasingly with international backers. According to IraqBodyCount.org, upwards of 200,000 Iraqis have died in sectarian conflict since the Iraq War began.

Chronology: Iraq

1975	Government of Iraq negotiates a deal with France to purchase an Osiris-class nuclear research reactor, to be named Osirak
1979	Saddam Hussein becomes president of Iraq; construction of the Osirak reactor begins near Baghdad; Israeli agents sabotage the Osirak reactor as it awaits shipment in France

1980	U.S. Defense Intelligence Agency reports that Iraq has been actively acquiring chemical weapons for several years; Israeli agents assassinate Yahya El Mashad, the scientist in charge of the Iraqi nuclear program
1980–1988	Iran-Iraq War
1986	Saddam orders a chemical weapons attack against Iraqi Kurds in northern Iraq
1988	Western media report an Iraqi chemical assault on Halabja in Iraqi Kurdistan
1981	Israeli warplanes destroy the Osirak reactor
1990	Iraqi forces invade Kuwait; UN Security Council imposes sanctions
1991	Gulf War; Iraqi forces expelled from Kuwait by U.S.-led coalition; UN Special Commission (UNSCOM) on Iraq established to inspect Iraqi weapons facilities, investigations by UNSCOM would find evidence of large-scale chemical and biological weapons development; encouraged by Iraq's defeat in Kuwait, southern Shi'a and northern Kurdish groups rebel, prompting a brutal crackdown
1995	Oil-for-Food Programme: UN Security Council Resolution 986 allows partial resumption of Iraqi oil exports in exchange for food and medicine
1998	Operation Desert Fox; Iraq ceases to cooperate with UNSCOM; after evacuating UN staff from Baghdad, United States and Britain begin a bombing campaign to destroy all of Iraq's nuclear, chemical, and biological weapons facilities
1999	UN Security Council creates the UN Monitoring, Verification and Inspection Commission to replace UNSCOM; Iraq rejects the resolution
2002	U.S. President George W. Bush addresses the UN General Assembly and encourages world leaders to confront the "grave and gathering danger" of Iraq or stand aside as the United States takes action; UN weapons inspectors return to Iraq

(*continued*)

2003	Chief UN weapons inspector Hans Blix reports that Iraq is cooperating with inspections, but that more time is needed to confirm compliance; arms inspectors are evacuated; United States gives Saddam and his family 48 hours to leave Iraq; Iraq War begins (March); Saddam toppled (April); Saddam captured (December)
2004	United States hands sovereignty to an interim government headed by Prime Minister Iyad Allawi; United States launches a major offensive against insurgents in Fallujah
2005	Eight million Iraqis vote in elections for a Transitional National Assembly; 114 are killed by a car bomb in the worst attack since the invasion; amid rising violence, Iraqi Parliament selects Kurdish leader Jalal Talabani as president, and Ibrahim al-Jaafari, a Shi'a, as prime minister; draft constitution endorsed by Shi'a and Kurdish negotiators, but not by Sunni representatives; elections for the first full-term post–invasion government (December)
2006	Talabani asks Nouri al-Maliki to form a new government, ending months of deadlock and tensions with Iraqi Shi'ites; Saddam executed for crimes against humanity
2008	Iraqi Parliament passes legislation allowing former Ba'ath Party officials to return to public life, ending the controversial policy of de-Ba'athification; security pact signed by which all U.S. troops are slated to leave the country by the end of 2011
2009	U.S. forces begin withdrawing from Iraqi cities and handing over security responsibility to Iraqi police; the Islamic State of Iraq and the Levant (ISIL) claims responsibility for several suicide bombings that kill hundreds
2010	Parliamentary elections take place, but nine months pass before the new government is approved; Talabani and al-Maliki re-appointed as president and prime minister, respectively; new government includes all major factions in Iraq
2013	Anti-government insurgency intensifies; full-scale sectarian war

2014	Islamist militants infiltrate Fallujah and Ramadi; government forces recapture Ramadi but face significant resistance in Fallujah; al-Maliki's coalition wins the parliamentary election but falls short of a majority government; led by ISIL, Sunni rebels seize Mosul and other key cities, causing thousands to flee; a coalition of U.S., Kurdish, and international forces assist the Iraqi government in repelling the attacks; ISIL declares a caliphate
2015	Iraqi government forces recapture Tikrit from ISIL

Iran

We have already touched on Iran and its historical role in regional conflict, and in particular on the Iran-Iraq War. In that instance, Iran was the victim. Today, many of Iran's neighbors, and many people in the United States as well, worry about Iran as a potential aggressor or at least as an aspiring regional hegemon. Following the Iranian Revolution and the fall of the shah, Iran was weak and could not possibly have threatened to dominate. To the extent that it was a "threat" at all, it was because the Iranian Revolution demonstrated that seemingly strong and secure secular authoritarian leaders were vulnerable to religiously inspired mass rebellion. Many countries in the Near East and Middle East had secular authoritarian leaders and large numbers of impoverished, disenfranchised, or outright oppressed believers, and it was for this reason, rather than any growth in Iranian power and the fear that it would cause in others, that Iran was treated as a pariah (you will recall from Chapter 3 that conservative monarchs in nineteenth-century Europe saw liberalism and nationalism as threats for precisely the same reason). But Iran is no longer weak, and realist balance-of-power considerations can largely explain regional wariness.

With a population of more than 77 million people (behind only Egypt and Turkey in the region) and a land mass second only to Saudi Arabia, Iran is naturally a country of consequence, and it could potentially become the most powerful country in the Middle East. First, Iran is poised strategically along the eastern shore of the Persian Gulf and dominates the narrow Strait of Hormuz, through which all sea traffic in and out of the gulf must pass. Second, it has massive proven oil reserves: 10 percent of the world's total, behind only Saudi Arabia and Canada. Third, Iran has an energetic ballistic missile program and is in principle now capable of striking targets virtually anywhere in the Middle East. Fourth, Iran now has a significant nuclear infrastructure that its leaders insist is for peaceful, civilian power-generation purposes, but that states wary of Iran—Israel and Saudi Arabia in particular—suspect is intended to give Iran independent nuclear capability.

Seen in one light, fear of Iran is puzzling. Unlike Iraq, Iran has never invaded a neighboring country or openly espoused regional hegemonic ambitions. The most it has done is support like-minded armed groups overseas, such as Hezbollah in Lebanon and Syria. Recently, it has also stepped up cyberattacks against Western and pro-Western targets. But Iranians describe these activities as defensive, not offensive, citing, for example, Western support for the shah, U.S. hostility to the Iranian Revolution, and so forth.

One thing Iran has done repeatedly, however, is declare its implacable hostility to Israel (because of Israel's treatment of Palestinians and occupation of sites holy to Islam). For example, Mahmoud Ahmadinejad, the incoming hardline Iranian president, was famously reported to have said in 2005 that Israel "must be wiped off the map."[7] Iranian leaders have also been vocal in their condemnation of what they consider corrupt, heretical, or Western-puppet regimes, such as the Sunni monarchs of Saudi Arabia. Hostile statements, rather than hostile actions, largely explain fears of Iran.

In recent years, the growth of Iranian hard power has amplified these fears, just as balance-of-power theory would predict. Of paramount concern to Israel, Saudi Arabia, and the United States is Iran's nuclear program, which is ambitious and less than fully transparent even though Iran is a signatory to the 1968 Treaty on the Non-Proliferation of Nuclear Weapons (NPT). Saudi Arabia has said that if Iran acquired nuclear weapons, it would be forced to acquire them as well. Israeli Prime Minister Benjamin Netanyahu has said that Israel cannot and will not tolerate a nuclear-armed Iran. Even countries not directly implicated in Near East or Middle East politics worry about Iran acquiring nuclear weapons because it would further weaken the nuclear nonproliferation regime.

It is not clear how close Iran is to nuclear weapons capability. Estimates vary from roughly a year at the earliest to many years, if ever (some analysts doubt that Iran would ever manage to acquire them).[8] Iran's spiritual leader, Ayatollah Ali Khamenei, has declared nuclear weapons *haram*, or forbidden under Islamic law, which suggests that Iran might be telling the truth that they neither seek nor desire them, but Iran's long-standing and elaborate investments in nuclear capability suggest that Iran is keeping a weapons option open. To hedge against the possibility, the West has used a mixture of hard power and soft power. The hard power comes in the form of deterrent threats, economic sanctions, and promises of rewards for good behavior. These carrots and sticks succeeded in getting Iran to the negotiating table to try to work out a compromise whereby Iran's nuclear program will be subject to limits and closely monitored in return for sanctions being lifted. Whether those negotiations will result in a durable deal remains uncertain at present.

One thing seems increasingly apparent: Opponents of Iran's nuclear program have limited military options. U.S. and Israeli intelligence has war-gamed military options repeatedly, and it is always clear that the costs outweigh the benefits, which are likely to prove short-lived. Perhaps the strongest arrows in

the Western quiver are soft-power arrows. The average Iranian is young, literate, and well-educated and craves the freedoms and opportunities that those in the West have come to take for granted. Most Iranians today have no memory of the shah's repressive regime and are increasingly weary of heavy-handed clerical rule. The more opportunity ordinary Iranians have to witness Western prosperity and Western freedom, the more it is possible that they will solve the West's Iran problem on their own.

Chronology: Iran

1953	The United States and Britain engineer a plot to overthrow Iranian Prime Minister Mohammad Mossadegh; the shah, Mohammad Reza Pahlavi, becomes an authoritarian monarch
1957	Iran and the United States sign civil nuclear cooperation agreement under U.S. Atoms for Peace program; the United States lends several kilograms of enriched uranium to Iran
1963	Iran signs and ratifies the Partial Nuclear Test Ban Treaty
1968	Iran signs the Treaty on the Non-Proliferation of Nuclear Weapons
1975	U.S. President Gerald Ford publishes a directive that permits Iran to use American technology to produce fuel for its reactors; German Kraftwerk Union begins construction on two nuclear reactors at Bushehr
1979	Climax of the Iranian Revolution; shah forced into exile; Ayatollah Ruhollah Khomeini returns to Tehran as the new supreme leader; construction on Bushehr reactors suspended; the United States withdraws support for Iranian nuclear program and stops supply of highly enriched uranium; Iranian nuclear progress slows dramatically until the late 1980s
1979	U.S. embassy in Tehran stormed by Iranian militants; 52 American diplomats and civilians taken hostage for 444 days; the United States imposes economic sanctions
1980	Iran-Iraq War begins

(*continued*)

1986	Iran-Contra Affair; U.S. President Ronald Reagan acknowledges that military supplies were sent to Iran in exchange for the release of American hostages in Lebanon, despite an arms embargo
1987	A Pakistani nuclear scientist offers his research to several countries, including Iran, and with a network of international suppliers begins transferring nuclear components to Iran; the United States intervenes in the Iran-Iraq War to protect Arab shipping, destroying the Iranian Navy
1988	United Nations brokers a ceasefire agreement ending the Iran-Iraq War
1989	Death of Ayatollah Khomeini; Ayatollah Ali Khamenei begins to rebuild the nuclear program
1995	Iran and Russia sign an agreement to cooperate on the construction of a nuclear power plant at Bushehr
2002	Evidence emerges that Iran has constructed a uranium enrichment plant and a heavy-water plant with Russian help; Iran signs a deal with Russia to speed up the completion of the Bushehr nuclear power plant; Iran invites International Atomic Energy Agency (IAEA) inspection, but shortly after removes IAEA cameras from its facilities; France, Germany, and Britain (EU3) begin negotiating with Iran to prevent nuclear weapons development
2004	IAEA adopts a resolution on Iran's failure to suspend enrichment program; Iran and EU3 reach a deal, with Iran promising to suspend most uranium enrichment
2005	Iran notifies IAEA that it intends to resume uranium conversion and removes IAEA seals from some plants; Iran maintains that nuclear activities are for peaceful purposes only; Mahmoud Ahmadinejad becomes president

2006	U.S. Director of National Intelligence John Negroponte tells Senate Select Committee on Intelligence that Iran will be capable of producing a nuclear weapon within ten years; Ahmadinejad announces that Iran has successfully enriched uranium at the Natanz plant; the United States offers to join European negotiations over Iranian nuclear program if Iran suspends all processing and enrichment; UN Security Council introduces legally binding sanctions against Iran; Iranian Foreign Ministry announces Iran is willing to negotiate with the United States on regional issues at Washington's invitation; IAEA discovers new traces of uranium at Iranian facilities and concludes that they cannot ensure compliance without improved cooperation from Iran
2007	United States and Israel cooperate on a cyberwarfare plan to attack the Natanz plant; IAEA cuts almost half of its aid to Iran in a second round of UN sanctions
2008	U.S.-Israeli Stuxnet cyberattack on the Natanz plant, crippling some centrifuges
2010	UN Security Council imposes fourth round of sanctions on Iran
2011	IAEA claims that it has evidence that Iran has conducted work on triggers for nuclear weapons; Iran's government downgrades diplomatic ties with Britain and calls for British ambassador to be expelled; Iranians storm the British embassy in Tehran, detaining six of the embassy's staff; the Natanz plant recovers, although the United States estimates that the cyberattacks have delayed Iran's progress by one to two years; the cyberwarfare program continues
2013	Hassan Rouhani becomes president of Iran; Iran and the IAEA sign a Joint Statement on a Framework for Cooperation; Iran signs an interim agreement (Joint Plan of Action) with UN Security Council members and Germany (P5+1) in Geneva, agreeing to a short-term reduction of its nuclear program in exchange for relaxed economic sanctions

(continued)

2014	Joint Plan of Action enters into effect; IAEA reports that Iran is meeting its obligations; six rounds of talks between the P5+1 and Iran fail to produce a final agreement, and the deadline is extended into 2015
2015	Talks between Iran and the United States, Britain, Russia, Germany, France, China, and the EU result in a partial framework agreement for Iran's nuclear activities

Afghanistan

Famously called "the graveyard of empires," Afghanistan has never been successfully conquered or governed from without. Arguably, it has never been successfully governed from within, either. Highly diverse ethnically and linguistically, Afghanistan has traditionally had a weak central government in its capital city, Kabul. Local tribal communities have enjoyed a high degree of autonomy, particularly in peripheral rural regions. Warlords holding sway in their particular territories would often contend with one another at the margins or for influence in Kabul. But unlike many other weak and divided states, Afghanistan has historically proven resilient to outside interference for a combination of geographical and ethnological reasons. Foreign armies have always found its remoteness, altitude, mountainous topography, and harsh climate challenging; those that have managed to get there have found its people both fearless and fiercely independent. Alexander the Great, the British Empire, the Soviet Union, and NATO have all attempted to impose their own particular kind of order in Afghanistan, and all have failed.

Afghanistan is a serious global flashpoint for a rather unusual reason. It is not a likely scene or catalyst for major interstate war, but an incubator and harbor for ideas and groups that other states often find threatening. The Soviet Union spent a decade trying to stabilize and pacify Afghanistan so as to prevent the spread of Islamic fundamentalism to its own heavily Muslim Central Asian republics. The United States and NATO intervened in Afghanistan in 2001 to destroy al-Qaeda's global headquarters in the country's eastern mountains, where Osama bin Laden enjoyed the patronage and protection of the fundamentalist Taliban regime and its leader, Mullah Omar. In attempting to protect themselves, both superpowers enjoyed but brief tactical successes; both suffered serious long-term strategic losses. Arguably, the cost in blood and treasure of the Soviet war in Afghanistan, as well as the corrosive effect it had on the legitimacy of the Soviet regime, played an important role in the collapse of the Soviet Union in 1991. Although the United States is not in danger of collapse as a result of its fruitless efforts to stabilize and democratize Iraq and Afghanistan, they are, in the words of economist Linda Bilmes, "the most expensive wars in U.S. history,"[9] totaling somewhere between $4 trillion and $6 trillion. This cost includes long-term medical care and disability compensation for service members, veterans and families, military replenishment, and social and economic costs. The largest portion of that bill is yet to be paid.

The legacy of decisions taken during the Iraq and Afghanistan wars will affect future federal budgets for decades to come. And the financial costs may well be even less significant than the damage these conflicts have done to U.S. soft power, the opportunity costs they have imposed on the United States' ability to handle serious foreign policy challenges elsewhere (e.g., in North Korea), and the effect they have had on the American people's willingness to engage overseas.

Chronology: Afghanistan

1978	The communist People's Democratic Party of Afghanistan (PDPA) seizes power; civil war erupts when the *mujahideen*, opponents of the communist government, mobilize; Soviet Union sends military advisors to support PDPA
1979	United States lends financial support to Afghan rebel groups; Soviets assassinate PDPA President Hafizullah Amin, whom they consider unreliable, and install Babrak Karmal; Soviet troops deploy to stabilize the country
1981	Mujahideen coalitions form to oppose the Soviet occupation
1983	United States and Pakistan develop a covert arms smuggling network to supply Afghan mujahideen with weapons to fight the Soviets
1985	Mikhail Gorbachev becomes president of the Soviet Union
1986	In a speech to the Soviet Politburo, Gorbachev calls for a phased withdrawal of Soviet troops from Afghanistan
1987	Soviets install a new Afghan government under Mohammad Najibullah; a new constitution is adopted; parliamentary elections called for the following year
1988	Geneva Accords pave the way for a phased withdrawal of Soviet troops
1989	The final contingent of Soviet troops leaves Afghanistan; mujahideen attack government forces in Jalalabad
1991	Collapse of the Soviet Union; direct aid to Najibullah's government ends
1992	Mujahideen leader Burhanuddin Rabbani becomes president of the Islamic State of Afghanistan

(continued)

1993	A short-lived power-sharing agreement between the new government and rival ethnic warlords made up of former mujahideen fighters collapses; ethnic warlords continue bombing Kabul
1994	Fundamentalist Pashtun-dominated Taliban emerges and receives funding and support from Pakistan, while ethnic warlords fight over Kabul; by the end of the year, the Taliban controls most of southern Afghanistan
1995	Taliban begins bombing Kabul; bin Laden expelled from Sudan and arrives in Jalalabad, joining forces with the Taliban
1996	Bin Laden calls for a *jihad* to purge the Middle East of U.S. influence and moves his family and allies to Afghanistan; Kabul falls to the Taliban; Najibullah killed; Islamic Emirate of Afghanistan proclaimed
2001	9/11 terror attacks on New York and Washington; the United States and allies invade Afghanistan, seizing Kabul and forcing al-Qaeda and the Taliban into the mountain regions; Hamid Karzai becomes the head of a new Afghan government
2002	NATO-led International Security Assistance Force deploys, marking the beginning of protracted counterinsurgency against the Taliban
2003	Afghanistan adopts new constitution
2004	First direct election in Afghan history; Karzai elected President
2006	Despite reports of election rigging and allegations of personal misconduct, Karzai elected to a second term as president
2009	In response to increased violence, U.S. President Barack Obama "surges" 30,000 additional troops into Afghanistan
2012	Enduring Strategic Partnership Agreement; the United States commits to providing economic and security aid to Afghanistan beyond the international troops withdrawal; NATO announces an exit strategy and a plan to transfer security to Afghan forces
2014	Afghanistan presidential election; Ashraf Ghani becomes president in first democratic transfer of power in Afghan history

Syria

Syria has emerged only recently as a significant flashpoint. For many decades a stable if somewhat brutal authoritarian state under the stern rule of Hafez al-Assad, Syria had few friends and many enemies because of what its neighbors saw as its troublemaker tendencies. In the wake of the Lebanese civil war, Syria seized the opportunity to exert its influence in the north and east (particularly in the Beqaa Valley) and played an active role destabilizing Lebanese politics so as to retain it. As we saw above, Syria participated in major wars against Israel three times (in 1948, 1967, and 1973) and has been a strong supporter of anti-Israeli groups such as Hamas and Hezbollah. Syria has angered its northern neighbor Turkey by providing sanctuary and support to the armed Kurdish independence group, the Kurdish Workers' Party. In addition, Assad was a major adversary of his fellow secular Ba'athist authoritarian ruler in Iraq, Saddam.

Today, however, Syria is a crucible, not an exporter, of conflict and instability. As the "Arab Awakening" protests began spreading through the region in 2010, beginning in Tunisia where an impoverished fruit seller who set himself on fire in protest of corrupt government officials relentlessly harassing him for bribes triggered massive demonstrations by frustrated citizens against oppressive Arab regimes, a relatively small number of Syrians were emboldened to demonstrate for the first time against the regime of Bashar al-Assad. Their demands were quite modest, but Assad reacted with an iron fist that sent the country into a downward spiral to civil war that has torn the country apart, reduced whole cities to rubble, resulted in millions of Syrian refugees or internally displaced persons, and created space for brutal radical groups such as the Islamic State of Iraq and the Levant (ISIL) to carve out and dominate territory where they commit horrific atrocities on a massive scale. The Syrian civil has also, in a more limited way, dragged in neighbors and outside powers who seek either to benefit from the chaos for their own particular purposes or who fear that it will become another hotbed of radicalism and transnational terrorism. Five years in, the Syrian civil war appears to have become a stalemate with no sign of the carnage or humanitarian catastrophe easing.

Chronology: Syria

1970	General Hafez al-Assad seizes power and declares himself president
2000	Death of al-Assad; succeeded by his son Bashar al-Assad
2001	Leading activists and civil rights campaigners arrested; criticism of Assad and his government increases
2010	Arab Awakening; massive antigovernment protests erupt in Tunisia and spread across the Arab world, including Syria

(continued)

2011	Beginning with mass protests in Damascus and Aleppo, unrest spreads across Syria; the United States and EU impose sanctions on Syrian regime and international community calls for Assad's resignation; Iran provides assistance to Assad's government; Free Syrian Army formed to oppose Assad regime; Arab League suspends Syria's membership
2012	Several Gulf states close their Syrian embassies; UN-Arab League envoy and former UN Secretary General Kofi Annan's peace plan fails; violence continues; parliamentary elections held but boycotted by opposition, majority of seats go to Assad and allies; Assad vows to use chemical and biological weapons if Syria is attacked by a foreign power; President Barack Obama declares that use of weapons of mass destruction by Syria would provoke U.S. military response
2013	Islamic State of Iraq and the Levant (ISIL) emerges; numerous countries and international groups announce clear evidence of chemical weapons use by Syrian government forces; Moscow persuades Assad to surrender Syria's chemical weapons to international control for destruction
2014	Two rounds of internationally brokered peace talks fail to make progress; government retakes Homs under a ceasefire agreement; evidence emerges that government forces have used chlorine gas bombs in rebel-held areas; ISIL declares itself a caliphate; Organization for the Prohibition of Chemical Weapons announces that the removal of chemical weapons from Syria is complete; American journalist James Foley is killed by ISIL; U.S. assembles an international coalition against ISIL; airstrikes against ISIL targets in Syria begin
2015	U.S. and Turkey agree to train and arm Syrian rebels fighting ISIL

Yemen

The newest flashpoint in the region is Yemen, a poor, overpopulated, politically unstable country that had been divided during the Cold War between a Marxist South supported by the Soviet bloc and a republican North supported by the West. Unified in 1990, the country has never enjoyed an extended period of genuine peace. In recent years, it has become a frontline state in three distinct battles: between the North and the South for influence; between Sunni and Shi'a Islam; and between al-Qaeda and the West. Most Yemeni experts consider the first battle the most important one. Much of the conflict we see in Yemen today can be understood as unfinished business from a less than fully inclusive reunification process. In 2015, the second battle became truly internationalized for the first time, pitting Saudi Arabia, the champion of the Sunni-dominated government of Yemen, against Iran, covertly supporting (albeit very modestly) Shi'ite Houthi rebels who have emerged as the most credible and best-organized political alternative to a series of corrupt and ineffective regimes. Finally, Yemen is one of the few places where al-Qaeda has managed to survive as an effective organization. Al-Qaeda in the Arabian Peninsula, as the Yemeni franchise is known, is one of the best organized, best funded, and most ambitious branches, organizing and mounting almost all the al-Qaeda operations against Western targets outside of North Africa. It is a small wonder that it has attracted the particular attention of the Obama administration, which has relied on an energetic drone warfare program to track, target, and destroy al-Qaeda operatives.

Geographically isolated as it is, it is unlikely that civil war in Yemen will spread. Still, it is a flashpoint for international conflict in much the same way as Afghanistan: as a stage for proxy war and as an incubator and haven for radicalism and transnational terrorism.

Chronology: Yemen

2010	Arab Awakening; massive antigovernment protests erupt in Tunisia and spread across the Arab world
2011	Arab Awakening spreads to Yemen; mass demonstrations and defections from the regime of President Ali Abdullah Saleh effectively neutralize the government's control of the country; by the end of the year, Saleh has survived an assassination attempt and has signed a political transition agreement; the United States reportedly begins construction of an airbase in the region to operate combat drones over Yemen; Yemeni media report at least 35 drone attacks in a two-month period
2012	Abd Rabbuh Mansur al-Hadi wins uncontested presidential election and is sworn in as president of Yemen; new government struggles to withstand challenges from al-Qaeda and Houthi militants; a U.S. drone strike in Lawder reportedly kills Abdel-Monem al-Fathani, a suspect in the USS *Cole* bombing in 2000

(*continued*)

2013	A U.S. drone strike mistakenly destroys a wedding convoy; intelligence had indicated that the vehicles were carrying al-Qaeda suspects; 5 of the 17 victims were confirmed to be al-Qaeda suspects
2014	Houthi militants enter the Yemeni capital, Sana'a, and force Hadi to negotiate a unity government; in April, three U.S. drone strikes target two dozen suspected al-Qaeda members and destroy one of their training camps in southern Yemen
2015	Hadi and his government resign, Hadi escapes to Aden; Houthis seize the government and dissolve parliament; Hadi flees the country as Houthi forces march toward Aden; in March, a Saudi-led coalition intervenes, using airstrikes to restore the former government

Uneasy Standoff: India and Pakistan

7.3 Assess the stability of nuclear deterrence in India-Pakistan relations.

Still further east is the site of a hotly contested territorial dispute over Kashmir. There are three main protagonists—India, Pakistan, and China—but the most dangerous axis of conflict is between the former two.

When Britain withdrew from South Asia in 1947, it divided the territory it had governed into two states. Predominantly Hindu areas were to become India, and predominantly Muslim areas were to become Pakistan (East Pakistan in the area of the Ganges River delta, West Pakistan in the Indus River watershed between Afghanistan and Iran on the West and India on the east). The criteria for partition were less than fully clear, however, and certain territories became subjects of dispute. Chief among them was Kashmir, a "princely state" in the remote mountainous northwest of the Indian subcontinent. Previously semiautonomous, Kashmir was reluctant to accede to either state. The First Indo-Pakistani War (1947–1948) was fought over control of Kashmir, but left India and Pakistan each in possession of only part of it. China controlled a portion as well: the high, remote, virtually unpopulated Aksai Chin, over which China and India fought a brief war in 1962 that resulted in a decisive Indian defeat.

The Second Indo-Pakistani War, also fought over Kashmir, broke out in 1965. In this instance, India's tepid military response to Pakistani incursions in a disputed portion of the Indian state of Gujarat encouraged the Pakistani military to believe that it could wrest control of Indian-occupied Kashmir. Pakistan overplayed its hand, however, and India responded forcefully, even going as far as to launch military operations into Pakistani territory in the Punjab. After the UN Security Council called for a cease-fire, hostilities ended, and the two countries agreed to meet to negotiate a settlement to the conflict, but ultimately failed to do so.

The Third Indo-Pakistani War (1971) was the deadliest. Some 9,000 Pakistani soldiers were killed, as well as 2,500 Indians. In contrast to the first two, however, it was not fought over Kashmir. It began as a domestic Pakistani dispute and ultimately resulted in East Pakistan seceding to become the state of Bangladesh.

What makes the conflict between India and Pakistan so dangerous today is that both countries now have nuclear arsenals. India developed nuclear weapons first, successfully conducting a "peaceful nuclear explosion" in 1974 intended primarily as a deterrent signal to China, with whom India had ongoing, if stable, territorial disputes. Prime Minister Indira Gandhi did not "weaponize" India's nuclear capability at the time, however. Pakistan began its nuclear weapons program in 1972 in response to its defeat in the Third Indo-Pakistani War, but it did not acquire the capability to build a nuclear weapon until the late 1980s. It received help from China, which had not yet become firm in its nonproliferation policies. Pakistan first tested nuclear weapons in 1998 immediately following a series of Indian nuclear tests, the motivation for which remains somewhat unclear: Indian Prime Minister Atal Bihari Vajpayee may have been attempting to send a deterrent signal to both China (at that time undergoing a nuclear modernization program) and Pakistan (whose nuclear ambitions were known and which had recently successfully tested a long-range missile), he may have been keen to develop some useful payload for India's own long-range missiles, or he may simply have sought to assert India's claim to great power status. Some combination of motivations is entirely plausible as well. Pakistan's response was very clearly deterrent in nature. Its tests were hasty and unimpressive.

Several additional factors render the ongoing Indo-Pakistani rivalry particularly worrisome. One is that the two countries have a long history of misperceptions and misjudgments leading to conflict. In one case, the 1999 Kargil confrontation, the two countries found themselves in direct conflict even after their nuclear tests. In this instance, in other words, Indian and Pakistani nuclear weapons proved to be of little deterrent value. Another worrisome consideration is that although India's nuclear arsenal appears to be under relatively secure civilian control, Pakistan's is under military control, and the Pakistani military is highly politicized and known for its risk-taking. Third, Pakistan does not have a culture or a history of responsible nuclear stewardship. Pakistan's chief nuclear scientist, A. Q. Khan, was at the hub of a major international proliferation network linking Pakistan to Libya, Iran, and North Korea, and he may well have done more harm to the global cause of nonproliferation than any individual on the planet. Fourth, although India is a relatively stable democracy, Pakistan is not, and significant elements within Pakistan are sympathetic to radical Islam. Most analysts believe that the most plausible way in which a terrorist group such as al-Qaeda might get its hands on a nuclear weapon, unlikely though it might be, would be a diversion from the Pakistani nuclear arsenal.

The international response to India and Pakistan's ascendancy to the nuclear club has been energetic if somewhat contradictory. Both countries were roundly condemned and initially sanctioned for violating a growing norm of nonproliferation (although not for violating the NPT, which neither had signed), yet both were ultimately rewarded for their transgressions. President George W. Bush made a deal with Indian Prime Minister Manmohan Singh in March 2006 granting India an exemption from U.S. laws prohibiting the sale of U.S. nuclear technology to nonsignatories of the NPT in return for India's agreement to open up its civilian nuclear facilities to international inspection. The United States has lavished Pakistan with military and economic aid intended to shore up its secular democracy and help it fight Islamic insurgents. There is no doubt that the United States (and possibly others) has tried to provide the Indian and Pakistani militaries with technology intended to help safeguard against the accidental or unintended use of nuclear weapons. But without a durable, permanent solution to the Kashmir problem, and with the ever-present danger of a transborder terrorist attack having a catalytic effect, the possibility of an Indo-Pakistani nuclear war can never be dismissed.

Chronology: India and Pakistan

1947	India granted independence from Britain, partitioned into India and Pakistan; territory of Jammu and Kashmir remains in dispute; First Indo-Pakistani War breaks out; Maharaja of Kashmir controversially accedes to India in return for military assistance against Pakistani infiltrators
1949	Fighting between India and Pakistan ends on January 1; Line of Control established
1962	Sino-Indian War
1965	Pakistan launches covert military offensive into Indian-held Kashmir; Second Indo-Pakistani War; three weeks into the fighting, UN-brokered cease-fire signed
1971	East Pakistan demands independence; Pakistan erupts into civil war; India invades East Pakistan to stem the flood of refugees into India; East Pakistan declared the sovereign state of Bangladesh
1974	Pakistan officially recognizes Bangladesh as an independent state; India detonates a "peaceful" nuclear device

1989	Armed resistance to Indian rule begins in Kashmir valley: some groups demand independence for Jammu and Kashmir, others accession to Pakistan
1992	Pakistan declares that it has acquired the scientific capability required to build nuclear weapons (after having acquired it de facto in the late 1980s)
1998	India conducts underground nuclear tests near Pakistani border; Pakistan retaliates with nuclear tests; the United States imposes sanctions against both countries
1999	Pakistani-backed forces cross the Line of Control into Indian territory at Kargil; India launches retaliatory air strikes; General Pervez Musharraf overthrows Pakistani government in military coup
2001	Militants attack Kashmiri assembly in Srinagar, killing 38; unidentified men attack Indian parliament in New Delhi, killing 14; India deploys troops to Kashmir in Operation Parakram; both sides escalate military presence in Kashmir
2002	After months of intermittent violence, India and Pakistan begin to demobilize
2003	India and Pakistan sign cease-fire agreement and restore diplomatic ties; Delhi-Lahore bus service resumes, helping defuse tensions
2006	President George W. Bush signs law permitting civilian nuclear cooperation with India in return for international inspections of Indian civilian nuclear facilities
2008	Pakistani members of Lashkar-e-Taiba mount terrorist attacks in Mumbai, killing more than 150 and escalating military tensions along the border
2010	Violent protests erupt in the Kashmir Valley against alleged Indian human rights abuses
2011	Indian and Pakistani troops exchange fire across the Line of Control, killing five Indian and three Pakistani soldiers
2012	Indian President Pranab Mukherjee visits Jammu and Kashmir within two months of taking office
2013	The prime ministers of India and Pakistan meet and agree to reduce the number of violent incidents taking place along the disputed border

(continued)

2014	India cancels talks with Pakistan, accusing it of interfering in India's internal affairs; state elections in Jammu and Kashmir; despite boycotts by separatist leaders voter turnout is high; Indian Prime Minister Narendra Modi accuses Pakistan of waging a proxy war against India in Kashmir

The Rise of China?

7.4 Identify the main threats to China's "peaceful rise" in East Asia and Southeast Asia.

As Figure 7.2 suggests, the most dramatic geopolitical development of the post–Cold War era has been the rise of China. Once a poor, underdeveloped, largely rural country, China has modernized at breakneck speed. It now boasts the world's second-largest economy, is predominantly urban, and has a large and growing wealthy middle class. Particularly under its new president, Xi Jinping, China has begun also to claim the rights and privileges normally accorded a great power. Exactly what rights and privileges China expects is a subject of debate. China's position is that it claims nothing more than the right to be treated with respect, which is certainly an understandable desire in view of the more than 150 years that China suffered humiliating treatment at the hands of others. Britain, the United States, France, Germany, Japan, Russia, and even lesser states such as Italy, Austria-Hungary, Belgium, and Portugal all held concessionary treaty rights in China for periods of time. Many of these treaties provided for extraterritorial jurisdiction, which was another way of saying that China was treated as less than fully sovereign. At times it was dismembered, dominated, and outright occupied. Japan and Russia contended for control of Manchuria in the early twentieth century, for example, and Chinese suffered horribly under Japanese occupation before and during World War II. As recently as 1999, Macau was Portuguese territory. Britain returned Hong Kong in 1997, but with restrictions designed to protect Hong Kong's democratic system for 50 years. It is no wonder that China is so sensitive to perceived affronts to its sovereignty, its territorial integrity, and its dignity.

Other countries, however, are suspicious that China seeks more than just respect. Some, particularly in Japan and Vietnam, suspect that China wishes to reimpose its ancient "Middle Kingdom" primacy, reducing neighbors to vassals and tributaries. Many Americans interpret Xi's call for a "new type of major power relationship" and his frequent insistence that Asian security should be provided by "Asians" without the "interference" of "outsiders" as indicating a desire or intention ultimately to drive the United States from the Western Pacific. China's increasingly assertive behavior in the South China Sea, the East China Sea, and elsewhere have set off alarm bells and triggered hedging and balancing behavior that China in turn interprets as hostile attempts at containment. In fact, the United States has no interest or desire in "containing" China. Unlike the Cold War when a containment policy toward the Soviet Union meant little economic or social contact, the United States has major trade and student exchanges with China. As U.S. officials say at every available opportunity, they welcome China's peaceful rise because a strong and wealthy China could make a major contribution toward solving some of the region's (and the world's) greatest challenges. But by a "peaceful" rise, they clearly mean one in which China accepts the basic rules of order as understood by Washington. That includes acknowledging that the United States has a vital interest in Asia-Pacific security and a leading role in providing it, which it has done for decades by means of a system of bilateral security alliances with Japan, South Korea, the Philippines, Thailand, and Australia, as well as security guarantees for Taiwan. President Barack Obama's "rebalance" of U.S. forces to Asia—colloquially known as the "pivot," to use a popular basketball metaphor—is intended to signal a continued U.S. commitment and acknowledge the strategic reality that Asia will only become more important to the United States as time goes on.

From Beijing's perspective, of course, the U.S. "rebalance" looks very much like containment. Although that is a largely a misperception—easily understood through the lens of perfectly normal human psychology (we tend to see what we most fear)—some very real conflicts of interest overshadow U.S.-China relations. One is China's increasing assertiveness on maritime and territorial claims, which is raising tensions with neighboring countries, some of whom the United States is bound by treaty to defend. A second, deeper conflict of interest is on the basic rules of world order. Increasingly, China pushes back against, or rejects outright, "Western" or "European" approaches to international law and dispute resolution, embracing Sino-centric principles that look very much like the Middle Kingdom to others.

To some analysts, none of it seems surprising. From a realist perspective, it is natural for a rising power to assert itself and a declining power to react warily. Some go even so far as to insist that conflict between the United States and China is inevitable. Political scientist John Mearsheimer, for example, flatly insists that "China cannot rise peacefully."[10] And as we saw in Chapter 1, if Sparta feared a rising Athens and risked war to protect its interests, might the United States fear a rising China and some day take similar risks? Power transitions can be dangerous, especially if people believe that conflict is inevitable and act in ways that make it a self-fulfilling prophecy.

It is possible, of course, that China's rise will run out of steam. Leaders in Beijing face a daunting set of long-term demographic, environmental, and economic challenges. They face increasingly strident demands for autonomy in Xinjiang, Tibet, and Hong Kong. As China's middle class grows, becomes wealthier, and is better educated, demands for political reform will increase, and the Communist Party's legitimacy will weaken.[11] But even if China does continue to rise, it is very hard to imagine the rational calculation that would lead to a modern-day version of war between Athens and Sparta. The U.S. and Chinese economies are highly interdependent, and the nuclear crystal ball effect means that leaders in Washington and Beijing can clearly imagine the horrific potential consequences of war. But rational calculation is not the only path to conflict. Leaders can also be pushed into war by public opinion; they can be pulled into war by allies; and they can stumble into war through misperception, misjudgment, or inadvertence. Thucydides wrote poignantly of these traps as well.[12]

The South China Sea

The South China Sea is one potential candidate for the push, pull, and stumble scenarios. Bordered on the north by China, on the east by the Philippines, on the west by Vietnam, and on the south by Malaysia and Brunei, the South China Sea is an area of enormous strategic and economic importance. One-third of the world's commercial shipping passes through it. Almost 8 percent of the world's fish are caught in it. It is also home to perhaps as much as an entire year's worth of global oil and natural gas consumption.

The danger of international conflict in the South China Sea is significant for three reasons. First, it is riddled with small islands, reefs, and atolls whose ownership is contested. These territorial disputes are the basis for overlapping claims to maritime space by all five littoral states (plus Taiwan). Indeed, China and Taiwan claim virtually the entire area (Figure 7.8). Second, the countries involved in these disputes have demonstrated a willingness to back up their claims with force. Third, there is ample opportunity for significant misperceptions or misjudgments that could lead to unintended conflict. Of particular concern is uncertainty over the role of the United States in any serious regional clash. Although the U.S. government has stated that it does not take sides in the territorial disputes, it regards the sea as international waters under the Law of the Sea Treaty and will keep important international sea lanes open. It also has treaty obligations to the Philippines and increasingly close relations with Vietnam that might incline one or both of these countries to misjudge the level of U.S. support that they might enjoy in a conflict with China and lead them to overplay their hand. China, for its part, may underestimate the willingness of Washington to resist Chinese attempts to become the dominant naval power in the region, an objective articulated by strategists in the People's Liberation Army.

Aware that the South China Sea is a powder keg, China and the Association of Southeast Asian Nations, or ASEAN, negotiated a Declaration of Conduct in the South China Sea in 2002 that, although not solving any of the territorial or maritime disputes, called on claimants to settle them peacefully through negotiation and to refrain from actions that would complicate or escalate them. But with China becoming more strident and assertive in the region, it remains an open question whether conflict or cooperation will prevail in this particularly important corner of the world.

Figure 7.8 Overlapping Claims in the South China Sea

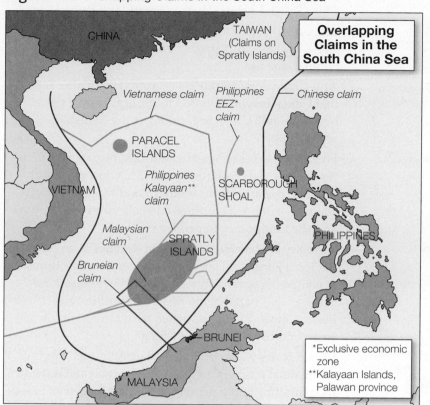

Chronology: The South China Sea

1976   China seizes the Paracel Islands from Vietnam

1988   Johnson Reef skirmish between China and Vietnam
                (Spratly Islands): 70 Vietnamese sailors killed

1992   Vietnam accuses China of occupying Da Lac Reef

1995   China occupies Philippine-claimed Mischief Reef

1996   Three Chinese vessels engage in a 90-minute gun battle
                with a Philippine patrol boat

1998   Philippine navy arrests Chinese fishermen near
                Scarborough Shoal; Vietnamese soldiers fire on
                Philippine fishing boat near Pigeon Reef

2002   China and the Association of Southeast Asian Nations
                (ASEAN) adopt the Declaration on the Conduct of
                Parties on the South China Sea to pave the way for
                possible commercial cooperation

(continued)

2003	Vietnam challenges Chinese ban on fishing in the South China Sea and asserts claims to Spratly and Paracel Islands
2005	Chinese, Vietnamese, and Philippine oil companies sign a deal to jointly protect oil and gas resources in the South China Sea
2007	Anti-China demonstrations occur in Hanoi after reports that China has consolidated its administrative rights over the South China Sea, calling it the "Sansha" administrative area
2009	Five Chinese vessels confront a U.S. research ship in the South China Sea, renewing U.S. concerns about freedom of navigation; Vietnam and Malaysia jointly claim an extended continental shelf, prompting China and the Philippines to protest
2010	Secretary of State Hillary Clinton declares at an ASEAN Regional Forum in Hanoi that the peaceful resolution of competing sovereignty claims to the South China Sea is a U.S. "national interest," prompting Yang Jiechi, China's foreign minister, to describe Clinton's comments as "an attack on China"
2011	United States warns of violent clashes unless multilateral mechanisms are strengthened and reiterates its commitment to defend the Philippines; Senate passes a resolution condemning China's use of force; China rebuffs U.S. statements and demands that the United States stay out of its regional disputes; the United States and Vietnam issue a joint call for freedom of navigation and a rejection of the use of force to resolve disputes; U.S., Japanese, Australian, and Vietnamese forces conduct exercises in the South China Sea
2012	Disagreement on the South China Sea derails ASEAN summit; China and the Philippines clash repeatedly over the Scarborough Shoal; National Assembly of Vietnam passes a law incorporating the Spratly and Paracel Islands as national territory
2013	The Philippines files a case with the Permanent Court of Arbitration seeking a ruling on China's "nine-dash line" and whether South China Sea reefs and islands support maritime jurisdiction claims under the UN Convention on the Law of the Sea; China refuses to participate

2014	Vietnamese and Chinese vessels collide after China deploys an oil rig to conduct drilling in disputed waters near the Paracel Islands; Vietnam releases video showing a Chinese vessel ramming and sinking a Vietnamese fishing boat; ASEAN expresses "serious concerns" over the tensions; China misses deadline to submit counterarguments in the Philippine arbitration case and releases a position paper stating that the tribunal has no jurisdiction
2015	Satellite images show that China is building artificial islands on coral reefs and building a runway in the Spratly Islands; at the ASEAN Summit, Philippine Foreign Affairs Secretary Albert De Rosario says that China is "poised to consolidate de facto control of the South China Sea"; the Summit results in a statement criticizing China's land reclamation activities; China rejects ASEAN's statement

The Taiwan Strait

Another important flashpoint is the Taiwan Strait, separating mainland China from Taiwan. As you will recall from Chapter 2, China considers Taiwan a renegade province and adamantly insists on the "One China" principle. Taiwan, however, has been a thriving sovereign state in all but name since Chinese Nationalist forces fled in the face of Mao Zedong's communist troops as they swept the mainland at the close of World War II. Because the Chinese Communist Party (CCP) and Nationalist Chiang Kai-shek's Kuomintang (KMT) both claimed to be the legitimate ruling party of all of China during most of the postwar period, the One China principle itself was never under serious contention; it was merely a question of who rightly claimed to represent it. The China seat at the United Nations was originally held by Taiwan, formally known as the Republic of China (ROC). But General Assembly Resolution 2758, passed on October 25, 1971, withdrew recognition of the ROC as the sole legitimate government of China, and the People's Republic of China (PRC) took its place at the United Nations shortly thereafter.

Even though no Taiwanese government has unilaterally declared independence, Taiwan has actively sought international recognition over the years. Since 1991, it has repeatedly, although unsuccessfully, applied for UN membership.

Three times in the postwar period serious international crises have erupted in the Taiwan Strait. In 1954–1955, Communist forces sought to dislodge Nationalist forces from a series of small islands close to the mainland. They succeeded in overrunning a few islands, but concentrated most of their effort on

Quemoy and Matsu, which suffered heavy artillery bombardment but did not fall. The PRC renewed its bombardment of Quemoy and Matsu in 1958, again unsuccessfully. In the third Taiwan Strait crisis (1995–1996), the PRC launched a series of missiles into waters near Taiwan intended to intimidate Taiwanese voters in the lead-up to the 1996 presidential election. Beijing had become convinced that KMT's president, Lee Teng-hui, if reelected, would abandon the One China principle and declare independence unilaterally. These fears proved unfounded, but the PRC's actions backfired, and Lee was reelected with a strong majority.

In all three crises, the United States has stood firm in its support of Taiwan. During the first two, the United States—but not the PRC—was a nuclear-armed state and held the upper hand. During the third, both were nuclear powers, but the United States was by far the more capable and could count on controlling the seas in the event of a major war. The PRC's options were severely limited.

The Taiwan Strait remains dangerous because the status of Taiwan is still unresolved. Although in recent years no Taiwanese government has asserted a unilateral declaration of independence (UDI), surveys indicate that the commitment to the One China principle is weakening among the Taiwanese. The One China principle is still very powerful on the mainland, where secession is unacceptable. Beijing fears that to allow Taiwan formally to secede would be to legitimize secessionist movements in Tibet or Xinjiang and to undermine the CCP as the sole legitimate ruler of China. Rather than allow Taiwan to secede, Beijing is likely to use force, and that could lead to conflict with the United States. Thus, ironically, Washington and Beijing share a strong interest in attempting to prevent a Taiwanese UDI. The United States has urged no use of force by Beijing, no declaration of independence by Taipei, and negotiations within that framework.

In recent years, cross-strait relations have improved dramatically. In his 2008 inaugural address, Taiwan's President Ma Ying-jeou promised to follow a policy of "no reunification, no independence, and no war." Ma's critics in Taiwan often voice the concern that he means only the last two, and officials in Beijing have certainly been willing to try to woo the Taiwanese with increased trade, investment, and travel. But there are worrying signs. China's insistence in 2014 on vetting candidates for Hong Kong's chief executive in the future, which would make a mockery of Beijing's commitment to the principle of "One Country, Two Systems" on the basis of which Britain withdrew in 1997, spooked Taiwanese voters, devastated Ma's party in local elections, and gave a significant boost to the Democratic Progressive Party, which rejects the One China principle. If China continues to rise and Taiwanese leaders begin to sense impatience for reunification from Beijing, it is conceivable that they would adopt the same kind of "better now than later on even less favorable terms" calculation that helped trigger World War I and take concrete steps toward full formal sovereignty, something that would almost certainly lead to war.

Chronology: The Taiwan Strait

1945   Japan returns territory of Taiwan to China at end of World War II

1949   Mao Zedong's Chinese Communist Party (CCP) declares victory over U.S.-backed Chinese Nationalist Kuomintang (KMT); Chiang Kai-shek flees to Taiwan (then called Formosa) with Nationalist supporters and establishes "provisional" capital; the United States recognizes Chiang as legitimate Chinese leader

1950   President Harry S. Truman claims that the United States will not become involved in conflict between Communists and Nationalists, even if the People's Republic of China (PRC) attacks the Republic of China (ROC); Korean War breaks out; Truman declares Formosa Strait neutral waters and deploys the Seventh Fleet, effectively putting Taiwan under U.S. protection

1953   Dwight D. Eisenhower inaugurated as U.S. president: withdraws U.S. naval blockade from Taiwan Strait

1954   Nationalists send troops to islands Quemoy and Matsu; PRC shells Quemoy and Matsu; Eisenhower rejects Joint Chiefs' recommendation to commit U.S. troops or use nuclear weapons; the United States and ROC sign mutual defense treaty, understood as U.S. pledge to aid Taiwan in the event of PRC attack

1955   PRC seizes Yijiangshan Islands; fighting continues along Chinese mainland and on Matsu and Quemoy; Congress approves Formosa Resolution, authorizing use of U.S. forces to defend Taiwan against armed attack; Secretary of State John Foster Dulles publicly admits that the United States is considering a nuclear strike against mainland China; PRC announces willingness to negotiate; cease-fire agreed

(continued)

1958	China shells islands of Quemoy and Matsu; Eisenhower sends U.S. naval contingent to the Taiwan Strait; facing a military stalemate, PRC and ROC agree to a cease-fire; message to the Compatriots in Taiwan issued by Defense Minister Peng Dehuai (actually drafted by Mao), calling for peaceful solution to the Taiwan issue and for Chinese unity in the face of "the American plot to divide China"; Dulles and Chiang issue a joint communiqué reaffirming their mutual support and intent to refrain from using military means to take back mainland China
1971	U.S. Ping-Pong team receives unexpected invitation to visit China while in Japan at World Table Tennis Championships, symbolic of thawing U.S.-PRC relationship; ROC expelled from China's UN seat, replaced by PRC
1972	Informal relationship between the United States and PRC established by President Richard Nixon's visit to mainland China; Shanghai communiqué issued stating "there is but one China and ... Taiwan is a part of China"
1979	Formal diplomatic ties established between the United States and PRC; mutual defense treaty signed in 1954 with Taiwan terminated; President Jimmy Carter signs the Taiwan Relations Act declaring U.S. commitment to Taiwan's security, to reassure ROC
1982	United States and China issue third joint communiqué; the United States declares intent to reduce arms sales to Taiwan
1987	Taiwan lifts martial law after 38 years; flow of goods and people between Taiwan and mainland China increases
1988	Native Taiwanese Lee Teng-hui assumes presidency of Taiwan and intensifies the pace of democratic reform
1989	Tiananmen Square crackdown in mainland China strains U.S.-Chinese relations

1992	Consensus on the "One China principle"; PRC and ROC appear to reach common ground, both sides recognize that there is only one China, and both agree to interpret the meaning of that separately
1995	Lee visits the United States to speak at his alma mater, Cornell University; the United States forced to reverse policy and issue travel visa to Lee; Chinese ambassador to the United States recalled in protest; PRC conducts missile tests near ROC-held Pengchiayu Island, mobilizes forces in Fujian; PRC conducts second set of missile tests, live ammunition exercises, and naval exercises; the United States sends USS *Nimitz* through Taiwan Strait, the first U.S. military presence in the Strait since 1976
1996	President Bill Clinton deploys the USS *Independence* carrier battle group to waters near Taiwan; PRC announces intent to complete live-fire exercises near Penghu; the United States deploys USS *Nimitz* carrier group to waters near Taiwan; China completes third set of missile tests preceding March 23 Taiwanese presidential election, announces simulated amphibious assault for March 18–25; PRC's attempt at intimidating Taiwanese voters backfires, Lee reelected with 54 percent majority; the United States increases military sales to ROC
2000	House of Representatives passes the Taiwan Security Enhancement Act, prompting strong Chinese protest
2001	President George W. Bush approves the largest sale of arms to Taiwan in a decade
2002	Taiwanese National Defense Report calls for enhanced confidence-building measures across the Strait

(*continued*)

2005	At a Security Consultative Committee meeting in Washington, the United States and Japan declare "the peaceful resolution of issues concerning the Taiwan Strait through dialogue" and increased military transparency in China to be among their common strategic objectives, eliciting a strong condemnation from the Chinese Foreign Ministry that Beijing "resolutely opposes the United States and Japan in issuing any bilateral document concerning China's Taiwan, which meddles in the internal affairs of China, and hurts China's sovereignty"; China passes an "Anti-Secession Law" requiring China to prevent a Taiwanese declaration of independence
2008	Ma Ying-jeou elected president of Taiwan; high-level contact resumes between PRC and ROC, Hu Jintao and Ma agree to conduct negotiations on the basis of the 1992 consensus; subsequent discussions result in the reinstatement of direct flights between the mainland and Taiwan
2009	Taiwan's Financial Supervisory Commission announces that Chinese investors will be permitted to invest in Taiwan's money markets for the first time since 1949
2012	United States announces a $6.4 billion sale of military equipment and hardware to Taiwan, prompting China to curtail military-to-military contact
2013	China announces 31 measures aimed at improving economic exchange between Taiwan and the mainland
2014	Wang Yu-chi, minister of the Mainland Affairs Council, and Zhang Zhijun, minister of the Taiwan Affairs Office, meet in Nanjing in the first official government-to-government contact since 1949; Hong Kong democracy protests; KMT devastated in local elections

The East China Sea

The end of World War II left a number of maritime and territorial issues unsettled in Asia, among them the status of a number of small, rocky, uninhabited islets in the East China Sea known as the Senkaku Islands in Japan and the Diaoyu Islands in China. Sitting near the southern end of the Ryuku Island chain, Japan had formally incorporated the islands into Japanese territory in 1895, but from 1945 to 1972, they were under the effective control of the U.S. military and were part of the territory that the U.S. transferred to Japan when it handed back Okinawa in 1972. China and Taiwan also claim sovereignty over the islands, and although the United States officially takes no position on the sovereignty dispute, it does recognize them as territory that falls under the protection of the U.S.-Japan Security Treaty.

For decades, all was calm. The islands had no real strategic value and relatively little economic value except to fishermen in Okinawa Prefecture and, to a lesser extent, Taiwan. When Tokyo and Beijing restored normal relations in 1972, they were happy to agree to disagree. Indeed, during the early postwar period, Beijing even occasionally forgot to disagree and listed the islands as Japanese territory, and used their Japanese names, on official maps and publications. But in the late 1970s, tensions began to rise when it first appeared that the East China Sea might hold significant oil and gas reserves. The stakes rose again in 1996 when China and Japan ratified the UN Convention on the Law of the Sea, which established for the first time a 200-mile offshore exclusive economic zone (EEZ), rendering all the more important who enjoyed sovereignty over the territory from which EEZs extend. More recently, these islands have come to symbolize, and to act as a lightning rod for, national hatreds, unresolved historical grievances, Japanese fears, and Chinese ambitions.

In fact, the maritime jurisdiction disputes in the East China Sea are mostly under good regulation. China and Japan disagree on the location of their maritime boundary and on rights to develop gas reserves, but they manage these disagreements well.[13] The islands, however, are another matter. Unlike maritime boundaries, islands are visible and tangible and more easily seen as zero-sum stakes. Accordingly, these islands have captured both public and official attention. Emotions run so high at present that analysts almost unanimously agree that a Japanese or Chinese attempt to settle the islands or to build permanent structures on them would trigger a military clash. The best solution for this generation is to continue to agree to disagree. Because the United States is committed by treaty to defend Japan's control of the islands, even a minor misstep could trigger a direct confrontation between two nuclear-armed great powers.

Chronology: East China Sea

1972	United States returns administrative control of the disputed Senkaku/Diaoyu Islands to Japan; Japan and China establish diplomatic relations; Deng Xiaoping proposes letting "future generations" resolve the territorial dispute
2005	Prime Minister Junichiro Koizumi visits Yasukuni Shrine, honoring Japanese war dead; violent anti-Japanese demonstrations erupt in China

(*continued*)

2008	China and Japan sign an agreement to jointly develop natural gas fields in the East China Sea; Japan later accuses China of drilling unilaterally
2010	A Chinese trawler collides with Japanese Coast Guard patrol boats near the Senkaku/Diaoyu Islands; Japan arrests the trawler's captain; China cancels high-level meetings when its demands for the captain's release are denied; China halts exports of crucial rare earth minerals to Japan; Japan releases the trawler and its captain
2012	Right-wing nationalist governor of Tokyo Shintaro Ishinara announces plans to purchase the Senkakus from their private owners; Japanese government preemptively purchases them to avoid antagonizing China; China perceives the nationalization as a deliberate provocation and warns that it will take "all necessary steps" to defend its sovereignty; activists from Hong Kong land on the islands and are detained by the Japanese Coast Guard; major anti-Japanese riots erupt across China; China steps up patrols in Japanese-controlled airspace and waters; China freezes high-level interaction with Japanese officials
2013	China proclaims an air defense identification zone (ADIZ) over the East China Sea covering the disputed islands and also overlapping both Japan's and South Korea's ADIZs; the United States, Japan, and South Korea refuse to comply with China's ADIZ requirements
2014	Japanese and Chinese military aircraft nearly collide in disputed airspace over the East China Sea; at the Asia-Pacific Economic Cooperation Summit, Japanese Prime Minister Shinzo Abe and Chinese President Xi Jinping finally meet and briefly discuss improving relations
2015	Chinese incursions continue; satellite imagery shows an increased Chinese military presence within range of the disputed islands, including a new airfield; deputy foreign ministers from both countries meet in Tokyo for the first bilateral security discussions since 2011

Rogue Wildcard: North Korea

7.5   Explain how North Korea threatens regional stability.

The last flashpoint we will examine is the Korean peninsula. As you will recall from Chapter 5, Korea has been divided since World War II into a communist

north (the Democratic People's Republic of Korea, or DPRK) and a capitalist south (the Republic of Korea, or ROK). North Korean leader Kim Il-Sung
launched a surprise invasion of South Korea in 1950 that prompted the United
Nations' very first collective-security action, made possible by a Soviet boycott
of the Security Council over the United Nations' failure to allow Beijing to occupy the China seat (a mistake that the Soviet Union would never make again).
An U.S.-led UN force pushed North Korean forces almost all the way to the Yalu
River, North Korea's border with China, prompting intervention by the PRC to
keep the United States at bay. Eventually, the war stalemated close to the thirty-
eighth parallel, the prewar border. Although the belligerents never formally concluded a peace, the border today between North Korea and South Korea falls
along the 1953 cease-fire line. Known as the demilitarized zone (DMZ), this narrow strip of land serves as a buffer zone between North Korean and South Korean forces. Despite its name, the concentration of soldiers on either side of the
DMZ is so great that in reality it is the most heavily militarized border in the
world.

In economic terms, North Korea has languished. Isolated and underdeveloped, its infrastructure crumbling, and its people malnourished, it is the world's
last remaining genuinely totalitarian state. Because the regime devotes an enormous proportion of the country's resources to the military and state security,
little remains for genuine economic development. Meanwhile, South Korea has
thrived. It is now a wealthy liberal democratic state that enjoys all the benefits of
being fully integrated into the world economy.

Why should an impoverished, underdeveloped DPRK represent such a serious regional security threat? The answer is twofold. First, North Korean policy
has traditionally been erratic, unpredictable, and aggressive. Not only did North
Korea launch a quixotic attack on South Korea in 1950, North Korean agents
have staged a bewildering array of bizarre operations over the years that include
bombings, hijackings, successful and attempted assassinations, and—perhaps
most puzzling—abductions of Japanese citizens from beaches near their homes.
In 1968, North Korea captured a U.S. intelligence ship in international waters,
the USS *Pueblo*, torturing and starving the crew before releasing them after the
United States offered an apology for spying (today the ship is a floating museum
in Pyongyang). In 2009, North Korea arrested, tried, and sentenced two American journalists to hard labor for allegedly spying along the Chinese border. Although they were eventually released following a diplomatic mission by former
U.S. president Bill Clinton, the incident served as a reminder that North Korea
remains unpredictable.

Second, North Korea has nuclear weapons and an active missile program.
North Korea's nuclear tests in 2006 and 2009 were unimpressive in military
terms—so much so that in both instances Western intelligence communities debated whether North Korea had successfully detonated nuclear weapons at all—
and its missile tests have also been failures more often than not. North Korea's
willingness to conduct provocative tests is a worrisome sign, however, and it is

difficult to deal with North Korea without having a sense of what it wants and why it does what it does.

For the most part, North Korean policy has been mysterious. The only patterns that seem tolerably clear are that North Korea will do something provocative when it feels ignored or under serious economic strain and that it will make commitments and keep them only as long as it takes to bilk the international community out of valuable resources. But the 2009 nuclear test illustrates the predicament facing foreign leaders attempting to deal with the North Korean "threat": It was equally plausibly a sign of aggressiveness and confidence, of weakness and desperation, of a desire to project an image of self-reliance (the concept at the core of the prevailing domestic juche ideology), of a need for attention, of a desire to be taken seriously, of petulance, or of a behind-the-scenes struggle over leadership succession. When a country is erratic, unpredictable, and mysterious, it is difficult to know how to manage the crises that its actions trigger.

In six rounds of "Six-Party Talks" between 2003 and 2009, the United States, China, Russia, South Korea, and Japan sought to address North Korea's security concerns in return for verifiable denuclearization. In the course of these talks, North Korea managed to extract from its interlocutors food aid, energy aid, and technical assistance of various kinds in return for nothing more than unfulfilled promises.

North Korea is today a veritable international pariah. Arguably, it is equally a threat to regional security whether it lashes out against its neighbor's military or implodes economically. It is without doubt one of the most challenging interstate conflict management problems facing the world today.

Chronology: North Korea

1945	World War II ends with Japan's unconditional surrender, liberating Korea from Japanese rule; Potsdam Conference cements multinational trusteeship of Korea; U.S. State Department issues General Order No. 1, dividing Korea along thirty-eighth parallel
1948	Democratic People's Republic of Korea established north of thirty-eighth parallel under rule of Kim Il-Sung
1950	North Korean troops invade South Korea, triggering Korean War
1953	Korean War ends in signing of temporary Armistice Agreement still in effect today; North Korea accepts aid from Soviet Union and China

1956	North Korea, China, and Soviet Union begin to engage in joint nuclear research projects
1967	Yongbyon nuclear research reactor, 54 miles from Pyongyang, becomes active
1977	North Korea signs Type 66 agreement with the International Atomic Energy Agency (IAEA), subjecting Yongbyon reactor to international scrutiny
1984	North Korea tests Scud-B missile
1985	North Korea signs Treaty on the Nonproliferation of Nuclear Weapons (NPT); the United States claims that North Korea is constructing a second secret nuclear reactor at Yongbyon, giving North Korea the complete fuel cycle required for weapons production
1989	North Korea tests long-range Scud-C missile
1991	United States withdraws nuclear weapons from South Korea; North Korea and South Korea sign Joint Declaration on the Denuclearization of the Korean Peninsula, banning nuclear weapons and calling for international inspections
1992	North Korea signs IAEA Full Scope Safeguards Agreement, granting IAEA monitors access to all nuclear facilities
1993	North Korea test-fires Nodong I missile with a range of 500 miles; Pyongyang threatens to withdraw from NPT and bars international monitors; IAEA director Hans Blix announces that IAEA can no longer meaningfully guarantee absence of North Korean nuclear weapons
1994	Kim Il-Sung dies, succeeded by his son Kim Jong-il; the United States and North Korea sign Agreed Framework, committing the United States to supply light-water reactors and alternative energy sources if North Korea shuts down Yongbyon plutonium reactor
1998	North Korea launches Taepodong I missile with a range of up to 1,200 miles
2002	President George W. Bush names North Korea as part of the "Axis of Evil" in his State of the Union address
2003	North Korea announces intent to withdraw from NPT; North Korea signals willingness to forgo insistence on bilateral talks with the United States and engage in multiparty talks; first round of Six-Party Talks begins

(continued)

2005	North Korea suspends participation in Six-Party Talks indefinitely in reaction to perceived U.S. bullying; North Korea and the United States issue joint statement: the United States commits not to attack North Korea in exchange for North Korea rejoining the NPT and ceasing nuclear activities; North Korea issues statement claiming that it will not scrap its nuclear program until given a civilian nuclear reactor
2006	North Korea detonates nuclear device; UN Security Council passes Resolution 1718 under Chapter VII imposing commercial and economic sanctions; North Korean plutonium stockpiles estimated to be sufficient for four to thirteen nuclear weapons
2007	Round five of Six-Party Talks concludes with agreement that North Korea will shut down Yongbyon reactor and allow IAEA inspections in exchange for aid and normalization of relations with the United States
2008	North Korea hands over 60-page review of nuclear capabilities for international inspection; the United States removes North Korea from its list of state sponsors of terrorism
2009	North Korea launches "satellite" believed to be Taepodong-2 intercontinental ballistic missile despite international pressure, but launch fails; UN Security Council expresses intent to strengthen sanctions; North Korea expels nuclear inspectors, withdraws from Six-Party Talks; North Korea tests second nuclear device
2010	46 sailors die when the South Korean corvette *Cheonan* explodes and sinks, probably as a result of a North Korean torpedo attack; two soldiers killed and dozens injured in North Korean artillery bombardment of Yeonpyeong Island; Kim Jong-il's son Kim Jong-un named a four-star general and given high-ranking political positions, signaling the beginning of a third-generation power transition
2011	Kim Jong-il dies, succeeded by Kim Jong-un
2012	North Korea launches Kwangmyongsong-3 "satellite," widely seen as a missile test

2013	UN Security Council condemns the "satellite" launch and strengthens sanctions; North Korea conducts an underground nuclear test; responding to international condemnation, North Korea withdraws from the armistice, severs all communication with South Korea, and declares a "state of war"; tensions thaw amidst discussion of resuming high-level talks, although talks fail to take place
2014	North Korea conducts midrange missile tests, the first in five years; North Korea and South Korea exchange artillery fire along the western sea borders; commercial satellite imagery shows evidence of weapons-grade plutonium production at the Yongbyon nuclear facility

Follow Up

- Vincent Pouliot, *International Security in Practice: The Politics of NATO-Russia Diplomacy* (Cambridge: Cambridge University Press, 2010).

- Andrei P. Tsygankov, *Russia and the West from Alexander to Putin: Honor in International Relations* (Cambridge: Cambridge University Press, 2012).

- *Global Connections: The Middle East* (online resource, PBS), http://www.pbs.org/wgbh/globalconnections/mideast/index.html.

- Joan Peters, *From Time Immemorial: The Origins of the Arab-Jewish Conflict over Palestine* (New York: Harper & Row, 1984).

- Ian J. Bickerton and Carla L. Klausner, *A History of the Arab-Israeli Conflict*, 7th ed. (Upper Saddle River, NJ: Pearson, 2015).

- F. Gregory Gause III, *The International Relations of the Persian Gulf* (Cambridge: Cambridge University Press, 2010).

- Dilip Hiro, *The Longest August: The Unflinching Rivalry between India and Pakistan* (New York: Nation Books, 2015).

- A. G. Noorani, *The Kashmir Dispute, 1947–2012* (New York: Oxford University Press, 2014).

- S. Paul Kapur, *Dangerous Deterrent: Nuclear Weapons Proliferation and Conflict in South Asia* (Stanford, CA: Stanford University Press, 2007).

- Bill Hayton, *The South China Sea: The Struggle for Power in Asia* (New Haven, CT: Yale University Press, 2014).

- Andrew T. H. Tan, ed., *Security and Conflict in East Asia* (New York: Routledge, 2015).

Study Questions

1. Each side blames the other for the decline in Russia's relations with the West since the 1990s. Is it possible to judge who is right and who is wrong? Is it useful to try?

2. In Chapter 6, we discussed the conditions under which intervention is justified. Does Russian intervention in Crimea meet those conditions? What about in eastern Ukraine?

3. What are the respective claims of the Palestinians and the Israelis to the territory that Israel now controls? Which group has a better argument, in your opinion, or are both equally valid?

4. What was the UN Palestine partition proposal? Why did the Arabs reject this plan?

5. What were the causes of the Middle East wars of 1956, 1967, 1973, and 1982? Were these wars inevitable? If so, when and why? Is another Arab-Israeli war inevitable?

6. How did the 1991 Gulf War and the 2003 Iraq War differ? What reasons were given for each war? What is the difference between preemptive war and preventive war?

7. Why did the United States intervene in Iraq and Afghanistan, but not in Syria?

8. What do realism, liberalism, and constructivism each contribute to your understanding of each of the flashpoints examined in this chapter?

9. What kinds of goods (public, private, club, or common) are at stake in each of the flashpoints we have examined in this chapter? How do the different types of goods complicate conflict management in each case?

10. Which interstate flashpoint is the most dangerous in the world today? Why?

Notes

1. John Mueller, *Retreat from Doomsday: The Obsolescence of Major War* (New York: Basic Books, 1989).

2. Robert B. Strassler and Richard Crawley, eds., *The Landmark Thucydides: A Comprehensive Guide to the Peloponnesian War* (New York: Free Press, 1996), 1.23. Recall from our discussion in Chapter 1 that Thucydides' interpretation here is a controversial one: according to Donald Kagan, Athens was not rising at the time. Donald Kagan, *The Outbreak of the Peloponnesian War* (Ithaca, NY: Cornell University Press, 1969), p. 354.

3. Although PPP provides an excellent price-adjusted comparison of countries' welfare, it is imperfect as an adjustment for comparing their hard power, because certain costs (such as arms imports) are priced at real exchange rates.

4. Sanjoy Banerjee, "Rules, Agency, and International Structuration," *International Studies Review* 17:2 (June 2015), p. 276.

5. Luke Harding, "Russia Threatening New Cold War over Missile Defence," *The Guardian* (April 11, 2007), http://www.theguardian.com/world/2007/apr/11/usa.topstories3; John Norris, *Collision Course: NATO, Russia, and Kosovo* (Westport, CT: Praeger, 2005).

6. *Fragmented Lives: Humanitarian Overview 2014* (East Jerusalem: United Nations Office for the Coordination of Humanitarian Affairs, Occupied Palestinian Territory, March 2015), http://www.ochaopt.org/documents/annual_humanitarian_overview_2014_english_final.pdf.

7. A literal translation of his remarks would be "the regime occupying Jerusalem must vanish from the page of time." "Corrections and clarifications," *The Guardian*, April 23, 2009, http://www.theguardian. com/theguardian/2009/apr/23/ corrections-clarifications.

8. Jacques E. C. Hymans, "Iran Is Still Botching the Bomb," *Foreign Affairs* (February 18, 2013), https://www.foreignaffairs. com/articles/iran/2013-02-18/ iran-still-botching-bomb.

9. Linda J. Bilmes, "The Financial Legacy of Iraq and Afghanistan: How Wartime Spending Decisions Will Constrain Future National Security Budgets," *HKS Faculty Research Working Paper RWP13-006* (March 2013), https://research.hks.harvard.edu/ publications/workingpapers/citation. aspx?PubId=8956&type=WPN.

10. John J. Mearsheimer, "The Gathering Storm: China's Challenge to US Power in Asia," *Chinese Journal of International Politics* 3:4 (Winter 2010), p. 382.

11. Minxin Pei, "Asia's Real Challenge: 'China's Potemkin' Rise," *The Diplomat* (2013), http://thediplomat. com/2013/05/asias-real-challenge- chinas-potemkin-rise; David Shambaugh, "The Coming Chinese Crackup," *Wall Street Journal* (March 6, 2015), http://www.wsj.com/articles/ the-coming-chinese-crack-up- 1425659198.

12. David A. Welch, "Can the United States and China Avoid a Thucydides Trap?," *e-International Relations* (2015), http://www.e-ir.info/2015/04/06/ can-the-united-states-and-china-avoid-a- thucydides-trap/.

13. James Manicom, *Bridging Trouble Waters: China, Japan, and Maritime Order in the East China Sea* (Washington, DC: Georgetown University Press, 2014).

Chapter 8

Globalization and Interdependence

Photo: Bloomberg/Getty Images

Shipping containers at the port of Singapore

Learning Objectives

8.1 Identify the similarities and differences in different types of globalization.

8.2 Understand interdependence as a general concept and complex interdependence as an analytical paradigm.

8.3 Explain how the concepts of globalization and interdependence illuminate the international politics of oil.

With the end of the Cold War in 1989, a number of observers argued that economic issues would become more central in world politics than they had been. Networks of economic interdependence that span the globe have increased as costs of communication and transportation have declined and shrunk the effects of distance. The role of markets has also increased as a result of new information and transportation technologies, as well as changed attitudes about the role of governments and states. Nearly half of all industrial output today is produced by multinational enterprises whose decisions about where to locate factories have a powerful effect on domestic economies and politics. As the economist Dani Rodrik points out, globalization is "exposing a deep fault line between groups who have the skills and mobility to flourish in global markets" and those who do not, "such as workers, pensioners, and environmentalists, with governments stuck in the middle."[1] Some theorists see a new competition— "geoeconomics"—replacing geopolitics and predict that economic sanctions and embargoes will become the key instruments of international politics.

It is important to keep these changes in perspective. Realists remind us that security can be taken for granted in peaceful times, but all markets operate within a political framework. Global markets depend on an international structure of power. Security is like oxygen: It is easy to take for granted until you begin to miss it, and then you can think about nothing else. Similarly, economic sanctions have been popular instruments because they avoid the use of force, but their effectiveness is mixed.[2] Multilateral sanctions were one factor in ending apartheid in South Africa and putting pressure on Serbia and Libya in the 1990s, but they failed to oust Iraqi troops from Kuwait, return an elected president to power even in a poor country such as Haiti, or force Russia to reverse its annexation of Crimea and its support for Russian separatists in eastern Ukraine. Moreover, globalization and economic interdependence were already growing rapidly when states followed relatively liberal policies toward trade, investment, and migration in the nineteenth century. That did not stop two world wars and an economic depression in the first half of the twentieth century from occurring and interrupting elements of these long-term trends.

The Dimensions of Globalization

8.1   Identify the similarities and differences in different types of globalization.

Globalization—defined as worldwide networks of interdependence—does not imply either universality or equity. Fewer than half of the people in the world use the Internet. Almost a third of Africans do not have access to telephones. The gap between the world's rich and the world's poor continues to widen. Even among rich countries, there is a lot less globalization than meets the eye. A truly globalized world market would mean free flows of goods, people, and capital, and similar interest rates everywhere. Even in North America, Toronto trades ten times as much with Vancouver as with Seattle, although the distance is the same and tariffs are minimal. Globalization has made national boundaries more porous, but not irrelevant.

Nor does globalization mean the creation of a universal community. Contacts among people with different religious beliefs and other deeply held values have often led to conflict: witness the great crusades of medieval times (the eleventh through the thirteenth centuries) or the current notion of the United States as "the Great Satan" held by some Islamic fundamentalists in the Middle East. Clearly, in social as well as economic terms, homogenization does not follow necessarily from globalization.

Globalization has a number of dimensions, although all too often economists write as if it and the world economy were one and the same. But other forms of globalization also have significant effects on our daily lives. The oldest form of globalization is environmental. For example, the first recorded smallpox epidemic began in Egypt in 1350 BCE. It reached China in 49 CE, Europe after 700, the Americas in 1520, and Australia in 1789. The bubonic plague, or "Black Death," originated in Asia, but it spread to Europe in the fourteenth century, where it killed a fourth to a third of the population. Europeans carried diseases to the Americas in the fifteenth and sixteenth centuries that destroyed up to 95 percent of the indigenous population. In 1918, a flu pandemic caused by a bird virus killed some 40 million people around the world, far more than died in World War I during the previous four years. Since 1940, scientists have discovered more than 80 new infectious diseases, including sudden acute respiratory syndrome, West Nile fever, Ebola, and HIV. Since HIV/AIDS was identified in the 1981, it has killed 39 million people, 1.5 million in 2013 alone. The spread of foreign species of flora and fauna to new areas has wiped out native species and may result in economic losses of several hundred billion dollars a year.

On the other hand, not all effects of environmental globalization are bad. For instance, both Europe and Asia benefited from the importation of such New World crops as the potato, corn, and the tomato, and today's "green revolution" agricultural technology has helped poor farmers throughout the world.

Global climate change will affect the lives of people everywhere. There is now virtual consensus in the scientific community that humans are responsible for most of the warming observed since the middle of the twentieth century, and that global temperatures are likely to rise between 2.5 and 10 degrees Fahrenheit by the end of the twenty-first century, depending upon how quickly the world can shift from fossil fuels to climate-friendly alternatives. It seems almost certain that we are in for several decades or centuries of more frequent extreme weather events, dramatic changes in rainfall patterns, periodic droughts and floods, and rising sea levels that will inundate small island states and low-lying coastal areas as glaciers and ice caps melt and as the world's oceans experience thermal expansion. It does not matter whether carbon dioxide is pumped into the atmosphere from China or the United States; it still warms the planet.

Military globalization consists of networks of interdependence in which force, or the threat of force, is employed. The world wars of the twentieth century are a case in point. During the Cold War, the global strategic interdependence between the United States and the Soviet Union was acute and well recognized. Not only did it produce world-straddling alliances, but either side could have used intercontinental missiles to destroy the other within the space of 30 minutes. It was distinctive not because it was totally new, but because the scale and speed of the potential conflict arising from military interdependence were so enormous. Today, al-Qaeda and other transnational actors have formed global networks of operatives, challenging conventional approaches to national defense in what has been called asymmetrical warfare.

Social globalization is the spread of peoples, cultures, images, and ideas. Migration is a concrete example. In the nineteenth century, some 80 million people crossed oceans to new homes, far more than in the eighteenth century. At the beginning of the twenty-first century, 32 million residents of the United States (11.5 percent of the population) were foreign-born. In addition, some 30 million visitors (students, businesspeople, tourists) enter the country each year. Ideas are an equally important aspect of social globalization. Four great religions of the world—Buddhism, Judaism, Christianity, and Islam—have spread across great distances over the last two millennia, as has the scientific method and the Enlightenment worldview over the past few centuries. Political globalization (a part of social globalization) is manifest in the spread of constitutional arrangements, the increase in the number of countries that have become democratic, and the development of international rules and institutions. Those who think that it is meaningless to speak of an international community ignore the importance of the global spread of political ideas. As constructivists point out, the antislavery movement in the nineteenth century, anticolonialism after World War II, and the environmental and feminist movements today have had profound effects on world politics. Of course, the world is a long way from a global community replacing people's loyalties to clans, tribes, and states, but such transnational political ideas affect how states construct their national goals and how they use their soft power.

What's New about Twenty-First-Century Globalization?

Although globalization has been going on for centuries, its contemporary form is "thicker and quicker." Globalization today is different from that of the nineteenth century, when European imperialism provided much of its political structure and when higher transport and communications costs meant that fewer people were involved directly with people and ideas from other cultures. But many of the most important differences are closely related to the information revolution. As the columnist Thomas Friedman argues, contemporary globalization goes "farther, faster, cheaper, and deeper."[3]

Economists use the term *network effects* to refer to situations in which a product becomes more valuable once many other people also use it. One telephone is useless, but its value increases as the network grows. That is why the Internet is causing such rapid change. Social networking sites such as Facebook, Twitter, and LinkedIn have burgeoned. The Nobel Prize–winning economist Joseph Stiglitz argues that a knowledge-based economy generates "powerful spillover effects, often spreading like fire and triggering further innovation and setting off chain reactions of new inventions. … But goods—as opposed to knowledge—do not always spread like fire."[4] Moreover, as interdependence has become thicker and quicker, the relationships among different networks have become more important. There are more interconnections among the networks. As a result, "system effects"—by which small perturbations in one area can spread throughout a whole system—become more important.

As government officials fashion foreign policies, they encounter the increasing thickness of globalism—the density of the networks of interdependence—which means that the effects of events in one geographical area, or the economic or ecological dimension, can have profound effects elsewhere. These international networks are increasingly complex, and their effects are therefore increasingly unpredictable. Moreover, in human systems, people are often hard at work trying to outwit one another, to gain an economic, social, or military advantage precisely by acting in an unpredictable way. As a result, globalization is accompanied by pervasive uncertainty. There will be continual competition between, on the one hand, increased complexity and uncertainty in global relationships and, on the other hand, efforts by governments, corporations, and others to comprehend them and manipulate them to their benefit. Frequent financial crises or sharp increases in unemployment could lead to popular movements to limit interdependence.

Quickness also adds to uncertainty and the difficulties of shaping policy responses. As mentioned, modern globalization operates at a much more rapid pace than its earlier forms. Smallpox took nearly three millennia to spread to all inhabited continents, finally reaching Australia in 1789. HIV took less than three decades to spread from Africa all around the world. And to switch to a metaphorical virus, the 2000 "love bug" computer virus, invented by hackers in the Philippines, needed only three days to straddle the globe. From three millennia to three decades to three days: that is the measure of the quickening of globalization.

Direct public participation in global affairs has also increased in rich countries. Ordinary people invest in foreign mutual funds, gamble on offshore Internet sites, and travel and sample exotic cuisine that used to be the preserve of the rich. Friedman termed this change the *democratization* of technology, finance, and information because diminished costs have made what were previously luxuries available to a much broader range of society. *Democratization* is not quite the right word, however, because in markets, money votes, and people start out with unequal stakes. There is no equality, for example, in capital markets, despite the new financial instruments that permit more people to participate. A million dollars or more is often the entry price for large hedge-fund investors. *Pluralization* might be a more accurate description of this trend, suggesting the vast increase in the number and variety of participants in global networks. In 1914, according to the English economist John Maynard Keynes, "the inhabitant of London could order by telephone, sipping his morning tea in bed, the various products of the whole earth, in such quantity as he might see fit, and reasonably expect their early delivery on his doorstep."[5] But Keynes's Englishman had to be wealthy to be a global consumer. Today, supermarkets and Internet retailers extend that capacity to the vast majority of people in postindustrial societies.

This dramatic expansion of transnational channels and contacts at intercontinental distances means that more policies, regulations, and practices are up for grabs internationally. Many of these—from pharmaceutical testing to accounting and product standards to banking regulation—were formerly regarded as the prerogatives of national governments.

What the information revolution has added to contemporary globalization is a quickness and thickness in the network of interconnections that makes it more complex. But such "thick globalism" is not uniform: It varies by region and locality and by issue.

Political Reactions to Globalization

Domestic politics channel responses to change. Some countries imitate success, as exemplified by democratizing capitalist societies from South Korea to Eastern Europe. Some accommodate change in distinctive and ingenious ways. For instance, small European states such as the Netherlands, Denmark, Norway, and Sweden have maintained relatively large governments and emphasized compensation for disadvantaged sectors, whereas the Anglo-American industrialized countries have, in general, emphasized markets, competition, and deregulation. Capitalism is far from monolithic, with significant differences between Europe, Japan, and the United States. There is more than one way to respond to global markets and to run a capitalist economy. There is even variation within countries. The United States used to have one of the world's most freewheeling financial systems, but when the subprime mortgage crisis became critical in 2008 and such seemingly unshakeable pillars of the U.S. financial industry as Bear Stearns and Lehman Brothers collapsed, a worldwide recession was triggered (precisely because of globalization) that forced several countries, including the United States, to intervene. Washington's response—spending billions of dollars to stimulate the economy, temporarily taking ownership stakes in firms such as General Motors that were considered too big to be allowed to fail completely, and even capping executive compensation packages in some cases—briefly took American capitalism back to the more assertive government intervention of the 1930s New Deal era.

In other societies, such as Iran, Afghanistan, and Sudan, conservative groups have resisted globalization strongly, even violently. Reactions to globalization help stimulate fundamentalism. Domestic institutions and divisions—economic or ethnic—can lead to domestic conflict, which can reformulate ethnic and political identities in profound and often unanticipated ways. As we saw in Chapter 6, political elites in Bosnia appealed to traditional identities of people in rural areas to overwhelm and dissolve the cosmopolitan identities that had begun to develop in the cities, with devastating results. And Iran has seen struggles between Islamic fundamentalists and their more liberal opponents, who are also Islamic but are more sympathetic to Western ideas.

Rising inequality was a major cause of the political reactions that halted a previous wave of economic globalization early in the twentieth century. The recent period of globalization, like the half century before World War I, has also been associated with increasing inequality among and within some countries. The ratio of incomes of the 20 percent of people in the world living in the richest countries compared with the 20 percent living in the poorest countries increased from 30 to 1 in 1960 to 74 to 1 in 1997. By comparison, it increased from 7 to 1 in 1870 to 11 to 1 in 1913. In any case, inequality can have political effects even if it is not increasing. According to the economist Robert Wade, "The result is a lot of angry young people, to whom new information technologies have given the means to threaten the stability of the societies they live in and even to threaten social stability in countries of the wealthy zone."[6] As increasing flows of information make people more aware of inequality, it is not surprising that some choose to protest, as we saw with the 2011 worldwide "Occupy" movement.

The political consequences of these shifts in inequality are complex, but the economic historian Karl Polanyi argued powerfully in his classic study *The Great Transformation* that the market forces unleashed by the Industrial Revolution and globalization in the nineteenth century produced not only great economic gains, but also great social disruptions and political reactions.[7] There is no *automatic* relationship between inequality and political reaction, but the former can give rise to the latter. Particularly when inequality is combined with instability, such as financial crises and recessions that throw people out of work, such reactions could eventually lead to restrictions on the pace of globalization of the world economy.

Protests against globalization are in part a reaction to the changes produced by *economic interdependence*. From an economist's view, imperfect markets are inefficient, but from a political view, some imperfections in international markets can be considered "useful inefficiencies" because they slow down and buffer political change. As globalization removes such inefficiencies, it becomes the political prisoner of its economic successes. In addition, as global networks become more complex, there are more linkages among issues that can create friction.

Liberals sometimes suggest that for states globalization means peace and cooperation, but unfortunately it is not that simple. Struggles over power go on, even in a globalized world. Because coalitions are more complex and different forms of power are used, the conflicts are often like playing chess on several boards at the same time. Conflicts in the twenty-first century involve *both* guns and butter.

Follow Up

- Manfred B. Steger, *Globalization: A Very Short Introduction* (Oxford: Oxford University Press, 2009).
- Dani Rodrik, *The Globalization Paradox: Democracy and the Future of the World Economy* (New York: W. W. Norton & Co., 2011).

The Concept of Interdependence

8.2 **Understand interdependence as a general concept and complex interdependence as an analytical paradigm.**

Interdependence is often a fuzzy term used in a variety of conflicting ways, like other political words such as *nationalism, imperialism,* and *globalization.* (Indeed, as noted above, globalization is the subset of interdependence that occurs at global distances.) Leaders and analysts have different motives when they use political words. The leader wants as many people marching behind his or her banner as possible. Political leaders blur meanings and try to create a connotation of a common good: "We are all in the same boat together; therefore, we must cooperate; therefore, follow me." The analyst, on the other hand, makes distinctions to understand the world better. He or she distinguishes questions of *good* and *bad* from *more* and *less.* The analyst may note that the boat we are all in may be heading for one person's port but not another's or that one person is doing all the rowing while another steers or has a free ride.

Interdependence is where the condition of one depends on another and vice versa. Simply put, interdependence means mutual dependence. Such a situation is neither good nor bad in itself, and there can be more or less of it. Marriages are a good example of highly interdependent relationships. The traditional Christian marriage vow commits both partners to stick with it "for richer, for poorer, for better, or for worse." Interdependence among countries sometimes means richer, sometimes poorer, sometimes for better, sometimes for worse. In the eighteenth century, Jean-Jacques Rousseau pointed out that along with interdependence comes friction and conflict. His "solution" was isolation and separation, but that is seldom possible in a globalized world. When countries try isolation, as with the cases of North Korea today and Myanmar (formerly Burma) until quite recently, it comes at enormous economic cost. It is not easy for countries to divorce the rest of the world.

Sources of Interdependence

Four distinctions illuminate the dimensions of interdependence: its sources, benefits, relative costs, and symmetry. Interdependence can originate in physical (natural) or social (economic, political, or perceptual) phenomena. Both are usually present at the same time. The distinction helps clarify the degree of choice in situations of reciprocal or mutual dependence.

Military interdependence is the mutual dependence that arises from military competition. There is a physical aspect in the weaponry, especially dramatic since the development of nuclear weapons and the resulting possibility of mutually assured destruction. An important element of perception is also involved in interdependence, though, and a change in perception or policy can reduce the intensity of the military interdependence. As we saw in Chapter 5, Americans lost little sleep over the existence of British nuclear weapons during the Cold War because there was no perception that those weapons would ever detonate on U.S. soil. Similarly, Westerners slept a bit easier in the late 1980s after Mikhail Gorbachev announced his "new thinking" in Soviet foreign policy. It was not so much the number of Soviet weapons that made the difference; rather, it was the change in the perception of Soviet hostility or intent. Indeed, American public anxiety about the Soviet nuclear arsenal virtually evaporated after the final collapse of the Soviet Union, even though at the twentieth century's close thousands of poorly guarded Soviet warheads seemed potentially to be at risk of falling into the hands of terrorists or "rogue" states such as Iran and North Korea. Today, some U.S. policy makers are increasingly alarmed by Chinese nuclear capability not because it has been improving dramatically (it has not), but because they are beginning to worry seriously about China's intentions.

Generally speaking, economic interdependence is similar to military interdependence in that it is the stuff of traditional international politics and has significant social, especially perceptual, aspects. Economic interdependence involves policy choices about values and costs. For example, in the early 1970s, there was concern that the world's population was outstripping global food supplies. Many countries were buying American grain, which in turn drove up the price of food in American supermarkets. A loaf of bread cost more in the United States than it used to because the Indian monsoons failed and because the Soviet Union mishandled its harvest. In 1973, in an effort to prevent price rises at home, the United States decided to stop exporting soybeans to Japan. As a result, Japan invested in soybean production in Brazil. A few years later, when supply and demand were better equilibrated, U.S. farmers greatly regretted that embargo because the Japanese were buying soybeans from a cheaper source in Brazil. Similarly, in 2008, as rich countries devoted more cropland to producing ethanol fuel, food prices rose globally. Social choices as well as physical shortages affect economic interdependence in the long run. It is always worth considering the long-term perspective when making short-term choices.

Ecological Interdependence

> Interdependence forces us to understand that today's challenges represent not just a dilemma for us [in our own country], but a shared dilemma for everybody. The environment brings that into a very tangible focus: there's no such thing as a stable climate for one country or one continent unless the climate is stable for everybody. Climate security is a global public good.
>
> —*John Ashton, UK Special Representative for Climate Change, September 27, 2006*[8]

Benefits of Interdependence

The benefits of interdependence are sometimes expressed as *zero-sum* and *non-zero-sum*. In a zero-sum situation, your loss is my gain and vice versa. In a *positive-sum* situation, we both gain; in a *negative-sum* situation, we both lose. Dividing a pie is zero-sum, baking a larger pie is positive-sum, and dropping it on the floor is negative-sum. Both zero-sum and non-zero-sum aspects are present in mutual dependence.

Some liberal economists tend to think of interdependence only in terms of joint gain; that is, positive-sum situations in which everyone benefits and everyone is better off. Failure to pay attention to the inequality of benefits and the conflicts that arise over the distribution of relative gains causes such analysts to miss the political aspects of interdependence. Both sides can gain from trade—for example, if Japan and South Korea trade computers and smartphones—but how will the gains from trade be distributed? Even if Japan and South Korea are both better off, is Japan a lot better off and South Korea only a little better off, or vice versa? The distribution of benefits—who gets how much of the joint gain—is a zero-sum situation in which one side's gain is the other's loss. The result is that there is almost always some political conflict in economic interdependence. Even when there is a larger pie, people can fight over who gets the biggest slices.

Some liberal analysts mistakenly think that as globalization makes the world more interdependent, cooperation will replace competition. Their reason is that interdependence creates joint benefits and that those joint benefits encourage cooperation. Although that is true, economic interdependence can also be used as a weapon: witness the use of trade sanctions against Serbia, Iraq, and Libya. Indeed, economic interdependence can be more usable than force in some cases because it may have more subtle gradations. And in some circumstances, states are less interested in their absolute gain from interdependence than in how the relatively greater gains of their rivals might be used to hurt them.

Some analysts believe that traditional world politics was always zero-sum, but that is misleading about the past. Traditional international politics could be positive-sum, depending on the actors' intentions. It made a difference, for example, whether Otto von Bismarck or Adolf Hitler was in charge in Germany. If one party sought aggrandizement, as Hitler did, politics was indeed zero-sum:

one side's gain was another's loss. But if all parties wanted stability, there could be joint gain in the balance of power. Conversely, the politics of economic globalization has competitive zero-sum aspects as well as cooperative positive-sum aspects.

In the politics of interdependence, the distinction between what is domestic and what is foreign becomes blurred. For example, the soybean situation mentioned earlier involved the domestic issue of controlling inflation at home, as well as U.S. relations with Japan and Brazil. In the late 1990s, on the other hand, an Asian financial crisis depressed world commodity prices, which helped the U.S. economy continue to grow without encountering inflationary pressures. In 2005, when Secretary of the Treasury John Snow visited China, he pleaded with the Chinese to increase consumer credit because the United States saw it "as going directly to the thing we have most on our minds—the global imbalances."[9] Chinese leaders replied that the Americans "need to get their own house in order by reducing their fiscal deficits."[10] Were Snow and his Chinese counterparts commenting on domestic or on foreign policy?

Or, to take another example, after Iran's 1979 revolution curtailed oil production, the U.S. government urged citizens to cut their energy consumption by driving 55 miles per hour and turning down thermostats. Was that a domestic or a foreign policy issue? Some social scientists have taken to calling such issues "intermestic," meaning international *and* domestic at the same time.

Interdependence also affects domestic politics in a different way. In 1890, a French politician concerned with relative economic gains pursued a policy of holding Germany back. Today, a policy of slowing economic growth in Germany is not good for France. Economic interdependence between France and Germany means that the best predictor of whether France is better off economically is when Germany is growing economically. Now with the two countries sharing a common currency, it is in the self-interest of the French politicians that Germany does well economically and vice versa. The classical balance-of-power theory, which predicts that one country will act only to keep the other down lest the other gain preponderance, is not valid in this situation. In economic interdependence, states are interested in absolute gains as well as gains relative to other states.

Costs of Interdependence

The costs of interdependence can involve short-run sensitivity or long-term vulnerability. *Sensitivity* refers to the amount and pace of the effects of dependence; that is, how quickly does change in one part of the system bring about change in another part? For example, in 1987, the New York stock market crashed suddenly because of foreigners' anxieties about U.S. interest rates and what might happen to the price of bonds and stocks. It all happened very quickly; the market was extremely sensitive to the withdrawal of foreign funds. In 1998, weakness in emerging markets in Asia had a contagious effect that undercut geographically distant emerging markets in Russia and Brazil. In 2008, the mortgage finance problem in the United States affected housing prices in other countries and eventually helped trigger a global recession in 2009.

A high level of sensitivity, however, is not the same as a high level of vulnerability. *Vulnerability* refers to the relative costs of changing the structure of a system of interdependence. It is the cost of escaping from the system or of changing the rules of the game. The less vulnerable of two countries is not necessarily the less sensitive; rather, it is the one for whom adjustment is less costly. During the 1973 oil crisis, the United States depended on imported energy for only about 16 percent of its total energy uses. On the other hand, in 1973, Japan depended about 95 percent on imported energy. The United States was sensitive to the Arab oil boycott insofar as prices shot up in 1973, but it was not as vulnerable as Japan was. In 1998, the United States was sensitive but not vulnerable to East Asian economic conditions. The financial crisis there cut half a percent off the U.S. growth rate, but with a booming economy, the United States could afford it. Indonesia, on the other hand, was both sensitive and vulnerable to changes in global trade and investment patterns. Its economy suffered severely and that, in turn, led to internal political conflict and a change of government.

Vulnerability is a matter of degree. When the shah of Iran was overthrown in 1979, Iranian oil production was disrupted at a time when demand was high and markets were already tight. The loss of Iran's oil caused the total amount of oil on the world markets to drop by about 5 percent. Markets were sensitive, and shortages of supply caused a rapid increase in oil prices. But Americans could reduce 5 percent of their energy consumption simply by turning down their thermostats and by driving on the highways at 55 rather than 60 miles per hour. It appears that the United States was sensitive but not very vulnerable if it could avoid damage by making such simple adjustments.

Vulnerability, however, depends on more than aggregate measures. It also depends on whether a society is capable of responding quickly to change. For example, the United States was less adept at responding to changes in the oil markets than Japan. Furthermore, private actors, large corporations, and speculators may each look at a market situation and decide to hoard supplies because they think that shortages are going to grow worse. Their actions will drive the price even higher because it will make the shortages greater and put more demand on the market. Thus degrees of vulnerability are not quite as simple as they first look.

Vulnerability also depends on whether substitutes are available and whether there are diverse sources of supply. In 1970, Lester Brown of the World Watch Institute expressed alarm about the increasing dependence of the United States on imported raw materials and therefore its vulnerability. Of thirteen basic industrial raw materials, the United States was dependent on imports for nearly 90 percent of aluminum, chromium, manganese, and nickel. Brown predicted that by 1985 the United States would be dependent on imports in ten of the basic thirteen.[11] He thought that this dependence would lead to a dramatic increase in U.S. vulnerability as well as a drastic increase in strength for the less developed countries that produced those raw materials.

Sensitivity Interdependence

We had begun to forget the danger of contagion and the speed with which [a financial crisis] takes place when it does occur. The current developments which began in a relatively minor segment of the financial market, the sub-prime mortgage segment [in the United States in 2007], have spread far and wide across continents.

—*Rakesh Mohan, Deputy Governor, Reserve Bank of India, September 20, 2007*[12]

But in the 1980s, raw materials prices went down, not up. What happened to Brown's prediction? In judging vulnerability, Brown failed to consider the alternative sources of raw materials and the diversity of sources of supply that prevented producers from jacking up prices artificially. Moreover, technology improves. Yesterday's waste may become a new resource, and miniaturization reduces inputs. Companies now mine discarded tailings because new technology has made it possible to extract copper from ore that was considered depleted waste years ago. Today's reduced use of copper is also due to the introduction of fiber-optic cables made from silicon, whose basic origin is sand. Far less copper was required to manufacture a state-of-the-art computer in 2010 than in 1980 because the newer one was much smaller and lighter than the older one. Thus projections of U.S. vulnerability to shortages of raw materials were inaccurate because technology and alternatives were not adequately considered.

Some analysts refer to advanced economies today as information-based in the sense that computers, communications, and the Internet are becoming dominant factors in economic growth. Such economies are sometimes called "lightweight" economies because the value of information embedded in products is often far greater than the value of the raw materials involved. Such changes further depreciate the value of raw materials in world politics. One of the few exceptions is oil, which still plays a significant role in most advanced economies, particularly for transportation, and in turn contributes to the strategic significance of the Persian Gulf, where a large portion of the world's currently known oil reserves are located.

Symmetry of Interdependence

Symmetry refers to situations of relatively balanced versus unbalanced dependence. Being less dependent than others can be a source of power. If two parties are interdependent but one is less dependent than the other, the less dependent party has a source of power as long as both value the interdependent relationship. Manipulating the asymmetries of interdependence can be a source of power in international politics. Analysts who say that interdependence occurs only in situations of equal dependence define away the most interesting political behavior. Such perfect symmetry is quite rare, as are cases of complete imbalance in which one side is totally dependent and the other is not dependent at all. Asymmetry is at the heart of the politics of interdependence (Figure 8.1).

Figure 8.1 The Asymmetric Nature of Interdependence

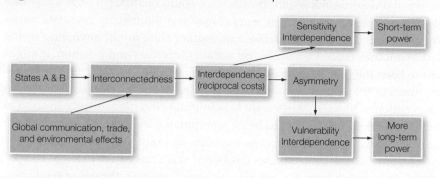

Asymmetry often varies according to different issues. In the 1980s, when President Ronald Reagan cut taxes and raised expenditures, the United States became dependent on imported Japanese capital to balance its federal government budget. Some argued that this dependency gave Japan tremendous power over the United States. But the other side of the coin was that Japan would hurt itself as well as the United States if it stopped lending to the United States. Japanese investors who already had large stakes in the United States would have found their investments devalued by the damage done to the U.S. economy if Japan suddenly stopped lending. Moreover, Japan's economy was a little more than half the size of the U.S. economy, which meant that the Japanese needed the U.S. market for their exports far more than vice versa (although both needed each other and both benefited from the interdependence). A similar relationship has developed today between the United States and China. The United States accepts Chinese imports, and China holds U.S. dollars and bonds, in effect making a loan to the United States. Although China could threaten to sell its holdings of dollars and damage the U.S. economy, a weakened U.S. economy would mean a smaller market for Chinese exports, and the U.S. government might respond with tariffs against Chinese goods. Neither side is in a hurry to break the symmetry of their vulnerability interdependence. In 2010, some Chinese generals suggested a massive sale of dollars to punish the United States for its arms sales to Taiwan, but top leaders refused. They knew that if China tried to bring the United States to its knees by dumping dollars, it would bring itself to its knees as well.

Moreover, security was often linked to other issues in the U.S.-Japanese relationship. After World War II, Japan followed the policy of a trading state and did not develop a large military capability or acquire nuclear weapons. It relied on the United States' security guarantee to balance the power of the Soviet Union and China in the East Asian region. Thus when a dispute seemed to be developing between the United States and Japan over trade in 1990, the Japanese made concessions to prevent weakening the overall security relationship.

When there is asymmetry of interdependence in different issue areas, a state may try to link or unlink issues. If each issue could be thought of as a separate poker game and all poker games were played simultaneously, one state might have most of the chips at one table, and another state might have most of the chips at another table. Depending on a state's interests and position, it might want to keep the games separate or create linkages between the tables. Therefore, much of the political conflict over interdependence involves the creation or prevention of linkage. States want to manipulate interdependence in areas in which they are strong and avoid being manipulated in areas in which they are relatively weak. Economic sanctions are often an example of such linkage. For example, in 1996, the United States threatened sanctions against foreign companies that invested in Iran, but when faced with European threats of retaliation through other linkages, the United States backed down.

By setting agendas and defining issue areas, international institutions often set the rules for the trade-offs in interdependent relationships. States try to use international institutions to set the rules that affect the transfer of chips among tables. Ironically, international institutions can benefit the weaker players by keeping some of the conflicts in which the poorer states are relatively better endowed separated from the military table, where strong states dominate. The danger remains, however, that some players will be strong enough to overturn one or more of the tables. With separate institutions for money, shipping, pollution, and trade, there is a danger that if the militarily strong players are beaten too badly, they may try to kick over the other tables. When the United States and Europe were beaten at the oil table in 1973, however, they did not use their preponderant military force to kick over the oil table because, as we will see below, a complex web of linkages held them back.

The largest state does not always win in the manipulation of economic interdependence. If a smaller or weaker state has a greater concern about an issue, it may do quite well. In 2013, for instance, the United States accounted for 53 percent of Canada's trade in goods, whereas Canada accounted for only 17 percent of the United States'. Put another way, Canada was more than twice as dependent on the United States for trade as vice versa. For most of the post–World War II period, this asymmetry was even more pronounced. Ottawa often prevailed in trade disputes with Washington, however, because Canada was willing to threaten retaliatory actions such as tariffs and restrictions that deterred the United States. The Canadians would have suffered much more than the United States if their actions had led to a full dispute, but Canada believed that it was better to risk occasional retaliation than to agree to rules that would *always* make it lose. Indeed, when it came to setting rules, that Canada had more to lose meant that it was motivated to negotiate more effectively and often came away from the bargaining table with the better end of the deal.[13] Deterrence via manipulation of economic interdependence is somewhat like nuclear deterrence in that it rests on a capability for effective damage and credible intentions. Small states can often use their greater intensity and greater credibility to overcome their relative vulnerability in asymmetrical interdependence.

A natural outgrowth of rising interdependence is the proliferation of trade pacts. The European Union is the most sophisticated of these agreements and requires its member states to relax not just some economic sovereignty, but political sovereignty as well. In 1994, the United States, Mexico, and Canada ratified the *North American Free Trade Agreement (NAFTA)*. For Mexico and Canada, NAFTA was appealing because it bound their economies more tightly to the larger U.S. economy and, in so doing, increased their access to U.S. markets and their ability to export their products to the United States. For the United States, NAFTA expanded the realm of U.S. exports and made it easier for U.S. companies to do business in Canada and Mexico.

Regional pacts such as NAFTA may increase interdependence and lessen the asymmetry in a relationship. By agreeing to intertwine its economy with that of Mexico, the United States assumed some of the liabilities of the Mexican economy along with the benefits of easier access. When the value of the Mexican peso plummeted, the Clinton administration rushed in early 1995 to shore up the flagging currency and assembled a multibillion-dollar aid package. At a time when the U.S. Congress was deadlocked over increased domestic spending for services such as health care, the administration saw little choice but to rescue the peso. With greater interdependence, even strong countries can find themselves sensitive to economic developments beyond their borders. In 1997, when Southeast Asia suffered its financial crisis, the United States was less vulnerable than in the Mexican case and responded primarily through multilateral institutions, yet fears of an economic domino effect in which collapse of some developing economies would undermine confidence in others meant that the United States and other advanced economies could not continue to stand idly by.

Leadership and Institutions in the World Economy

By and large, the rules of the international economy reflect the policies of the largest states (Figure 8.2). In the nineteenth century, Britain was the strongest of the major world economies. In the monetary area, the Bank of England adhered to the gold standard, which set a stable framework for world money. Britain also enforced freedom of the seas for navigation and commerce and provided a large open market for world trade until 1932. After World War I, Britain was severely weakened by its fight against the kaiser's Germany. The United States became the world's largest economy, but it turned away from international affairs in the 1930s. The largest player in the world economy behaved as if it could still take a free ride rather than provide the leadership its size implied. Some economists believe that the Great Depression of the 1930s was aggravated by bad monetary policy and lack of American leadership. Britain was too weak to maintain an open international economy, and the United States was not living up to its new responsibilities.

Figure 8.2 Overview of Major International Economic Institutions

MAJOR INTERNATIONAL ECONOMIC INSTITUTIONS

International Monetary Fund (IMF)

Location: Washington, DC
Founded: 1945, as a result of the International Monetary and Financial Conference held at Bretton Woods, NH, in 1944
Members: 187 countries
Staff: Approx. 2,500 from 160 countries
Assets: $376 billion USD

Organizational Structure:
- Board of Governors, with one representative from each member, which meets annually
- International Monetary and Finance Committee, consisting of 24 members, which meets twice a year
- Executive Board, consisting of 24 members, which carries out daily business of the IMF

System of Voting: Majority—Weighted based on size of membership quota (payment)
Primary Goals:
- Promoting international monetary cooperation
- Facilitating the expansion and balanced growth of international trade
- Promoting exchange stability
- Assisting in the establishment of a multilateral system of payments
- Making its resources available (under adequate safeguards) to members experiencing balance-of-payments difficulties

The World Bank

Location: Washington, DC
Founded: 1945, as a result of the International Monetary and Financial Conference held at Bretton Woods, NH, in 1944
Members: 187 countries
Staff: More than 10,000 from 160 countries
Budget: $44.2 billion USD in commitments; $28.9 billion gross disbursements

Organizational Structure:
- Board of Governors, with one representative from each member, which meets annually
- President from the largest shareholder (the United States) elected to a renewable five-year term and responsible for overseeing the Board of Directors
- Board of Directors, consisting of 24 members who meet twice weekly
- Executive Directors carry out daily operations and decision making

System of Voting: Majority—Weighted based on size of each member's economy
Subagencies:
- International Bank for Reconstruction and Development
- International Development Association
- International Finance Corporation
- Multilateral Investment Guarantee Agency
- International Center for the Settlement of Investment Disputes

Primary Goals:
- Reducing poverty through efforts to promote economic growth and employment
- Debt relief for developing and least developed countries
- Improving the quality of governance and capacity of governing institutions
- Reducing the spread of diseases, including HIV/AIDS and malaria
- Increasing child access to primary education
- Reducing environmental degradation

(continued)

Figure 8.2 (*continued*)

The World Trade Organization (WTO)

Location: Geneva, Switzerland

Founded: 1995, as a result of the Uruguay Round of multilateral trade negotiations (formerly known as Generalized Agreement on Tariffs and Trade [GATT], which entered force in 1948)

Members: 153 member countries, 31 observer countries
Staff: 629 (Secretariat Staff)

Budget: 196 million CHF (approx. $264 million USD)

Organizational Structure:

- General Council, with one representative from each member, which convenes several times a year to negotiate agreements; also convenes as the Dispute Settlement Body and Trade Policy Review Body
- Appellate Body, consisting of seven permanent members who hear disputes referred to it by the Dispute Settlement Body (i.e., General Council)
- Secretariat, led by a Secretary, which has no formal decision-making powers and thus works to facilitate the daily business of the General Council and various subcommittees

System of Voting: Consensus based—One member, one vote

Primary Goals:

- Administering WTO trade agreements
- Providing a forum for multilateral trade negotiations
- Handling trade disputes
- Monitoring national trade policies
- Providing technical assistance and training to developing countries
- Cooperating with other international development organizations

Organization for Economic Cooperation and Development (OECD)

Location: Paris, France

Founded: 1960, as an economic counterpart to NATO; was preceded by the Organization for European Economic Cooperation founded after World War II to coordinate the Marshall Plan

Members: 34 countries (mostly developed countries)
Staff: 2,500 (Secretariat Staff)

Budget: 342 million EUR (approx. $486 million USD)

Organizational Structure:

- Council, with one representative from each member, which provides guidance regarding OECD activities and establishes the group's annual budget
- Secretary General, who oversees the Council and the Secretariat, which is responsible for the group's daily operations

System of Voting: Consensus based

Primary Goals:

- Promoting good governance
- Conducting economic surveys and offering economic policy recommendations
- Promoting economic development
- Providing a forum for multilateral discussion of economic, development, social, and governance challenges related to globalization

---

After World War II, the lessons of the 1930s were on the minds of American leaders, and in 1944, an international conference at *Bretton Woods*, New Hampshire, established institutions to maintain an open, international economy. The *International Monetary Fund (IMF)* lends money, usually to developing countries and new market economies, to help when they have difficulties with their balance of payments or with paying interest on their debts. The IMF generally conditions its loans on the recipient country reforming its economic policies, such as reducing budget deficits and price subsidies. Although its policies are sometimes controversial and not always effective, the IMF played a role in helping the Russian economy in the early 1990s as well as in the Asian financial crisis later in the decade. The *World Bank* lends money to poorer countries and new market economies for development projects. (There are also regional development banks for Asia, Latin America, Africa, and Eastern Europe.)

The *General Agreement on Tariffs and Trade (GATT)*, later transformed into the *World Trade Organization (WTO)*, established rules for liberal trade and has served as the locus for a series of rounds of multilateral negotiations that have lowered trade barriers. The Organization for Economic Cooperation and Development (OECD) serves as a forum for 34 of the most developed countries to coordinate their international economic policies. Since the mid-1970s, the leaders of the seven largest economies, which accounted for two-thirds of world production at the time, have met at annual G7 summit conferences (expanded to the G8 from 1998–2014 to include Russia) to discuss conditions of the world economy. In 1999, an even larger and more geographically representative group of countries—the G20—was created, and it played an important role in the 2008–2009 global financial crisis. These institutions have helped reinforce government policies that allow rapid growth of private transnational interactions. The period has seen a rapid increase in economic interdependence. In most of the period after 1945, trade grew between 3 and 9 percent per year, faster even than the growth of world product. International trade, which represented 5.6 percent of the U.S. gross domestic product (GDP) in 1960, more than doubled to 11.2 percent of the U.S. GDP by 1995 and reached 27.97 percent of GDP in 2009. Large multinational corporations with global strategies became more significant as international investments increased by nearly 10 percent per year.

Critics have argued that the major international economic institutions are biased in favor of rich rather than poor countries. The IMF and the *World Bank*, for example, have weighted voting that gives a preponderant influence to the United States, Europe, and Japan. The IMF has always been directed by a European and the World Bank by an American (although that may change in the future). The United States is able to run fiscal and trade deficits with only the mildest of criticism, but when poor countries incur similar debts, IMF bureaucrats insist on a return to market discipline as a condition for help. One reason is that the poor countries often need the IMF's help to borrow money, but the United States can borrow without the IMF. In other words, the institutions reflect the underlying power of the asymmetrical interdependence of financial markets. Abolishing the IMF would not change that underlying power reality in financial markets. If anything, leaving matters to private bankers and fund managers might make it even more difficult for poor countries to borrow.

The WTO does not have weighted voting. It provides a forum in which 161 member countries can negotiate trade agreements on a nondiscriminatory basis, as well as panels and rules to help arbitrate their trade disputes. Critics argue that the agreements that countries negotiate within its framework (such as the current Doha "development round" of multilateral trade talks) have allowed rich countries to protect areas such as agriculture and textiles from developing-country competition and thus are unfair to the poor. The critics' descriptions are correct, and the protectionist policies hurt poor countries. But the causes of such protectionism lie in the domestic politics of the rich countries and might be even greater if the WTO did not play a role. Again, international institutions can alleviate but not remove the underlying power realities. If anything, that the United States, Europe, and China have abided by costly decisions made against them by WTO panels suggests that institutions can make a difference, at least at the margin.

Even among the rich and powerful countries, there are problems in managing a transnational economy in a world of separate states. In the 1980s and again after 2001, the United States became a net debtor when it refused to tax itself to pay its bills at home and instead borrowed money from abroad. Some analysts believed that this policy was setting the scene for a repeat of the 1930s in that the United States would experience decline as Britain had. But the United States did not decline, and other countries continued to be willing to lend it money because they had confidence in its economy and because it suited their interests. China, for example, continues to hold large reserves in dollars as a means to facilitate its exports to the United States. In 2009, although Chinese officials spoke of a desire to reduce China's holding of dollars, its practice changed very little.

Financial volatility, however, remains a potential problem. Global financial markets have grown dramatically in recent years, and their volatility poses risks to stability. Much will depend on the willingness of governments to pursue policies that maintain stability in the international economic system. In any case, the global political and economic system is more complicated and complex than before. More sectors, more states, more issues, and more private actors are involved in interdependent relationships. It is increasingly unrealistic to analyze world politics as occurring solely among a group of large states, solid as billiard balls, bouncing off one another in a balance of power.

Realism and Complex Interdependence

What would the world look like if realism were wrong about some of its fundamental propositions? Realism holds that states are the only significant actors, that military force is their dominant instrument, and that power (or security) is their dominant goal. What if states were not the only significant actors? What if *transnational actors* working across state boundaries were also major players? What if force were not the only significant instrument and, instead, economic manipulation and the use of international institutions were dominant? What if welfare, rather than security, were the primary goal? Such an antirealist world could be characterized as a situation of *complex interdependence*. Social scientists call complex interdependence an "ideal type." It is an imaginary concept

Figure 8.3 Spectrum from Realism to Complex Interdependence

```
                Israel/Syria        U.S./China       U.S./Canada        Complex
Realism   ◄──────────────────────────────────────────────────────►   Interdependence
                India/Pakistan                     France/Germany
```

that does not perfectly describe the real world; but then, neither does realism. Imagining a world in a condition of complex interdependence allows us to imagine a different type of global politics, one in which the liberal paradigm would presumably perform much better.

In fact, both realism and complex interdependence represent ideal types. The real world lies somewhere between the two. We can ask where certain country relationships fit on a spectrum between a Hobbesian state of nature and a condition of complex interdependence (Figure 8.3). The Middle East is closer to the realist end of the spectrum, but relations between the United States and Canada and relations between France and Germany today come much closer to the complex interdependence end of the spectrum. Different politics and different forms of the power struggle occur depending on where on the spectrum a particular relationship between a set of countries is located. In fact, countries can change their position on the spectrum. During the Cold War, the U.S.-Soviet relationship was clearly near the realist end of the spectrum, but at the end of the Cold War, the Russia-U.S. relationship moved closer to the center between realism and complex interdependence for a while before drifting back toward the realist end in recent years.

A prime example of the interaction in the real world between complex interdependence and realism is the U.S. relationship with China. As with Japan, U.S. imports from China far outstrip U.S. exports to China. The result is a significant trade deficit. Although the bilateral trade relationship between the United States and China is asymmetrical in China's favor, the United States is not particularly vulnerable to potential Chinese trade embargoes because it could compensate for the potential loss of Chinese goods by purchasing them elsewhere, and China has strong domestic incentives to export to the United States. Moreover, as we saw above, Chinese threats to sell the large holdings of dollars it earns for its exports would hurt Chinese sales to the United States. At the same time, the potential size of the Chinese market for American goods and the domestic demand for Chinese goods in the United States mean that the ability of the U.S. government to act against China is somewhat constrained by transnational actors, including U.S. multinational corporations that have pressured the U.S. government not to implement sanctions against China for unfair trade practices and human rights violations. As we saw in Chapter 7, however, the rapid growth of China's economic and military strength and its more assertive actions in maritime and territorial disputes have had a strong effect on the perceptions of the balance of power in East Asia and have contributed to the reinvigoration of U.S. alliances with Japan, the Philippines, and Australia.

Before the 2003 Iraq War, columnist Robert Kagan argued that many European countries were less willing to confront dangerous dictators such as Saddam Hussein because they had become accustomed to the peaceful conditions of complex interdependence that prevailed inside Europe and tended to generalize them to the Hobbesian world outside Europe, where they were less appropriate. In his words, "Americans were from Mars, and Europeans were from Venus."[14] Of course, this clever phrase was too simple (witness the role of Britain in the Iraq War), but it captured different perceptions across the Atlantic. It also illuminated a larger point. In their relations with one another, all advanced democracies form liberal islands of peace in the sea of Hobbesian realism. In its relations with Canada, Europe, and Japan, even the United States is from Venus. It is equally mistaken to pretend that the whole world is typified by Hobbesian realism or by complex interdependence.

Follow Up

- Robert O. Keohane and Joseph S. Nye, Jr., *Power and Interdependence*, 4th ed. (New York: Longman, 2011).

- Mark J. C. Crescenzi, *Economic Interdependence and Conflict in World Politics* (Lanham, MD: Lexington Books, 2005).

The Politics of Oil

8.3   **Explain how the concepts of globalization and interdependence illuminate the international politics of oil.**

For the last 100 years, oil has been the most important raw material in the world, in both economic and political terms, and it is likely to remain an important source of energy well into the twenty-first century. The United States consumes roughly a fifth of the world's oil (compared with 11 percent for China, although Chinese consumption is growing rapidly). Even with high Chinese growth, the world is not about to run out of oil in the short run. Since the early 2000s, technological advances in horizontal drilling and hydraulic injection have unleashed major reserves of oil and gas trapped in shale rock that had once be considered inaccessible. More than 1.6 trillion barrels of conventional oil reserves have been proven, and more are likely to be found. But half of the proven reserves are in the Persian Gulf and are therefore vulnerable to political disruption, which could have devastating effects on the world economy. Oil was not the primary cause of the Gulf War or the Iraq War in the simple sense of seizing and owning it, but the strong positive relationship between the stability of Middle East oil supplies and global economic stability was a major consideration of policy makers when they debated policy toward Iraq. As one wag put it, if the Persian Gulf produced broccoli instead of oil, the wars might not have occurred. Thus oil not only is important in itself, but is also an issue that illustrates aspects of both realism and complex interdependence.

Interdependence in a given area often occurs within a framework of rules, norms, and institutions that are called a *regime*. The international oil regime has changed dramatically over the decades. In 1960, the oil regime was a private oligopoly with close ties to the governments of the major consuming countries. Oil at that time sold for about $2 a barrel, and seven large transnational oil companies, sometimes called the "seven sisters," determined the amount of oil that would be produced. The price of oil depended on how much the large companies produced and on the demand in the rich countries where most of the oil was sold. Transnational companies set the rate of production, and prices were determined by conditions in rich countries. The strongest powers in the international system in traditional military terms occasionally intervened to keep the system going. For example, in 1953, when a nationalist movement tried to overthrow the shah of Iran, Britain and the United States covertly intervened to return the shah to his throne. The oil regime was then largely unchanged.

As mentioned above, there was a major turning point in the international regime governing oil after 1973. The producing countries set the rate of production and therefore had a strong effect on price, rather than price being determined solely by the market in the rich countries. There was an enormous shift of power and wealth from rich to relatively poor countries. Confidential documents released in 2004 showed that in response to the Arab oil embargo of 1973, the United States had considered the use of force to seize Persian Gulf oil fields, as realist theory might have predicted. But it did not do so, and the regime changed in favor of the weaker countries. How could such a dramatic change be explained?

A frequently offered explanation is that the oil-producing countries banded together and formed the *Organization of Petroleum Exporting Countries (OPEC)*. The trouble with this explanation is that OPEC was formed in 1960, and the dramatic change did not occur until 1973. Oil prices fell despite OPEC, so there is more to the story. There are three ways to explain these changes in the international oil regime: the overall balance of power, the balance of power in the oil issue, and international institutions.

Realists look at changes in the balance of power resting primarily on military force, particularly with regard to the Persian Gulf, the major oil-exporting region of the world. Two changes affected that balance: the rise of nationalism and decolonization. In 1960, half the OPEC countries were colonies of Europe; by 1973, they were all independent. Accompanying the rise in nationalism was a rise in the costs of military intervention. It is much more expensive to use force against a nationalistically awakened and decolonized people. When Britain and the United States intervened in Iran in 1953, it was not very costly, but if the United States had tried to keep the shah on his throne in 1979, the costs would have been prohibitive.

Relative changes in U.S. and British power also affected the balance of power in the Persian Gulf. When OPEC was formed, and even earlier, Britain was to a large extent the police officer of the Persian Gulf. In 1961, it prevented an earlier Iraqi effort to annex Kuwait. But by 1971, Britain was economically weakened, and the British government was trying to cut back on its international defense commitments. In 1971, Britain ended what used to be called its role "east of Suez." That may sound a bit like 1947, when Britain was unable to maintain its role as a power in the eastern Mediterranean. At that time, the United States stepped in to help Greece and Turkey and formulated the Truman Doctrine. But in 1971, the United States was not well placed to step in to replace Britain as it did in 1947. The United States was deeply embroiled in Vietnam and unwilling to accept an additional major military commitment in the Persian Gulf. As a result, President Richard Nixon and then–National Security Adviser new Henry Kissinger designed a U.S. strategy that relied heavily on regional powers. Their chosen instrument was Iran. By using Iran as the regional hegemon, they thought that they could replace the departing British police cheaply. A realist would point to these changes in the overall structure of power, particularly the balance of military power in the Persian Gulf region, to explain the change in the oil regime.

A second way of explaining the change is a modified form of realism that focuses on the relative symmetry of economic power of various countries in a given issue area. Between 1950 and 1973, serious changes occurred in global oil consumption that altered U.S. dependence on foreign oil. Specifically, the United States, until 1971, was the largest oil producer in the world. But U.S. production peaked in 1971; U.S. imports began to grow thereafter, and the United States no longer had any surplus oil. During the two Middle East wars of 1956 and 1967, the Arab countries tried an oil embargo, but their efforts were easily defeated because the United States was producing enough oil to supply Europe when it was cut off by the Arab countries. Once U.S. production peaked in 1971 and the United States began to import oil, the power to balance the oil market switched to countries such as Saudi Arabia and Iran. No longer was the United States the supplier of last resort that could make up any missing oil.

A third way to explain the difference in the oil regime after 1973 relies less on realism than on changes in the role of international institutions, particularly the multinational corporations and OPEC that are emphasized by liberal and constructivist approaches. The "seven sisters" gradually lost power over this period. One reason was their *obsolescing bargains* with the producer countries. When a multinational corporation goes into a resource-rich country with a new investment, it can strike a bargain in which the multinational gets a large part of the joint gains. From the point of view of the poor country, having a multinational come in to develop its resources will make it better off. Even if it gets only 20 percent of the revenues and the multinational gets 80 percent, the poor country has more than it had before. So, at the early stages when multinationals have a monopoly on capital, technology, and access to international markets, they strike a bargain with the poor countries in which the multinationals get the larger share by far. Over time, however, the multinationals inadvertently transfer resources to the poor countries, not out of charity but in the normal course of business. They train locals. Thus Saudis, Kuwaitis, and others learned how to run oil fields, pumping stations, and loading docks. Locals also developed expertise in marketing and associated tasks.

Eventually, the poor countries wanted a better division of the profits. The multinationals could threaten to pull out, but the poor countries could credibly threaten to run the operations by themselves. Thus, over time, the power of the multinational companies, particularly in raw materials, diminished in terms of their bargaining with host countries. It was the "obsolescing bargain." From the 1960s to 1973, the multinationals inadvertently transferred technology and skills that developed the poor countries' capacity to run oil operations themselves.

There were other developments. The seven sisters were joined by "little cousins" when new transnational corporations entered the oil market. Although they were not as large as the seven sisters, they were still big, and they began to strike their own deals with the oil-producing countries. Thus, when an oil-producing country wanted to get out of the hands of the seven sisters, it could strike a deal with smaller independent multinationals. That again reduced the bargaining power of the largest multinationals.

Institutionally, there was a modest increase in the effectiveness of OPEC as a cartel. Cartels restricting supply had long been typical in the oil industry, but in the past, they had been private arrangements of the seven sisters. Cartels generally have a problem because there is a tendency to cheat on production quotas when markets are soft and the price drops. Cartels work best when there is a shortage of oil, but when there is a surplus, people want to sell their oil and tend to cut the price to get a bigger share of the market. With time, market forces tend to erode cartels. OPEC represented an effort to shift from a private to a governmental cartel of the oil-producing countries. In its early years, OPEC had trouble exercising power because there was plenty of oil. As long as oil was in surplus, the OPEC countries had incentives to cheat to get a larger share of the market. OPEC was unable to enforce price discipline from the year it was founded, 1960, until the early 1970s. But after oil supplies tightened, OPEC's role in coordinating the bargaining power of the producers increased.

The Middle East War of 1973 gave OPEC a boost, a signal that now it could use its power. The Arab countries cut off access to oil during the 1973 war for political reasons, but that created a situation in which OPEC could become effective. Iran, which is not an Arab country, was allegedly the instrument of the United States for policing the Persian Gulf, but the shah of Iran moved to quadruple oil prices, and the other OPEC countries followed suit. Over the long term, OPEC could not maintain permanently high prices because of market forces, but there was stickiness on the downside that was an effect of the OPEC coalition.

A more important institutional factor was the role that the oil companies played in "smoothing the pain" in the crisis itself. At one point in the crisis, Kissinger, by now secretary of state, said that if the United States faced "strangulation," force might have to be used. Fifteen percent of traded oil was cut, and the Arab embargo reduced oil exports to the United States by 25 percent. Oil companies, however, made sure that no one country suffered much more than any other. They redistributed the world's traded oil. When the United States lost 25 percent of its Arab oil imports, the companies shipped it more Venezuelan or Indonesian oil. They smoothed the pain of the embargo so that the rich countries all lost about 7 to 9 percent of their oil, well below the strangulation point. They helped prevent the economic conflict from becoming a military conflict.

Why did they do that? It was not out of charity. Transnational companies are profit maximizers who do not want to risk their valuable investments in production. Accordingly, they want reliable access to markets and stable political and economic conditions. The multinational companies feared situations in which they would be nationalized in a country if they refused to sell to that country. For example, Prime Minister Edward Heath of Britain demanded that British Petroleum (BP) sell only to Britain and not to other countries. The head of BP replied that if he followed such an order, oil-producing countries would nationalize BP's assets and destroy the company. The British prime minister backed down.

In short, oil is an illustration of an issue that falls between the ideal types of realism and complex interdependence. Changes in three dimensions—the overall balance of military power, the symmetry of interdependence within the issue structure of economic power, and the institutions within the oil issue area—help explain the dramatic difference between the oil regime of 1960 and the oil regime after 1973.

Oil as a Power Resource

How powerful was the oil weapon at the turning point of 1973? By cutting production and embargoing sales to countries friendly to Israel, Arab states were able to bring their issues to the forefront of the U.S. agenda. They also created temporary disarray in the alliances between Japan, Europe, and the United States, each of whom responded somewhat differently. The oil weapon encouraged the United States to play a more conciliatory role in arranging the settlement of the Arab-Israeli dispute in the aftermath of the Yom Kippur War, but it did not change the basic policy of the United States in the Middle East: Washington did not suddenly switch from its alliance with Israel to support of the Arab cause. Oil was a power resource that had an effect, but not a strong enough effect to reverse U.S. policy.

Why was the oil weapon not more effective? Part of the answer is reciprocity in interdependence. Saudi Arabia, which became the key country in oil markets, had large investments in the United States. If the Saudis damaged the U.S. economy too much, they would also hurt their own economic interests. In addition, Saudi Arabia depended on the United States for security. In the long run, the

Photo: Epa/Landov

The Deepwater Horizon offshore oil drilling platform, which exploded and sank in the Gulf of Mexico in April 2010, causing the largest oil spill in U.S. history

United States was the only country able to keep a stable balance of power in the Persian Gulf region. The Saudis knew that, and they were careful about how far they pushed the oil weapon. Moreover, in the aftermath of the oil crisis, major oil consumers took measures to reduce somewhat their sensitivity and vulnerability in the future. The United States, for example, established a Strategic Petroleum Reserve—an oil stockpile, in effect—and with other OECD countries established the International Energy Agency to promote transparency in world energy markets and sound energy policy.

What was the role of force as a power resource in the oil crisis of 1973? There was no overt use of force. There was no military intervention, because strangulation never occurred. Moreover, the Saudis were benefiting from the long-run security guarantee provided by the United States. Thus force played a background role. There was an indirect linkage between security interdependence and oil interdependence. Force was too costly to use overtly, but it played a role as a power resource in the background.

This complex set of factors persists. Oil remains an exception among raw materials, and that contributed indirectly to the Gulf War and the Iraq War as well as to the continuing strong U.S. naval presence in the Persian Gulf. But oil prices are sensitive to global market forces, and multinationals' exploration for new supplies has increased supply.

The nightmare oil scenarios predicted during the 1970s failed to materialize. The U.S. Department of Energy, for instance, forecast that oil would routinely cost more than $100 a barrel by 2000.[15] Although the nominal spot price of oil did shoot up briefly to $145 in July 2008, the average annual inflation-adjusted price actually peaked in 1980 (at $107), and in 2015 it dropped below $50.[16] A number of factors helped keep these earlier predictions from coming true. On the demand side, policy measures and price increases led to more efficient use of energy. For example, the Corporate Average Fuel Efficiency law in the United States mandated that automakers manufacture cars that achieved minimum standards for gas mileage. In this example, a domestic policy had a clear, intended effect on foreign policy. (Cost-conscious drivers who had felt the pinch of high gasoline prices also contributed to this effect.) On the supply side, the emergence of non-OPEC oil sources that were unavailable during the Cold War meant that OPEC faced more competition on the world market. Many of these new sources were made possible by advances in extraction technology. Since 1999, for example, Canada has been the United States' single largest source of imported oil, a development made possible by new tar-sands processing techniques. The development of hydraulic fracturing of shale (mentioned above) gave the U.S. domestic oil industry an enormous boost as well. These changes have all hurt OPEC's capacity to influence the global market. Whereas OPEC accounted for more than 70 percent of global crude oil production in 1973, today it accounts for only about 40 percent.

Although people in the 1980s and 1990s used to fret about the world running out of oil, the key worry now is that we will burn too much of it. As climate science improves, the imperative to reduce our reliance on fossil fuels (not only oil, but also coal and natural gas) becomes clearer and clearer. As we will see in Chapter 9, this situation represents both a major challenge and a major opportunity. But as far as the politics of oil are concerned, a shift away from fossil fuels and toward climate-friendly sources of energy will have dramatic geopolitical effects as oil-producing regions lose importance and clout.

Follow Up

- Francisco R. Parra, *Oil Politics: A Modern History of Petroleum* (New York: I. B. Tauris, 2004).

- Daniel Yergin, "Ensuring Energy Security," *Foreign Affairs*, March/April (2006), pp. 28–36.

Study Questions

1. What are the major types of globalization? Is globalization an irreversible process? How is contemporary globalization different from past periods of globalization?

2. What are the implications of globalization in the cultural realm? Does globalization necessarily result in global cultural homogenization? More specifically, will globalization ultimately lead to universal "Westernization"?

3. What kinds of political responses has globalization sparked? What is the relationship between antiglobalization sentiment and economic inequality in the international sphere?

4. What is "complex interdependence"? How does it differ from simple "interdependence"? What paradigm is best at making sense of it? Where do we find complex interdependence most closely approximated today?

5. What makes economic interdependence a source of power? How do sensitivity and vulnerability differ?

6. What were the underlying and immediate causes of the 1973 oil crisis? Why didn't it occur earlier, say, in 1967? Was it a unique event or the beginning of a revolution in international politics? Why was force not used? Could it be used today?

7. Liberal theory was optimistic that increasing international commerce would seriously decrease the attractiveness of military force as a tool in international politics. What does the international oil regime indicate either to support or to falsify this thesis?

8. Under classical realist assumptions, we would not expect to see cooperation among states under conditions of anarchy. How can you explain the degree of cooperation achieved by states in international economic relations? Do institutions play a role?

Notes

1. Dani Rodrik, *Has Globalization Gone Too Far?* (Washington, DC: Institute for International Economics, 1997), p. 2.

2. Jonathan Masters, "What Are Economic Sanctions?," *CFR Backgrounders* (April 8, 2015), http://www.cfr.org/sanctions/economic-sanctions/p36259.

3. Thomas Friedman, *The Lexus and the Olive Tree: Understanding Globalization* (New York: Farrar, Straus & Giroux, 1999), pp. 7–8.

4. Joseph Stiglitz, "Weightless Concerns," *Financial Times* (London), February 3, 1999, p. 14.

5. John Maynard Keynes, *The Economic Consequences of the Peace* (New York: Penguin, 1988), p. 11.

6. Robert Wade, "Winners and Losers" and "Of Rich and Poor," *The Economist*, April 28, 2001, pp. 72–74, 80. Global inequality is difficult to measure, and there is always a degree of uncertainty; but although it is clear that income inequality has risen dramatically since the Industrial Revolution, there is reason to believe that it may have declined slightly in recent decades. See Branko Milanovic, *Global Income Inequality by the Numbers: In History and Now*, World Bank Development Research Group Policy Research Working Paper 6259 (November 2012), http://elibrary.worldbank.org/doi/pdf/10.1596/1813-9450-6259.

7. Karl Polanyi, *The Great Transformation: The Political and Economic Origins of Our Time* (Boston, MA: Beacon Press, 2001).

8. UK Special Representative for Climate Change John Ashton, Speech at the School of Oriental and African Studies (SOAS) in London, September 27, 2006.

9. Edmund L. Andrews, "Snow Urges Consumerism on China Trip," *International New York Times* (October 14, 2005), http://www.nytimes.com/2005/10/14/business/snow-urges-consumerism-on-china-trip.html.

10. Edmund Andrews, "Snow Urges Consumerism on China Trip," *New York Times*, October 14, 2005, p. 1.

11. Lester Brown, *World without Borders* (New York: Random, 1972), p. 194.

12. Rakesh Mohan, Valedictory Address, Reserve Bank of India, Asia Regional Economic Forum, September 20, 2007.

13. The 1959 Defense Production Sharing Arrangements, the 1965 Auto Pact, and the 1988 Canada-U.S. Free Trade Agreement. Michael Hart, *A Trading Nation: Canadian Trade Policy from Colonialism to Globalization* (Vancouver: UBC Press, 2002), pp. 214–217, 240–247, 367–393.

14. Robert Kagan, *Of Paradise and Power: America and Europe in the New World Order* (New York: Vintage, 2004), p. 1.

15. "Still Holding Customers over a Barrel," *The Economist*, October 25, 2003, pp. 61–63.

16. Adjusted to March 2015; http://inflationdata.com/inflation/inflation_rate/historical_oil_prices_table.asp.

Chapter 9

The Information Revolution and Transnational Actors

Photo: Lefteris Pitarakis/AP Images

An International Committee of the Red Cross/Red Crescent tent supports refugees from the Libyan civil war in the spring of 2011

Learning Objectives

9.1 Describe the distinctive features of the modern information revolution and their effects on interstate politics.

9.2 Explain how transnational actors affect interstate politics.

9.3 Identify four likely future effects of the information revolution and the rise of transnational actors.

reduction in the *cost* and a mind-boggling increase in *capacity*. For all practical purposes, the cost of transmitting and receiving information has become negligible. At the same time, storage and bandwidth have exploded. Siemens estimates that by 2020, approximately 26 billion things—everything from cars and appliances to smartphones, watches, tablets, and computers—will be connected to the Internet, generating a total information flow of 40 zettabytes (40 trillion gigabytes).[1] These dramatic changes have led to what some call the "third industrial revolution," which is changing the nature of governance, affecting sovereignty, and creating a diffusion of power.

Lessons from the Past

Technology has always had an important effect on how human beings interact and organize their world. The invention of writing 5,000 years ago in Mesopotamia (specifically, in ancient Sumeria) made rudimentary bureaucracy possible for the very first time. The invention of movable type in Europe permitted the transformation of medieval fiefdoms into modern states.[2] Revolutions in communications, transportation, and military technology permitted governance over larger and larger areas. It is no accident that in Western Europe, where the modern sovereign state was first invented, countries are physically small.[3] France—the largest—ranks only forty-second in the world. You could fit 12 Frances into Australia and 15 into the United States or Canada. What will ongoing technological developments mean for world politics in the future?

We can get some idea of where we are heading by looking back at the past. In the first industrial revolution around the turn of the nineteenth century, the application of steam to mills and transportation had a powerful effect on the economy, society, and government. Patterns of production, work, living conditions, social class, and political power were transformed. Public education arose, with literate, trained workers being needed for increasingly complex and potentially dangerous factories. Police forces such as London's "bobbies" were created to deal with urbanization. Subsidies were provided for the necessary infrastructure of canals and railroads.

Around the turn of the twentieth century, the "second industrial revolution"—electricity, synthetics, and the internal combustion engine—brought similar economic and social changes. The United States went from a predominantly agrarian to a primarily industrial and urban nation. In the 1890s, most Americans still worked on farms or as servants. A few decades later, the majority lived in cities and worked in factories. Social class and political cleavages were altered as urban labor and trade unions became more important. And again, with lags, the role of government changed. The bipartisan progressive movement ushered in antitrust legislation, early consumer protection regulation by the forerunner of the Food and Drug Administration, and economic stabilization by the Federal Reserve Board. The United States rose to the status of a great power in world politics. Some expect the third industrial revolution to produce analogous transformations in the economy, society, government, and world politics.

These historical analogies help us understand some of the forces that will shape world politics in the twenty-first century. Economies and information networks have changed more rapidly than governments have. The political scales of sovereignty and authority have not yet grown at a similar rate. As the sociologist Daniel Bell noted, "If there is a single overriding sociological problem in postindustrial society—particularly in the management of transition—it is the management of scale."[4] Put more simply, the basic building blocks of world politics are being transformed by the new technology. If we focus solely on the hard power of states, we will miss the new reality.

We are still at an early stage of the current information revolution, and its effects on economics and politics are uneven. As with steam in the late eighteenth century and electricity in the late nineteenth century, productivity growth lagged as society had to learn to fully use the new technologies. Social institutions change more slowly than technology. For example, the electric motor was invented in 1881, but it was nearly four decades before Henry Ford pioneered the reorganization of factory assembly lines to take full advantage of electric power. Similar lags were true for information technology and computers. The increase in productivity of the U.S. economy began to register only as recently as the mid-1990s.

The advent of truly mass communications and broadcasting a century ago, which was facilitated by newly cheap electricity, provides some lessons about possible social and political effects today. It ushered in the age of mass popular culture. The effects of mass communication and broadcasting, although not the telephone, tended to have a centralizing political effect. Although information was more widespread, it was more centrally influenced even in democratic countries than in the age of the local press. President Franklin Roosevelt's use of radio in the 1930s worked a dramatic shift in U.S. politics. These effects were particularly pronounced in countries where they were combined with the rise of totalitarian governments that were able to suppress competing sources of information. Indeed, some scholars believe that totalitarianism would not have been possible without the mass communications that accompanied the second industrial revolution.

In the middle of the twentieth century, people feared that the computers and communications of the current information revolution would create the central governmental control dramatized in George Orwell's novel *1984*. Mainframe computers seemed set to enhance central planning and increase the surveillance powers of those at the top. As Edward Snowden's revelations about the National Security Agency have made clear, modern technology has indeed given governments an astonishing capacity to collect information, to identify persons of interest, and to conduct surveillance. But at the same time, private companies collect more information than many governments, and improvements in encryption technology and programs that allow people to share information anonymously

Photo: Xinhua / Landov

Traders working at the New York Mercantile Exchange

have limited governments' capacity. In many ways, governments had an easier time controlling information during the second information revolution than they are having in the third.

As computing power has decreased in cost and computers have shrunk in size and become more highly mobile, their decentralizing effects have outweighed their centralizing effects. The Internet creates a system in which power over information is much more widely distributed. Compared to radio, television, and newspapers, controlled by editors and broadcasters, the Internet creates unlimited one-to-one (via e-mail), one-to-many (via a personal homepage, blog, or Twitter feed), and, perhaps most important, many-to-many (via online chat rooms or message boards) communication. Comparing these electronic methods of communication to previous advances in communication, political scientist Pippa Norris wrote, "Internet messages have the capacity to flow farther, faster, and with fewer intermediaries."[5] Central surveillance is possible, but governments that aspire to control information flows through control of the Internet face high costs. What that means is that world politics will decreasingly be the sole province of governments. Both individuals and private organizations, ranging from corporations to nongovernmental organizations (NGOs) to criminals to terrorists, will be empowered to play direct roles in world politics. The spread of information means that power will be more widely distributed and that informal networks will undercut the monopoly of traditional bureaucracy. The speed of Internet time means that governments everywhere will have less control of their agendas. Political leaders will enjoy fewer degrees of freedom before they must respond to events, and then they will have to share the stage with more actors. Constructivists warn that we will have to avoid being mesmerized by terms such as *balance of power* and *hegemony* and by measures of strength that compare only the hard power of states run by centralized governments. They say that realist images of sovereign states balancing and bouncing off one another like billiard balls will blind us to the new complex reality.

A New World Politics?

The effects of the information revolution are still in their early stages. Is it really transforming world politics? Realists would say no; states will remain the most important actors, and the information revolution will still disproportionately benefit the most powerful ones. That may be so, but liberals and constructivists are right to note that the information revolution is making world politics more complex by empowering nonstate actors. It is also important to note that the effects of the information revolution are not the same everywhere. In 2014, for example, 77 percent of the people who lived in countries that belonged to the Organization for Economic Cooperation and Development used the Internet, compared with only 24 percent in the African Union. At almost 98 percent, wealthy Bermuda has the world's single highest Internet participation rate; at less than 1 percent, Eritrea has the lowest of the countries for which there are data. The world remains a mixture of agricultural, industrial, and service-dominated economies. The postindustrial societies and governments most heavily affected by the information revolution coexist and interact with countries still far less affected. And as dependency theorists first pointed out, although a relatively small number of people in poor "periphery" countries are well plugged into the "core," most are not. Inequality is not merely a matter of money; it is also a matter of access to information, both between and within states.

Will this digital divide persist? Decreasing costs may allow poor countries to leapfrog or skip over certain stages of development. For example, in many African countries, inexpensive cell phones provide banking and monetary as well as communications roles. Wireless communications are already replacing costly landlines, and voice recognition technologies can give illiterate populations access to computer communications. Technology spreads over time, and many countries are keen to develop their own Silicon Valleys. But it is easier to identify the virtual keys to the high-tech kingdom than to open the actual gates. Well-developed communications infrastructure, secure property rights, sound government policies, an environment that encourages new business formation, deep capital markets, and a skilled workforce, many of whom understand English (still the dominant language of the Internet outside China) will come to some poor countries in time, but not quickly. Even in India, which meets some of the criteria, software companies employ hundreds of thousands, but more than a fourth of India's 1.2 billion people are illiterate.

The information revolution has an overall decentralizing and leveling effect, but will it also equalize power among states? In principle, as it reduces costs and barriers of entry into markets, it should reduce the power of large states and enhance the power of small states and nonstate actors. But in practice, international relations are more complex than such technological determinism implies. Some aspects of the information revolution help the small, but some help the already large and powerful. Realists give several reasons why.

First, size still matters. What economists call barriers to entry and economies of scale remain in some of the aspects of power that are related to information. For example, soft power is strongly affected by the cultural content of what is broadcast or what appears in movies and television programs. Large, established entertainment industries often enjoy considerable economies of scale in content production and distribution. The dominant U.S. market share in films and television programs in world markets is a case in point. It is hard for newcomers to compete with Hollywood (although India's "Bollywood" has a wide following). Moreover, in the information economy, there are "network effects" with increasing returns to scale. As we know, one telephone is useless. The second adds value, and so forth as the network grows.

Second, even though it is now cheap to disseminate existing information, the collection and production of new information often requires major investment. In many competitive situations, *new* information matters most. In some dimensions, information is a public good: One person's consumption does not diminish that of another. Thomas Jefferson used the analogy of a candle. If you give someone a light, it does not diminish your light. But in a competitive situation, it may make a big difference if someone else has the light first and sees things before you do. Intelligence collection is a good example. The United States, Russia, Britain, France, and China have capabilities for collection and production that dwarf those of other countries. The United States spends $50 billion a year on non-defense-related intelligence alone. In some commercial situations, a fast follower can do better than a first mover, but in terms of power among states, it is usually better to be a first mover than a fast follower. It is ironic, but no accident, that for all the discussion of the Internet shrinking distance, firms still cluster in Silicon Valley, a congested little area south of San Francisco, because of what is called the "cocktail party effect." What makes for success is informal access to new information before it becomes public. As Douglas McGray notes, "In an industry where new technology is perpetually on the verge of obsolescence, firms must recognize demand, secure capital, and bring a product to market quickly or else be beaten by a competitor."[6] Market size and proximity to competitors, suppliers, and customers still matter in an information economy.

First movers are often the creators of the standards and architecture of information systems. As in Robert Frost's famous poem, once two paths diverge in the wood and one is taken, it is difficult to get back to the other. Sometimes, crude low-cost technologies open shortcuts that make it possible to overtake the first mover, but in many instances, the path-dependent development of information systems reflects the advantage of the first mover. The use of the English language and the pattern of top-level domain names on the Internet is a case in point. Partly because of the transformation of the U.S. economy in the 1980s and partly because of large investments driven by Cold War military competition, the United States was often the first mover and still enjoys a lead in the application of a wide variety of information technologies. But being a first mover also makes the United States more dependent on the Internet and thus more vulnerable to disruption than isolated countries such as North Korea.

Finally, as we have seen, military power remains important in critical domains of international relations. Information technology has some effects on the use of force that benefit the small and some that favor the already powerful. The off-the-shelf commercial availability of formerly costly military technologies benefits small states and nongovernmental actors and increases the vulnerability of large states. For example, today anyone can order satellite images from commercial companies or simply use Google Earth to see what goes on in other countries at little or no cost. Commercial firms and individuals can go to the Internet and get access to satellite photographs that were top secret and cost governments billions of dollars just a few years ago. When a nongovernmental group believed that U.S. policy toward North Korea was too alarmist a few years ago, it published private satellite pictures of North Korean rocket launch pads. Obviously, other countries can purchase similar pictures of U.S. bases.

Global positioning system (GPS) devices that provide precise locations, once the property of the military alone, are readily available to all and make possible the navigation systems that are available now in many new cars. What is more, information systems create vulnerabilities for rich states by adding lucrative targets for terrorist (including state-sponsored) groups. It is conceivable that a sophisticated adversary (such as a small country with cyberwarfare resources) will decide that it can blackmail large states. There is also the prospect of freelance cyberattacks, and deterrence becomes more difficult when a country cannot be sure of the origin of an attack.

Other trends, however, strengthen already powerful countries. Information technology has produced a revolution in military affairs. Space-based sensors, direct broadcasting, high-speed computers, and complex software provide the ability to gather, sort, process, transfer, and disseminate information about complex events that occur over a wide geographic area. This dominant battle-space awareness combined with precision targeting and networking of military systems produces a powerful advantage. As the Gulf War and Iraq War showed, traditional assessments of balances of weapons platforms such as tanks or planes become irrelevant unless they include the ability to integrate information with those weapons. That was the mistake that Saddam Hussein made in 1990, as well as those in Congress who predicted massive U.S. casualties. Many of the relevant technologies are available in commercial markets, and weaker states can be expected to purchase many of them. The key, however, will not be possession of fancy hardware or advanced systems, but the ability to integrate a system of systems or to dominate crucial nodes of the modern military information infrastructure. Although anyone can purchase a GPS receiver, for example, the U.S. military, in time of emergency, has the ability to alter the signals that make them work because the satellites that broadcast them are American. Aware that at a moment's notice the United States could throw into disarray anything that used GPS devices for navigation, Russia, China, India, Europe, and Japan set about developing global or regional positioning systems of their own. From a realist perspective, their moves make perfect sense.

Liberals agree that states will remain the basic units of world politics, but they argue that the information revolution will increase the role of democratic states and thus the eventual prospects of a Kantian democratic peace. As far as countries are concerned, most information shapers are democracies, which is not accidental. Their societies are familiar with the free exchange of information, and their institutions of governance are not threatened by it. They can shape information because they can also take it. Authoritarian states, typically among the laggards, have considerably more trouble. Governments such as China's attempt to control their citizens' access to the Internet by controlling Internet service and content providers and by monitoring and censoring users. It is possible, but costly, to route around such restrictions, and control does not have to be complete to be effective for political purposes, but the attempt to control information domestically puts China at a disadvantage when it comes to shaping it globally. Singapore, a state that combines political control with economic liberalism, has thus far combined its political controls with an increasing role for the Internet. But as societies such as Singapore reach levels of development in which a broader range of knowledge workers want fewer restrictions on access to the Internet, they run the risk of losing their creative knowledge workers, their scarcest resource for competing in the information economy. Thus, for example, Singapore is reshaping its educational system to encourage the individual creativity that the information economy will demand while at the same time relaxing controls over the flow of information. Closed systems become more costly, as Egypt discovered when it briefly disconnected from the Internet during the demonstrations of February 2011.

Another reason that closed systems become more costly is that it is risky for foreigners to invest funds in an authoritarian country in which the key decisions are made in an opaque fashion. Liberals point out that transparency is becoming a key asset for countries seeking investments. The ability to keep information from leaving, which once seemed so valuable to authoritarian states, undermines the credibility and transparency necessary to attract investment on globally competitive terms. This point was illustrated by the 1997 Asian financial crisis. Governments that are not transparent are not credible, because the information they offer is seen as biased and selective. Moreover, as economic development progresses and middle-class societies develop, repressive measures become more expensive not only at home, but also in terms of international reputation. Both Taiwan and South Korea discovered in the late 1980s that repressing rising demands for democracy and free expression would be expensive in terms of their reputation and soft power. By beginning to democratize, they strengthened their capacity to cope with economic crisis. One of the great questions for China will be how it manages increased demands for political participation as it grows wealthier, but at a sharply declining pace.

Whatever the future effects of interactivity and virtual communities, one political effect of increased flows of free information through multiple channels is already clear: States have lost much of their control over information about their own societies. States that seek to develop need foreign capital and the technology and organization that go with it. Geographical communities still matter most, but governments that want to see rapid development will have to give up some of the barriers to information flows that protected officials from outside scrutiny. No longer will governments that want high levels of development be able to afford the comfort of shielding their domestic affairs from prying eyes and foreign influences. For decades, Myanmar tried and has all but given up. North Korea still tries, but is having a harder and harder time.

Constructivists provide a more radical perspective on whether the information revolution is transforming world politics. Some even see the beginnings of the end of the Westphalian state system. Heidi Toffler and Alvin Toffler as well as Peter Drucker argue that the information revolution is bringing an end to the hierarchical bureaucratic organizations that typified the age of the industrial revolution.[7] In civil societies, as decentralized organizations and virtual communities develop on the Internet, they cut across territorial jurisdictions and develop their own patterns of governance.

If these prophets are correct, the result would be a new cyberfeudalism, with overlapping communities and jurisdictions laying claim to multiple layers of citizens' identities and loyalties. In short, these transformations suggest the reversal of the modern centralized state that has dominated world politics for more than 350 years. Instead of "international" politics, we may have a broader "world politics." A medieval European might have owed equal loyalty to a local lord, a duke, a king, and the pope. A future European might owe loyalty to Brittany, Paris, and Brussels, as well as to several cybercommunities concerned with religion, work, and various interests.

Although the international system is still best understood as a system of sovereign states, constructivists argue that we can begin to discern a pattern of cross-cutting communities and governance that resembles the situation before the Peace of Westphalia in 1648. Transnational contacts across political borders were typical in the feudal era, but they were gradually constrained by the rise of centralized states. Now the world is changing. In the 1980s, transnational contact at a distance was growing, but it involved relatively small numbers of elites involved in multinational corporations, scientific groups, and academic institutions. Now the Internet offers a low-cost means of transnational communication to billions of people.

Sovereignty and Control

The issue of sovereignty is hotly contested in world politics today. Many political leaders resist anything that seems to diminish national autonomy. They worry about the political role of the United Nations in limiting the use of force, the economic decisions handed down by the World Trade Organization, and efforts to develop environmental institutions and treaties. Many countries seek more sovereign control over the Internet. In their eyes, the notion of an international or transnational community of opinion is illusory.

But the debate over the fate of the sovereign state has been poorly framed. As the constructivist political scientist John Ruggie puts it, "There is an extraordinarily impoverished mind-set at work here, one that is able to visualize long-term challenges to the system of states only in terms of entities that are institutionally substitutable for the state."[8] A better historical analogy is the development of markets and town life in the early feudal period. Medieval trade fairs were not substitutes for the institutions of feudal authority. They did not tear down the castle walls or remove the local lord. But they did bring new wealth, new coalitions, and new attitudes summarized by the maxim, "Town air brings freedom."

Medieval merchants developed the *Lex Mercatoria* ("Merchant Law") that governed their relations largely as a private set of rules for conducting business. Similarly, today, everyone from hackers to large corporations is developing the code and norms of the Internet partly outside the control of formal political institutions. The development of transnational corporate intranets behind firewalls and encryption represent "private appropriations of a public space."[9] These private systems, such as corporate intranets or worldwide newsgroups devoted to specific issues such as the environment, do not frontally challenge the governments of sovereign states; they simply add a layer of relations that sovereign states do not effectively control. People will participate in transnational Internet communities without ceasing to be loyal citizens, but their perspectives will be different from those of typical loyal citizens before the Internet.

Even in the age of the Internet, the roles of political institutions are likely to change gradually. After the rise of the territorial state, other successors to medieval rule such as the Italian city-states and the Hanseatic League in northern Europe persisted as viable alternatives, able to tax and fight for nearly two centuries. The real issue today is not the continued existence of the sovereign state, but how its centrality and functions are being altered. As Stephen Krasner puts it, "The reach of the state has increased in some areas but contracted in others. Rulers have recognized that their effective control can be enhanced by walking away from some issues they cannot resolve."[10] All countries, including the largest, are facing a growing list of problems that are difficult to control within sovereign boundaries, problems such as financial flows, drug trade, climate change, HIV/AIDS, refugees, terrorism, and cultural intrusions. Complicating the task of national governance is not the same as undermining sovereignty. Governments adapt. In the process of adaptation, however, they change the meaning of sovereign jurisdiction, control, and the role of private actors.

Take, for example, the problems of controlling U.S. borders. Airports, seaports, and land border crossings all pose their own particular challenges. In 2014—at land crossings alone—236 million people, 102 million cars, 11 million trucks, 318,000 buses, and 39,000 trains entered the United States. By some estimates, half a million undocumented migrants simply walk, ride, or swim across the border from Mexico or Canada each year. As 9/11 illustrated, terrorists can easily slip across borders, and it is easier to bring in a few pounds of a deadly biological or chemical agent than to smuggle in the tons of illegal heroin and cocaine that arrive annually. The best ways for the Department of Homeland Security to cope with such flows are to expand intelligence sharing with and cooperation inside the jurisdiction of other states and to rely on private corporations to develop transparent systems for tracking international commercial flows so that enforcement officials can conduct "virtual" audits of inbound shipments before they arrive. Today, customs officers are working throughout Latin America to help businesses implement security programs that reduce the risk of being exploited by drug smugglers, and cooperative international mechanisms are being developed for policing trade flows. The sovereign state adapts, but in doing so, it transforms the meaning and exclusivity of governmental jurisdiction. Legal borders do not change, but they blur in practice.

National security—the absence of threat to major values—is another example. Damage done by climate change or imported viruses can be larger in terms of money or lives lost than the effects of some wars. But even if one restricts the definition of national security more narrowly to organized violence, the nature of military security is changing. No foreign army has invaded the United States in more than 200 years, and the U.S. military is designed to project force and fight wars far from our shores. But the U.S. military was not well equipped to protect against an attack on the homeland by terrorists using civilian aircraft as weapons. In absolute numbers, the United States suffered more casualties from the transnational terrorist attacks on 9/11 than from the Japanese attack on Pearl Harbor in 1941 (although, in proportion to the total population of the United States, Pearl Harbor was almost twice as deadly). Today, attackers may be states, nonstate groups, individuals, or some combination. The al-Qaeda network that attacked the United States on 9/11 involved individuals and groups from many countries and is alleged to have had cells in as many as 50 (including the United States). Some aggressors, though, may be anonymous and may not even come near the targeted country. Cyberattacks, as we will see below, can pose a real transnational threat to security. Hence, nuclear deterrence, border patrols, and stationing troops overseas to shape regional power balances will continue to matter in the information age, but they will not be sufficient to ensure national security.

Competing interpretations of sovereignty arise even in the domain of law. As we saw in Chapter 6, Article 2.7 of the UN Charter says that nothing shall authorize the United Nations to intervene in matters within domestic jurisdiction.

But as we saw in our earlier discussion of the Responsibility to Protect (R2P; see Chapter 6), there has been a trend, although not monotonic, toward understanding nonintervention as a privilege states must earn through good behavior rather than as a right to which they are absolutely entitled. Thus evolving global norms of antiracism and repugnance at the South African practice of apartheid led a large majority at the United Nations to abridge the principle of nonintervention. In 2011, the UN Security Council authorized military intervention in the Libyan civil war on the basis of the doctrine of the R2P, even though the United Nations failed to authorize the intervention by the North Atlantic Treaty Organization (NATO) in Kosovo in 1999 under what were, in fact, very similar circumstances (and has not even tried to authorize intervention in the ongoing Syrian civil war). From the very beginning, the UN Charter enshrined principles of human rights as well as provisions that protect the sovereignty of states, but the former are gaining at the expense of the latter. And new actors are projecting themselves into these debates. In 1998, General Augusto Pinochet was detained in Britain in response to a Spanish magistrate's request for extradition based on human rights violations and crimes committed while he was president of Chile. Britain ultimately denied the request, but on narrow legal grounds, not by invoking British or Chilean sovereignty.

Information technology, particularly the Internet, has eased the tasks of coordination and strengthened the hands of human rights activists. But political leaders, particularly in formerly colonized countries, cling to the protections legal sovereignty provides against outside interventions. Tensions between the principle of state sovereignty and emerging human rights norms are likely to coexist for many years to come.

For many people, the state provides an important source of political identity. People are capable of multiple cross-cutting identities—family, village, ethnic, religious, national, cosmopolitan—and which one predominates often depends on the context. In many preindustrial countries, subnational identities at the tribe or clan level prevail. In some postindustrial countries, including the United States and the countries of Europe, cosmopolitan identities such as "global citizen" or "custodian of planet Earth" are beginning to emerge. It is still too early to understand the full effects of the Internet, but the shaping of identities can move in contradictory directions at the same time—up to Brussels, down to Brittany, or fixed on Paris—as circumstances dictate.

A fascinating use of the Internet to wield soft power can be found in the politics of diaspora communities. In the words of communications expert David Bollier, "The Internet has been a godsend to such populations, because it enables large numbers of geographically isolated people with a shared history to organize into large virtual communities."[11] The Internet enables them to present attractive alternative ideas to those back home. Internet connections between foreign nationals and local citizens helped spark protests in Beijing against anti-Chinese riots taking place in Indonesia in 1998. The frustration of ethnic Chinese living in Indonesia was transferred to Beijing with remarkable speed. Similarly, in Zimbabwe in 2008 and in Iran in 2009, the Internet was crucial in spreading news about government manipulation during disputed elections. At the same time, although cell phones and social media helped bring repression and violation of human rights to the world's attention, they did not alone lead to a change of government.

The Internet has also allowed protests to be quickly mobilized by freewheeling amorphous groups rather than hierarchical organizations. In the Vietnam War era, planning a protest required weeks and months of pamphlets, posters, and phone calls, and it took four years before the size of rallies reached half a million people in 1969. In contrast, 800,000 people turned out in the United States and 1.5 million in Europe on one weekend in February 2003 to protest the looming war in Iraq.[12] Protests do not represent the "international community," but they often affect the attitudes of editorial writers, parliamentarians, and other influential people in important countries whose views are summarized by that vague term.[13] The continual contest for legitimacy illustrates the importance of soft power.

The result may be greater volatility rather than consistent movement in any one direction. As Pippa Norris puts it, "The many-to-many and one-to-many characteristics of the Internet . . . seem highly conducive to the irreverent egalitarian, and libertarian character of the cyber-culture."[14] One effect is "flash movements"—sudden surges of protest—triggered by particular issues or events, such as antiglobalization protests, the sudden rise of the anti–fuel tax coalition that captured European politics in the autumn of 2000, or the protests around the world at the start of the 2003 Iraq War.[15] Politics becomes more theatrical and aimed at global audiences. In the mid-1990s, the Zapatista rebels in Mexico's Chiapas province relied less on bullets than on transnational publicity, much of it coordinated on the Internet, to pressure the Mexican government for reforms. In 2004, activists used cell phones to organize peaceful revolutions in the former Soviet states of Georgia and Ukraine.

Perhaps the most spectacular examples of the power of the Internet to mobilize efforts for political change may be found in the recent Arab Awakening uprisings. Unplanned and unforeseen by anyone anywhere, a tidal wave of protest and discontent swept North Africa and the Middle East in 2011. It was triggered by a lone, desperate act on December 17, 2010, of a young street vendor in Tunisia named Mohamed Bouazizi. Frustrated and humiliated by corrupt officials repeatedly harassing him and ultimately confiscating his wares, Bouazizi set himself on fire in protest. Within weeks, mounting public outrage at his mistreatment and pent-up anger at systemic malfeasance and corruption ended the 23-year rule of President Zine El Abidine Ben Ali and inspired similar mass uprisings in Egypt, Yemen, Syria, Bahrain, and Libya. Egypt's longtime strongman Hosni Mubarak fell shortly thereafter, on February 11, 2011. Other besieged secular autocrats tried to hold on to power, either by making small concessions or cracking down with violence (and sometimes both). Hopes of lasting change have been dashed in most cases; the early label "Arab Awakening" now seems grossly inappropriate. But although governments did not topple everywhere, politics nowhere would ever be quite the same.

In what sense was the Arab Awakening a demonstration of the transformative political power of the Internet? Along with satellite television networks such as Al Jazeera, Internet connectivity made it easy for North African and Middle Eastern youths and young adults to see that life prospects were dramatically better for others in their age brackets with similar levels of education elsewhere, such as in Europe and North America. By enabling them to interact with and see how much better were the material lives and opportunities of emigrants in their diaspora communities, or even just their Facebook friends, Internet penetration in the Arab world made it harder and harder for kleptocratic regimes to hide their own sins and underperformance as leaders. In addition, once protests began to break out, social media made it easy to mobilize and coordinate them.

We can use the very same concepts of deep, intermediate, and precipitating causes to explain the Arab Awakening that we used to explain the outbreak of World War I in Chapter 3. Among them are demographic considerations (the enormous proportion of young people in North Africa and the Middle East), economic considerations (massive underemployment, growing inequality, and perceptions of relative deprivation), and political causes (a sense of powerlessness and loss of identification with national leaders, resulting in declining levels of legitimacy). A single Tunisian street vendor provided the precipitating cause, but the information revolution provided a set of crucial intermediate causes. Communications technology and social media enabled an explosion of economic and political disaffection that simply would not have been possible in the 1980s or 1990s.

All that seems clear enough in retrospect, but it is interesting and important to note that no one saw it coming. Most likely, it is simply because our understanding of political dynamics in areas such as North Africa and the Middle East had simply not yet absorbed the implications of the new information revolution. It often takes a shocking failure of foresight to make one notice that one's eyeglass prescription is out of date.

Although the Arab Awakening made clear that the information revolution has fundamentally changed regional political dynamics, there is little evidence yet that it has affected political identities. In every country experiencing upheaval, the dominant political cleavages during and after were the same as the dominant political cleavages before: for example, secular/religious in Egypt, tribal in Libya, and Sunni/Shi'a in Bahrain. But as people more easily identify with members of different kinds of groups, both at home and abroad, connectivity can soften the hard edges of these distinctions. Political scientist James Rosenau has tried to capture this notion by inventing a new word, *fragmegration*, to express the idea that both integration toward larger identities and fragmentation into smaller communities can occur at the same time.[16] But one need not alter the English language to realize that apparently contradictory movements can occur simultaneously. They do not spell the end of the sovereign state, but they do make its politics more volatile and less self-contained within national shells.

The Information Revolution and Complex Interdependence

The information revolution has not equalized power among states. Thus far, it has had the opposite effect, and realists might feel vindicated. But what about reducing the role of governments and the power of all states? Here the changes are more along the lines predicted by liberals and constructivists. Complex interdependence is certainly much greater in the dimension of multiple channels of contact between societies.

The explosion of information has produced a "paradox of plenty."[17] Plenty of information leads to scarcity of attention. When people are overwhelmed with the volume of information confronting them, they have difficulty discerning what to focus on. Attention rather than information becomes the scarce resource, and those who can distinguish valuable information from background clutter gain power. Editors and cue givers are in increasingly high demand, and this increasing demand is a source of power for those who can tell us where to focus our attention. Brand names and the ability to bestow an international seal of approval will become increasingly more important in the future.

In addition, the public has become more wary and sensitized about propaganda. Propaganda as a form of free information is not new. Adolf Hitler and Josef Stalin used it effectively in the 1930s. Slobodan Milošević's control of television was crucial to his power in Serbia in the 1990s. Credibility is the crucial resource and an important source of soft power. Reputation becomes even more important than in the past, and political struggles occur over the creation and destruction of credibility. Governments compete for credibility not only with other governments, but with a broad range of alternatives, including news media, corporations, NGOs, intergovernmental organizations, and networks of scientific communities.

Politics has become a contest of competitive credibility. Narratives are more important than ever before. The world of traditional power politics is typically about whose military or economy wins, but in an information age, it is increasingly important whose story wins. Governments compete with one another and with other organizations to enhance their own credibility and weaken that of their opponents.

Witness the struggle between Serbia and NATO to frame the interpretation of events in Kosovo in 1999 and the events in Serbia a year later. Prior to the demonstrations that led to the October 2000 overthrow of Milošević, 45 percent of Serb adults were tuned to Radio Free Europe and the Voice of America radio broadcasts. In contrast, only 31 percent listened to the state-controlled radio station, Radio Belgrade.[18] Moreover, the domestic alternative radio station, B92, provided access to Western news, and when the government tried to shut it down, the station continued to provide such news on the Internet. In another example, in both the 2006 war between Israel and the nonstate actor Hezbollah and the 2014 war between Israel and the nonstate actor Hamas, Israel enjoyed military superiority but lost the propaganda war because of the extensive media coverage of the civilian casualties and destruction of property caused by Israeli air strikes.

Information that appears to be purely propaganda may not only be scorned, but it may also turn out to be counterproductive if it undermines a country's reputation for credibility. In 2003, exaggerated claims about Hussein's weapons of mass destruction (WMDs) and ties to al-Qaeda may have helped mobilize domestic support for the Iraq War, but polls showed that the subsequent disclosure of the exaggeration dealt a costly blow to British and U.S. credibility. Under the new conditions more than ever, a soft sell may prove more effective than a hard sell.

The Iraq example illustrates that power does not necessarily flow to those who can withhold information. Under some circumstances, private information can cripple the credibility of those who have it. As the Nobel Prize–winning economist George Ackerlof has pointed out, sellers of used cars have more knowledge about their defects than potential buyers. Moreover, owners of bad cars are more likely to sell than owners of good ones.[19] These facts lead potential buyers to discount the price that they are willing to pay to adjust for unknown defects. Hence, the result of the superior information of sellers is not to improve the average price they receive, but instead to make them unable to sell good used cars for their real value. Unlike asymmetrical interdependence in trade, in which power goes to those who can afford to hold back or break trade ties, information power flows to those who can edit and credibly validate information to sort out what is both correct and important.

One implication of the abundance of free information sources, and the role of credibility, is that soft power is likely to become less a function simply of material resources than in the past. When the ability to produce and disseminate information is the scarce resource, limiting factors include the control of printing presses, radio stations, and newsprint. Hard power—for instance, using force to take over the radio station—can generate soft power. In the case of worldwide television, wealth can also lead to soft power. For instance, CNN was based in Atlanta rather than Amman or Cairo because of the United States' leading position in the industry and in technology. When Iraq invaded Kuwait in 1990, that CNN was basically a U.S. company helped frame the issue worldwide as aggression (analogous to Hitler's actions in the 1930s) rather than as a justified attempt to reverse colonial humiliation (analogous to India's widely accepted "liberation" of the Portuguese colony of Goa in the 1960s). But by 2003, the rise of cable networks in the region, such as Al Jazeera and Al Arabiya, undercut the U.S. monopoly and provided a local framing of the issues involved in the Iraq War. In an information age, the occupation of Iraq and its coverage were very costly for U.S. soft power.

The close connection between hard power and soft power is likely to be somewhat weakened under conditions of complex interdependence in an information age. The power of broadcasting persists, but it will be increasingly supplemented by the Internet with its multiple channels of communication controlled by multiple actors who cannot use force to control one another. Conflicts will be affected not only by which actors own television networks, radio stations, and websites, but also by who pays attention to which fountains of information and misinformation.

Broadcasting is a type of information dissemination that has long had an effect on public opinion. By focusing on some conflicts and human rights problems, broadcasters have pressed politicians to respond to some foreign conflicts rather than others, such as Somalia rather than southern Sudan in the 1990s. Not surprisingly, governments have sought to influence, manipulate, or control television and radio stations and have been able to do so with considerable success, mainly because a relatively small number of physically located broadcasting sites were used to reach many people with the same message. The shift from broadcasting to "narrowcasting" has major political implications, however. Cable television and the Internet enable senders to segment and target audiences. Even more important for politics is the interactive role of the Internet; it not only focuses attention, but also facilitates coordination of action across borders. YouTube videos can affect how political issues are perceived and framed. Interactivity at low cost allows for the development of new virtual communities: people who imagine themselves as part of a single group regardless of how far apart they are physically from one another. Transnational communications have made borders more porous.

"Man Bites Dog"

Defense Secretary Robert M. Gates called Monday for the United States government to commit more money and effort to "soft power" tools, including diplomacy, economic assistance, and communications, because the military alone cannot defend America's interests around the world. . . . Mr. Gates joked that having a sitting secretary of defense travel halfway across the country to make a pitch to increase the budget of other agencies might fit into the category of "man bites dog."

—New York Times, *November 27, 2007*[20]

Follow Up

- Ronald J. Deibert, *Parchment, Printing, and Hypermedia: Communication in World Order Transformation* (New York: Columbia University Press, 1997).

- Elizabeth C. Hanson, *The Information Revolution and World Politics* (Lanham, MD: Rowman & Littlefield, 2008).

Transnational Actors

9.2 Explain how transnational actors affect interstate politics.

As noted above, a characteristic of the global information age is the increased role of *transnational actors*, nonstate entities acting across international borders. Traditional international politics is discussed in terms of states. We use shorthand expressions such as "Germany wanted Alsace" or "France feared Britain." That shorthand is a useful simplification, especially in the classical period of international politics. In the eighteenth century, the monarch spoke for the state. If Frederick the Great wanted something for Prussia, Frederick was Prussia. In the nineteenth century, a broader elite class controlled foreign policy decisions, but even on the eve of World War I, European diplomacy was a relatively narrowly held, cabinet-level affair. In addition, in the classical period of international politics, the agenda was more limited. Military security issues dominated, and they were handled primarily by the foreign office or its equivalent.

Qualitatively, transnational actors have played a role for centuries, but the quantitative shift in the last half of the twentieth century marks a significant change in the international system. In a world of global interdependence, the agenda of international politics is broader than it was, and everyone seems to want to get into the act. In the United States, for example, almost every domestic agency has some international role. The Department of Agriculture is interested in international food issues, the Environmental Protection Agency is interested in acid rain and climate change, the Coast Guard is interested in ocean dumping, the Department of Commerce is interested in trade, and the Treasury Department is interested in exchange rates. The State Department does not control all these issues. Every bureau of the U.S. government has its own little foreign ministry. In fact, if we look at the representation of the United States abroad, only a minority of the Americans in most embassies are from the State Department.

In complex interdependence, societies interact at many points. There is too much traffic for one intersection or for one police officer at one intersection. These interactions across state borders outside the central control of the foreign policy organs are called *transnational relations*. They include but are not limited to migration of populations, the rapid transfer of capital from one country to another that occurs daily in the world stock and money markets, illicit trafficking in weapons and drugs, and certain forms of terrorism. Governments can try to control these activities—and in the case of terrorism or smuggling, they need to—but control often comes at a very high price. For example, the Soviet Union closely controlled transnational relations, and the Soviet economy suffered gravely for it. In circumstances with high degrees of interdependence and a large number of transnational actors, we can be led astray by the shorthand that was so useful in the classical period. We say things like "Japan agreed to import more" or "The United States opposed broad claims to the continental shelf under the ocean," but looking more carefully, we notice that Japanese firms

Power and the Information Revolution: From the Invention of Writing to the Arab Awakening

9.1 Describe the distinctive features of the modern information revolution and their effects on interstate politics.

An information revolution is currently transforming world politics. Four centuries ago, the English statesman-philosopher Francis Bacon wrote that knowledge is power. In the twenty-first century, a much larger portion of the population both within and among countries has access to this power. Governments have always worried about the flow and control of information, and the current period is not the first to be strongly affected by changes in information technology. In the fifteenth century, Johann Gutenberg's (1398–1468) invention of movable type, which allowed printing of the Bible and made it accessible to large portions of the European population, is often credited with playing a major role in the onset of the Reformation. Pamphlets and committees of correspondence paved the way for the American Revolution. As constructivists point out, rapid changes in information flows can lead to important changes in identities and interests.

The current information revolution is based on rapid technological advances in computers, communications, and software that in turn have led to dramatic decreases in the cost of processing and transmitting information. Computing power has doubled every two years since the invention of the integrated circuit in 1958, and by the beginning of the twenty-first century, it cost one-thousandth of what it did in the early 1970s. If the price of automobiles had fallen as quickly as the price of semiconductors, a car today would cost less than $5.

In 1993, there were about 50 websites in the world; in September 2014, there were more than 1 billion. Between 2000 and 2014, global Internet usage grew by more than 700 percent, with Africa and the Middle East experiencing some of the largest gains. Communications bandwidths are expanding rapidly, and communications costs continue to fall even more rapidly than computing power. As late as 1980, phone calls over copper wire could carry only one page of information per second; today, a thin strand of optical fiber can transmit 90,000 *volumes* in a second. In terms of current dollars, the cost of a brief transatlantic phone call had fallen from $250 in 1930 to considerably less than $1 at the beginning of the new century. Now with Voice over Internet Protocol (VoIP), it can be virtually free. Webcams allow people to have personal video conferences from the comfort of their home office. In 1980, a gigabyte of storage occupied a room; now an iPod Touch that fits in your shirt pocket comes with up to 64 gigabytes of storage.

The key characteristic of the information revolution is not the *speed* of communications between the wealthy and powerful: Since the late 1800s, virtually instantaneous communication has been possible, at least between Europe and North America, via telephones. The two crucial changes are an enormous acted transnationally to export more or that some U.S. citizens lobbied internationally to promote a broad definition of the continental shelf at the same time that the U.S. Navy sought the opposite.

This complexity of interests has always existed, but it is greater in economic and social issues than in the traditional military security issues. Security issues are often more collectively shared. The survival of a people as a whole is obviously a collective good. Social and economic issues are often less broadly shared; there are more differences of interest. Thus, with the rise of economic interdependence and the rise of economic issues on the agenda of international politics, we find that our traditional shorthand less adequately describes the political process.

A useful illustration is the case of oil, which we examined in Chapter 8. Consumer countries wanted low prices and the producer countries wanted high prices in 1973. But the politics was a lot more complex than that. Producing interests inside the consumer countries wanted high oil prices. Small Texas oil producers were not at all unhappy that the Organization of Petroleum Exporting Countries raised oil prices because they had the same economic interests as the Arabs, not as the consumers freezing in New England. Producers of nuclear energy were not unhappy to see oil prices rise because that might help nuclear energy become a more competitive energy source. Those affected by the declining coal industry in Europe and unemployed coal miners were not unhappy about the rise of oil prices either. Neither were ecologists who believed that higher prices would curtail consumption and pollution (until they realized that coal consumption would increase!). So inside the consumer countries there were enormous differences in the interests over oil prices. In a situation of interdependence, politics looks different if we lift the veil of national interest and national security. One of the reasons consumer countries did not use more extreme measures such as force during the oil crisis was that the sensitivity interdependence that led to high energy prices was regarded as good by important political actors inside the consumer countries. There was a de facto transnational coalition that was not unhappy with higher oil prices.

Of course, the existence of contradictory interests inside states is not new. In the United States in the nineteenth century, politics was marked by differences over tariffs between southern farmers and northern industrialists. When President George W. Bush raised tariffs on steel in 2002, he pleased companies and unions that produce steel, but hurt those companies, such as car manufacturers, who use it. As we saw in Chapter 2, domestic politics has always been important to foreign policy, but with the expansion of participation in domestic politics, it becomes more so. Moreover, as some of those domestic interests develop the capability to communicate and interact directly with other interests in other countries, they develop a different type of world politics.

Two forms of world politics are illustrated by Figure 9.1. The traditional form of international politics is represented on the left. If people in Society 1 want to put pressure on Government 2, they ask Government 1 (through regular domestic

Figure 9.1 Traditional versus Transnational World Politics

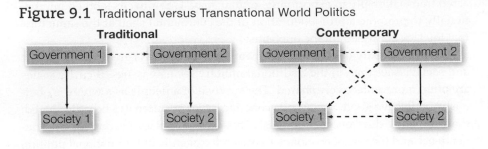

politics, the vertical line) to talk to Government 2 (through regular intergovernmental politics, the horizontal line). But in transnational relations, shown in the right-hand diagram, people in Society 1 put pressure on Government 2 directly or may put pressure on people in Society 2 directly. The transnational links are the diagonal lines and the lower horizontal line in the right-hand diagram, which represent direct contacts across borders between individuals or NGOs. (Not shown in Figure 9.1 are the increasingly diverse and important direct connections between subunits of different governments, called *transgovernmental relations*. Sometimes, departments or ministries have warmer ties with their foreign counterparts than either of them has with their own political leaders. This phenomenon was illustrated in the Cuban missile crisis when the U.S. and Canadian militaries cooperated seamlessly despite tensions between the White House and the Pentagon on the one hand and between the Canadian Armed Forces and 24 Sussex Drive on the other.)[21]

When we talk about the politics of interdependence, we must not assume that everything is captured by the traditional model of government-to-government relations. One of the distinguishing characteristics of complex interdependence is the significance of other actors in addition to the states. The traditional shorthand is not wrong; it remains the best first approximation even for the politics of interdependence. States usually are the major actors. But "global civil society" actors are increasingly important. As constructivists remind us, when you have said that states are the major actors, you have not said everything that is important to know about the politics and conflicts of interdependence.

Nongovernmental Organizations

Private organizations also increasingly cross national boundaries (Figure 9.2). Transnational religious organizations opposed to slavery date back to 1775, and the nineteenth century saw the founding of the Socialist International, the Red Cross, peace movements, women's suffrage organizations, and the International Law Association, among others. Before World War I, there were 176 *international nongovernmental organizations* (sometimes called INGOs, although for our purposes, because we are interested only in NGOs that operate across borders, the more common designation NGO will suffice). In 1956, there were nearly 1,000 NGOs; in 1970, nearly 2,000. There are more than 38,000 active NGOs today. There even meta-NGOs—NGO NGOs, in other words!—such as the Union of International Associations and the World Association of NGOs.

The numbers do not tell the full story, because they represent only formally constituted organizations. Many NGOs claim to act as a "global conscience" representing broad public interests beyond the purview of individual states or interests that states are wont to ignore. Although they are not democratically

---

Figure 9.2 Overview of Select Nongovernmental Organizations (NGOs)

Human Rights Watch
Website: http://www.hrw.org
Founded: 1978
Headquarters: New York
Budget: $87.6 million USD (total support and revenue, 2014)
- Largest U.S.-based human rights organization
- Shames human rights offenders by documenting human rights abuses in more than 80 countries, generating media attention regarding abuses and lobbying governments and institutions to pressure offending governments diplomatically
- Was part of a coalition for groups and individuals that won the Nobel Peace Prize in 1997 for work related to the Campaign to Ban Landmines

International Crisis Group
Website: http://www.crisisgroup.org
Founded: 1995
Headquarters: Brussels
Budget: $21.9 million USD (total expenses, 2013)
- Analyzes countries "at risk of outbreak, escalation or recurrence of violent conflict" and offers policy recommendations, targeted to policy makers, regarding ways to reduce tensions and resolve specific conflicts
- Board includes influential figures from politics, diplomacy, business, and media who help shape the group's operations and lobby for implementation of its policy recommendations

Amnesty International
Website: http://www.amnesty.org
Founded: 1961
Headquarters: London
Budget: £53.4 million GBP (approx. $81.5 million USD, 2013)
- Mobilizes a network of more than 3 million members, supporters, and activists in more than 150 countries to help prevent and end "grave abuses of the rights to physical and mental integrity, freedom of conscience and expression, and freedom from discrimination" and promote human rights

Doctors Without Borders (Médecins Sans Frontières)
Website: http://www.msf.org
Founded: 1971
Headquarters: Geneva
Budget: $282.7 million USD (Total expenses, 2014)
- International humanitarian aid organization assisting more than 70 countries
- Assistance provided to "populations in distress, to victims of natural or man-made disasters and to victims of armed conflict, without discrimination and irrespective of race, religion, creed or political affiliation"

(continued)

Figure 9.2 (*continued*)

Bill and Melinda Gates Foundation
Website: http://www.gatesfoundation.org
Founded: 2000
Headquarters: Seattle
Budget: $3.6 billion USD (total direct grantee support, 2013)

- Founded by Microsoft founder Bill Gates and his wife, Melinda
- Works to "promote greater equity in four areas: global health, education, public libraries, and support for at-risk families"

Oxfam International
Website: http://www.oxfam.org
Founded: 1942
Headquarters: Oxford, UK
Budget: €631 million EUR (approx. $700 million USD, program expenditure, 2014)

- A confederation of "13 organizations working together to find lasting solutions to poverty and injustice"

International Committee of the Red Cross (ICRC)
Website: http://www.icrc.org
Founded: 1863
Headquarters: Geneva
Budget: 1.6 billion CHF (approx. $1.7 billion USD, 2015)

- Tasked by the Geneva Convention with responsibility for "visiting prisoners, organizing relief operations, re-uniting separated families and similar humanitarian activities during armed conflicts"
- An "impartial, neutral and independent organization whose exclusively humanitarian mission is to protect the lives and dignity of victims of war and internal violence and to provide them with assistance"

Greenpeace International
Website: http://www.greenpeace.org
Founded: 1971
Headquarters: Amsterdam
Budget: €75.6 million EUR (approx. $84 million USD)

- 2.9 million supporters in more than 40 countries
- Supports efforts against climate change, degradation of land and oceans, whaling, and genetic engineering as well as efforts to preserve ancient forests, eliminate toxic chemicals, and encourage sustainable trade

---

elected, they sometimes help develop new norms by directly pressing governments and business leaders to change policies and indirectly by altering public perceptions of what governments and firms should be doing. In terms of power resources, these new groups rarely possess much hard power, but the information revolution has greatly enhanced their soft power.

Governments now have to share the stage with actors who can use information to enhance their soft power and press governments directly or indirectly by mobilizing their publics. Given the power of credible editors and cue givers who can cut through the avalanche of available information in the Internet age, a rough way to gauge the increasing importance of transnational organizations is to look at the number of mentions these organizations receive in mainstream media publications. By this measure, the biggest NGOs have become established players in the battle for the attention of influential editors. For example, after Human Rights Watch released its "2003 World Report," which included strong criticism of the U.S. government for its conduct in the war on terrorism, articles appeared in 288 newspapers and magazines over the next ten days mentioning the organization.[22]

News coverage has reflected the growth of this general sector. The term *nongovernmental organization* or *NGO* appeared 70 times in English-language newspapers in July 1991, 576 times in July 2001, and 4,371 times in July 2011, an increase of 62 times in 20 years. In addition to Human Rights Watch, other NGOs, such as Amnesty International, the International Red Cross, Greenpeace, Doctors Without Borders (*Médecins Sans Frontières*), and Transparency International, have undergone exponential growth in terms of mainstream media mentions. As the information revolution has lowered the costs of global communication, the barriers to entry into world politics have been lowered.

Not only is there a great increase in the number of transnational and governmental contacts, but there has also been a change in type. Earlier transnational flows were heavily controlled by large bureaucratic organizations such as multinational corporations or the Roman Catholic Church that could profit from economies of scale. Such organizations remain important, but the lower costs of communication in the Internet era have opened the field to loosely structured network organizations with a small headquarters staff and even to individuals. These NGOs and networks are particularly effective in penetrating states without regard to borders. Because they often involve citizens who are well placed in the domestic politics of several countries, they are able to focus the attention of the media and governments on their preferred issues. The treaty banning landmines, as mentioned above, was the result of an interesting mixed coalition of Internet-based organizations working with middle-power governments such as Canada and some individual politicians and celebrities such as the late Diana, princess of Wales. On global poverty issues, rock stars, NGOs, and political leaders worked together to press for debt relief for heavily indebted poor countries.

Environmental issues are another example. NGOs have played an important role at every major climate change conference since Kyoto in 1997, either acting as channels of communication between official delegations, as agenda setters, or as mobilizers of public pressure. For example, former U.S. vice president Al Gore's Live Earth coalition organized concerts over a period of 24 hours in eight major cities across the world in 2007. This event brought together a global audience to try to persuade governments to take action against climate change.

Geographical communities and sovereign states will continue to play the main role in world politics for a long time to come, but they will be less self-contained and more porous than in the past. They will have to share the stage with actors who can use information to enhance their soft power and press governments directly or indirectly by mobilizing their publics. Governments that want to see rapid development will find that they have to give up some of the barriers to information flow that historically protected officials from outside scrutiny. As we noted above, no longer will governments that want high levels of development be able to afford the comfort of keeping their financial and political situations inside a black box, as Myanmar and North Korea have done. That form of sovereignty proves too expensive. Even large countries with hard power, such as the United States, find themselves sharing the stage with new actors and having more trouble controlling their borders. Cyberspace will not replace geographical space and will not abolish state sovereignty, but like the town markets in feudal times, it will coexist and greatly complicate what it means to be a sovereign state or a powerful country.

The New Global Actors

It is almost as if the world has arrived at a sort of neomedievalism in which the institutions and sources of authority are multifarious. Just as the leaders of the Knights Templar or the Franciscan order outranked all but the most powerful of princes, so too the secretary general of Amnesty International and the chief executive officer of Royal Dutch Shell cast far longer shadows on the international stage than do leaders of Moldova, Namibia, or Nauru. The state may not be quite ready to wither away, but it's not what it used to be.

—*Peter J. Spiro*[23]

Transnational Terrorism and the "War on Terror"

Not all transnational actors are benign. Drug cartels, human smuggling rings, and cyberspace crime syndicates are all cases in point. For such groups, the information revolution has opened up new opportunities for action over longer distances than ever before. Terrorist groups, however, have captured the public's imagination as particularly dangerous transnational actors. When in the wake of 9/11 President George W. Bush proclaimed a "war on terror" in his speech to a joint session of Congress (on September 20, 2001), he signaled a fundamental change in U.S. foreign policy that would have far-reaching implications for the world as a whole.[24]

The terrorist attacks of 9/11 took the lives of 2,974 innocent citizens from more than 90 countries, not counting the 19 hijackers. Horrific video of the second plane to hit the World Trade Center circulated the globe almost instantly, generating a massive outpouring of shock, anger, grief, and sympathy for the United States almost everywhere in the world. One thing that made the attacks so horrifying was that they were so low-tech. Armed only with box cutters available at any hardware store, the hijacker terrorists managed to avoid detection and turn civilian airliners into weapons. The ease with which they did so made it seem likely to be repeated.

Kenneth Waltz's first image, the individual level of analysis, helps us understand why 9/11 had such a profound effect on the American psyche and hence on U.S. policy.[25] As psychologist Daniel Gilbert explains, human beings are hard-wired to be particularly sensitive to threats that are intended by others, that trigger moral outrage, that seem clear and present, and that catch us by surprise. Terrorism is like theater, and terrorists rely on the dramatic effect of their actions to magnify the action. Thus a terrorist group such as the Islamic State of Iraq and the Levant (ISIL) posts videos of beheading captives online. As Gilbert notes, global warming will almost certainly kill many times as many people as terrorism and will probably also cause much more damage to U.S. property, but it will do so anonymously, unintentionally, and gradually.[26] Thus we have a war on terror, but not a war on climate change.

How serious a threat to world order is transnational terrorism? The answer depends on the angle one takes and the time scale one considers. If one is primarily concerned with transnational terrorism as a cause of premature death, it is not, at present, a serious global problem. Globally, transnational terrorist attacks peaked in the 1990s.[27] Not counting 9/11 and insurgent attacks against foreign targets in Afghanistan and Iraq—made possible precisely because the war on terror placed foreigners in vulnerable positions there—transnational terrorism has killed fewer than 5,000 people per year globally since the start of the twenty-first century. Terrorist attacks take place at a rate far less than once per day. As a cause of premature death transnational terrorism is well down the list, behind such things as unsafe drinking water, infectious disease, traffic accidents, tobacco, allergic reactions, and obesity.

Of the total amount of transnational terrorism in the world, groups such as al-Qaeda and ISIL represent only a part. Drug cartels and paramilitaries in Latin America account for dramatically more. Al-Qaeda's operational tempo, not including Afghanistan and Iraq, has historically been roughly two attacks per year. Aside from 9/11, the average al-Qaeda attack has killed approximately 50 people. Although reliable information about counterterrorist operations is hard to come by—governments do not like to release information that might compromise future operations—it is clear that many al-Qaeda attacks are prevented by timely interdiction. Others fail because of incompetence or unprofessionalism. Al-Qaeda's attack on the USS *Cole* was actually its second attempt on a U.S. warship in the Yemeni port of Aden: The first failed when terrorists overloaded their boat with so many explosives that it sank when they attempted to launch it. U.S. authorities captured the so-called millennium bomber, Ahmed Ressam, when he lost his nerve in his plans to bomb Los Angeles International Airport and attempted to flee upon being questioned at his port of entry in Washington state. Al-Qaeda's first attack on the World Trade Center in 1993—a truck bombing of the underground parking garage—was partially successful in the sense that it managed to kill six and wound 1,400, but it failed in its goal of toppling the towers, and the terrorists involved in the attack were caught when they foolishly returned to the rental agency in New Jersey to get their deposit back without the truck. ISIL has proven to be more efficient and more deadly than al-Qaeda, but it has two crucial advantages: It operates almost entirely in territory that it controls, and many of its members are trained soldiers who used to serve in national armies, such as that of Iraq. It is certainly much easier to conduct military-style operations when you have internal lines of communication than it is to try to project terror over long distances by infiltrating operatives or relying on lone wolves with virtually no supporting infrastructure. ISIL is not unique in this regard. Al-Shabaab in Somalia, Boko Haram in Nigeria, and al-Qaeda in the Islamic Maghreb in North Africa have been at their deadliest and most terrifying when operating as proto-state insurgencies and least effective when attempting to mount distant transnational terror attacks.

Although transnational terrorists succeed in causing a relatively low level of death and destruction today, they could cause calamitous levels of death and destruction if they managed to acquire, transport, and detonate WMDs. It is for this reason that Western governments take counterterrorism so seriously, and rightly so, yet even if al-Qaeda or some other transnational terrorist group managed to get its hands on a nuclear, chemical, or biological weapon, it would not pose an existential threat to a modern developed state. During the latter half of the Cold War, the Soviet Union had the capacity to destroy the United States as a functioning society within half an hour of deciding to do so. The most al-Qaeda could do is wreak havoc within a U.S. city in an area of perhaps a few miles' radius. There are many reasons for this conclusion. First, the organizational characteristics required for a successful transnational terrorist operation are very different from the organizational characteristics needed to mount an existential threat. Terrorist groups must operate under the radar, which requires small groups of loosely connected operatives with minimal financial requirements and minimal communications needs. To acquire, transport, and detonate a weapon of mass destruction requires a significant number of well-resourced people, a sophisticated security team, and the ability to design around or thwart the detection and interdiction capabilities of modern sovereign states. Such things are expensive and require a great deal of technical expertise. Al-Qaeda's annual operations budget is probably not more than about $30 million, or less than five one-hundredths of 1 percent of the U.S. defense budget. In addition to face-to-face meetings, terrorists operate through a communications infrastructure (cell phone, radio, and Internet) that can relatively easily be monitored by national intelligence communities, making it harder to avoid being thwarted or caught.

What al-Qaeda can do, however, is destroy the character of American democracy, tie down its hard-power assets, and erode its soft-power attractiveness. Terrorism is like the sport of jiu jitsu, in which the small attacker leverages the strength of the larger defender against himself. Arguably, al-Qaeda has already accomplished much of that by provoking the United States to overreact to 9/11. Although Operation Enduring Freedom (the use of air power and special forces to topple the Taliban regime and destroy al-Qaeda's infrastructure in Afghanistan) enjoyed a UN mandate and broad-based international support, Operation Iraqi Freedom—the 2003 invasion and occupation of Iraq—did not. The 2002 National Security Strategy of the United States, which proclaimed a right and intention to wage preventive war to deal with distant possible future threats (inaccurately called "preemptive" war in the document itself), struck the international community as dangerously unilateral and provocative. Some provisions of the Patriot Act and the creation of the terrorist detention facility at Guantánamo Bay, Cuba, struck many around the world as a retreat from the principles of democracy, individual freedom, and rule of law that represented the United States' most attractive soft-power asset. According to some, in other words, 9/11 was an unusually "successful" terrorist attack not so much because of the death and destruction that it caused, but because of the reaction that it provoked.

All countries have an interest in protecting their citizens and their territory from terrorist attack, as well as an obligation to do so. The United States is no exception. But the most effective way of combating transnational terrorism is through steady, painstaking security and intelligence work, conducted in collaboration with friends and allies, combined with policies designed to starve terrorist groups of recruits and cut off their access to the material and financial resources necessary to mount deadly attacks. Although military operations in Iraq and Afghanistan have attracted the bulk of the world's attention, the behind-the-scenes conduct of the war on terror has, in fact, been relatively successful. President Barack Obama's decision in August 2009 to drop "war on terror" was not a declaration of victory, but an acknowledgment that emphasizing the muscular, visible, and militarized dimensions of counterterrorism policy has been somewhat counterproductive. As many critics have long noted, one cannot wage war on a noun; one can only ever hunt down and thwart terrorists.

The great danger is that al-Qaeda or an affiliate group will get its hands on a "loose nuke" and manage to detonate it somewhere. Accordingly, the United States has spent millions of dollars to help ensure that the former Soviet Union's nuclear weapons are properly accounted for and securely stored. Also of particular concern is Pakistan, the one nuclear power whose military and intelligence communities harbor radical Islamic sympathizers. It is no wonder that Pakistan has consistently been one of the largest recipients of U.S. financial and technical assistance. But Pakistan is, at best, a half-hearted ally, and U.S. attempts to thwart Islamic terrorism in the region have on more than one occasion threatened to undermine this important strategic relationship. For example, U.S. attempts to kill known or suspected Taliban or al-Qaeda leaders on Pakistani soil by means of remotely controlled unmanned Predator drones that sometimes kill civilians have been a major point of contention for years. In January 2011, the killing of two Pakistanis in Lahore by Raymond Davis, an agent of the Central Intelligence Agency with diplomatic accreditation (and hence diplomatic immunity), triggered a national uproar. But by far the most serious strain on the U.S.-Pakistani strategic relationship was Operation Neptune Spear, the U.S. special forces mission on May 2, 2011, that resulted in the killing of Osama bin Laden in his compound in Abbottabad, where he had been living for years just blocks away from the Pakistan Military Academy. Outraged by Washington's lack of prior consultation and its violation of Pakistani airspace and sovereignty, and embarrassed also by the failure of its own military to detect the operation, the government of Pakistan condemned U.S. high-handedness and throttled back its cooperation in U.S. antiterror operations. U.S. officials were equally outraged by, and unusually blunt about, what they inferred must have been Pakistani complicity in bin Laden's hiding. This delicate relationship, which is important yet frustrating to both sides, illustrates very clearly that sometimes the hardest part of fighting unconventional wars is not engaging and defeating your adversaries, but engaging and managing your allies.

Follow Up

- Peter Mandaville and Terence Lyons, eds., *Politics from Afar: Transnational Diasporas and Networks* (New York: Columbia University Press, 2011).
- Christer Jönsson and Jonas Tallberg, eds., *Transnational Actors in Global Governance: Patterns, Explanations, and Implications* (New York: Palgrave Macmillan, 2010).

Conclusions

9.3 Identify four likely future effects of the information revolution and the rise of transnational actors.

Although we are at such an early stage of the information revolution, the discussion in this chapter suggests four tentative conclusions that may help us understand how recent developments will influence global conflict and cooperation in the future. First, realists are correct to challenge predictions that the information and communications revolutions will have an equalizing effect on the distribution of power among states. In part it is because economies of scale and barriers to entry persist with regard to commercial and strategic information, and in part it is because with respect to free information, larger states are often well placed in the competition for credibility. Second, cheap flows of information have created an enormous change in channels of contact across state borders, and this change may have liberalizing effects over time. Nongovernmental actors operating transnationally have much greater opportunities to organize and propagate their views than ever before, sovereign states are more easily penetrated and less like black boxes than in the past, and political leaders will find it more difficult to maintain a coherent ordering of foreign policy issues than they ever have. Third, the information revolution is changing political processes in a way that enables open democratic societies and transnational actors to compete more successfully than authoritarian states for the key power resource of credibility. Finally, soft power is becoming more important in relation to hard power than it was in the past as credibility becomes a key power resource for both governments and NGOs. Although the coherence of government policies may diminish in more pluralistic and penetrated states, those same countries may be better placed in terms of credibility and soft power. In short, geographically based states that realists emphasize will continue to structure politics in an information age, but the constructivists are correct that the processes of world politics within that structure are undergoing profound changes. States remain the most important actors on the stage of world politics, but in an information age, the stage has become more crowded.

Study Questions

1. What is the third industrial revolution? How does it differ from previous industrial revolutions?

2. How are the information revolution and the Internet affecting world politics?

3. Which have been stronger, the centralizing of advances in information technology or the decentralizing effects?

4. What kind of effect has the information revolution had on state sovereignty? What kind of changes in the international system of states and in global governance is it producing?

5. Has the information revolution brought about an equalizing effect in terms of power and wealth among states?

6. What is the "digital divide"? What implications does it have for developing countries in particular?

7. What do realists, liberals, and constructivists see as the main effects of the information revolution?

8. What are transnational actors? Are they likely to gain in importance? What are some examples of the power of transnational actors in the information age?

9. What is the role of large states in the governance of the international economy? What is the role of institutions?

10. What has been the relationship between the information revolution and democracy? Have globalization and the information revolution strengthened civil societies in nondemocratic states? What kind of effect have they had on political participation?

11. How does the information revolution enable terrorism? How does it facilitate counterterrorism? Who has the upper hand in the war on terror, states or transnational terrorist groups?

Notes

1. Gitta Rohling, "Facts and Forecasts: Billions of Things, Trillions of Dollars," *Pictures of the Future* (October 1, 2014), http://www.siemens.com/innovation/en/home/pictures-of-the-future/digitalization-and-software/internet-of-things-facts-and-forecasts.html.

2. Ronald J. Deibert, *Parchment, Printing, and Hypermedia: Communication in World Order Transformation* (New York: Columbia University Press, 1997).

3. Daniel Deudney, *Bounding Power: Republican Security Theory from the Polis to the Global Village* (Princeton, NJ: Princeton University Press, 2007).

4. Daniel Bell, *The Coming of Post-Industrial Society: A Venture in Social Forecasting* (New York: Basic Books, 1999), pp. 94, 97.

5. Pippa Norris, *The Digital Divide: Civic Engagement, Information Poverty, and the Internet Worldwide* (New York: Cambridge University Press, 2001), p. 232.

6. Douglas McGray, "The Silicon Archipelago," *Daedalus* 128:2 (Spring 1999), p. 167.

7. Alvin Toffler and Heidi Toffler, *The Politics of the Third Wave* (Kansas City, MO: Andrews & McMeel, 1995); and Peter Drucker, "The Next Information Revolution," *Forbes*, August 24, 1998, pp. 46–58.

8. John G. Ruggie, "Territoriality and Beyond: Problematizing Modernity in International Relations," *International Organization* 47:1 (Winter 1993), pp. 143, 155.

9. Saskia Sassen, "On the Internet and Sovereignty," *Indiana Journal of Global Legal Studies* 5 (Spring 1998), p. 551.

10. Stephen Krasner, "Sovereignty," *Foreign Policy* 121 (January/February 2001), p. 24; see also Linda Weiss, *The Myth of the Powerless State* (Ithaca, NY: Cornell University Press, 1998).

11. David Bollier, "The Rise of Netpolitik: How the Internet Is Changing International Politics and Diplomacy," http://www.aspeninstitute.org/sites/default/files/content/docs/cands/NETPOLITIK.PDF, p. 21.

12. Jennifer Lee, "How Protesters Mobilized So Many and So Nimbly," *New York Times*, February 23, 2003, "Week in Review," p. 4.

13. For various views of what it means, see "What Is the International Community?" in the September 2002 issue of *Foreign Policy*.

14. Norris, *The Digital Divide*, p. 191.

15. Ibid.

16. James N. Rosenau, *Distant Proximities: Dynamics Beyond Globalization* (Princeton, N.J.: Princeton University Press, 2003), p. 11.

17. Herbert A. Simon, "Information 101: It's Not What You Know, It's How You Know It," *Journal for Quality and Participation* 21:4 (July/August 1998), pp. 30–33.

18. Edward Kaufman, "A Broadcasting Strategy to Win Media Wars," *The Washington Quarterly* 25:2 (Spring 2002), p. 118.

19. George Akerlof, "The Market for 'Lemons': Quality Uncertainty and the Market Mechanism," *Quarterly Journal of Economics*, Vol. 84, No. 3 (August 1970), pp. 488–500.

20. "Defense Secretary Urges More Spending for U.S. Diplomacy," *New York Times*, November 27, 2007.

21. Peter T. Haydon, *The 1962 Cuban Missile Crisis: Canadian Involvement Reconsidered* (Toronto: Canadian Institute of Strategic Studies, 1993).

22. Search of Factiva/Dow Jones database, January 14–25, 2003.

23. Peter J. Spiro, "New Global Communities, Nongovernmental Organizations in International Decision-Making Institutions," *The Washington Quarterly* 18:1 (Winter 1995), pp. 45–46.

24. David A. Welch, *Painful Choices: A Theory of Foreign Policy Change* (Princeton, NJ: Princeton University Press, 2005), pp. 1–4.

25. Kenneth N. Waltz, *Man, the State and War* (New York: Columbia University Press, 1959).

26. Daniel Gilbert, "If Only Gay Sex Caused Global Warming," *Los Angeles Times*, July 2, 2006; http://articles.latimes.com/2006/jul/02/opinion/op-gilbert2.

27. Walter Enders, Todd Sandler, and Khusrav Gaibulloev, "Domestic versus Transnational Terrorism: Data, Decomposition, and Dynamics," *Journal of Peace Research* 48: 3 (May 2011), pp. 319–337.

Chapter 10

What Can We Expect
in the Future?

Osama bin Laden (1957–2011) as seen in a video captured by U.S. special forces in his hideout in Abbottabad, Pakistan, May 2011

∨ Learning Objectives

10.1 Relate novel challenges to competing visions of the future of world politics.

10.2 Explain how the changing nature of power affects possible future world orders.

10.3 Articulate how theory and history can help us explain, understand, and evaluate world politics.

Alternative Visions

10.1 **Relate novel challenges to competing visions of the future of world politics.**

International politics remains a realm of self-help in which states face security dilemmas and force plays a considerable role. There are mitigating devices such as the balance of power and international norms, law, and organization, but they have not prevented all wars. The Prisoner's Dilemma logic of international conflict that we see reflected even in the writings of Thucydides still applies in some parts of the world today.

With the end of the Cold War, there was a good deal of talk about the prospects for a "new world order." As we later found, there was far less clarity about what that meant than optimism that it could be so. There was a new world order in the sense that the bipolar system established after World War II had broken down. But that was order within the anarchic state system, and it was not necessarily a just order. Others thought that a new world order meant escaping from the problems of the anarchic state system. Is such a world possible? British historian Arnold Toynbee wrote at the beginning of the Cold War that the sovereign state and the atom bomb could not coexist on the same planet. In a world of sovereign states, where the ultimate form of defense is war and the ultimate weapons are nuclear, he believed that something had to go, preferably the state. And as we saw in Chapters 8 and 9, globalization and the information revolution present new challenges to state sovereignty, for better and for worse.

The territorial state has not always existed, so it need not necessarily exist in the future. Fragmented units and state systems have existed since the days of Thucydides, but the large territorial state as the basis of international politics developed only after the Renaissance of the fourteenth and fifteenth centuries. The Thirty Years' War (1618–1648) still had some features of a feudal war and was thus both the last of the wars of feudalism and the first of the wars of the territorial state. The large territorial state as we know it today has been the dominant institution of modern world politics for only three and a half centuries.

Five Future Worlds

A number of futurists have predicted the decline of the territorial state. Their new world order involves structures that overcome the dilemmas of anarchy. Since World War II, there have been five major efforts to develop alternatives that go beyond the sovereign state as the model for world politics.

WORLD FEDERALISM One of the oldest traditions of European thought, federalism posits a solution for the problem of anarchy by way of an international federation: States would agree to give up their national armaments and accept some degree of central government. Federalists often draw analogies to the way the 13 American colonies came together in the eighteenth century. Some believe that history is a record of progress toward larger units. But federalism has not proven to be a very successful design at the global level. Peace is not the only thing that people value. People also want justice, welfare, and autonomy, and they do not trust world government to protect them. People of different cultures often cannot agree on what these concepts mean. In addition, few people are convinced that the federal remedy would work, that it would be a cure for the problem of war. Even if the anarchic system of states is part of the cause of war, getting rid of independent states would not necessarily be the end of war. As we have seen, most wars in recent years have been *internal* to states.

FUNCTIONALISM   Because of the inadequacies of federalism, the idea of international functionalism was developed. Popular in the 1940s, functionalism held that if issue-specific international institutions were created that had real decision-making power for handling global problems, states would have less reason to squabble, and war would be eliminated. Sovereignty would become less relevant than ever. Even though the formal shell of the state would continue to exist, its hostile content would be drained away. At the end of World War II, functionalist thinking gave rise to some of the specialized UN agencies such as the Food and Agricultural Organization and the World Health Organization (WHO). Functionalism exists to some extent today, and even where genuine international institutions are weak or underdeveloped, transnational actors of various kinds, such as nongovernmental organizations (NGOs) and multinational corporations, often step in to fill the need to promote coordinated management of issue-specific conflicts. So the spirit of functionalism is very much alive and well and responsible for a considerable amount of the international cooperation that we see in the world. But functionalism in the grand sense has not proven a sufficient design for *world* order, because most states are reluctant to allow themselves to become so interdependent that they become highly vulnerable to others.

REGIONALISM   Regional integration became very popular in the 1950s and 1960s. Jean Monnet, head of the French Planning Commission, thought that the functional approach at a regional level might lock Germany and France together and thereby prevent a resurgence of the conflicts that had led to World Wars I and II. In 1950, Europe started the process with the Schumann Plan, integrating Western European coal and steel industries. After 1957, the *Treaty of Rome* established the European Common Market, which provided a step-by-step reduction of trade barriers and harmonization of a whole range of agricultural and economic policies that culminated in the creation of the European Union (EU) in 1992. As we saw in Chapter 8, other regions have tried to emulate European regionalism, with the North American Free Trade Agreement as the most significant example in the Western Hemisphere.

In 1965, however, Charles de Gaulle, then president of France (and later, in the 1980s, Margaret Thatcher, then prime minister of Britain), set limits on how far regional integration could go. By the mid-1990s, there was widespread ambivalence in the EU countries over just how much sovereignty to cede to a regional government. The new common currency, the euro, began to circulate in 2002, but not in all countries, and since 2009, it has been under severe strain as heavily indebted eurozone countries in the Mediterranean (primarily Greece) struggled to avoid default on their sovereign debts. Efforts to create a new constitution for the EU faltered when voters in France and the Netherlands rejected a proposed draft in referendums held in 2005. Prime Minister David Cameron, a Conservative, campaigned in 2015 on a platform of renegotiating the terms of Britain's membership in the EU and won a majority government. But despite these bumps in the road, Europe has changed for the better compared with the earlier periods we have studied. The EU represents an ongoing and dynamic experiment in international relations. As its members continue to painstakingly negotiate a thick web of multilateral institutions that deal with issues from agriculture to a common defense force, a distinctly European identity has emerged. Although national differences certainly remain at the policy-making level, public opinion polls show that many EU citizens regard themselves as *European* as well as French, German, or Spanish. This attitude fits with constructivist theory, which emphasizes the role ideas and culture play in the construction of political identities and interests. EU members have chosen to increase their complex interdependence in the belief that the cost-benefit ratio favors cooperation over full national independence. In today's Europe, not everybody is in the same boat, but the boats are lashed together in a variety of ways that are very different from those of earlier periods. For example, in many areas, EU laws now supersede national laws. The EU represents a new type of international polity, but it is only a regional one.

ECOLOGISM   In the 1970s, ecologism provided a new brand of hope for a different type of world order. Richard Falk's *This Endangered Planet* argued that two things could provide the basis of a new world order: the growing importance of transnational, nonterritorial actors and growing interdependence under conditions of scarcity.[1] Falk argued that there would be a gradual evolution of grassroots, populist values that would transcend the state. Anticolonialism, antiracialism, greater equality, and ecological preservation would lead not only to the strengthening of majorities in the United Nations, but to the creation of new regimes for handling the world's dwindling resources. The result would be international norms of peace, justice, and ecological balance and a new form of world order.

Technological change and economic growth have accentuated ecological problems. Global resource supplies have become further stretched, and as biological diversity decreases, further harm has occurred to the oceans and atmosphere that are part of the global commons. The International Environmental Agreements Database Project at the University of Oregon provides information on approximately 1,200 multilateral and more than 1,500 bilateral agreements on subjects of shared concern, including fisheries, acid rain, ozone depletion, endangered species protection, Antarctica, and ocean pollution. Most have been signed since the first UN Environmental Conference in Stockholm in 1972. The United Nations has held major conferences on the environment and climate change in Brazil in 1992, in Japan in 1997, in Indonesia in 2007, in Denmark in 2009, in Mexico in 2010, in South Africa in 2011, in Peru in 2014, and in Paris in 2015. Environmental issues have also spawned numerous NGOs with transnational lobbying efforts. Citizens and politicians in developed countries are expressing increased awareness and concern regarding matters of environmental degradation and protection. As we discuss further below, the science on climate change is rapidly improving. The more we learn, the more urgent containing and ultimately reducing greenhouse gas emissions seems. Falk, however, overestimated how scarce resources would become and underestimated how much new technologies can compensate for the scarcity there is, and in many countries, ecological concerns take second place to a desire for rapid economic development. In addition, greenhouse gas emissions reductions are a classic international collective action problem. Finding our way to an ecologically sustainable future is perhaps the single greatest cooperation challenge facing the world today.

CYBERFEUDALISM   As we saw in Chapter 9, some theorists of organization in the information age—Peter Drucker, for example, and Alvin Toffler and Heidi Toffler[2]—argue that the information revolution is flattening hierarchies and replacing them with network organizations. They predict that the centralized bureaucratic governments of the twentieth century will become decentralized organizations in the twenty-first century and that more governmental functions will be handled by private markets as well as by nonprofit organizations. Moreover, Esther Dyson argues that as decentralized organizations and virtual communities develop on the Internet, they will cut across territorial jurisdictions and develop their own patterns of governance.[3] Although states will continue to exist, they will become much less important and less central to people's lives. People will live by multiple voluntary contracts and drop in and out of communities at the click of a mouse. The new pattern of cross-cutting communities and governance will become a modern and more civilized analogue to the feudal world that existed before the Westphalian system of states became dominant.

Although we can discern trends in this direction, this vision of how to get beyond the sovereign state leaves open questions about how the claims of virtual and geographical communities will conflict and how issues of violence and security will be handled. Moreover, as we saw in Chapter 9, new information technologies can be used for evil as well as for good. Today's terrorists use computers and the Internet to recruit members, obtain instructions for building weapons, transfer funds, and expand their networks. And remote hackers can create damage in other countries without ever crossing borders. In such situations, citizens may want stronger, not weaker, states whose governments can provide protection. As Thomas Hobbes pointed out centuries ago, the anarchy of states has its dangers, but it may be the least of the available evils.

Contrary to the predictions of these five models, the sovereign state has not yet become obsolete. Those who believe that it has often use a simple analogy. They say that the state today is penetrable by both rockets and electronic messages that can cross its borders in no time. Just as gunpowder and infantry penetrated and destroyed the medieval castle, so have nuclear missiles and the Internet made the sovereign state obsolete. But people want three things from their political institutions: physical security, economic well-being, and communal identity. Changes in international processes are shifting the locus of these values slowly, but thus far, the sovereign state has provided more of all three than any other institution. Multinational corporations, NGOs, and international organizations lack the force to provide for security and the legitimacy to provide a focus for communal identity. Moreover, at this stage of human history, democracy has flourished only within the context of sovereign states. Virtual communities are still weaker than geographical ones. So, despite the long tradition of efforts to design alternatives, the territorial state remains central to world politics.

States will persist, but the context of world politics is changing. Revolutionary changes in technology make the world seem smaller and more closely knit than ever before, yet many people are reacting to rapid change with divisive ethnic, religious, and nationalistic responses. As we saw in Chapter 8, globalization can create both economic integration and political fragmentation at the same time.

Communications are changing the world. Diplomacy is carried out in real time. In the Gulf War, both Saddam Hussein and George H. W. Bush were watching CNN for the latest news. During the fighting in Afghanistan, both Osama bin Laden and George W. Bush watched CNN and the Arabic station Al Jazeera. During the Iraq War, television reporters were embedded with frontline troops and broadcast battles in real time to a global audience. Human rights problems and mass suffering in distant parts of the globe are brought into our living rooms by television. People living on $1 a day in poor countries are becoming more aware of the lifestyles of people earning millions of dollars a year.

But economic integration does not mean political integration. Most people who watched the wars in Afghanistan and Iraq on Al Jazeera had different views of events than those who watched them on CNN. Similarly, the Internet makes more information available to more people, but people do not always seek the same types and sources of information. The Internet, cable, and satellite television all encourage "narrowcasting" of information to specific groups rather than the common denominator that typified television network broadcasting in the past. The Canadian communications theorist Marshall McLuhan once argued that modern communications was producing what he called a "global village."[4] But the metaphor of a global village can be misleading because global political identity remains weak. In much of the world, national, religious, and ethnic identities seem to be getting stronger, not weaker. Instead of a global village, we have villages around the globe that are more aware of one another. And villages connote parochialism as well as community. This simultaneous process of integration and disintegration gave rise to two popular oversimplified visions of the future of world politics after the Cold War.

The End of History or the Clash of Civilizations?

In 1989, Francis Fukuyama published an article titled "The End of History." He did not mean that literally, but rather argued that with the demise of communism we had reached the end point of ideological evolution and the emergence of Western liberal democracy as "the final form of human government."[5] Deep ideological cleavages drove international conflict over the twentieth century, and movements such as fascism and communism were responses to the disruption of traditional life by modernization. Industrialization tore people from their villages or small communities and made them available for mobilization by large ideological movements. Over time, however, liberal capitalism proved more successful in producing a higher level of welfare and citizen participation. The end of the Cold War suggested that liberal capitalism had prevailed. In one sense, Fukuyama was correct. There is no longer one single competitor to liberal capitalism as an overarching ideology. And the relations among rich democracies have been profoundly transformed. Neither Germany and France nor the United States and Japan expect or plan for war with each other. Their complex interdependence forms large islands of democratic peace in the world today, along the lines of Immanuel Kant's liberal predictions.

But in another sense, rather than the "end of history," the post–Cold War world could be described as the *return* of history. The return of history means more normal circumstances in which a single ideological cleavage does not drive the larger conflicts in international politics. Liberal capitalism has many competitors, albeit fragmented ones. China and Russia use capitalism and global markets, yet neither is liberal nor fully capitalist. In other areas, religious fundamentalism challenges the norms and practices of liberal capitalism. We sometimes lump all religious fundamentalisms together, but there are many fundamentalisms. What many have in common is a reaction against and a resistance to secular liberal capitalism. The major response and competitor to liberal capitalism after the Cold War is ethnic, religious, and national communalism.

In 1993, Samuel P. Huntington published an article (later a book) titled "The Clash of Civilizations" that became a well-known counter to Fukuyama's vision.[6] Huntington argued that rather than the fundamental sources of conflict in the new world being primarily ideological or economic, the great divisions that would dominate conflict would be cultural. Building on the work of the British historian Arnold Toynbee, Huntington divided the world into eight great "civilizations" (Western and Latin American, African, Islamic, Sinic, Hindu, Orthodox, Buddhist, and Japanese). He predicted conflict along the fault lines of those civilizations. In contrast to realists who used balance-of-power theory to predict that interstate conflicts would reemerge between Germany and its neighbors or to some liberals who expected the democratic peace to spread around the globe, Huntington saw culture as a source of conflict.

Huntington oversimplified his vision by adopting Toynbee's rather arbitrary categorization of civilizations. As constructivists point out, cultures are neither homogeneous nor static; they are overlapping and fluid.[7] More conflicts have occurred within the large "civilizations" in Huntington's map of the world (e.g., within Africa or Islam) than between them. Some observers argue that bin Laden's terrorist attacks and his call for an Islamic jihad against the West proved that Huntington was correct, but one can more plausibly see the events following 9/11 as a civil war within Islam between extreme fundamentalists and mainstream Muslims. Many faithful Muslims have more in common with moderate Christians and Jews than with bin Laden.

Both Fukuyama's and Huntington's visions suffer from trying to fit the post–Cold War world into a single, simple pattern. But one size does not fit all. Not only are there multiple cultures, but there are very different types of states in terms of levels of economic modernization. Fukuyama's triumph of liberal capitalism and democratic peace fits well with much of the postindustrial world. Huntington's focus on cultural conflict fits better with the preindustrial world and its relations with the rest of the world. Neither fits anywhere perfectly.

Ethnic and cultural conflict tends to rise when identities are challenged by major social changes that accompany modernization and globalization. Ethnic characteristics are a powerful bond, but so are state identities. In the Middle East, Egyptian and Syrian leaders have more readily acted on the basis of traditional state interests than on pan-Arabism or their common identity as Muslims. Indeed, Egyptian and Syrian leaders are currently engaged in major struggles against transnational Islamic fundamentalism.

Even when states prevail, nationalism varies in intensity. It is instructive to look at the difference between Eastern Europe and Western Europe. Under communist rule, nationalistic and ethnic conflicts in the East were frozen for a half century. The end of the Cold War and the removal of Soviet hegemony thawed many of these tensions. For example, with the end of the Cold War and the demise of its communist government, competition between Serbs, Croats, Muslims, and Kosovar Albanians came to the fore with terrible consequences in the former Yugoslavia. Throughout the former Soviet Union, many ethnic groups spill across borders, stirring up more potential for further ethnic conflict and revivals of nationalism. Contrast this scene with post–Cold War Western Europe, where intrastate conflict is negligible and countries that previously held strong national rivalries have formed a larger European Union. What can explain it?

Much of the explanation fits well with liberal theories. When people are better off, animosities become less tense than they were. Part of the answer may be democracy because when people have a chance to resolve disputes openly, passions can be better managed. Some Western animosities were exorcised through democratic processes; witness the debate that went on in West Germany at the end of World War II that led to changes in the textbooks and a new understanding of German history. And part of the answer lies in the regional institutions that pulled Western Europeans together in a larger framework in which the more extreme nationalist views were discouraged. Fortunately, the desire of many Eastern European countries to join the EU had an important moderating effect on their leaders and peoples. Indeed, the soft power of the EU has helped spur significant economic and political reforms in Eastern Europe, at a pace once considered unachievable.

But even in Western Europe, nationalism is far from dead. Many Europeans do not want their national identity submerged completely in a European identity. There are still residual concerns between the French and Germans. One reason the French support European integration is to tie the Germans down. In addition, many Western Europeans are concerned about the effect of immigration on their national cultures, as we have seen so clearly in the recent Syrian refugee crisis. They fear migration from the north of Africa as well as from Eastern Europe. Experts point to 9/11 and subsequent attacks in Madrid, London, Copenhagen, and Paris as evidence that European citizens and leaders have failed to adequately address the political and economic grievances of Europe's sizable Muslim immigrant community. And riots in France have demonstrated that many North African immigrants have not been successfully assimilated into the French economy and society. Simultaneously, right-wing parties in Western Europe increasingly appeal to xenophobia and provide a warning signal that the problems of nationalism and ethnic tensions are not totally banished from Western Europe. And as the tragic events in Norway demonstrated in July 2011, xenophobes are just as capable of acts of terrorism as the most extreme members of the groups they hate.

With declining birthrates and porous borders, Europe cannot cut off all immigration from its poorer neighbors across the Mediterranean Sea. Resolving the tensions between a desire to preserve a European identity and the need to better integrate immigrants into society is an ongoing challenge for Europe, as it will increasingly be for wealthy countries with low birthrates everywhere.

Technology and the Diffusion of Power

A third vision of the future is less determinate than that of Fukuyama or Huntington, but comes closer to reality: the view that technology, particularly information technology, is leading to a diffusion of power away from central governments. Just as the twentieth century was the era of centralizing power in national capitals, which reached its peak with the totalitarian governments in the Soviet Union and Nazi Germany, economic and information networks are moving some functions of governance to higher and lower levels of government and some from formal government to the private and nonprofit sectors, as Table 10.1 illustrates.

Table 10.1 The Diffusion of Governance in the Twenty-First Century

	Private	Public	Third Sector
Supranational	Transnational corporations (e.g., IBM, Shell)	Intergovernmental organizations (e.g., UN, WTO)	Nongovernmental organizations (e.g., International Committee of the Red Cross, Greenpeace)
National	National corporations (e.g., Southwest Airlines)	21st-century central government	National nonprofit organizations (e.g., American Red Cross)
Subnational	Local businesses	State/local government	Local groups

As we saw in Chapter 9, information affects power, and governments of all kinds will find their control eroding during the twenty-first century as information technology gradually spreads and costs continue to decrease. In the middle of the twentieth century, people worried that computers might produce the centralized, authoritarian world of George Orwell's novel *1984*, but the decentralizing effects have proven to be more powerful.

How far and how fast the information revolution causes decentralization will vary across countries, and countervailing forces may arise. But the general propositions that governments are losing their monopoly over foreign policy and that they will have to share the stage in world politics with the nonstate actors described in Chapter 9 seem highly likely.

This diffusion of power can have both positive and negative consequences. A benign vision paints a picture in which technology will encourage economic development and make authoritarian regimes less tenable. The result will be to speed the spread of islands of democratic peace. A malign vision sees a new feudalism in which destructive individuals, terrorist groups, and otherwise weak states gain access to weapons of mass destruction (WMDs), creating true anarchy rather than the anarchy of the interstate system. In such an insecure world, a negative reaction may slow down or reverse economic globalization; citizens may sacrifice democratic liberties in favor of Hobbesian autocratic governments that provide basic personal security.

The benign vision points out that because of transnational communications, there is much more awareness of what is going on in other parts of the globe, and groups are better able to organize on a global basis. As noted above, NGOs are able to mount transnational campaigns for environmental and human rights causes. The Internet provides information to citizens that undercuts the controls of authoritarian regimes.

The most impressive transnational actor, of course, is the multinational corporation. By spreading investments around the world and making profits in different parts of the global market, the transnational corporation is producing a different type of world economy. Governments compete to attract international investments. A large part of international trade is trade within multinational corporations. Honda now produces more automobiles in the United States than it does in Japan, and it transports American-made automobiles back to Japan. The U.S. government even pressed the European Union to accept Honda vehicles made in the United States. In other words, the United States defined the export of Japanese cars made in the United States to Europe as a U.S. national interest. Similarly, IBM was once the largest producer of mainframe computers in Japan, and IBM/Japan does its research in Japan and hires Japanese employees. (In 2004, IBM sold its personal computer division to the Chinese computer manufacturer Lenovo, furthering the globalized nature of the computer industry.) When an American calls a multinational company's toll-free service number in the United States, the call is likely to be answered by an Indian in Bangalore.

This change has led former secretary of labor Robert Reich to ask, "Who is us?"[8] Should analysts focus on the identity of the headquarters of a company, or should they focus on where it does its research and production? Reich argues that in terms of what is good for the people living within the borders of the United States, a foreign company working inside the United States may be more important than an American company working in Japan. Critics have responded to Reich by saying that he is looking further into the future than is currently justified. Most multinational corporations have a predominant national identity, and three-fourths of U.S. production is done by companies with headquarters in the United States. It is nonetheless an interesting way of thinking about the future. Transnational investment is helping confuse identities—helping confuse the question of "Who is us?"—and along with ecological interdependence might affect long-run views of global problems.

If the United States responded by excluding foreign firms from U.S. markets, it would simply create inefficient firms that could no longer compete on a global basis. The trouble with protectionist responses is that they may hurt the protector as much as they hurt the other side. So, in the 1990s, the United States and Japan negotiated over domestic impediments to trade. The United States pressed Japan over something strictly within Japanese domestic jurisdiction. Japan had laws restricting supermarket size and other practices restricting access of foreign firms to the distribution system. A number of Japanese politicians and consumers were delighted to have this U.S. pressure because it benefited the Japanese consumer. In a sense, there was a transnational coalition between U.S. producers and Japanese consumers. The Japanese government in turn pressed the United States to reduce its budget deficit, arguing correctly that the U.S. trade deficit was related to the government budget deficit. In other words, U.S. and Japanese officials were dealing with each other not at water's edge, but on matters that were deep within the sovereign jurisdiction of each country.

Proliferation of Weapons of Mass Destruction

The malign vision of the effects of technology on the diffusion of power focuses on a different dimension of the transnational spread of technology. As we saw in the oil case in Chapter 8, companies spread technologies and skills. Technology can also be spread through trade, migration, education, and the flow of ideas. What will this dispersal do to security? Already, 40 countries have the potential to make nuclear, chemical, or biological weapons. The technology of chemical weaponry is nearly a century old; nuclear weaponry and ballistic missiles are more than half-century-old technologies. To some extent, policies of nonproliferation have slowed the rate of spread of nuclear weapons. But the problem of proliferation was exacerbated when the Soviet Union collapsed, and its successor states have been less able to control the outflow of technology.

Before the Soviet collapse, eight countries had nuclear weapons. Five were formally declared nuclear weapons states in the 1968 Treaty on the Non-Proliferation of Nuclear Weapons (NPT): the United States, the Soviet Union, Britain, France, and China. Three states remained outside the treaty and were widely reputed to have developed nuclear weapons covertly: Israel, India, and Pakistan. In 1998, both India and Pakistan openly tested their nuclear weapons. Three other countries—Iraq, Iran, and North Korea—signed the NPT but were widely viewed as trying to develop weapons anyway. North Korea eventually withdrew from the treaty and exploded two small nuclear devices. Five other countries—South Africa, South Korea, Argentina, Brazil, and Libya—started down that path but changed their minds. Interestingly, more than 30 countries could have produced nuclear weapons but did not; that is, three or four times more states were able to have nuclear weapons than actually had them. That is quite a contrast to President John F. Kennedy's fear, which he articulated when he signed the Limited Test Ban Treaty in 1963, that 25 countries would have nuclear weapons by the 1970s.

Why wasn't there more nuclear proliferation? After all, in an anarchic world of sovereign states, nuclear weapons are the ultimate form of self-help. There are several major answers. Realists point to the alliances that arose during the Cold War in which each superpower gave security guarantees to its allies. For example, Germany and Japan did not develop nuclear weapons because they had U.S. security guarantees. Promises by the United States to prevent any country from using nuclear blackmail against these allies reassured the Japanese and the Germans that they did not have to develop nuclear weapons. Alliances also made a difference to some of the smaller states. For example, South Korea and Taiwan each began to develop nuclear weapons when it looked as if the United States might withdraw from Asia in the 1970s in the aftermath of Vietnam, but they stopped when the United States protested and promised continued protection. Similarly, the Soviet Union constrained its Eastern European allies and developing world client states from developing nuclear weapons.

Another explanation, favored by liberals, was superpower cooperation and the development of a nonproliferation regime of norms and institutions. In the early stages of the nuclear era, the superpower attitude toward nuclear weaponry was highly competitive. The superpowers tried to use nuclear technology to earn points in the ideological competition. In 1953, President Dwight D. Eisenhower announced with great fanfare the Atoms for Peace program to help other countries develop nuclear technology for peaceful purposes, emphasizing the benign face of the atom to win more points for the United States. Similarly, the Soviet Union extended nuclear assistance to China. But by 1968, the United States and the Soviet Union learned to cooperate to the point that they could agree on a nonproliferation treaty. In 1977, the United States, the Soviet Union, and 13 other countries that supplied nuclear technology set up the Nuclear Suppliers Group to set guidelines on what sorts of nuclear technology could be exported.

Liberals point out that nuclear proliferation was curbed by the existence of treaties and institutions. So far, 189 states have ratified or acceded to the NPT, obliging them to develop or to transfer nuclear weapons. Nonnuclear states have agreed to have inspectors from the UN's International Atomic Energy Agency in Vienna (which was awarded the 2005 Nobel Peace Prize) visit their peaceful nuclear facilities to ensure that they are not being misused. As just noted, only a few countries such as Israel, India, and Pakistan did not sign the treaty, and a few signatories cheated. After Iraq lost the Gulf War in 1991, coalition forces and UN inspectors dismantled its nuclear programs. Constructivists would add that the development of a norm against the use of nuclear weapons since 1945 has helped reinforce the effects of the treaties and institutions. Finally, the history of many authoritarian states' attempts to acquire nuclear weapons shows quite simply that it is more difficult for most states than Kennedy imagined. In particular, as political scientist Jacques Hymans has argued, badly run states tend to have badly run nuclear weapons programs.[9] Still, these programs are among the most dangerous. Nuclear weapons in the United States and the Soviet Union were equipped with elaborate technological devices—"permissive action links"—that required a code from a higher authority to activate the weapon, but many of the countries with active nuclear weapons programs may not have these elaborate technological devices. The end of the Cold War and the transnational spread of technology may produce a larger prospect of nuclear weapons being used in some of the new countries trying to enter the nuclear race than has been true since the 1950s.

Two open questions about proliferation remain. One concerns the future of alliances, institutions, and security guarantees; the other asks whether nuclear technology would leak from countries such as Russia, Pakistan, and North Korea to would-be proliferators and terrorist groups. Neorealists, such as Kenneth Waltz, have argued that the spread of nuclear weapons to more states may be stabilizing because deterrence will work. If nuclear weapons helped prevent the Cold War from becoming hot, why wouldn't their crystal ball effect produce prudence and order in other parts of the world such as the Middle East and South Asia? The trouble with this view is that it rests almost entirely on a rational model of deterrence among coherent unitary actors. But if the real danger of nuclear weapons in the post–Cold War period is likely to be loss of control, these rational models that provide the basis for confident predictions may be largely irrelevant. Many of the countries that may develop nuclear weapons will have a history of coups and political instability.

Transnational Challenges to Security

One fact about the future seems quite clear: Many of the security challenges that states will face will be transnational in character. For most of the Westphalian era, sovereign states had only to worry about other sovereign states. Today, there are a range of actors and issues that pose security challenges. Globalization and the information revolution may make possible many wonderful new opportunities, but they have also made possible many new threats, not just to states, but to other possible referent objects of security, including individuals ("human security").

TRANSNATIONAL TERRORISM   In Chapter 9, we discussed transnational terrorism in the context of the information revolution and concluded that although transnational terrorism is exaggerated as a security threat today, it is worth taking seriously because of the danger—small though it may seem—of terrorists acquiring and using WMDs.

What is terrorism? Under U.S. law, it is premeditated, politically motivated violence against noncombatant targets by subnational groups. The United Nations has passed conventions to suppress terrorist bombings, assassinations, hostage taking, and the financing of terrorism. A UN Security Council resolution in September 2001 that obligated all member states to deny terrorists safe harbor helped legitimize U.S. actions in Afghanistan. The General Assembly has nonetheless found it difficult to agree on a resolution defining terrorism. Arab governments led by Egypt and Syria blocked any text that did not exempt groups such as the Palestinians, whose political goals they endorsed, from being defined as terrorists. As skeptics sometimes put it, "One man's terrorist is another man's freedom fighter."

When President George W. Bush addressed the UN General Assembly in 2001, he said that the world must unite in "opposing all terrorists, not just some of them. No national aspiration, no remembered wrong can ever justify the deliberate murder of the innocent." His statement was consistent with just war doctrine discussed in Chapter 1 and with international law. Some acts of nonstate political resistance perhaps should not be considered terrorism; for example, much of the antiapartheid struggle in South Africa did not kill civilians. But even if a political group can argue that the absence of democratic procedures for change make violence necessary in a "war of national liberation," the taking of innocent life is not morally or legally acceptable under just war doctrine. Similarly, if states deliberately kill noncombatants to terrorize a population, it is a war crime. If terrorism is defined as the substate use of violence for political purposes, states are excluded (by definition), but they are not thereby exculpated if they engage in similar immoral and illegal behavior. For all the difficulties at the margins of defining terrorism, the core evil of deliberately killing innocent people for political purposes is broadly condemned by the mainstream moral codes of all major religions as well as by international law. In 2004, a high-level panel appointed by the UN secretary-general agreed unanimously that terrorism is any action intended to cause death or serious bodily harm to civilians or noncombatants for the purpose of intimidation.

Transnational terrorism is to the twenty-first century somewhat as piracy was to an earlier era. Some governments gave pirates and privateers safe harbor to earn revenues or to harass their enemies. Today, some states harbor terrorists to attack their enemies or because they are too weak to control such groups. At the same time, the technology of miniaturization of explosives, the vulnerability of modern systems such as air travel, and the increasing ease of communication via the Internet provide opportunities for nonstate actors to do great harm across borders even without state support. Ironically, the common threat felt by many people may enhance their appreciation of the role of states and the importance of their cooperation in providing security. The anarchy of the interstate system is usually more bearable than the chaotic anarchy of a nonstate actor's war of all against all.

Because transnational terrorists cannot do a great deal of physical damage without WMDs, it is vital to be on guard against this danger. We know that bin Laden and the al-Qaeda network were making efforts to obtain such weapons and made contact with scientists working in Pakistan's nuclear program. We also know that al-Qaeda operatives made contact with arms dealers claiming to have access to material stolen from former Soviet states and smuggled abroad. As we saw in Chapter 9, fissile material is difficult and costly to produce, and transnational terrorist groups lack the organizational characteristics and resources required to do it. There are reasons to doubt whether they would even be capable of acquiring nuclear weapons from someone else, transporting, and detonating them. But they have certainly tried. Moreover, nuclear weapons are not the only threat. Biological agents have been developed by states. Even though they are unreliable on the battlefield (think of the effect of wind on an aerosol cloud of anthrax spores), biological weapons are easier to make than nuclear weapons—recipes are available on the Internet—and can be used to create terror among defenseless civilian populations. In 1993, if the terrorists who detonated a truck bomb in the basement garage of New York's World Trade Center had used anthrax or the chemical agent sarin in addition to high explosives, they could have claimed thousands of victims. In 2001, terrorists turned hijacked civilian airliners into gigantic cruise missiles to accomplish that purpose. In contrast, however, if the 9/11 terrorists had had access to a nuclear weapon, they could have killed hundreds of thousands of people. More alarmingly, the problem of transnational actors seeking to acquire WMDs is not likely to vanish if the al-Qaeda network is destroyed. In 1995, a religious cult in Japan, Aum Shinrikyo, killed a dozen people with sarin in the Tokyo subway system, sending shock waves of fear through Japanese society. Interestingly, eight years later, a deranged mental patient killed more than ten times as many people without triggering a similar wave of fear or panic simply by setting fire to a milk carton full of flammable liquid in a subway car in Daegu, South Korea. The contrast between the two attacks demonstrates that it is not the consequences as much as the nature of the attack and the identity of the attacker that provoke terror.

Terrorist groups could also wreak havoc by attacking the information systems that control electricity for hospitals, air traffic radar, or banking transactions. Such attacks could be perpetrated with high explosives at the sites of key server computers, but they could also be carried out transnationally by computer hackers tens of thousands of miles away.

Deterrence does not provide adequate protection against terrorist threats because there is sometimes no return address against which to retaliate, unless a foreign state can be proven to have assisted the terrorists, as Afghanistan's Taliban regime did. And the worst case of terrorism in the United States before 2001, the bombing of the federal building in Oklahoma City in 1995, was purely homegrown. In other cases, criminal groups may take control of the government of a state but ostensibly behave according to international law and claim the rights of sovereign protection against interference in their internal affairs. In such circumstances, other states may feel justified in intervening. Some situations in Latin America and the Caribbean have come close to that: witness the 1989 U.S. invasion of Panama; the capture of its president, Manuel Noriega; and his trial in the United States on drug-smuggling charges. In 2002, President George W. Bush issued a new national security strategy that argued in favor of preventive war against state sponsors of terrorism, but intelligence agencies estimate that the subsequent invasion of Iraq increased rather than decreased the number of transnational terrorists.

Terrorism is not new in world politics. It is a method of violence with roots stretching far back in history. Terror means "great fear," and governments as varied as the French First Republic (1792–1804) and Josef Stalin's Soviet Union have used it to control their populations. Terrorism was also used by anarchists and other transnational revolutionaries in the nineteenth century, as we saw in Chapter 3. They killed half a dozen heads of state, and World War I was triggered in part by a terrorist assassin. What is new today is that technology could potentially put into the hands of deviant individuals and groups destructive powers that were once reserved primarily to governments. In the twentieth century, heads of government such as Stalin and Adolf Hitler could kill large numbers of people. If terrorists are able to obtain WMDs, they will develop similar capabilities. That is why some observers refer to terrorism as the privatization of war. Moreover, technology has made the complex systems of modern societies more vulnerable to large-scale attack. As Walter Laqueur argues, "This trend toward increased vulnerability was occurring even before the Internet sped it along."[10]

One of the hardest things for terrorists to do is organize trustworthy cells across borders that cannot be taken down by intelligence and police agencies. By moving from the physical sanctuaries of the 1990s to virtual sanctuaries on the Internet, the terrorists reduce their risk. No longer does recruiting occur only in physical locations such as mosques and jails. Instead, alienated individuals in isolated national niches can make contact with a new virtual community of fellow believers around the world. The number of jihadist websites is reported to have grown from a dozen in the late 1990s to thousands today. Such websites not only recruit; they also train. They include detailed instructions on how to make bombs, how to cross borders, and how to plant and explode devices to kill soldiers and civilians. And experts use chat rooms and message boards to answer trainees' questions. Plans and instructions are then sent through coded messages. Of course, such websites can be monitored by governments. Some sites are shut down, others left open to monitor. But the cat-and-mouse game between police agencies and terrorists is a close one.

CYBERWARFARE Another threat related to the information revolution combines both governments and transnational actors. Cyberthreats and potential cyberwarfare illustrate the increased vulnerabilities and loss of control of modern societies. As a very distinguished group of scientists put it in a letter to then-President George W. Bush, "The critical infrastructure of the United States, including electrical power, finance, telecommunications, health care, transportation, water, defense and the Internet, is highly vulnerable to cyberattack. Fast and resolute mitigating action is needed to avoid national disaster."[11] And in the murky world of the Internet, attackers are difficult to identify.

In today's interconnected world, an unidentified cyberattack on nongovernmental infrastructure might be severely damaging. For example, some experts believe that electric power grids may be a particularly susceptible target. The control systems that electric power companies use are thought to be vulnerable to attacks, which could shut down entire cities and regions for days or weeks. Moreover, cyberattacks may interfere with financial markets and cause immense economic loss by closing down commercial websites.

Some scenarios, including an "electronic Pearl Harbor," sound alarmist, but they illustrate the diffusion of power from central governments to individuals. In 1941, the powerful Japanese navy used many resources to inflict damage thousands of miles away. Today, an individual computer hacker using malicious programs has the potential to inflict considerable damage and chaos in faraway places at very little cost to himself. The so-called love bug virus launched by a hacker in the Philippines in 2000 is estimated to have cost billions of dollars in damage to information systems. Sabotage is not a new phenomenon, but the information revolution enables individuals to perpetrate sabotage at unprecedented speed and scope. As we have seen, terrorists can engage in asymmetrical warfare with governments and exploit new vulnerabilities in cyberspace.

In 2007, the government of China was accused of sponsoring thousands of hacking incidents against German federal government computers as well as against Pentagon and private-sector computer systems in the United States. But it was difficult to prove the source of the attack, and the Pentagon had to shut down some of its computer systems. Google has accused the government of China of stealing its intellectual property as well, but China has denied it. In

2007, when the government of Estonia moved a World War II statue commemorating Russian war dead, hackers retaliated with a costly denial of service attack that closed down Estonia's access to the Internet. There was no way of proving whether this transnational attack was aided by the Russian government, a spontaneous nationalist response, or both, and in the 2008 war between Russia and Georgia, similar claims were made about cyberattacks on Georgia. In 2009, when Canadian scholars cracked GhostNet—an elaborate back-door cyberespionage network—they were unable to prove that the government of China was behind it, even though the network clearly targeted groups and movements of particular concern to Beijing. In 2010, Iranian nuclear centrifuges were destroyed by a mysterious computer worm called Stuxnet, which some attributed to Israel or the United States. More recently, in 2013, the U.S. government accused the Chinese military of conducting cyberattacks and engaging in industrial espionage, issuing arrest warrants for five Chinese nationals; and in 2014, U.S. cybersecurity experts claimed to have back-traced an attack on Sony's servers to North Korea, which had been enraged by the planned 2014 release of Sony Pictures' comedy *The Interview*, a film about a madcap plot to assassinate Kim Jong-un. Such examples clearly illustrate both the capabilities and limits of state and nonstate actors to engage in offensive and defensive cyberoperations for both economic and political goals. A new theater of conflict has emerged in our increasingly interconnected and interdependent world.

PANDEMICS   As we saw in Chapter 3, World War I was devastating for Europe and is estimated to have killed more than 15 million people worldwide. What is less often remembered is that in 1918, a transnational avian flu pandemic killed far more people than died in World War I. Episodes of flu recur on an annual basis; occasionally, though, a new strand is transmitted across borders by trade, travelers, or migratory birds and has a devastating effect. Because transnational pandemics can kill more citizens than a world war, governments have to develop a broader conception of national security and new sets of policies to cope with this threat.

Microbes are constantly racing science. Not only do well-known bugs develop resistance to drugs, but new diseases emerge every year. As we saw in Chapter 8, scientists have discovered more than 80 new infectious diseases that have killed tens of millions of people since 1940. The most recent epidemic, the deadliest outbreak of Ebola since its discovery in 1976, caused more than 11,000 deaths in West Africa since the first case was discovered in March 2014—a fatality rate of 50 percent—and overwhelmed the capacities of both affected states and key international actors such as the WHO to contain it in a timely way. In dealing with these transnational challenges, governments need to think of foreign policies in new ways. Aid to other countries' public health systems may be the most cost-effective form of defense. Work must be done to improve their databases and surveillance. Stockpiles of vaccines and antibiotics must be developed, along with distribution systems. Just as natural and human-made threats overlap, so too are the national and global public health systems closely connected by direct and indirect linkages.

Microbes do not respect borders. The West Nile virus spread to nearly all states east of the Mississippi within a few years after it was first detected in New York in the 1990s. It could have entered the United States by a mosquito carried in a plane or in the blood of passenger who was subsequently bitten by a local mosquito. The H1N1 virus that by the summer of 2009 had infected people on every continent probably first evolved in Mexico less than a year earlier. Roughly 140 million people enter the United States by plane each year. At least half of U.S. cases of tuberculosis come from abroad, some with resistance to antibiotics because of faulty foreign health care systems. And, of course, terrorists can obtain microbes and viruses from inadequately protected foreign laboratories, by bribing underpaid scientists in the remnants of the Russian biological warfare system, or from natural sources.

Effective response to these infectious diseases lies in the global public health system of surveillance, detection, communication, and response. The WHO has developed international public health regulations and a reporting system for its 194 members. Its global alert network is supplemented by reports from nongovernmental organizations such as Doctors Without Borders. The WHO has created a network of national laboratories that do early detection work, and it manages all that on a modest annual budget of less than $2.5 billion. There are also indirect connections between the national and global public health systems. Many poor states need assistance in developing the laboratories and institutions necessary for surveillance, detection, communication, and response to infectious diseases. In addition to a humanitarian concern, developing their capacity is in the wealthy countries' interest, not only for early warning but also to ensure that improper care does not lead to creation of resistant strains. Even states with better-developed public health systems are more likely to cooperate if assistance meets their broader health needs as well as narrow pandemic concerns. Because there is increasing evidence that improved public health contributes to economic development and greater stability in poor countries, farsighted policies by donor governments can serve their own interests and the interests of others at the same time. With transnational threats, policies to enhance security do not start or stop at the national border.

Only a few years ago, lack of funding was the main constraint to improving global health. Thanks to private and public giving (from organizations such as the Gates Foundation), more money is being donated and spent today. But these funds often go to high-profile cases of diseases and pandemics, not to general improvements in public health and infrastructure, and higher spending is unlikely to lead to improvements if it continues in an unsystematic and disorganized way.[12]

CLIMATE CHANGE   In Chapter 8, we examined climate change as an environmental dimension of globalization. In the public debate, the issue has been viewed mainly as an environmental problem with economic implications, but as scientific models that predict future changes in the climate become more reliable and precise, climate change is increasingly being framed as a transnational threat and potential international security issue. When the Nobel Committee awarded the 2007 Peace Prize jointly to former vice president Al Gore and to the UN's Intergovernmental Panel on Climate Change, it cited climate change as a source of "increased dangers of violent conflicts and wars, within and between states."[13]

According to leading scientists, global warming today is to a large extent caused by human activities. Carbon dioxide, a greenhouse gas that accumulates in the atmosphere and is a major cause of rising temperatures, is emitted by a wide range of normal economic activities. Carbon emissions are what economists call a negative externality, which means that emitters do not bear the full cost of the damage that they cause and hence produce too much carbon dioxide. A domestic analogy is tobacco smoking. Smokers do not face the full costs of their action because society has to bear part of the increased health care costs that are incurred. As a result, governments try to discourage smoking through taxes and regulations. But in the case of global warming, such moves are far more difficult; there is no global government that can immediately regulate excessive carbon emission, and countries are tempted to take a free ride and leave expensive remedies to others. Moreover, some countries such as Russia, which believes that it stands to benefit economically from a warmer Siberia, have different incentives than Bangladesh, a poor country that is likely to be flooded by rising sea levels that will accompany global warming. In 2001, the United States decided not to ratify the Kyoto Protocol, an agreement to cap greenhouse gas emissions, because it would be too damaging to the U.S. economy and would not involve limits on less-developed emitters such as China.

What are the expected consequences of climate change? Some scientists predict severe disruptions such as weather-related natural disasters, droughts, and famines that may lead to enormous loss of life. Global warming between 2.5 and 10 degrees Fahrenheit would raise sea levels by a foot and a half. That estimate is conservative, and if warming proceeds more rapidly because of the loss of the reflectivity of Arctic ice and the release of carbon dioxide and methane from thawing permafrost, rising sea levels could lead to the submersion of low-lying islands and hence threaten the survival of entire countries such as the Maldives and Tuvalu. At the same time, in other places such as Africa and Central Asia, water will become scarcer, and drought will reduce food supplies. External shocks brought about by climate change will directly affect advanced economies, but they may also have indirect effects by aggravating the disparities between developed and developing countries and creating additional incentives for mass migration to rich, less affected, and more adaptable regions. In addition, climate change will put stress on weak governments in poor countries and may lead to an increase in the number of failed states.

All these consequences make climate change a transnational issue with potentially high economic, environmental, and human costs. But is it also a transnational threat from an international security perspective? If we think of security as protecting vital interests, climate change has both direct and indirect effects on security. If the Maldive Islands ceases to exist as a country, the effects of climate change would be as devastating to them as a nuclear bomb. Even for the United States, the damage to Florida, the Chesapeake Bay area, and the San Francisco Bay area could be as costly as the effects of bombing. Such direct effects of human activities, although not malevolent in intention like terrorism or cyberwarfare, argue for a broadening of our concept of security and the adoption of new policies. But climate change may also be an indirect source of international conflict. UN Secretary-General Ban Ki Moon argued in 2007 that the Darfur conflict "began as an ecological crisis, arising in part from climate change." Some scholars argue that climate change will cause international and civil wars, terrorism, and crime and that increasingly scarce food and water will lead to violent conflict and mass migration from poor to rich countries. Other scholars play down these effects and see climate as just one of many factors that lead to conflicts. Some realists argue that climate change is a scientific and technological challenge, but that it should not be confused with intentional and organized violent conflict. Other scholars and practitioners concerned with traditional security issues, such as a panel of retired generals from the U.S. military, pay more heed to the indirect effects and call climate change a "threat multiplier for instability in some of the most volatile regions of the world."[14] The Bush administration's 2002 National Security Strategy argued that in an age of transnational terrorism, the United States may face a greater threat from failed states than from great powers, and to the extent that climate change accelerates state failure, the indirect effects as well as the direct effects of climate change must be taken into account in security policies.

There are four basic ways of reducing carbon emissions and mitigating global warming: technological innovation, substitution, economic instruments, and conservation. An example of technological innovation is carbon sequestration, which allows the capture and storage of carbon in underground geological formations so that less carbon dioxide is released into the atmosphere. An example of substitution is switching from coal-, oil-, or natural gas–fired electricity generation to other sources of energy that do not involve combustion, such as hydro, nuclear, wind, geothermal, tidal, and solar power. Each source has advantages and disadvantages from both economic and environmental points of view. Nuclear power generation is undoubtedly the most reliable and arguably the least environmentally costly, but the partial meltdowns at the Fukushima Daiichi nuclear power plant in the wake of the March 2011 earthquake and tsunami in Japan have made nuclear power generation suddenly far less popular worldwide. Economic instruments include both incentives and disincentives. "Cap and trade" systems limit the amount of greenhouse gases that corporations can emit but allow them to buy emissions permits from corporations that reduce their emissions below their allowed caps. This approach has also been used successfully in other cases of environmental pollution. A different method is a carbon tax, which would be a tax on the use of energy resources and, if set accurately, would reflect the cost of the negative externality. A carbon tax would induce individuals to lower the use of fossil fuels in particular, whose consumption leads to high carbon emissions. Finally, there is conservation. Greenhouse gas emissions can be lowered if people simply learn to use less energy. As the Japanese public response to the immediate shutdown of the country's nuclear power plants in the wake of "3/11" dramatically illustrated, people are capable of getting by with far less energy than we might imagine.

Photo: Kyodo News/Newscom

Melting icebergs, Greenland, 2006

Seeing transnational climate change as a security issue requires a reframing of security policy. For example, in 2007, China surpassed the United States as the world's leading emitter of carbon dioxide. China points out, however, that on a per capita basis, each of its citizens is responsible for only one-fifth the emissions of the average American. China uses coal, a particularly carbon-dioxide-intensive fuel, for 68 percent of its commercial energy supply, whereas coal accounts for roughly a third of the United States' total energy. China builds more than one new coal-fired power plant each week. Coal is cheap and widely available in China, which is important as the country scrambles for energy resources to keep its many energy-intensive industries running. What can the United States do about this security threat? The bombs, bullets, and embargoes of traditional security policy are irrelevant. A 2007 report from the International Energy Agency (which was created after the 1973 oil crisis to provide policy advice to industrial countries) urged a cooperative approach to helping China and India become more energy efficient. In other words, to promote its own security, the United States may have to forge a partnership with China to develop creative ideas, technologies, and policies for preventing dangerous climate change.

As realists would argue, the anarchical nature of the international system makes it difficult to address the issue of climate change comprehensively. If a number of states decide to impose costs on their economies to slow global warming, other nonparticipating states will benefit from a better climate while paying none of the costs. That is a typical example of the free-rider problem, which we can also observe in a variety of other situations in international politics. Free-riding is often rational behavior from the point of view of the individual country. Moreover, state leaders are first and foremost responsible for their own people and not for others who may be more severely affected by climate change. Hence, a leader may choose to free-ride by not participating in mitigation policies while reaping the benefits of other states' efforts.

Overall, however, the issue of climate change is increasingly being recognized as one of the transnational challenges with the greatest environmental, economic, and perhaps security implications. As many governments take action, a powerful global environmental movement constantly highlights the importance of addressing global climate change. Such environmental issues and other transnational challenges will become much more important in the future and inspire new ways of thinking about international conflicts beyond the limited military dimension. In any case, transnational challenges will intensify the already enormously complicated nature of contemporary international politics.

As transnational challenges and threats grow, states will not only begin to question the Westphalian norms that make clear distinctions between what is domestic and international, but they will also find themselves broadening their concepts of security and defense. Many new threats will not be susceptible to solution by armies wielding high-explosive weaponry. Close cooperation of intelligence, customs, and police agencies will play a major role, as will private-sector measures of protection of facilities critical to the global economy. If democracies fail in these tasks and terrorists using WMDs create an anarchy of individuals rather than states, Fukuyama's vision of the future becomes less relevant. But even if governments rise to the challenge and contain transnational threats, more traditional problems of interstate order still remain.

Follow Up

- Francis Fukuyama, "The End of History," *National Interest* 16 (Summer 1989), pp. 3–18; Francis Fukuyama, "Second Thoughts: The Last Man in a Bottle," *National Interest* 56 (Summer 1999), pp. 16–33; and "Responses to Fukuyama," *National Interest* 56 (Summer 1999), pp. 34–44.

- John Mearsheimer, "Back to the Future," *International Security* 15:1 (Summer 1990), pp. 5–56; and Stanley Hoffmann, Robert Keohane, and John Mearsheimer, "Back to the Future: Part II," *International Security* 15:2 (Fall 1990), pp. 191–199.

- Samuel P. Huntington, "The Clash of Civilizations?" *Foreign Affairs* 72:3 (Summer 1993), pp. 22–49.

- Charles W. Kegley and Gregory A. Raymond, *The Global Future: A Brief Introduction to World Politics* (Boston: Wadsworth, 2011), pp. 377–392.

A New World Order?

10.2   Explain how the changing nature of power affects possible future world orders.

Given the contradictory forces at work, how will world order change over the course of the twenty-first century? The end of the Cold War certainly altered the international system, but claims of the dawning of a "new world order" were undermined by the profoundly different ways in which people interpret the word *order*. Realists argue that wars arise from the effort of states to acquire power and security in an anarchic world (one in which there is no ultimate arbiter of order other than self-help and the force of arms). In this view, order refers primarily to the structure or distribution of power among states. Liberals and constructivists argue that conflicts and their prevention are determined not only by the balance of power, but by the domestic structure of states; their values, identities, and cultures; transnational challenges; and international institutions for conflict resolution. In contrast to realists, liberals argue that institutions such as the United Nations can help prevent conflict and establish order by stabilizing expectations, thereby creating a sense of continuity and a feeling that current cooperation will be reciprocated in the future. Order for liberals, then, is tied to values such as democracy and human rights, as well as to institutions. Constructivists focus attention on the norms, interests, and identities of actors and remind us that "orders" evolve over time through interaction between agents and social structures. Order thus understood is always contested, never a value-neutral term, and not entirely predictable. The United States' vision of a preferred world order may be quite different, for example, from China's, and is certainly very different from that of the Islamic State of Iraq and the Levant, or ISIL.

For some, order has sinister connotations. In the view of nativist or nationalist groups such as those led by Pat Robertson in the United States or by Jean-Marie Le Pen in France, "new world order" suggests a conspiracy among financial and political elites to dominate the world. In this view, multinational corporations, in league with the financial markets of Wall Street, London, and Tokyo, enrich themselves at the expense of the rest. In the view of certain Islamic fundamentalists, order is a purely Western concept designed to dominate the non-Western world.

These differing conceptions of order mean that a new world order is tricky to define. None of these schools of thought is adequate by itself in understanding the causes of conflict in the current world. The realist emphasis on the balance of power is necessary but not sufficient when long-term societal changes are eroding the norms of state sovereignty, as constructivists might expect. The view that peace has broken out among the major liberal democracies is accurate, but it is not a panacea because most states, including some rising great powers, are not liberal democracies. The old, bipolar Cold War order provided a stability of sorts. The Cold War exacerbated a number of conflicts in the developing world, but economic conflicts among the United States, Europe, and Japan were dampened by common concerns about the Soviet military threat, and bitter ethnic divisions were kept under the tight lid of the Soviet presence in Eastern Europe. With the passing of that bipolar order, conflict did not end. It did, however, have different sources.

Future Configurations of Power

As historians and political observers since Thucydides have noted, rapid power transitions are one of the leading causes of great power conflict and hegemonic wars. Such power transitions were a deep structural cause of recent great power conflicts, including Germany's rise before each of the two world wars and the relative rise and resulting rivalry of the United States and the Soviet Union after World War II. There is a strong consensus that the period after the Cold War was one of rapid power transitions with the rise of the United States and China and the decline of Russia. Considerable debate remains over the description and magnitude of the transitions, however, and these debates indicate the unpredictability that makes such transitions a potential source of conflict.

One alternative is multipolarity. Former French President Jacques Chirac, for example, called for a return to a multipolar world. If the term *multipolarity* implies a historical analogy with the nineteenth century, it is highly misleading. That order rested on a balance of power between roughly five equal powers, whereas the great powers after the Cold War are far from equal. Russia declined faster and further after 1991 than almost anyone expected, although it retains an immense nuclear arsenal and, owing to its large natural resource base, remains an energy superpower. China has risen faster than most anticipated, with a long period of double-digit economic growth, but remains a developing country with a formidable set of domestic challenges, not least of which is a declining rate of growth. Japan and Germany have not become the full-fledged superpowers that some incorrectly predicted in 1990. And India, despite its great economic progress, must overcome several hurdles before achieving its full potential as a major world power. The United States is the only military superpower, although the European Union is a peer in economic terms.

Some realists warn that the rapid rise of China will present a hegemonic challenge to the United States in the twenty-first century analogous to what the kaiser's Germany posed to Britain on the eve of World War I. But the historical analogy is flawed. Germany had already surpassed Britain in industrial strength by 1900, whereas China's economy is only about 60 percent the size of that of the United States (measured at official exchange rates). If the Chinese economy continued to grow at a spectacular rate of 10 percent and the United States at 3 percent, China would catch up by 2025; but China is already bumping up against limits to growth—including environmental and demographic changes—and its growth rate is already slowing down. In any case, the two countries' economies are so interdependent that they have every incentive to avoid conflict. Although conflict is possible if the two governments mismanage their relations, hegemonic war is far from inevitable.

Some analysts predict the world will be organized around *three economic blocs*: Europe, Asia, and North America. Even here, however, global technological changes and the increase of nonbloc, nonstate actors such as multinational corporations and ethnic groups will resist the capacity of these three blocs to constrain their activities. And we have already discussed the problem with describing world order in terms of civilizations.

In the aftermath of the 2003 U.S. invasion of Iraq, other analysts described the international order as a U.S. world empire. In many ways, the metaphor of empire is seductive. The U.S. military has a global reach with bases around the world, and its regional commanders sometimes act like proconsuls. English is a *lingua franca* just as Latin was during the heyday of Rome. The U.S. economy is the largest in the world, and American culture serves as a magnet. But it is a mistake to confuse the politics of primacy with the politics of empire. The United States is certainly not an empire in the way we think of the European overseas empires of the nineteenth and twentieth centuries, because the core feature of such imperialism was political control. Although unequal relationships certainly exist between the United States and weaker powers and can be conducive to exploitation, in the absence of formal political control, the term *empire* is inaccurate and misleading.

The United States has more power resources than Britain had at its imperial peak, but the United States has less power in the sense of direct control over the behavior that occurs inside other countries than Britain did when it ruled a fourth of the globe. For example, Kenya's schools, taxes, laws, and elections—not to mention its external relations—were controlled by British officials. The United States has little such control today. In 2003, the United States could not even get Mexico and Chile to vote for a second UN Security Council resolution authorizing the invasion of Iraq. The imperial analysts reply that the term *empire* is merely a metaphor. But the problem with the metaphor is that it implies a control from Washington that fits poorly with the complex ways in which power is distributed today. As we saw in Chapter 7, the United States found it far easier to win the initial battle in Iraq than to manage the occupation.

In the global information age, power is distributed among countries in a pattern that resembles a complex three-dimensional chess game in which you play vertically as well as horizontally. On the top chessboard of political-military issues, military power is largely unipolar with the United States as the sole superpower, but on the middle board of economic issues, the United

Photo: David Leeson/Dallas Morning News

Iraq War, 2003

States is not a hegemon or an empire, and it must bargain as an equal when Europe acts in a unified way. For example, on antitrust or trade issues, the United States must meet Europe halfway to reach agreements. On the bottom chessboard of transnational relations that cross borders outside the control of governments and include actors as diverse as bankers and terrorists, power is chaotically dispersed. To take a few examples in addition to terrorism, private actors in global capital markets constrain the way interest rates can be used to manage the U.S. economy, and the drug trade, pandemics, migration, and climate change have deep societal roots in more than one country and are outside U.S. governmental control. It makes no sense to use traditional terms such as *unipolarity*, *hegemony*, or *U.S. empire* to describe such transnational issues.

Those who portray an empire based on traditional military power are relying on a one-dimensional analysis. In a three-dimensional game, however, you lose if you focus only on one board and fail to notice the other boards and the vertical connections among them; witness the connections in the war on terrorism between military actions on the top board where the United States removed a tyrant in Iraq, but simultaneously increased the ability of the al-Qaeda network to gain new recruits on the bottom transnational board. Representing the dark side of globalization, these issues are inherently multilateral and require cooperation for their solution. To describe such a world as a U.S. empire fails to capture the real nature of the world that the United States faces.

Another issue, often ignored by proponents of the empire model, is whether the American public will tolerate a classical imperial role. The United States was briefly tempted into real imperialism when it emerged as a world power in 1898, but the interlude of formal empire did not last. Unlike in Britain, imperialism was not a comfortable experience for Americans. Polls have consistently shown little taste for empire. Instead, the public continues to say it favors multilateralism and using the United Nations. Perhaps that is why Michael Ignatieff, a Canadian advocate of the empire metaphor, qualifies it by referring to the U.S. role in the world as "Empire Lite."[15]

The current distribution of power is one of *multilevel interdependence*. No single hierarchy adequately describes a world politics that is like a three-dimensional chess game. None of this complexity would matter if military power were as fungible as money and could determine the outcomes in all areas. But military prowess is a poor predictor of the outcomes on the economic and transnational playing boards of current world politics. The United States has a more diversified portfolio of power resources than other countries, but the current world order is not an era of U.S. empire in any traditional sense of the word. The world's only superpower cannot afford to go it alone. Globalization is elevating issues on the international agenda that not even the most powerful country can address on its own; witness international financial stability; global climate change; the spread of infectious diseases; and transnational drug, crime, and terrorist networks. The paradox of U.S. power in the twenty-first century is that the strongest military power the world has seen since the days of Rome is unable to provide security to its citizens by acting alone.

The Prison of Old Concepts

The world after the Cold War is unlike any other time. Constructivist theorists are correct that we should not overly constrain our understanding by trying to force it into the procrustean bed of traditional metaphors with their mechanical polarities. Power is becoming more multidimensional, structures more complex, and states themselves more permeable. This added complexity means that world order must rest on more than the traditional military balance of power alone.

The realist view of world order is necessary but not sufficient to explain today's geopolitical order, because it does not take into account the long-term societal changes that have been slowly moving the world away from the early Westphalian system. In 1648, after 30 years of tearing one another apart over religion, the European states agreed in the Peace of Westphalia that the ruler, in effect, would determine the religion of a state regardless of popular preferences. Order was based on the sovereignty of rulers, not the sovereignty of peoples.

The mechanical balancing of states treated as billiard balls was slowly eroded over the ensuing centuries by the growth of nationalism and democratic participation, but the norms of state sovereignty persisted. Now the rapid growth in transnational communications, migration, and economic interdependence is accelerating the erosion of the classical conception of order and state control and is increasing the gap between old norms and reality.

This evolution makes more relevant the liberal conception of a world politics of peoples as well as of states and of order resting on values and institutions as well as on military power. Liberal views that were once regarded as hopelessly utopian, such as Kant's plea for a peaceful league of democracies, seem less far-fetched now that political scientists report virtually no cases of liberal democracies going to war with each other. In the debates over the effects of German reunification, for example, the predictions of realists who saw Europe going "back to the future" have fared less well than those of liberals who stressed that the new Germany would be democratic and deeply enmeshed with its Western neighbors through the institutions of the European Union. As political scientists Edward Mansfield and Jack Snyder point out, however, young democracies can be more prone to war,[16] and so increased democratization in tumultuous regions, such as the Middle East, should not be expected to yield instant security dividends.

Indeed, liberal conceptions of order are not entirely new, and they do not apply to all countries. The Cold War order had norms and institutions, but they played a limited role. During World War II, Franklin Roosevelt, Josef Stalin, and Winston Churchill had agreed to a United Nations that assumed a multipolar distribution of power. The UN Security Council would enforce the doctrine of collective security and nonaggression against smaller states, whereas the five great powers were protected by their vetoes.

Even this abbreviated version of Woodrow Wilson's institutional approach to order was hobbled, however, by the unforeseen rise of bipolarity. The superpowers vetoed each other's initiatives, and the organization was reduced to the more modest role of stationing peacekeepers to observe cease-fires rather than repelling aggressors. When the decline of Soviet power led to a new Kremlin policy of cooperation with the United States in applying the UN doctrine of collective security against Iraq in 1990–1991, it was less the arrival of a new world order than the reappearance of an aspect of the liberal institutional order that was supposed to have come into effect in 1945.

But just as the 1991 Gulf War resurrected one aspect of the liberal approach to world order, it also exposed an important weakness in the liberal conception. The doctrine of collective security enshrined in the UN Charter is state-centric, applicable when borders are crossed, but not when force is used among peoples within a state. Liberals try to escape this problem by appealing to the principles of democracy and self-determination: Let peoples within states vote on whether they want to be protected behind borders of their own. But self-determination is not as simple as it sounds. Who decides what self will determine? Less than 10 percent of the states in today's world are ethnically homogeneous. Only half have one ethnic group that accounts for as much as 75 percent of their population. Most of the states of the former Soviet Union have significant minorities, and many have disputed borders. Africa might be considered a continent of roughly a thousand peoples squeezed within and across more than 50 countries. In multilingual or multiethnic states such as Canada, Spain, and Britain, minority groups that have majorities within their provinces or regions (Québécois, Basques and Catalans, Scots) demand special status or agitate for outright independence. Once such multiethnic, multilingual states are called into question, it is difficult to see where the process ends. In such a world, local autonomy and international surveillance of minority rights hold some promise, but a policy of unqualified support for national self-determination could turn into a principle of enormous world disorder.

The Evolution of a Hybrid World Order

How, then, is it possible to preserve some order in traditional terms of the distribution of power among sovereign states while also moving toward institutions based on "justice among peoples"? International institutions are gradually evolving in such a post-Westphalian direction. Human rights and the broader concept of human security are becoming more important than ever before. International humanitarian law, and within it the notions both that states have an obligation to protect their citizen's human rights and that the international community has a "Responsibility to Protect" (R2P) those who are victimized by their own governments, is gaining increased influence. Already in 1945, Articles 55 and 56 of the UN Charter pledged states to collective responsibility for observance of human rights and fundamental freedoms. Even before the 1991 Security Council resolutions authorizing postwar interventions in Iraq, UN recommendations of sanctions against apartheid in South Africa set a precedent of not being strictly limited by the Charter's statements about sovereignty. In Europe, the 1975 Helsinki Accords codified minority rights, and violations could be referred to the European Conference on Security and Cooperation and the Council of Europe. International law is therefore gradually evolving. In 1965, the American Law Institute defined international law as "rules and principles . . . dealing with conduct of states and international organizations." Two decades later, the institute's lawyers added, "as well as some of their relations with persons."[17] Human rights are increasingly treated as more than just national concerns. In 2005, the UN General Assembly agreed that although states have the primary responsibility to protect the human rights of their citizens, the international community should take up this responsibility if states are unable or unwilling to do so. In 2011, for the first time, the international community acted on the basis of R2P to protect civilians in the Libyan civil war.

In many, perhaps most, parts of the world, human rights are still flouted, and violations go unpunished. To mount an armed multilateral intervention to right all such wrongs would be another enormous principle of disorder. But, as we saw in Chapter 6, intervention is a matter of degree, with actions ranging from statements and limited economic measures at the low end of the spectrum to full-fledged invasions at the high end. Limited interventions and multilateral infringements of sovereignty may gradually increase without suddenly disrupting the distribution of power among states.

On a larger scale, the Security Council may act under Chapter VII of the UN Charter if it determines that internal violence or development of weapons of mass destruction are likely to spill over into a more general threat to the peace in a region. Such definitions are somewhat elastic and may gradually expand over time. In other instances, groups of states may act on a regional basis, as Nigeria and others did in the 1990s by sending troops to Liberia and Sierra Leone under the framework of the Economic Community of West African States, as NATO did in Kosovo in 1999, and as Niger and Chad did to combat Boko Haram militants in neighboring Nigeria in 2015.

Such imperfect principles and institutions will leave much room for domestic violence and injustice among peoples. But the moral horrors will be less than would be the case if policy makers were to try either to right all wrongs by force or, alternatively, to return to the unmodified Westphalian system. Liberals must realize that the evolution of a new world order beyond the Westphalian system is a project of decades and centuries; realists must recognize that the traditional definitions of power and structure in purely military terms ignore the changes that are occurring in a world of global communications and growing transnational relations.

One thing is clear: World government is not around the corner. There is too much social and political diversity in the world and not a sufficient sense of community to support world government. Reform of the United Nations and the development of new institutions offer new ways for states to work with one another as well as for nonstate actors to facilitate cooperation. In some instances, transnational networks of government officials will foster such cooperation; in other instances, mixed coalitions of governments and private actors will do the job. But what does that mean for democracy?

Democracy is government by officials who are accountable and removable by the majority of people in a jurisdiction, albeit with provisions for protections of individuals and minorities. Who are "we the people" in a world in which political identity at the global level is so weak? "One state, one vote" is not democratic. Using that formula, as we saw in Chapter 6, a citizen of the Maldive Islands would have close to 600 times the voting power of a citizen of Brazil. On the other hand, treating the world as one global constituency implies the existence of a political community in which citizens of most states would be willing to be continually outvoted by more than a billion Chinese and more than a billion Indians. Minorities acquiesce to a majority when they believe that they participate in a larger community. In the absence of such community, the extension of domestic voting procedures to the global level makes little practical or normative sense. A stronger European Parliament may reduce a sense of "democratic deficit" as a European community evolves, but it is doubtful that the analogy makes sense under the conditions that prevail on the global scale. Thus far in world history, democracy has flourished only in the context of sovereign states.

Accountability, however, is not assured only through voting, even in well-functioning democracies. In the United States, for example, the Supreme Court and the Federal Reserve System are responsive to elections only indirectly through a long chain of delegation. Professional norms and standards can help keep the judges and central bankers accountable, but transparency is essential if they are to play this role. In addition to voting, publics communicate and agitate over issues through a variety of means ranging from letters and polls to protests. Interest groups and a free press can play an important role in increasing transparency at the local, national, and transnational levels.

The private sector can also contribute to accountability. Private associations and codes, such as those established by the international chemical industry in the aftermath of the 1984 explosion of a plant in Bhopal, India, can create common standards. The NGO practice of naming and shaming companies that exploit child labor has helped consumers hold accountable transnational firms in the toy and apparel industries. And although people have unequal votes in markets, in the aftermath of the 1997 and 2009 financial crises, accountability to markets may have led to more increases in transparency by governments than any formal agreements did. Open markets can help diminish the undemocratic power of local monopolies and can reduce the power of entrenched and unresponsive government bureaucracies, particularly in countries in which parliaments are weak. Moreover, efforts by investors to increase transparency and legal predictability can have beneficial spillover effects on political institutions. Hybrid networks that combine governmental, intergovernmental, and nongovernmental representatives are likely to play a larger role in the future than ever before.

There is no single answer to these questions of global governance. We need to think hard about norms and procedures for the governance of globalization. Denial of the problem, misleading domestic analogies, and platitudes about democratic deficits will not do. We need changes in processes that take advantage of the multiple forms of accountability that exist in modern democracies. International institutions are not international government, but they are crucial for international governance in a global information age.

Follow Up

- Daniel Deudney, *Bounding Power: Republican Security Theory from the Polis to the Global Village* (Princeton, NJ: Princeton University Press, 2007), pp. 1–26, 193–277.

- T. V. Paul and John A. Hall, eds., *International Order and the Future of World Politics* (Cambridge: Cambridge University Press, 1999).

- Heikki Patomäki, *The Political Economy of Global Security: War, Future Crises and Changes in Global Governance* (London: Routledge, 2008).

Thinking About the Future

10.3 **Articulate how theory and history can help us explain, understand, and evaluate world politics.**

What kind of world would you like to live in? You will almost certainly live in a world that will be anarchic in the sense stated at the beginning of the book: a world without a single overarching political authority. With luck, that world will not be a Hobbesian anarchy, or a war of all against all. Order will be provided by the realists' balance of power among states, by the liberals' evolving international institutions, and by the constructivists' evolution of new norms and ideas. That order will not always be just. Justice and order are often at odds with each other, even in issues of self-determination. Is it more important to keep borders intact or to pursue humanitarian causes and protection of human rights that violate territorial integrity? What do these choices do to principles of order? Will the role of legitimacy and soft power become more important than that of hard power? These debates are not easily resolved.

But change is occurring. Robert Gilpin argued that international politics has not changed over two millennia and that Thucydides would have little trouble understanding our world today. If Thucydides were plopped down in the Middle East or East Asia, he would probably recognize some aspects of the situation quite quickly, but if he were set down in Western Europe, he would probably have a more difficult time understanding the relations between France and Germany. Globally, there has been a technological revolution in the development of nuclear weaponry, an information revolution that reduces the role of geography and territory, an enormous growth in economic interdependence, and an emerging global society in which there is increased consciousness of certain values and human rights that cross national frontiers. Interestingly, similar changes were anticipated by Kant in his eighteenth-century liberal view of international politics. He predicted that over the long run, humans would evolve beyond war for three reasons: the greater destructiveness of war, the growth of economic interdependence, and the development of what he called republican governments and what we call today liberal democracies.

To understand the current world, we must understand both the realist and liberal views of world politics and be alert to social and cultural changes that constructivists emphasize. We need to be able to think about different ideal types at the same time. Neither realism nor complex interdependence exists in pure form; both are abstract models of the world. The realist sees a world of states using force to pursue security. Reversing that produces complex interdependence in which nonstate actors, economic instruments, and welfare goals are more important than security. Those two views are at the opposite ends of a conceptual continuum on which we can locate different real-world relationships. All three approaches—realism, liberalism, and constructivism—are helpful and necessary to understand international politics in a changing world. What we have done is provide an example of how to think about the complex and changing domains of world politics. We have shown you how to combine the tools of theory and history to explain (i.e., show the causes), interpret (give the meanings), and evaluate (both politically and morally) the world in which you will live. The rest is up to you.

Study Questions

1. What does Francis Fukuyama mean by the "end of history"? What are the strengths and weaknesses of his concept?

2. Are conflicts more likely to occur between large civilizations or within them? What are the strengths and weaknesses of Samuel P. Huntington's argument?

3. Is there a new world order distinct from that which came to be after World War II? Can we characterize it as multipolar? Bipolar? Unipolar? Does it matter?

4. Is nationalism fading in importance in world politics, or is it stronger than ever? Cite examples. Is empire possible in an era of nationalism?

5. Is the threat of nuclear war a thing of the past? What would happen if terrorists obtained weapons of mass destruction?

6. What are the arguments for and against a diffusion of power away from central governments? Why does it matter? What are the implications for democracy?

7. What kinds of power are important and will be important in coming decades? How will this affect the role of the United States in the world? How would your answers to these questions differ if you looked only at the 1991 Gulf War, the 1999 Kosovo crisis, the 2003 Iraq War, or the ongoing war in Afghanistan?

8. What does realist theory predict about the future of Europe? Of Asia? What other factors might affect events? What do liberal and constructivist approaches add?

9. What is the difference between global government and global governance? What role do institutions play? What are the implications for democracy?

10. What are arguments for and against portraying the current world order as a U.S. empire?

11. If the Internet strengthens transnational groups, would it affect world politics? If so, how?

12. How does security in the twenty-first century differ from security in the twentieth century? Will transnational challenges such as climate change and pandemics transform the nature of world politics?

13. Are human rights becoming more important in world politics than in the past? How can humanitarian law be reconciled with the norm of sovereignty at the heart of the Westphalian system?

Notes

1. Richard A. Falk, *This Endangered Planet: Prospects and Proposals for Human Survival* (New York: Random House, 1971).

2. Peter Drucker, "The New Information Revolution," *Forbes*, August 24, 1998, pp. 1–17; Alvin Toffler and Heidi Toffler,

Creating a New Civilization: The Politics of the Third Wave (Atlanta: Turner Pub., 1995).

3. Esther Dyson, *Release 2.0: A Design for Living in the Digital Age* (New York: Broadway Books, 1997).

4. Marshall McLuhan and Bruce R. Powers, *The Global Village: Transformations in World Life and Media in the 21st Century* (New York: Oxford University Press, 1992).

5. Francis Fukuyama, "The End of History," *National Interest* 16 (Summer 1989), p. 3.

6. Samuel P. Huntington, "The Clash of Civilizations?," *Foreign Affairs* 72:3 (Summer 1993), pp. 22–49; Samuel P. Huntington, *The Clash of Civilizations and the Remaking of World Order* (New York: Simon & Schuster, 1996).

7. Peter J. Katzenstein, ed., *Civilizations in World Politics: Plural and Pluralist Perspectives* (London: Routledge, 2010).

8. Robert B. Reich, "Who Is Us?," *Harvard Business Review* 68:1 (January–February 1990), pp. 53–65.

9. Jacques E. C. Hymans, *Achieving Nuclear Ambitions: Scientists, Politicians and Proliferation* (Cambridge: Cambridge University Press, 2012).

10. Walter Laqueur, "Left, Right, and Beyond: The Changing Face of Terror," in James F. Hogue and Gideon Rose, eds., *How Did This Happen? Terrorism and the New War* (New York: PublicAffairs, 2001), p. 73.

11. "Letter from Scientists to President Bush Regarding Cybersecurity, February 2002," Council on Foreign Relations, February 27, 2002, http://www.cfr.org/cybersecurity/letter-scientists-president-bush-regarding-cybersecurity-february-2002/p21160 (accessed October 21, 2015).

12. Laurie Garrett, "The Challenge of Global Health," *Foreign Affairs* 86:1 (January/February 2007), p. 14.

13. Michael T. Klare, "Global Warming Battlefields: How Climate Change Threatens Security," *Current History* 106:703 (November 2007), p. 355.

14. Center for Naval Analyses, "National Security and the Threat of Climate Change," p. 3; https://www.cna.org/cna_files/pdf/National%20Security%20and%20the%20Threat%20of%20Climate%20Change.pdf (accessed October 21, 2015).

15. Michael Ignatieff, *Empire Lite: Nation-Building in Bosnia, Kosovo and Afghanistan* (Toronto: Penguin Canada, 2003).

16. Edward D. Mansfield and Jack Snyder, "Democratization and the Danger of War," *International Security* 20:1 (Summer 1995), pp. 5–38.

17. Richard A. Mann and Barry S. Roberts, *Essentials of Business Law and the Legal Environment*, 11th ed. (Mason, OH: South-Western, Cengage Learning, 2013), p. 905.

Glossary

Terms with their own glossary entries are in **bold**, to make cross-referencing easy.

Actor   Any person or body whose decisions and actions have repercussions for international politics. **States**, **nongovernmental organizations (NGOs)**, multinational corporations, and even occasionally individuals can qualify as international **actors**.

Alliance   A formal or informal arrangement made by two or more **sovereign states** to achieve a common objective jointly, usually to ensure mutual security. An example is **NATO**.

Anarchy   The absence of hierarchy. The current **system** of **sovereign states**, inaugurated by the **Peace of Westphalia** in 1648, is anarchic because there is no authority above **states**. When used in the study of international politics, anarchy is generally not used as a synonym for chaos because anarchic **systems** can be very orderly.

Appeasement   Generally, the act or policy of accommodating another's demands so as to prevent conflict. Often used very specifically to refer to the British policy between the two world wars of attempting to satisfy Germany's legitimate grievances arising from the harsh terms of the highly punitive Treaty of Versailles that concluded World War I.

Arab Awakening   (Sometimes called Arab Spring or Arab Renewal.) The wave of protests and uprisings against authoritarian regimes in North Africa and the Middle East that began in Tunisia in December 2010.

Asymmetry   Situations in which **states** or other **actors** with unbalanced **power** are in opposition to one another. The U.S. war against al-Qaeda is widely regarded as an asymmetrical conflict.

Balance of power   A term commonly used to describe (1) the distribution of **power** in the international **system** at any given time, (2) a policy of allying with another **state** or group of **states** so as to prevent some other **state** (or group of **states**) from gaining a preponderance of **power**, (3) a "**realist**" theory about how **states** behave under **anarchy**, or (4) the **multipolar system** of Europe in the nineteenth century.

Bipolarity   The structure of an international **system** in which two **states** or **alliances** of **states** dominate world politics. During the **Cold War**, the international **system** was **bipolar** because the United States and the Soviet Union (the two **superpowers**) were by far the two most powerful **states**, each sitting atop its own **alliance system** (**NATO** in the case of the United States and the Warsaw Pact in the case of the Soviet Union).

Bretton Woods   New Hampshire resort where a 1944 conference established the **International Monetary Fund (IMF)** and the **World Bank**. The post–World War II international financial system is often called the Bretton Woods system.

Cold War   The standoff between the United States and the Soviet Union that lasted from roughly the end of World War II until the fall of the Berlin Wall in 1989. Although proxy wars were fought on behalf of both sides around the globe, U.S. and Soviet troops did not engage in direct combat, making it a "cold" war rather than a "hot" shooting war.

Collective security   An agreement between two or more **states** to respond jointly to aggression (i.e., to treat an attack upon one as an attack upon all). The **United Nations** is founded on the principle of **collective security**, as is **NATO**. Two examples of **collective security** actions conducted under the auspices of the **United Nations** were the Korean War (1950–1953) and the Persian Gulf War (1991).

Concert of Europe   A mechanism adopted by European **great powers** at the **Congress of Vienna** in 1815 for attempting to keep the peace in Europe by periodic consultation and by maintaining a **balance of power**; to restore and reintegrate France as a nonrevolutionary, monarchical **great power**; and to deal proactively with **nationalist** threats to the integrity and legitimacy of European **great powers**.

Congress of Vienna   A conference of European statesmen in 1815 that marked the end of the Napoleonic Wars and established a general framework for the nineteenth-century European international **system** known as the **Concert of Europe**.

Constructivism   An analytical approach to international relations that emphasizes the importance of ideas, norms, cultures, and social **structures** in shaping **actors'** identities, interests, and actions. John Ruggie, Alexander Wendt, and Peter Katzenstein are prominent constructivists.

Containment   A foreign policy designed to prevent a potential aggressor from expanding its influence geographically. **Containment** was the cornerstone of U.S. foreign policy toward the Soviet Union and Soviet-supported communist movements during the **Cold War**.

Cosmopolitanism   The view that individuals, not **sovereign states**, are the relevant moral units in world affairs and that moral principles such as human rights are universal rather than culture-specific. Charles Beitz is a prominent cosmopolitan theorist.

Counterfactuals   Thought experiments that imagine situations with a carefully selected change of facts. They are often phrased as "what-if" questions and are employed in the analysis of scenarios in international relations to explore causal relationships.

Crisis stability   A measure of the pressure leaders feel to escalate to war during an international crisis. Whenever leaders believe that military technology or doctrine favors the offense, **crisis stability** is low. When they believe that the defense holds the advantage, **crisis stability** is high. It is much easier to resolve an international crisis when **crisis stability** is high because leaders believe that they can afford to take time to work out a solution.

Cuban missile crisis   A standoff in October 1962 between the United States and the Soviet Union over the deployment of Soviet nuclear missiles in Cuba. The crisis was resolved when the Soviets removed their missiles, partly in exchange for a secret agreement that the United States would remove similar missiles based in Turkey and Italy.

Dependency theory   A theory of development inspired by Marxism, popular in the 1960s and 1970s, that predicted wealthy countries at the "center" of the international system would hold back "peripheral" developing countries.

Deterrence   A strategy of dissuading a potential aggressor by deploying enough force to credibly thwart an attack ("**deterrence** by denial") or to punish an attack so severely that an attacker will believe that the costs of attacking would outweigh the benefits ("**deterrence** by punishment").

Economic interdependence   Situations characterized by reciprocal economic effects among countries or **actors** in different countries.

Fourteen Points   Woodrow Wilson's blueprint for a settlement at the end of World War I. Among its most important features was a call for an **intergovernmental organization** that would safeguard **collective security**, the **League of Nations**.

Game theory   The analysis of how rational **actors** will behave in contexts of strategic interaction.

GATT (General Agreement on Tariffs and Trade)   An international agreement on tariffs and trade that began in 1947 and was replaced in 1994 by the **World Trade Organization (WTO)**.

Geopolitics   A theory of international politics that considers the location, proximity, and power of a **state** to be the key causes of its behavior.

Globalization   At its broadest, the term is used to describe worldwide networks of **interdependence**. It has a number of dimensions, including economic, cultural, military, and political globalization. It is not a new phenomenon—it dates back at least to the Silk Road—but due to the information revolution, its contemporary form is "thicker and quicker" than previous ones.

Global Public Goods   Extension of the public goods concept in economics, which refers to goods that are nonrival and nonexcludable. Examples include knowledge and a stable climate.

Great power   A **state** of unusual consequence that can only be checked by other great powers, not by smaller **states**.

Hard power   The ability to obtain desired outcomes through coercion or payment.

Hegemony   The ability to exercise a specific kind of control within a **system** of **states** (military, financial, or both). The United States is often said to be both a military and a financial **hegemon** today. An international **system** with a true **hegemon** is said to be **unipolar**.

IGO (intergovernmental organization)   An organization whose members are **sovereign states**. The **United Nations**, **IMF**, and **World Bank** are examples of IGOs. Commonly referred to as **international institutions**.

IMF (International Monetary Fund)   An **international institution** set up after World War II at **Bretton Woods** to lend money, primarily to developing countries, to help stabilize currencies or cover balance-of-payments problems.

INGO (international nongovernmental organizations)   A subset of **NGOs** with an international focus.

Interdependence   Situations characterized by reciprocal effects among **states** or other **actors**.

International Court of Justice (ICJ)   An international tribunal for settling disputes between **states** and for providing legal opinions on questions submitted to it by the **UN** General Assembly and other authorized bodies. The Statute of the International Court of Justice is an integral part of the **UN** Charter (Chapter XIV). Based in The Hague, the ICJ is the successor to the **League of Nations'** Permanent Court of International Justice.

International Criminal Court (ICC)   A permanent tribunal of last resort for trying individuals charged with genocide, crimes against humanity, or war crimes. Established by the Rome Statute (1999) and in operation since July 1, 2002.

International Criminal Tribunal for Rwanda (ICTR)   An ad hoc tribunal established by the **UN** Security Council to prosecute those charged with committing genocide, crimes against humanity, or war crimes in Rwanda (1994).

International Criminal Tribunal for the Former Yugoslavia (ICTY)   An ad hoc tribunal established by the **UN** Security Council to prosecute those charged with committing genocide, crimes against humanity, or war crimes during the violent breakup of Yugoslavia (1991–1995).

International institutions See **IGO**.

International law The collective body of treaties and accepted customary practices that regulate the conduct of **states**. International law can also apply to individuals who act in an international context.

International society A way of conceptualizing the international **system** that stresses the importance of international law, norms, and rules (including rules of protocol and etiquette), as well as the rights and obligations of **states**. **Constructivists** and British scholars of the "English School" of International Relations theory (some of whom are classical **realists**) generally prefer to speak of international society rather than the international **system**. **Neorealists** prefer the opposite.

International system See **System**.

Intervention External actions that influence the domestic affairs of a **sovereign state**. Most often, this term is used to refer to forcible interference by one or more **states** in another **state's** domestic affairs.

Jus ad bellum The part of **just war doctrine** that specifies the conditions under which **states** may morally resort to war. Traditionally, they include just cause, right intention, legitimate authority, last resort, and reasonable chance of success. From the Latin "justice to war."

Jus in bello The part of **just war doctrine** that specifies the ways in which wars may morally be fought. Traditionally, they include observing the laws of war, maintaining proportionality between the amount of force used and the objective sought, and observing the principle of noncombatant immunity. From the Latin "justice in war."

Just war doctrine An intellectual tradition with origins in ancient Rome and the early Christian church that provides moral guidelines for the resort to force and the use of force in war. St. Augustine and St. Thomas Aquinas are important historical figures in this tradition; Michael Walzer is a well-known modern just war theorist. Sometimes called "just war theory." See *jus ad bellum* and *jus in bello*.

League of Nations An **intergovernmental organization** founded at the end of World War I and dedicated to **collective security**. Woodrow Wilson, the League's chief advocate, called for its creation in his **Fourteen Points** at the end of the war. The League failed owing to its inability to prevent or to respond effectively to Italian aggression in Africa, Japanese aggression in Manchuria, and German aggression in Europe in the 1930s. The League of Nations was the forerunner of the **United Nations**, which was designed to address some of the flaws of the League.

Liberalism An analytical approach to international relations in which **states** function as part of a global **society** that sets the context for their interactions and that stresses the domestic sources of foreign policy. Classical liberalism has intellectual roots in the writings of Immanuel Kant, Jeremy Bentham, and John Stuart Mill. Richard Rosecrance is a prominent liberal.

Marxism An analytical approach to international relations, inspired by the writings of Karl Marx and Friedrich Engels, that sees economic classes as the primary **actors** and that explains patterns and events in world affairs in terms of the interactions between classes. Immanuel Wallerstein is a prominent Marxist international relations theorist.

Milieu goals Intangible goals such as democracy or human rights, in contrast to tangible possession goals such as territory.

Multipolarity The structure of an international **system** in which three or more **states** or **alliances** dominate world politics. Nineteenth-century Europe was a **multipolar system**.

NAFTA (North American Free Trade Agreement) A 1994 agreement among the United States, Canada, and Mexico that created a free-trade zone in North America.

Nation A group of individuals who have some combination of common language, culture, religion, history, mythology, identity, or sense of destiny, as well as strong ties to a particular territory and, usually, aspirations for political autonomy. All **nations** are **peoples**. It is good practice to distinguish **nation** and **state**, but unfortunately, these words are often used interchangeably.

National interest A **state's** perceptions of its goals in the international **system**. **Realists**, **liberals**, and **constructivists** all have different accounts of how states formulate their national interests.

Nationalism A celebration or assertion of a **nation's** identity that commonly finds political expression in the claim of a right to **self-determination** or **self-government**.

Nation-state An ethnically homogenous **state**; that is, a **state** whose citizens are all, or virtually all, members of a single **nation**. Used both descriptively (e.g., with respect to Korea, Japan, and other ethnically homogenous **states**) and prescriptively (i.e., as a philosophical ideal—impossible to realize in practice—that all **nations** should have **states** of their own).

NATO The North Atlantic Treaty Organization, a military **alliance** formed in 1948 on the principle of **collective security** that currently has 28 member **states** in Europe and North America, including Canada and the United States.

Neoliberalism An analytical approach to international relations in which the actions of **states** are constrained by economic **interdependence** and **international institutions**. Robert Keohane is a prominent neoliberal.

Neorealism An analytical approach to international relations, inspired by the objectivity and rigor of natural science, that sees the actions of **states** as constrained primarily by the distribution of **power** in the international system. Prominent neorealists include Kenneth Waltz and John Mearsheimer.

NGO (nongovernmental organization) In the broadest definition, any organization that represents interests other than those of a **state** or multinational corporation. Most references concern transnational or international groups (sometimes referred to as **INGOs**). Examples of well-known NGOs include the Roman Catholic Church, Greenpeace, and the International Committee of the Red Cross.

Nuclear deterrence A strategy used by both the United States and Soviet Union during the **Cold War** to dissuade each other from provocative acts by threat of annihilation (i.e., through **deterrence** by punishment).

OPEC (Organization of Petroleum Exporting Countries) An organization of some of the world's largest oil-producing **states** that tries to coordinate policy on oil production and pricing among its members.

Peacebuilding A term coined by **UN** Secretary-General Boutros Boutros-Ghali in 1992 describing a range of activities by foreign military and civilian personnel intended to stabilize war-torn societies; build durable governance structures; and lay the groundwork for long-term peace, security, and development.

Peace enforcement The deployment of well-armed foreign troops to compel one or more warring parties to comply with **UN** resolutions calling for a cessation of hostilities.

Peacekeeping The deployment of neutral, lightly armed foreign troops or police to prevent conflict or maintain peace in a state or between states. Many peacekeeping operations are conducted under **UN** auspices, but peacekeeping can also be conducted by a regional organization or a group of countries acting outside the **United Nations**.

Peace of Westphalia The 1648 treaties that formally concluded the **Thirty Years' War** and established **state sovereignty** as the chief organizing principle of the international **system**.

Peloponnesian War More accurately, the Second Peloponnesian War, documented by **Thucydides**; a conflict between Athens and Sparta lasting from 431 to 404 BCE that resulted in the defeat of Athens and the end of the Golden Age of Athenian democracy.

People A group of individuals united by common culture, tradition, or sense of kinship (although not necessarily by blood, race, or political ties), typically sharing a language and set of beliefs. A **people** with a sense of territorial homeland and a shared political identity is a **nation**.

Power Generally, the ability to achieve one's purposes or goals; more specifically, the ability to affect others to get the outcomes one wants. In a more restricted definition, Robert Dahl defined **power** as "the ability to get others to do what they otherwise would not do." **Hard power** involves carrots and sticks, such as the threat or use of force or economic or other kinds of sanctions or inducements. **Soft power**, or the "power of attraction," involves setting an example that others will seek to emulate, persuading by argument, or cultivating goodwill or trust.

Prisoner's Dilemma A classic strategic interaction analyzed by **game theory** in which two independent decision makers, each attempting to pursue his or her rational self-interest, will choose not to cooperate with each other (i.e., to defect) and will thereby end up worse off than if they had both chosen to cooperate. Because the best possible outcome in the Prisoner's Dilemma is to defect while the other cooperates, the noncooperative outcome is a function of their inability to trust.

Realism The view that international politics is inherently a struggle for **power** and security and, at least potentially, what Thomas Hobbes called "a war of all against all." Prominent nineteenth-century realists include Austrian Foreign Minister Prince Klemens von Metternich and British Foreign Secretary Lord Castlereagh. Prominent twentieth- and twenty-first-century realists include Hans Morgenthau, Henry Kissinger, and Kenneth Waltz.

Self-determination The right of a **people** to decide their own political fate (which may or may not involve ruling themselves; they may choose to be part of a larger political community).

Self-government The right of a **people** to rule themselves (i.e., a specific form of **self-determination**).

Sensitivity The degree and rapidity of the effects of **interdependence**. Describes how quickly a change in one part of a **system** leads to a change in another part.

Skeptics Those who believe that moral categories have no place in discussions of international relations because of the lack of an international community that can establish rights and duties.

Soft power The ability to obtain desired outcomes through attraction or persuasion rather than coercion or payment.

Sovereignty An absolute right to rule. In a traditional monarchy, the king or queen is **sovereign**; in a democracy, the people are **sovereign**. **States** are **sovereign** because no other **state** has formal authority over them, which makes the international **system anarchic**. It is true whether the right to rule within the **state** rests with a monarch or with the people. (A constitutional monarchy such as Canada or Britain is actually democratic; the queen is merely a symbol of the **state's sovereignty** and does not actually exercise it.)

Stability   See **Crisis stability** and **System stability**.

State   A **sovereign**, territorial political unit.

State moralism   The view that international morality depends on a society of **sovereign states** playing by certain rules, even if those rules are not always obeyed, and that moral obligations within state borders are much greater than across them.

Structure   The configuration of units within a **system**. Structures characterize how units relate. **Realists** consider the distribution of power the most important structural feature of the international **system**; **constructivists** emphasize its social dimensions (e.g., norms, rules, and identity relationships).

Superpower   An unusually strong **great power** with global military reach. Historically, there have only been two genuine **superpowers**: the United States (1945 to the present) and the Soviet Union (1945–1991).

Symmetry   Situations in which **states** or agents with relatively balanced power capabilities are in opposition to one another. The latter half of the **Cold War** is widely regarded as a symmetrical conflict because of the rough nuclear balance between the United States and the Soviet Union.

System   A set of interrelated units that interact in a regular way. The international system is a particular system whose units are international **actors**, of which **sovereign states** are currently the most significant, and whose processes of interaction include such things as diplomacy, negotiation, trade, and war.

System stability   Generally, a measure of the ability of a **system** to absorb shocks without breaking down or becoming disorderly; with respect specifically to the international **system**, a measure of its war-proneness.

Thirty Years' War   A series of European wars fueled by international, religious, and dynastic conflicts that took place from 1618 to 1648 and were finally concluded by the **Peace of Westphalia**.

Thucydides   An Athenian commander whose book *History of the Peloponnesian War*, a chronicle of the war

between Athens and Sparta, is one of the earliest known works of history and international relations. Thucydides is widely considered the father of **realism**.

Transgovernmental relations   Relations between subunits of national governments.

Transnational actor   Any nonstate **actor** that acts across international borders.

Treaty of Rome   The 1957 treaty that laid the groundwork for European integration, which led first to the creation of a European Common Market and eventually to the European Union and the common euro currency.

Treaty of Utrecht   The 1713 treaty that ended the Wars of Spanish Succession and established the legitimacy of both British and French holdings in North America.

Treaty of Westphalia   See **Peace of Westphalia**.

UN (United Nations)   An **intergovernmental organization** founded at the end of World War II and dedicated to **collective security**, designed in such a way as to correct for the flaws of the failed **League of Nations**.

Unipolarity   The structure of an international **system** in which one state exercises preponderant **power**. Some analysts consider the current international **system** to be **unipolar** because the United States enjoys military predominance; economically, however, the world is clearly **multipolar**.

Virtual history   A particular style of **counterfactual** analysis that infers what would have happened had something been different (the counterfactual) from what actually did happen beforehand.

Vulnerability   The relative cost of changing the **structure** of a **system** of **interdependence**. Can also be thought of as the cost of escaping or changing the rules of the game.

Westphalia   See **Peace of Westphalia**.

World Bank   An institution set up after World War II at **Bretton Woods** to provide loans, technical assistance, and policy advice to developing countries.

WTO (World Trade Organization)   An international organization created in 1994 to regulate trade and tariffs among its member **states**; successor to the **GATT**.

Index